SHAKESPEARE
STUDIES

EDITORIAL BOARD

SHAKESPEARE STUDIES
Volume XXXVI

EDITED BY

SUSAN ZIMMERMAN
Queens College
The City University of New York
and
GARRETT SULLIVAN
Pennsylvania State University

ASSISTANT TO THE EDITORS
LINDA NEIBERG
The Graduate Center, CUNY

Madison • Teaneck
Fairleigh Dickinson University Press

Associated University Presses
2010 Eastpark Boulevard
Cranbury, NJ 08512

The paper used in this publication meets the requirements of the American National Standard for Permanence of Paper for Printed Library Materials Z39.48-1984.

International Standard Book Number: 978-0-8386-4179-8
International Standard Serial Number: 0-0582-9399

All editorial correspondence concerning *Shakespeare Studies* should be addressed to the Editorial Office, *Shakespeare Studies,* English Dept., Queens College, CUNY, Flushing, NY 11367. Orders and subscriptions should be directed to Associated University Presses, 2010 Eastpark Boulevard, Cranbury, New Jersey 08512.

Shakespeare Studies disclaims responsibility for statements,
either of fact or opinion, made by contributors.

Contents

6   *Contents*

Articles

Reviews

Foreword

VOLUME 36 OF *Shakespeare Studies* is pleased to continue its tradition of Forums on theoretical, historical, and critical issues of importance to scholars of early modern literature and culture. In this issue, a forum entitled "The Return of the Author," organized by Patrick Cheney, revisits the vexed question of Shakespearean authorship in a post-structural critical environment. As Cheney puts it, "for many working in the field today, the author has either died or disappeared, but for some the author has now returned"; accordingly, the premise currently under debate is that "Shakespeare is a literary author, both a playwright and a poet, who took an interest in the publication not just of his poems but of his plays, and thus in his own literary legacy." Scholars contributing opinions on this issue include Lukas Erne, David Scott Kastan, Jeffrey Knapp, Wendy Wall, Richard Wilson, Heather James, Leah S. Marcus, Brian Vickers, Richard Dutton, and Michael D. Bristol.

The four articles in volume 36 all deal with early modern drama (three with plays of Shakespeare, and one with Marlowe's *Faustus*), each from an unusual theoretical perspective. Hugh Grady's "*Hamlet* as Mourning-Play: A Benjaminesque Interpretation" addresses Shakespeare's tragedy through Benjamin's difficult theory of *Trauerspiel,* reading play and theory against each other in a mutually reinforcing analysis; Heather Anne Hirschfeld's "'The verie paines of hell': *Doctor Faustus* and the Controversy over Christ's Descent" examines Faustus's obsession with hell in terms of Reformation concerns about the sufficiency of Christ's sacrifice as debated in the controversy over his post-Crucifixion descent into hell; Bradley Greenburg's "'O for a muse of fire': *Henry V* and Plotted Self-Exculpation," identifies "discourse networks" operative in 1.1 that reveal the subtexts of Henry's self-presentation, here and throughout the play; and Jeremy Lopez's "Eating Richard II" challenges "entrenched habits" of interpreting the historical dimensions of Shakespeare's history plays without reference to Shakespeare's "deliberate effacement of historical narrative for the sake of theatrical effect."

The book reviews in volume 36 are unusually varied, reflecting the aim of *Shakespeare Studies* to include works of methodological and theoretical interest to scholars of early modern culture. Accordingly, in addition to several books whose primary focus is Shakespeare's works, the review section includes, for example, two medieval studies that offer revisionist perspectives on issues of interest to Renaissance scholars. In *Empire of Magic,* Geraldine Heng rethinks the origin of the medieval romance, connecting it to "projects of imperialism, nation-building, racial and religious purification, and protocapitalist economics"; and in *Lacan's Medievalism,* Erin Felicia Labbie demonstrates conceptual affinities between medieval scholasticism and post-structural psychoanalytical theory, affinities no longer in evidence in Reformation theology, so that, interestingly, it seems possible to use Lacanian theory to address an important conceptual shift in early Renaissance theological discourse. Other critical books of wide-ranging interest include a study of the multiple manifestations of the human voice as (often unruly) early modern cultural agent; studies of the relationship of geographical localities to politics and cultural identity—specifically, a new argument for the "failed" Jamestown colony as prototype for subsequent American colonies—and a consideration of early modern London and Paris as cultural centers; a collection of essays examining the relationship of discourses about the passions to political structures and to theories of subjectivity; an interdisciplinary analysis of early modern perspectives on the animal/human divide; and a study of "the advent of the New Philosophy and the attendant cross-fertilization of scientific and literary thinking" in the age of Shakespeare.

SUSAN ZIMMERMAN, Co-Editor

Contributors

ELIZABETH JANE BELLAMY is Professor of English and John C. Hodges Chair of Excellence in the Department of English at the University of Tennessee, Knoxville.

MICHAEL D. BRISTOL is Greenshields Professor Emeritus at McGill University. His books include *Carnival and Theater* and *Big-Time Shakespeare*. He currently aspires to become a flâneur.

GLENN BURGER is Professor of English and Medieval Studies at Queens College and The Graduate Center, City University of New York. He has edited Hetoum's *A Lytell Cronycle* and (with Steven Kruger) *Queering the Middle Ages* (2000). He is the author of *Chaucer's Queer Nation* (2003) and numerous articles on queer, gender, and postcolonial issues in Chaucerian texts. He is currently completing a book entitled *Conduct Becoming: Representing the Good Wife in the Late Middle Ages*.

DYMPNA C. CALLAGHAN is Dean's Professor in the Humanities at Syracuse University. She has written extensively on the drama and poetry of the early modern period.

PATRICK CHENEY is Distinguished Professor of English and Comparative Literature at Pennsylvania State University. He is the author of *Shakespeare, National Poet-Playwright* and *Shakespeare's Literary Authorship* as well as editor of *The Cambridge Companion to Shakespeare's Poetry*.

JONATHAN CREWE is Willard Professor of English at Dartmouth College.

RICHARD DUTTON is Humanities Distinguished Professor of English at the Ohio State University. He has a book on *Volpone* and the Gunpowder Plot (forthcoming) and is working on a study of the influence of cast performance on Shakespeare's texts.

JIM EGAN is Associate Professor of English at Brown University. He is currently completing a book on figures of the East in early American literature.

LUKAS ERNE is Professor of English at University of Geneva. He is the author of *Shakespeare's Modern Collaborators* (2008) and *Shakespeare as Literary Dramatist* (2003) and the editor of *The First Quarto of Romeo and Juliet* (2007) and, with M. J. Kidnie, of *Textual Performances: The Modern Reproduction of Shakespeare's Drama* (2004).

HUGH GRADY is Professor of English at Arcadia University. He is the author of *The Modernist Shakespeare* (1991), *Shakespeare's Universal Wolf* (1996), and *Shakespeare, Machiavelli, and Montaigne* (2002).

BRADLEY GREENBURG is Associate Professor of English at Northeastern Illinois University in Chicago. He has articles published or forthcoming on T. S. Eliot and *Hamlet* in *Criticism;* on *1 Henry IV,* Wales, and romance *Quidditas;* on Troilus; on *Troilus and Cressida* and Ovid in *Studies in Medieval and Renaissance History;* and on Shakespeare's reading of John Foxe in an edited collection. He is currently completing a book on the Henriad, romance, chronicle history, and Wales titled *Romancing the Chronicles.*

HEATHER ANNE HIRSCHFELD is Associate Professor of English at the University of Tennessee, Knoxville. Her book on collaborative drama, *Joint Enterprises,* was published in 2004. She is currently working on a project on revenge and Reformation theology.

JEAN E. HOWARD is George Delacorte Professor in the Humanities at Columbia University where she teaches early modern literature and feminist studies. She is co-editor of *The Norton Shakespeare* and author of several books on Renaissance drama, the most recent being *Theater of a City: The Places of London Comedy, 1598–1642.*

WENDY BETH HYMAN is Assistant Professor of English at Ithaca College. She has essays on Nashe and Spenser in *Studies in English Literature* and *English Literary Renaissance* and is currently editing a collection of essays on early modern literary automata.

HEATHER JAMES is Associate Professor of English and Comparative Literature at the University of Southern California. Her publications include *Shakespeare's Troy: Drama, Politics, and the Translation of Empire* (1997), and numerous articles on Shakespeare, Marlowe, Milton, Castiglione, and Marguerite de Navarre, and questions of classical reception in the early modern period. She is presently completing a book on Ovid in Renaissance poetry and political thought.

DAVIS SCOTT KASTAN is the George M. Bodman Professor of English Literature at Yale University. He is currently working on a book on publishers and the invention of English Literature.

JEFFREY KNAPP is Professor of English at the University of California, Berkely. He is currently completing a companion volume to his previous book, *Shakespeare's Tribe,* entitled *Shakespeare Only.*

CHRIS R. KYLE is Associate Professor of the Humanities and History at Syracuse University. He is currently completing a book on Parliament and political culture in Early Modern England.

JEREMY LOPEZ is Assistant Professor of English at the University of Toronto. He is currently completing a book on *Richard II* for the *Shakespeare Handbooks* series.

LYNNE MAGNUSSON is Professor of English at the University of Toronto. She is the author of *Shakespeare and Social Dialogue* and is completing a book on early modern English letters.

LEAH S. MARCUS is Edwin Mims Professor at Vanderbilt University. Her current projects include a Norton Critical Edition of *As You like It* and an Arden edition of *The Duchess of Malfi.*

JOHN PARKER is Associate Professor of English at Macalester College. He is the author of *The Aesthetics of Antichrist: From Christian Drama to Christopher Marlowe.*

KATHERINE ROWE is Professor of English at Bryn Mawr College and co-editor of *Reading the Early Modern Passions: Essays in the Cultural History of Emotion.*

CAROLYN SALE is Assistant Professor of English at the University of Alberta. She is currently completing a book on early modern writers and the law.

SUZANNE M. VERDERBER is Associate Professor of English and Humanities at Pratt Institute. She is currently completing a book on the emergence of the individual in the Middle Ages.

BRIAN VICKERS is Distinguished Senior Fellow of the School of Advanced Study, London University, a Fellow of the British Academy, and a foreign Honorary Member of the America Academy of Arts and Sciences. He is the General Editor of *The Complete Works of John Ford.*

WENDY WALL is Professor and Chair of the English Department at Northwestern University. She is author of *The Imprint of Gender: Authorship and Publication in the English Renaissance* and *Stage Domesticity: Household Work and English Identity in Early Modern Drama.*

RICHARD WILSON is Professor of English Literature at Cardiff University. He is the author or editor of numerous books on Shakespeare and Renaissance culture, most recently *Secret Shakespeare: Studies in Theatre, Religion and Resistance* and *Shakespeare in French Theory: King of the Shadows.*

SHAKESPEARE
STUDIES

FORUM

The Return of the Author

Introduction

Patrick Cheney

THE OCCASION FOR THIS FORUM is indeed the "return of the author" in Shakespeare studies. I'm grateful to the editors, Susan Zimmerman and Garrett A. Sullivan Jr., for the opportunity to convene ten distinguished scholars who represent a variety of viewpoints on the topic.

While the return of the author is a complex and even delicate topic, we might begin rather simply, with the binary it implies: for many working in the field today, the author has either died or disappeared, but for some the author has now returned. Most of the contributors present their own version of this change, but a short version might run as follows. Through the convergence of two branches of scholarship and criticism—what we might call the *bibliographical* and the *theatrical*—the twentieth century succeeded in reclassifying Shakespeare, not as the autonomous genius of "dramatic poesy," but as the consummate "man of the theater," so engaged in the collaborative enterprise of the new commercial stage that he took no interest in the literary career of an English author (such as Spenser or Jonson), eschewing print like the plague and thus failing to concern himself with the legacy of artistic fame. During the first years of the twenty-first century, however, principally through Lukas Erne's groundbreaking 2003 monograph, *Shakespeare as Literary Dramatist,* scholars and critics have challenged the twentieth-century view with a new classification: Shakespeare is a literary author, both a playwright and a poet, who took an interest in the publication not just of his poems but of his plays, and thus in his own literary legacy.[1]

As readers will learn in these pages, most of the contributors don't think the Shakespearean author ever died, and thus they find that to speak of his return is something of a discomfiting misnomer. Having acknowledged that, we may then record that each of the contributors lines up fairly clearly on one side of the divide or the other, whether *individuation* or *collaboration, literary authorship* or *socially constructed theatricality.* And no one seems to be budging. Those who previously argue for a collaborative theatrical Shakespeare committed to performance and opposed to print continue to do so; those who acknowledge collaboration but argue for the space of an individuated print Shakespeare also continue to do so. Perhaps for the first time, however, the opponents appear together formally in dialogue, working through the issues genially in public, occasionally giving up some ground (but not all of it), and making available to the rest of us the fruit of their civil conversation. It is an astonishing *read,* by many of the major voices in the field. (My principal regret is that I did not succeed in securing a contributor from the field of performance criticism.)

Nearly all of the contributors identify Lukas Erne as the lightning rod of the conversation. With characteristic wit (and goodwill), David Scott Kastan calls Erne "the new sheriff in town." Accordingly, the forum opens with an essay by Erne, in which he clarifies his argument about Shakespeare as a "literary dramatist" but also reviews other recent criticism supporting his argument (freeing me from the need to do so here). For Erne, Shakespeare is "a self-conscious literary author" who "wanted his dramatic productions to be read and was aware of the eloquence of his printed playbooks." Citing a surge of both publications and conferences, Erne makes a strong "case for a significant Shakespearean literary authorship." He also makes a more specific contribution: in contradistinction to the 1986 Oxford *Complete Works,* which monumentalized the plays as they were originally performed, Erne lays out an "editorial policy" that "attempts to recover the full, unabridged authorial play texts . . . as Shakespeare wanted them to be read, and as he repeatedly saw them published and republished during his lifetime."

The next essay, by Kastan, offers a formal response to Erne's pioneering book. Acknowledging that "Authorship matters," and that the "author lives," Kastan sticks to his 2001 argument in *Shakespeare and the Book*:[2] "in the early modern theater the author was not of primary importance." In particular, he rejects Erne's two major arguments to the contrary. First, Kastan sifts through Erne's evidence for a "coherent strategy to get Shakespeare's plays into print" to conclude that "at best" the evidence "point[s] . . . to an acting company eager to control the publication of plays, but . . . not, therefore, evidence of an affirmative commitment to print or of an identity of interest between the acting company and the playwright." Second, Kastan reviews the evidence Erne provides for seeing the short quartos of Shakespeare's plays as representing works to be performed and the long quartos as plays to be read: "the publication history . . . offers at best ambiguous evidence for Erne's thesis." In the end, for Kastan, Shakespeare can be no "*author,* as the word was becoming gradually defined in the cultural and legal institutions of the day": "There is no evidence of his own desire for his plays to be printed and read."

The next two essays also form an opposing pair, but introduce a complication to the binary between individuated literary author and collaborative theatrical professional. In "Shakespeare as Coauthor," Jeffrey Knapp rejects the received collaborative model and accepts the return of the author, but he does so in order to argue for a new model not of individuated but of coauthorship. In particular, Knapp rejects the critical narrative in which "collective playwrighting was both the practical and the theoretical norm in English theaters until around 1600, when the idea of single dramatic authorship first began to surface." As evidence for the weakness of this narrative, Knapp cites the fact that Shakespeare "returned to collaborative writing after its heyday was past, and, even more bafflingly, after he had already achieved fame as a single author"—that is to say, at the end of his career in such plays as *Pericles* and *The Two Noble Kinsmen.* Proposing a new model, Knapp argues that at the very time Jonson is consolidating single authorship Shakespeare is opening coauthorship up: "Shakespeare's return to collective playwrighting coincided with a major change in his dramaturgy: his abandonment of tragedy and his adoption of romance." In a close analysis of *Pericles,* Knapp demonstrates how Shakespeare and George Wilkins each retool John Gower's story of family succession and inheritance as a story about coauthorship: "More than Wilkins, Shakespeare . . . stressed the sheer variety of authorial models that *Pericles* evokes. Throughout his portion . . . , collective writing draws strength as a conceptual project." Thus, in this fable of authorship Shakespeare outlines the "disintegration" of single authorship even as he acknowledges its cultural power.

Wendy Wall begins her essay as a response to Knapp's 2005 *Representations* essay on Shakespearean coauthorship, which had objected to her own argument about collaboration in *The Imprint of Gender*.³ In particular, she takes issue with Knapp's assessment that she got all the "facts wrong," reporting that to her "the 'facts' are not unambiguous," and questioning any argument that depends on phenomena so lacking in transparency. Like Kastan, she sticks to her previous argument, but she carefully emphasizes the validity of both sides: "single authorship was functional in the period, as were other modes of production. The other modes have been more interesting to me . . . because they allow us to imagine literature and writing and being other than they are now." Like Kastan as well, Wall finds Erne's use of the facts "speculative," and, in an important conclusion, she chooses "*interpretive* rather than *empirical* analyses" as the most "useful," citing recent work that examines "how Shakespeare's texts themselves meditate on different models of authorship": "If all scholarly narratives about early modern authorship, including my own, remain conjectural, then why not foreground the *fictive* realm where ambiguity and contradiction are so richly productive?"

The next five essays each outline a model of Shakespearean authorship from a particular perspective. While most line up either in favor of Erne's thesis or against it, all end up challenging the simplicity of the binary. Richard Wilson's essay is an acute example. He accepts Shakespeare as the founder of modern authorship, yet he objects to Erne's thesis, favoring one akin to Kastan's, while remaining consistent with Wall's directive to turn from empiricism to interpretation. For Wilson, the plays of Shakespeare write modern authorship *fictively* through "self-concealment" and "self-erasure." Everywhere we look, melancholic figures lament the advent of individuated print authorship. Thus, *Cymbeline* mourns "the falling away of the blackened page": "This is a writer who never forgets that ink is made of wormwood and gall. . . . Shakespeare's apprehension about the stigma of print deepens, . . . and the printing-press becomes . . . yet another scene of death." Relying on Bourdieu, Derrida, and others to meditate on the phrase from the Epilogue to *Henry V,* "our bending author," Wilson finds "Shakespeare" taking a bow, "his authority . . . 'bent' by the same bonds of subjection he gave his protagonists, who in scene after scene he imagines in an attitude not of self-determination or intentionality" but of "wily or peasantlike subservience." Finally, "the originator of modern authorship insured his freedom of expression by remaining invisible."

Heather James also finds the presence of authorship within Shakespeare's texts but does so "from the perspective of the classics." By looking at the plays' "rhetorical forms," she shows how "maxim, adage, sentence, and marginal gloss"—not the usual "imitation"—"detach . . . authority from the classical author and his works." For instance, "sententiae break apart poetic or prose works in search of the valuable fragment, . . . largely indifferent and sometimes even hostile to the issues of authorial intentions and personal agency taken up by imitation." Such rhetorical forms "make it clear that Renaissance writers were not necessarily waiting for the Author to Return." Offering a valuable history of the "tacit deal about authors and authority" during the 1980s between the "humanist poetics" of Thomas Greene and the "cultural poetics" of Stephen Greenblatt, James emphasizes how the two "share the view that the classical text and author enjoy a privileged but suspect monumentality." She thus finds that "the time is ripe for scholars to revisit the old idea of the classical text as a monument to the poet or Author and inspect its foundations anew." She does so here by looking at the engraving to George Sandys's 1632 *Ovid's Metamorphoses:* whereas humanist poetics would emphasize the iconography of the author's fame, cultural poetics would underscore the iconography of political exile and death: "The poem-as-monument-to-the-author . . . is a trope in a political discourse about princes, poets, poetry, and readers." Relying on a recent essay by Peter Stallybrass and Roger Chartier, James concludes that "Authority, not authors, made the man": "The key to the Author's return in Shakespeare studies . . . is to recognize the complex and deep history of the tropes of authorship."

Leah S. Marcus brings the complementary perspective of a textual editor. Again objecting to Erne's thesis, she emphasizes how much of his evidence for Shakespeare as a literary dramatist comes from John Webster, whose *Duchess of Malfi* Marcus is now editing. Focusing on the question of Shakespeare's interest in publication, she turns to a case where the text makes such an interest patently clear: whereas the first state of Webster's play attributes a "Hymne" to the author, the second state inserts a comment announcing that he didn't write it. Echoing Roland Barthes, Marcus writes, "Here we have a likely case of the author entering quite literally as guest into his text as it is being printed." No such evidence emerges for Shakespeare: "the sad fact is that Shakespeare, unlike Webster, appears to have had relatively little interest in being a critic as well as an author; he has left us no body of commentary . . . on his own achievement independent of the evidence provided within the plays and poems themselves." In contradistinction to Wall, Wilson, and James, Marcus concludes that we may have invited Shakespeare as a guest into his plays "but we have not yet invented a reliable way to gauge his presence."

Brian Vickers does not directly enter the Erne fray, but instead joins Knapp in looking into "the plays . . . themselves" for the presence of Shakespeare's coauthorship. Reminding us that "the single-author paradigm . . . does not fit the material conditions under which drama was produced in London between 1579 and 1642," Vickers introduces "three case studies"—*Titus Andronicus, 1 Henry VI,* and *Pericles*—to conclude that "those who deny the very idea of Shakespeare as a coauthor have opted out of the [Baconian] process by which knowledge grows." While Vickers rejects the collaborative model of post-structuralism with its abhorrence of individuation, complexly he locates individuation right within Shakespearean collaborative works.

Like Vickers, Richard Dutton tacitly accepts the idea of the Shakespearean author, but he joins others like Kastan, Wilson, and Marcus in objecting to Erne's thesis. For Dutton, "the most intriguing, frustrating, and perplexing question at the heart of any meaningful Shakespearean authorship debate" concerns the "multiple versions of many (nearly half) of Shakespeare's plays." Acknowledging that "we do not *know* why there are multiple versions," Dutton identifies this phenomenon as "an utterly distinctive defining characteristic of Shakespeare as an 'author.'" Invaluably, he uses the two versions of *Henry V* to suggest that "the 'theater-centric' side of the argument . . . might be reconciled with the 'reader-focused' side" more than "the usual division of the kingdoms allows." Starting with his determination that the 1600 quarto of *Henry V* "was an original independent version of the play" and "the 1623 text . . . a later recasting of it," he replaces Erne's model of stage and page with a model of both commercial and court performance. Thus, "the nature of the Shakespearean 'author' need not . . . be confined to the traditional extremes of 'reader-focus' and 'performance-focus'" but might include different forms of performance that both get into print: "Attention to the fact of multiple versions of so many of the plays is the essential first step in any 'authorship' debate."

The last essay in the forum, by Michael Bristol, serves as an intriguing retrospective on the return of the author. Offering an "essentialist view," he leans harder than does Kastan or Marcus on the fact that the author never died, and so need not return, and he does so by taking the argument of Erne and others to heart: "Much of what is being offered as an alternative to the notion that Shakespeare is the author of his works strikes me as equivocating and question-begging; and some of it seems just plain begrudging." Echoing his important postrevisionist model of authorship in *Big-Time Shakespeare*,[4] Bristol writes, "I think it makes pretty good sense to say that Shakespeare is an author, but it's not a good idea to have an inflated notion of what that means . . . My own view . . . retains the traditional view of Shakespeare as an 'author' in the sense that his 'singular creative agency' determines the specific ordering of language that constitutes his specific achievement. This does not imply that Shakespeare lived in a bubble or that other people weren't involved in the transmission and even the composition of his plays and poems."

As my review of the ten essays suggests, the forum may not solve the question of Shakespearean authorship, but it does clarify the lines of battle, while also indicating just how complex and fruitful the received binary between individuation and collaboration can be. The conclusion drawn here is that the author is alive and well in Shakespeare studies, but that we need to be careful when concluding that this particular author is either simply literary or purely commercial. From the evidence assembled here, we might expect subsequent criticism and scholarship to continue to advance the case for a literary poet-playwright, for a collaborative man of the theater, and for differing ways to see both.

Notes

1. Lukas Erne, *Shakespeare as Literary Dramatist* (Cambridge: Cambridge University Press, 2003).
2. David Scott Kastan, *Shakespeare and the Book* (Cambridge: Cambridge University Press, 2001).
3. Jeffrey Knapp, "What is a Co-Author?" *Representations* 89 (2005): 1–29; Wendy Wall, *The Imprint of Gender: Authorship and Publication in the English Renaissance* (Ithaca: Cornell University Press, 1993).
4. Michael Bristol, *Big-Time Shakespeare* (New York: Routledge, 1996), 58.

Reconsidering Shakespearean Authorship

Lukas Erne

Shakespeare's sonnet 23, which I quote from the edition by G. Blakemore Evans,[1] constitutes an eloquent comment on Shakespearean authorship but also on the traditional resistance to the view of Shakespeare as a self-conscious, literary author:

> As an unperfect actor on the stage,
> Who with his fear is put beside his part,
> Or some fierce thing replete with too much rage,
> Whose strength's abundance weakens his own heart;
> So I, for fear of trust, forget to say
> The perfect ceremony of love's rite,
> And in mine own love's strength seem to decay,
> O'ercharged with burthen of mine own love's might:
> O let my looks be then the eloquence
> And dumb presagers of my speaking breast,
> Who plead for love, and look for recompense,
> More than that tongue that more hath more expressed.
>   O learn to read what silent love hath writ:
>   To hear with eyes belongs to love's fine wit.

Sonnet 23 as quoted above appears not only in Evans's 1996 edition, but also in Helen Vendler's *The Art of Shakespeare's Sonnets* (1997), as well as in many other editions.[2] Their text departs in an important way from the quarto of 1609 in which the poem was first published. In line 9, where Evans, Vendler, and others have "looks," the 1609 quarto has "books." The emendation from "books" to "looks" has a long history, going back all the way to George Sewell who edited the unauthorized seventh volume that was added to Pope's Shakespeare edition of 1725. Sewell has found countless followers in the course of the last three centuries. By the

26

early twentieth century, "looks," as one editor had it, was "an almost certain emendation," and another editor, twenty years later, thought that "looks" was "entirely necessary."[3] Reassuringly, others have disagreed, pointing out that "Books alone agrees with line 13," "O! learn to *read* what silent love hath writ."[4] As Stephen Booth writes, "books is the Q reading and makes sense," so there is no need to emend it.[5] Some have argued that books can hardly be "presagers of [someone's] speaking breast," but Colin Burrow rightly points out that "The word is a new one in the 1590s, and Shakespeare seems to be using it as a near synonym for 'ambassador,' rather than exploiting its associations with understanding of the future."[6]

In fact, the sonnet carefully constructs an opposition between the oral and the literate: the "actor on the stage" (1), the "ceremony of love's rite" (6), "eloquence" (9), "dumb" (10), "speaking" (10), and "tongue" (12) all contribute to the notion of orality to which the sonnet opposes that of literacy: "books" (9), "read" (13), "writ" (13), and "hear with eyes" (14). Yet even when editors realize how important the word "book" is in establishing one of the sonnet's central oppositions and thus do not emend "books" to "looks," their annotation at times seems tendentious. "Books" refers exclusively to Shakespeare's *Venus and Adonis* and *The Rape of Lucrece,* the argument goes. Since both narrative poems are dedicated to the Earl of Southampton, the so-called Southamptonites—who argue that the famous "Mr. W. H." in the prefatory material to the sonnets corresponds to the Earl of Southampton—have been particularly keen to argue this case. Others have maintained that "books," which could refer to any kind of text on paper, even to a single handwritten sheet, in fact refers to the sonnets themselves.[7]

Considering the theatrical context of the sonnet's opening lines, however, it seems significant that editors have generally failed to investigate a rather more plausible reading, namely, that "books" refers to printed Shakespearean playbooks. Stephen Booth is the only exception of which I am aware, pointing out that "Shakespeare may intend a play on 'book' meaning the written text of a stage play."[8] Indeed, just as the speaker, incapable of adequately expressing his love in speech, asks the addressee to witness his written profession of love, so the speaker, an imperfect actor, says that his true eloquence is apparent in his playbooks. To discount this possibility fails to register a simple but powerful analogy established by the sonnet. If we take seriously recent arguments about the dating of the sonnets,[9] then we realize that many of the sonnets addressed to the young man may have been written or revised around the middle of the first decade of the seventeenth century, a time in which a good number of Shakespeare's playbooks had been published. It seems clear that the editorial history of Shakespeare's Sonnet 23 has much to do with the traditional resistance to the view that William Shakespeare wanted his dramatic productions to be read and was aware of the eloquence of his printed playbooks.

I have sketched elsewhere what seems to have sustained this resistance for so long, namely, the interaction of four misassumptions that, by mutually reinforcing each other, contributed to keeping each other in place:

> Firstly, printed playbooks, mostly in quarto format, roughly the equivalent of the modern paperback, allegedly represented mere ephemera. . . . Secondly, Shakespeare had no interest in the publication of his plays. . . . Thirdly, the Shakespeare playbooks that have come down to us supposedly give us the texts as they would have been performed, even in the case of very long plays such as *Richard III* or *Antony and Cleopatra.* And fourthly, when we have plays that survive in both long and short versions—like *Romeo and Juliet, Henry V,* and *Hamlet*—the long texts are thought to represent the "normal" stage version whereas the short ones, which scholars sometimes refer to as "bad quartos," represent anomalies of some kind.[10]

It is easy to see how these misassumptions supported each other: the ephemeral nature of playbooks allegedly explained why Shakespeare was indifferent to their publication. The supposition that Shakespeare only wrote for the stage meant that even Shakespeare's longest plays were thought to have been designed for performance in their entirety. And the idea that these long play texts were performed meant that shorter versions of the same plays had to reflect something different and inferior. This mechanism of mutual reinforcement may well be an important reason why belief in Shakespeare's indifference to his literary reputation, his authorial standing, and his works' survival long remained in place.

The present forum in the pages of *Shakespeare Studies* is one among a number of signs testifying to the fact that our view of Shakespearean authorship has recently received an overdue revaluation. Several publications since the turn of the century have made plausible a Shakespeare who cared about his standing as published dramatic author. In a monograph of 2001, James Bednarz sees the Shakespeare who was involved in the poets' war around the turn of the century as self-consciously literary, aware of his authorial standing, competitive.[11] Even slightly earlier, Richard Dutton was arguing that "in writing plays which were in some respects unplayable . . . [Shakespeare] was effectively writing for a readership no different in essence from that of his sonnets and epyllia," and that "Shakespeare had readers in mind too, however much practical theatrical applications must also have shaped his thoughts."[12] Building on the work of Dutton as well as on that of Peter Blayney, Andrew Gurr, and Stephen Orgel,[13] my *Shakespeare as Literary Dramatist* (2003) similarly argues for an alternative to the exclusively theatrical Shakespeare in whom many have long believed, opposing the beliefs that he was indifferent to the publication and afterlife of his plays and that the only form of publication he ever sought for his plays was the stage. I suggest instead that Shakespeare was acutely aware of and cared about his rise to prominence as a print-published dramatic author, that he and his fellow actors of the Lord Chamberlain's Men had a policy of having his plays published, and that he anticipated and catered to a readership for his plays. Shakespeare's long play texts, I argue, thus give us access to literary versions of his plays that would have been significantly abridged—to something like the length of short quartos such as Q1 *Romeo and Juliet* or *Hamlet*—before reaching the stage.

Scholarship published since 2003 may suggest that the time was right for the view presented in *Shakespeare as Literary Dramatist*. In his British Academy Shakespeare Lecture of 2004, Henry Woudhuysen—one of the general editors of the Arden Shakespeare—holds that printed playbooks were not the "ephemeral items" they have often been taken to be.[14] He argues instead that "Shakespeare must have been aware that his plays had reached print, and this may have influenced the ways in which he wrote," adding that "It is possible to argue, on textual as well as aesthetic or historical grounds, that distinct authorial versions of [Shakespeare's] plays were produced for reading rather than performance."[15] Woudhuysen's argument that Shakespeare "cannot have been entirely indifferent to the phenomenon of seeing plays, including his own, printed" is corroborated by an article by MacD. P. Jackson published in 2005, "Francis Meres and the Cultural Contexts of Shakespeare's Rival Poet Sonnets," which establishes a wealth of telling connections between Meres's "Comparative Discourse" in *Palladis*

Tamia (1598) and the Rival Poet sonnets (78–86), for which recent research strongly suggests a composition date of ca. 1598–1600.[16] Meres compares English and ancient writers, singling out for repeated praise a number of contemporary or recent English authors, including Shakespeare (whose name, it may be well to recall, had not appeared on a single title page prior to 1598). Jackson convincingly demonstrates that "Shakespeare read Meres's 'Comparative Discourse' attentively" and argues that "[t]he Rival Poet sonnets originated . . . in a general sense of rivalry fuelled by Francis Meres's glib inventory of England's top poets and playwrights."[17] Jackson's article considerably strengthens our sense of Shakespeare's self-awareness as a print-published poet and dramatist who profoundly cared about seeing his name and his works in print.

Two recent monographs by Patrick Cheney, *Shakespeare, National Poet-Playwright* (2004) and *Shakespeare's Literary Authorship* (2008), lend further support to this view by demonstrating how the works themselves are preoccupied with an inscription of Shakespearean authorship.[18] Of further significance is *The Cambridge Companion to Shakespeare's Poetry,* for which Cheney served as editor, in which several contributions pay attention not only to the freestanding poems but also to the poetry in the plays.[19] Cheney's work convincingly establishes that Shakespeare was not simply a playwright who occasionally happened to write poems, but that he was a poet and a dramatist throughout his career, writing poetry that could be lyric, narrative, or dramatic, and drama that could function as poems on the page or be adapted and abridged to function as plays onstage.

Shakespeare's standing as a literary author has also been rendered more plausible by Alan H. Nelson who, in an article of 2005, surveys individuals who, during Shakespeare's lifetime, owned libraries that contained at least one book by Shakespeare. He concludes, "against the grain of much modern criticism, that Shakespeare's poems and plays ought to be approached, if we are to respect history . . . as verbal and dramatic art, as—dare I think it?—English Literature."[20] Whether in terms of literary production or of its contemporary reception, the case for a significant Shakespearean literary authorship has been considerably strengthened in the last few years.

Publications have done most to establish Shakespeare's new authorial standing, but work presented at several conferences has duly followed in their wake. In July 2004, Richard Wilson organized a conference at the University of Lancaster with the title "The New Shakespeare: A Writer and His Readers; The Return of the Author in Shakespeare Studies."[21] In March of the following year, a paper session at the conference of the Shakespeare Association of America (SAA), 2005, in Bermuda, was devoted to "Shakespeare's Literary Aspirations," while a seminar at the conference of the British Shakespeare Association (BSA) in Newcastle, in September of the same year, investigated to what extent Shakespearean drama constitutes "an almost oral art" or, conversely, "is already a fully literary art."[22] In 2006, at the World Shakespeare Congress in Queensland, Australia, a panel session addressed the topic of "Shakespeare for Reading," which invited a reconsideration of "the received wisdom of the last fifty years that Shakespeare's texts are, without question, play-texts intended primarily for the stage."[23] The scholarly dissemination of Shakespeare's new authorial standing at conferences and in publications has become such that Catherine Belsey has diagnosed "a quiet revolution in Shakespeare studies": "More than two decades after New Historicism turned our attention away from close reading and toward locating Shakespeare more firmly in his own culture, scholarship is shifting our focus onto Shakespeare's own place in that culture itself, and the case is founded firmly on the texts."[24]

If the beginning of this century is witnessing "a quiet revolution" with the advent of a "New Shakespeare," then it may be asked how this advent ought to affect, or is already affecting, Shakespeare as he is commonly mediated to us in modern editions. As the unwarranted emendation of "books" to "looks" in Sonnet 23 illustrates, we do well not to underestimate the power of editors in shaping our conception of Shakespeare. John Jowett has recently commented on "a new emphasis at the beginning of the twenty-first century, one that pares back the theatrical dimension and asserts on new grounds the presence of Shakespeare the author in the field of textual study." Jowett goes on to evoke the possibility of an immanent "restatement of an authorial orientation" in editorial policy.[25] Such a restatement would need to counter in the first place the policy of the influential Oxford *Complete Works* (of which Jowett himself was an editor), the aim of which was "recovering and presenting texts of Shakespeare's plays as they were acted in the London playhouses." Being given the choice between "a text which is as close as possible to what Shakespeare originally wrote" and "a text presenting the play as it appeared when performed,"

the Oxford editors emphatically opted for the latter.[26] A number of
reputed scholars have recently argued that this policy is in fact profoundly flawed, not only because it relies on an increasingly dated
view that threatens to reduce Shakespeare to "a man of the theatre," but also because the recovery of "Shakespeare's plays as they
were acted in the London playhouses" is simply impossible or, to
use Paul Werstine's word, "quixotic."[27] As David Scott Kastan has
rightly asked, "how are we to know how '[the plays] were acted'?
How can this information be recovered from the witness of the
early printed play texts?"[28] The answer is that we can't. All we have
access to is "the early printed play texts," not early modern performances. Of the two options outlined above, the only one that can
thus be undertaken is editing the text that takes us as close as possible to Shakespeare's authorial composition, not his and his fellow
actors' theatrical adaptation. In other words, an editorial policy in
line with the recent revaluation of Shakespearean authorship attempts to recover the full, unabridged authorial play texts, the play
texts as Shakespeare wanted them to be read, and as he repeatedly
saw them published and republished during his own lifetime.

The second edition of the Oxford *Complete Works* (2005) shows
no change in editorial policy, which has prompted Brian Vickers to
lament "The Oxford editors' stubborn adherence to their theatrical
paradigm."[29] Elsewhere, however, it is apparent that the paradigm
has started to shift. For instance, whereas the Oxford editors based
their *Hamlet* on the supposedly theatrical Folio text, Ann Thompson and Neil Taylor, in the Arden 3 (2006) edition of the same play,
rightly point out that only the much-abridged First Quarto is of a
length that could have been performed, therefore choosing to base
the main volume not on the Folio but on the Second Quarto, the
version reflecting the play as Shakespeare originally conceived it.[30]

Revising the Oxford editors' theatrical paradigm is not only a
matter of copy text, however, but also requires a reconsideration of
the editorial mediation of dramatic action. Early modern play texts
usually contain few stage directions, which has led modern editors
to add their own. As Wells put it, "the editor needs to identify
points at which additional directions, or changes to those of the
early texts, are necessary to make the staging intelligible."[31] As a
result, modern Shakespeare editions suggest that the printed play
texts are surrogate performances, performances of the mind in
which (added) stage directions encourage readers to imagine a theatrical performance. Yet as far as we know, printed play texts were

conceived of rather differently not only by Shakespeare (who could have, but did not, provide additional stage directions) but also by his readers: what we know about their reading habits suggests that they were particularly interested in poetic, "purple" passages or in sententiae, which they highlighted or excerpted, but showed little interest in inferring stage action from the play text.[32] Modern editions with stage directions that are added to the main text (rather than suggested in the commentary) thus arguably fabricate a more theatrical and less literary play text than Shakespeare ever intended.[33]

Even if we grant the usefulness of added stage directions for certain kinds of editions, the exact makeup of these stage directions may still deserve reconsideration. Wells argues that an editor, when adding stage directions, "has to think in terms of the Elizabethan stage," and takes it "as axiomatic that the plays take place, not on heaths, in forests, in castles, in palaces, in ante-rooms, or bedrooms, or throne-rooms, but on a stage."[34] Much editorial practice since the Oxford *Complete Works* conforms to these ideas. Yet if we want to do editorial justice to a Shakespeare who not only wrote play scripts for the stage but also dramatic texts for the page, there is no reason why added directions should be conceived of exclusively in terms of the theatrical representation (i.e., the stage), and not the represented dramatic fiction (i.e., the castles, etc.). *Pace* Wells, what takes place onstage is not simply plays but theatrical performances, whereas a play text that is read (as is the case with modern editions) takes place in the reader's imagination, which can easily picture the dramatically represented instead of the theatrical representation. An editorial practice that encourages readerly engagement with the fictionally represented seems all the more appropriate as Shakespeare's early modern play texts contain not only theatrical but also fictional stage directions: in *Coriolanus,* characters "*enter the City*" (TLN 568); in *Timon of Athens,* the protagonist enters "*out of his Caue*" (TLN 2360); in *Julius Caesar,* Brutus enters "*in his Orchard*" (TLN 615); and a stage direction in *2 Henry VI* records a "*Fight at Sea*" (TLN 2168).[35] Examples could be multiplied at will.[36] What this means is that an editorial practice that adds not only theatrical but also literary stage directions does better justice to a Shakespeare who was not only a playwright but also a literary dramatist.

If Shakespeare, to return to Sonnet 23, not only cared about the "actor on the stage" but also about his own dramatic "books" and their "eloquence," then it seems important that modern editions reflect the Shakespeare that a growing body of recent scholarship has proposed to us. By avoiding a policy that unduly privileges the theatrical over the literary, editors thus play a vital role in mediating to us the plays in a form that does justice to Shakespeare's early modern authorial standing.

Notes

1. G. Blakemore Evans, ed., *The Sonnets,* the New Cambridge Shakespeare (Cambridge: Cambridge University Press, 1996).

2. Helen Vendler, *The Art of Shakespeare's Sonnets* (Cambridge, MA.: Harvard University Press, 1997). For other editions reading "looks," see Hyder Rollins, ed., *The New Variorum Edition of Shakespeare: The Sonnets,* 2 vols. (Philadelphia: Lippincott, 1944), 1:66–67.

3. H. C. Beeching, ed., *The Sonnets of Shakespeare* (Boston: Athenaeum Press, 1904); T. G. Tucker, ed., *The Sonnets of Shakespeare* (Cambridge: Cambridge University Press, 1924).

4. Sidney Lee, ed., *The Complete Works of William Shakespeare,* 40 vols. (New York: George D. Sproul, 1907), vol. 38.

5. Stephen Booth, ed., *Shakespeare's Sonnets* (New Haven: Yale University Press, 1977), 172.

6. See Rollins, ed., *The Sonnets,* 1:66–67; Colin Burrow, ed., *The Complete Sonnets and Poems,* the Oxford Shakespeare (Oxford: Oxford University Press, 2002), 426.

7. See Rollins, ed., *The Sonnets,* 1:66–67.

8. Booth, ed., *Shakespeare's Sonnets,* 172. For an incisive recent discussion of the sonnet in the light of Shakespearean authorship, see Patrick Cheney, " 'O, let my books be . . . dumb presagers': Poetry and Theater in Shakespeare's Sonnets," *Shakespeare Quarterly* 52 (2001): 222–54, revised and reprinted in *Shakespeare, National Poet-Playwright* (Cambridge: Cambridge University Press, 2004), 207–38, in particular 220–25.

9. See Katherine Duncan-Jones, ed., *Shakespeare's Sonnets,* Arden Shakespeare (Walton-on-Thames, Surrey: Thomas Nelson, 1997), 1–28.

10. Lukas Erne, "For the Stage *and* the Page," *Around the Globe* 26 (2004): 36–37.

11. See James P. Bednarz, *Shakespeare and the Poets' War* (New York: Columbia University Press, 2001). Scholars working on Shakespearean coauthorship have also strengthened our sense of Shakespeare's proprietary sense of his own writings. See, in particular, Brian Vickers, *Shakespeare, Co-Author: A Historical Study of Five Collaborative Plays* (Oxford: Oxford University Press, 2002); and Jeffrey Knapp, "What Is a Co-Author?" *Representations* 89 (2005): 1–29.

12. Richard Dutton, "Shakespeare: The Birth of the Author," in *Licensing, Censorship and Authorship in Early Modern England: Buggeswords* (Basingstoke: Palgrave, 2000), 111–12.

13. See, in particular, Peter Blayney, "The Publication of Playbooks," in *A New*

History of Early English Drama, ed. John D. Cox and David Scott Kastan, 383–422 (New York: Columbia University Press, 1997); Andrew Gurr, "Maximal and Minimal Texts: Shakespeare v. the Globe," *Shakespeare Survey* 52 (1999): 68–87; and Stephen Orgel, "Acting Scripts, Performing Texts," in *Crisis in Editing: Texts of the English Renaissance,* ed. Randall McLeod (New York: AMS Press, 1994), 251–94, repr., Orgel, *The Authentic Shakespeare and Other Problems of the Early Modern Stage* (London: Routledge, 2002), 21–47.

14. H. R. Woudhuysen, "The Foundations of Shakespeare's Text," in *Proceedings of the British Academy: 2003 Lectures* (Oxford: Oxford University Press, 2004), 74–77 and 88–89.

15. Ibid., 92, 99.

16. Ibid., 84; MacD. P. Jackson, "Francis Meres and the Cultural Contexts of Shakespeare's Rival Poet Sonnets," *Review of English Studies* 56 (2005): 224–46 and "Vocabulary and Chronology: The Case of Shakespeare's Sonnets," *Review of English Studies* 52 (2001): 59–75.

17. Jackson, "Francis Meres," 236, 243.

18. Patrick Cheney, *Shakespeare, National Poet-Playwright* (Cambridge: Cambridge University Press, 2004), and *Shakespeare's Literary Authorship* (Cambridge: Cambridge University Press, 2008). Of related interest is Charlotte Scott's *Shakespeare and the Idea of the Book* (Oxford: Oxford University Press, 2007). See also Jason Gleckman, "Shakespeare as Poet or Playwright? The Player's Speech in *Hamlet,*" *Early Modern Literary Studies* 11.3 (January 2006): 2.1–13 (http://purl.oclc.org/emls/11–3/glechaml.htm), which finds in the fiction of *Hamlet,* more specifically in the player's speech in act 2, scene 2, an enactment of the tension between the literary drama by Shakespeare, the author, and the theatrical play by Shakespeare, the playwright.

19. Patrick Cheney, ed., *The Cambridge Companion to Shakespeare's Poetry* (Cambridge: Cambridge University Press, 2007).

20. Alan H. Nelson, "Shakespeare and the Bibliophiles: From the Earliest Years to 1616," in *Owners, Annotators and the Signs of Reading,* ed. Robin Myers, Michael Harris, and Giles Mandelbrote, 70 (London: Oak Knoll Press, 2005).

21. Some of the work presented at this conference is published in Richard Meek, Jane Rickard, and Richard Wilson, eds., *Shakespeare's Book: Essays in Reading, Writing and Reception* (Manchester: Manchester University Press, 2008).

22. I quote from the seminar description posted on the conference Web site at http://www.ncl.ac.uk/niassh/shakespeare. The BSA seminar was led by Neil Rhodes. The SAA paper session was chaired by the present author and featured papers by Patrick Cheney, Katherine Duncan-Jones, and Richard Helgerson.

23. I quote from the panel description posted on the conference's Web site, www.shakespeare2006.net. The panel featured contributions by Sukanta Chaudhuri (chair), Paul Eggert, and Lena Cowen Orlin.

24. Catherine Belsey, review of *Shakespeare, National Poet-Playwright, Shakespeare Studies* 34 (2006): 170.

25. John Jowett, "Editing Shakespeare in the Twentieth Century," *Shakespeare Survey* 59 (2006): 18–19.

26. Stanley Wells, introduction to *William Shakespeare: The Complete Works,* ed. Stanley Wells and Gary Taylor, with John Jowett and William Montgomery (Oxford: Oxford University Press, 1986), xxxvii, xxxiii.

27. Ibid., xxxiv; Paul Werstine, "McKerrow's 'Suggestion' and Twentieth-

Century Shakespeare Textual Criticism," *Renaissance Drama* 19 (1988): 149–73. See also Andrew Gurr, "A New Theatre Historicism," in *From Script to Stage in Early Modern England,* ed. Peter Holland and Stephen Orgel, 71–72 (Basingstoke: Palgrave Macmillan, 2004).

28. David Scott Kastan, *Shakespeare after Theory* (London: Routledge, 1999), 65.

29. Brian Vickers, "Are all of them by Shakespeare?" *Times Literary Supplement,* August 11, 2006, 10.

30. Ann Thompson and Neil Taylor, eds., *Hamlet,* Arden Shakespeare (London: Thomas Learning, 2006), 8–13, 506–9. The companion volume by the same editors—*Hamlet: The Texts of 1603 and 1623* (London: Thomas Learning, 2006)—contains the First Quarto and the Folio texts.

31. Stanley Wells, *Re-Editing Shakespeare for the Modern Reader* (Oxford: Clarendon Press, 1984), 68.

32. See Erne, *Shakespeare as Literary Dramatist,* 227–30.

33. For an essay that argues against added stage directions and advocates instead discussion of staging options in the commentary, see John D. Cox, "Open Stage, Open Page? Editing Stage Directions in Early Dramatic Texts," in *Textual Performances: The Modern Reproduction of Shakespeare's Drama,* ed. Lukas Erne and M. J. Kidnie, 178–93 (Cambridge: Cambridge University Press, 2004). For the argument that editors should do more to mediate to modern readers the specificities of the early modern printed play text, see Lukas Erne, "Shakespeare for Readers," in *Alternative Shakespeares 3,* ed. Diane E. Henderson (London: Routledge, 2007), 78–94.

34. Wells, *Re-Editing Shakespeare for the Modern Reader,* 70, 69.

35. I refer to the through-line numbering (TLN) adopted in Charlton Hinman, ed., *The First Folio of Shakespeare: The Norton Facsimile,* 2nd ed. (1968; New York: Norton, 1996).

36. For a fuller development of the present argument, see Lukas Erne, *Shakespeare's Modern Collaborators* (London: Continuum, 2008).

"To think these trifles some-thing": Shakespearean Playbooks and the Claims of Authorship

David Scott Kastan

—Who's that?
—No one. The author.
         —*Shakespeare in Love*

AUTHORSHIP MATTERS. It is not merely that we want to know who has written what we read (think of the recent excitement over the outing of Laura Albert as "J. T. LeRoy") or sometimes who has written what we don't read (as is the case with much of the interest in the Shakespeare authorship question), but, more abstractly, if also more consequentially, the concept of authorship is tightly tied to the urgent claims of individuality against the impersonal forces of history. The widely proclaimed "Death of the Author," as authorship threatened to dissolve into discourse or into the collaborative forms of textual production, has in recent years been vehemently denied, in the case of Shakespeare, by the spate of recent biographies and the sudden critical focus on "Shakespeare the Thinker."[1] The author lives; the postmodern understanding of discourse is denied, as is the New Historical understanding of a premodern literary system.

In truth, the historical author only ever died, one could say, historically. That is, Shakespeare died in 1616, but as a writer he lived (*pace* Barthes), active, thoughtful, and willful, even as his intentions were sometimes compromised in the necessary collaborations of the theater and the printing house, and as his thought was necessarily affected (not imprisoned) by the discourses that circulated and by the language in which he did his thinking. One needn't

37

choose between two false alternatives: a Shakespeare unfettered by history or language, or a Shakespeare who is a mere epiphenomenon of one or the other.

But that is the way things have largely gone, or at least the way things have been construed by those few who would take one or the other of the extreme and indefensible positions. More sensible is to recognize Shakespeare's agency within the conditions of possibility for writers in his time. The difficulty posed by this, however, is that this seems to leave us with a Shakespeare whose plays have granted him an iconic cultural position as an author but that were written, performed, and published in artistic, legal, and institutional circumstances that do not quite allow the idea of authorship in any robust, historically specific sense to be applied—not least because Shakespeare (unlike, say, Jonson) seems to have had no interest in it. As my epigraph above, from the film *Shakespeare in Love,* suggests, in the early modern theater, the author was not of primary importance.

This is not, of course, to say that playwrights always happily acceded to this fact. There is indeed evidence of playwrights (and not just Jonson) using print to assert the authority of their creation against the reshapings of the theater or to defend it from the hostility of its audiences. The title page of Webster's *Duchess of Malfi* (1623) announces that the published text appears "with diuerse things Printed, that the length of the Play would not beare in the Presentment" (although it, contradictorily, also insists that it offers the text "As it was Presented priuatly, at the Blackfriars, and publiquely at the Globe, By the Kings Maiesties Seruants"). Robert Daborne, in his preface to *A Christian Turn'd Turk* (1612), admits, "I haue, so farre as my weake power extended, procured the publishing this oppressed and martird Tragedy" (sig. A3r), just as Webster, in the same year, includes a preface to *The White Devil* in which he defends his actions: "In publishing this Tragedy I do but challenge to my selfe that liberty, which other men haue tane before mee . . . since it was acted, in so dull a time of Winter, presented in so open and blacke a Theater, that it wanted . . . a full and understanding auditory" (sig. A2r). Playwrights did occasionally assert their right to publish their plays (Heywood noting that "some have used a double sale of their labours, first to the Stage, and after to the presse"), but the number of these is small and the authors almost always at least overtly apologetic for, what John Ford calls, "My presumption of coming in Print."[2]

It has been usual, however, to insist, since Shakespeare was not one of those who presumptuously claimed "that liberty" to publish (perhaps because, as a sharer, he didn't have to), that print was not the form of publication he sought for his plays. Scholars, of course, have long made much of the distinction between the Shakespeare who wrote for the stage and the one whose two long poems appeared published by Richard Field, carefully printed and with dedications by Shakespeare. Shakespeare the poet wrote for readers and seemed (except perhaps in the case of his sonnets) eager for print; Shakespeare the playwright wrote for spectators and cared nothing for publication. To the degree Shakespeare the playwright is an author (rather than a writer), it has been argued, he became so unwittingly, constructed as such by the efforts of the early modern book trade rather than through his own efforts or ambitions.[3]

Recently, however, this familiar story has been upended. Lukas Erne has written a bold, provocative, and unquestionably important book arguing for a Shakespeare who was not merely a man of the theater but who was always writing for readers and who, along with his company, "had a coherent strategy" (115) to get his plays into print—arguing, that is, for a Shakespeare who was indeed an author, committed both to his readers and to print publication.[4] Most of the evidence for the claim is divided over two chapters, one on the publication history of the plays before Elizabeth's death and one on the history under James. The first of these argues that one can discern a regular pattern of publication, normally two years after a play was performed, with the aim of serving as "publicity" for continued performances of the play. The second tries to account for the fact that the pattern clearly breaks around 1600. Only five new plays appeared in print between 1600 and Shakespeare's death in 1616, and Shakespeare's works as a percentage of overall play publication drops from 18 percent in the decade before 1603 to only 4 percent in the decade following (109). Nonetheless, Erne insists that this later history cannot be taken to undermine his thesis about Shakespeare's continuous commitment to publication, because "such indifference would be difficult to account for after a policy of regular and systematic publication from 1595 to 1603" (114), leading to his hypothesis that "Shakespeare and his fellows" (and much is occluded in this conflation) had begun to imagine "a collected edition and therefore refrained from publishing in cheap quartos" (114).

Though somewhat circular in its defense, it is an attractive thesis, not least because it points to what indeed took place (i.e., the publication of the Folio in 1623)—though that might also make us suspicious of it. Knowing what happened, it is easy to imagine that it had to be that way. But there is no evidence that Shakespeare, the acting company, or its patrons in the early seventeenth century imagined a collected edition, and, by Erne's own admission, none that publication was much on any of their minds in that period. Heminge and Condell, in their dedication of the Folio to the Herberts, commend the brothers for having "been pleas'd to think these trifles some-thing, heeretofore" (sig. A2r), and, while Erne observes that "these suggestive words do nothing to rule out the possibility that Pembroke and his brother had been for some time Shakespeare's most important readers" (112), they do nothing to prove it either, being offered as evidence, as the Folio says, of the two earls' "likings of the severall parts, when they were acted" (sig. A2v). The argument, then, rests on two pillars: (1) what we know did happen; and (2) the claim about the "regular and systematic publication from 1595 to 1603." The first seems to me clearly a common error of historical thinking, the second at least worthy of another look.

Erne's vision of "a coherent strategy to get Shakespeare's plays into print" (87) depends largely on the claims that "of the first dozen or so plays Shakespeare wrote for the Lord Chamberlain's men, not a single one that could legally have been printed remained unprinted by 1602" (86) and that each appeared in print "at an interval of roughly two years between composition and entrance" (84). While the first is arguably true (although some things are quickly passed over in the phrase "that could legally have been printed"), the latter depends on a highly conjectural dating of the plays, and, in any case, the history of these early publications might easily be used to suggest conclusions different from those Erne reaches about the motives of "Shakespeare and his fellows."

Erne's eagerness to argue for a literary Shakespeare leads him to reject the familiar narrative of the actors' resistance to having the play texts they owned appear in print. Thomas Heywood's well-known claim that actors "thinke it against their peculiar profit to haue [their plays] come in Print" is disregarded (125).[5] The "Articles of Agreement" for the sharers in the Whitefriars Theatre, insisting that "noe man of the said company shall at any time hereafter put into print, or cause to put into print any matter of playe book now in use, or that hereafter shalbe sould unto them" (upon the severe penalty of forty pounds or the loss of the share),[6] is explained away as referring only to the licensed copy that the company needed to keep in their possession (126–27). The epistle introducing the quarto of *Troilus and Cressida* (1609), which seems to say that the intentions of the Lord Chamberlain's Men as owners of the play text ("the grand possessors' wills") were to keep the play from being published, is dismissed as a marketing ploy (123). Brome's 1635 contract with the Salisbury Court theater enjoining him from publishing without the sharers' permission is not considered. There is no mention of the letter from the then Lord Chamberlain, Philip, Earl of Pembroke, noting the unauthorized publication of plays in the repertory of the King's Men and ordering "the stay of any further impression of any of the playes and interludes of his majesties servants without their consents," since, by the unauthorized publication, "not only they themselves had much prejudice, but the books much corruption, to the injury and disgrace of the authors."[7] But the letter from his brother, the previous Lord Chamberlain, of May 3, 1619, which has not survived but which is minuted in the court records of the Stationers' Company, and which resulted in an order that no plays of the company were to be printed without the "consents" of "some" of the sharers in the acting company,[8] is discussed, though taken as a pointer to Pembroke's support for the Folio project (112) rather than as an indication of his opposition to unauthorized printing.

Though this evidence all comes from the seventeenth century, it is hard to imagine that conditions and attitudes had completely changed from the last decade of the sixteenth century. At the very least, it suggests that we should be wary of too quickly replacing an old insistence upon the players' opposition to print with a new account of their systematic engagement with it. The evidence suggests something far less consistent and coherent (and that may very well vary from company to company), at best pointing here to an acting company eager to control the publication of plays, but that is not, therefore, evidence of Shakespeare's affirmative commitment to print or of an identity of interest between the acting company and the playwright.

We all agree that nineteen of Shakespeare's plays were individually published before the Folio appeared in 1623. By 1603, fifteen of these were already in print. Six of the fifteen—*2 Henry VI, 3 Henry VI, Romeo and Juliet, Henry V, Hamlet, The Merry Wives of Windsor*—appeared first in versions once known as "bad quartos,"[9] and, setting aside the judgmental language and all the assumptions it carries with it, seem almost certainly to have arrived at the printing house without Shakespeare's initiative or even his knowledge. Of these, two, *Romeo and Juliet* and *Hamlet,* were soon succeeded by new versions designed to replace deficient and apparently unauthorized printings. Possibly a third is in that category. If *Love's Labor's Lost,* which appeared in 1598 with a title page announcing it as "Newly corrected and augmented," was designed to replace a now lost unauthorized printing of the play, as many believe, it would mean that before 1603, seven plays had appeared first in unauthorized editions.[10] If publicity was indeed the motive for publication, it is not, in any case, immediately clear why a "bad" quarto would serve this end less well than a "good" one, while the evidence of the publication of the seemingly authorized replacement quartos of *Romeo and Juliet* and *Hamlet* (and perhaps *Loves Labor's Lost*) but not the others suggests less a conscious strategy of publicity at work than an unsystematic, if unusually vigorous, reaction to the appearance of defective texts.

The other eight plays published before 1603—*Titus Andronicus, Richard II, Richard III, 1 Henry IV, A Midsummer Night's Dream, The Merchant of Venice, 2 Henry IV,* and *Much Ado About Nothing*—appeared in editions that might plausibly be thought to reflect the desire or at least the willingness of Shakespeare to see them in print in the form they were published. (Of these, *Richard III* is the most contested, with many thinking the quarto some kind of reconstruction by actors.)[11] But even if all eight appeared with the approval of Shakespeare and by the design of the company, that would mean that nearly one-half of the plays of Shakespeare that appeared in print by this time were not printed as part of a regular publication strategy by Shakespeare or his company, rendering it, therefore, something less than "regular."

And even of these eight that might have been offered to the press by Shakespeare, several seem unlikely candidates for Erne's thesis. The first edition of *Titus,* as Erne realizes, can hardly be taken as evidence for it, since the play was published soon after it was first performed, appearing without Shakespeare's name on the title page and advertising it "As it was Plaide by the Right Honourable the Earle of *Darbie,* Earle of *Pembrooke,* and Earle of *Sussex* their seruants." It had been entered in the Stationers' Register by John Danter on September 6, three days after an order shutting the theaters beginning on the seventh because of an outbreak of plague. Later that year, the play appeared in print, printed by Danter and published by Edward White and Thomas Millington. The publication history, like the performance history, is complex, but almost certainly publication was motivated by the closing order in an effort to salvage something from the termination of performances of what was a successful new play. Republished in 1600 and again in 1611, it appears still without Shakespeare's name, but with the theatrical auspices updated: in 1600, it is identified as having been played "sundry times" by the Lord Chamberlain's company, and in 1611, as having been played by the King's Men, as the company became upon the accession of James in 1603. Although by 1598, Shakespeare's name had begun to appear with some regularity on the title pages of his playbooks, in the case of *Titus Andronicus* Shakespeare's name never seemed either necessary or sufficient to vend the playbook in the reprintings, nor did the Chamberlain's Men quickly turn to publication to publicize either the play or the company itself.

But it is the group of plays entered in the Stationers' Register provisionally or formally "stayed" that we should turn to, since these have often been taken as compelling evidence for the thesis that the company tried to prevent unauthorized printing of its plays. This seems certainly to be the case with *Patient Grissel,* a new play in 1600 for the Admiral's Men. On March 18, Henslowe's account book records a loan of forty shillings "to geue vnto the printer to staye the printing of patient grisell."[12] On March 28, Cuthbert Burby entered the play, presumably to prevent any other stationer from printing it. In the event, in 1603, the play was published by Henry Rocket, a former apprentice of Burby, but whether this was now with permission of the company is unknown.

There is nothing quite so clear in the Shakespeare canon, but on July 22, 1598, James Roberts "Entred for his copie vnder the handes of bothe the wardens, a booke of the Marchaunt of Venyce or otherwise called the Jewe of Venyce. Prouided that yt bee not prynted by the said James Robertes or anye other whatsoeuer without lycense first had from the Right honorable the lord Chamberlin."[13] Little of this is odd. Roberts was presumably known to the company (having a monopoly on the printing of playbills), and conditional entries in the Register are not uncommon, granting a stationer the right to print once proper authorization has been received (e.g., John Marriot's entry for John Donne's poems on September 13, 1632, which gives Marriot the right to publish "when he brings lawfull authority" [Arber, 4:285]). But here the entry's term, "lycense," cannot mean what it normally does, that is, the Stationers' permission to print; nor can it refer to the ecclesiastical license (what Marriot must get before he can publish Donne) that was necessary after the copyright law of 1586. For *The Merchant of Venice,* the authorization needed for publication is the Lord Chamberlain's, and not only Roberts but also "any other whatsoeuer" is enjoined from printing the play without the Lord Chamberlain's approval, presumably not in his governmental capacity, which had no direct control of the book trade, but in his role as patron of the acting company that owned the play texts, though the former would no doubt increase the reluctance of any stationer to ignore the order.

This looks to be a different strategy to accomplish the same thing as the Admiral's Men payment. The acting company has effectively kept control of its play text. On October 28, 1600, "A booke called the booke of the merchant of Venyce" was entered by Thomas Hayes "under the handes of the Wardens and by Consent of James Roberts" (Arber, 3:175), and the play was published later that year, published by Hayes and printed by Roberts. Here the company seemingly did, as was perhaps the case with *Patient Grissel,* allow publication of the play several years after it was played. But it seems far less likely that either stay of publication was intended as the initial step of a publicity campaign designed over time to revitalize interest in the play than that it was designed to prevent more immediate threats to an asset from unauthorized printing.[14] Even authors sometimes took preemptive action, as Chapman does in selling his *All Fools* to Thomas Thorpe, as he says, "Lest by others stealth it be imprest" (sig. A2r).

The four plays "staied" in the summer of 1600—*As You Like It, Henry V* (in fact almost certainly *2 Henry IV), Much Ado About Nothing,* and Jonson's *Every Man In His Humor*—seem to me to reflect a similar concern.[15] Erne argues that the order came about because the plays lacked the necessary ecclesiastical license (103), but, as that was clearly not the case with the provisional entrance of *The Merchant of Venice,* and as all four of these are here specifically identified as "My lord chamberlens menns plaies," it seems more probable that these also were set aside, like *The Merchant,* until the acting company was ready to authorize publication, preventing stationers who had not at least paid them for the texts to bring them into print. In any case, as three of these (excepting only *As You Like It,* which did not appear in print until the Folio) were soon entered and published, none can be used to support the putative strategy of delayed publication.

So we are left with perhaps no more than four plays of the fifteen published before 1603 that can easily be said to contribute to Erne's "recognizable pattern which bespeaks a coherent strategy" (101) and none that gives evidence of Shakespeare's own commitment to it. The pattern claimed to be "too regular to be accidental" (100) is in reality too haphazard to show a pattern at all, and hardly enough to bear the burden of explaining away the absence of any evidence for the interest in publication after 1603 (114). And, even if such a pattern could be more clearly discerned, surely it says far more about the acting company's theatrical interests than any literary ones of Shakespeare.

For the acting company, print might indeed be a form of advertising. Peter Blayney has made a compelling argument of this sort to explain various spikes in the publication of plays that correspond to the reopenings of the theaters after outbreaks of plague that closed them for substantial periods of time: print as publicity.[16] But it isn't clear how such publicity would advance the literary ambitions of a dramatist. Indeed the now familiar claim that print turned drama into literature or at least (as I think even I have argued in print) becomes literature with the publication of the Jonson and Shakespeare folios, is worth reconsideration, if only from the fact that booksellers' catalogs well into the eighteenth century continue to separate plays from poems (Moseley, for example, separating "incomparable Comedies and Tragedies" from "Choise Poems"), and that Shakespeare's poems, which do appear in various unauthorized supplements soon after Rowe's 1709 edition, must wait another eighty years for Malone's *Plays and Poems of William Shakespeare* (1790) to appear together. The evidence really suggests that, as it gets published, the printed drama becomes a category of its own, competing in the marketplace with other recognizable categories of reading material like literature, religion, and history.[17]

But if the publication history, then, offers at best ambiguous evidence for Erne's thesis, his contention that "about a dozen of Shakespeare's plays are too long to have been performed—or to have been intended to be performed—in their entirety" (175) is unarguable and suggestive. For Erne, this is the flip side of the earlier argument: the internal evidence of Shakespeare's literary ambitions. These long texts (over 2800 lines, but interestingly including none of the comedies) record what Erne, following some contemporary usage, calls "the poem" (190), the version written to be published and read, but it seems to me that, although the focus on length is valuable, the conclusions drawn from it are unjustified. These long plays indeed will not fit into "the two hour's traffic of our stage" (*Romeo and Juliet,* Prologue, l.12), even into the "three hours spectacle" mentioned in James Shirley's preface to the 1647 Beaumont and Fletcher Folio, but that fact itself says nothing about Shakespeare's commitment to print and readership, only about his own exercise of his writerly interests and integrity.

Erne, however, holds that the length of Shakespeare's long plays is incomprehensible if Shakespeare had "no considerations for their appearance in print" (140), but his own evidence shows that plays were routinely abridged for the theater. Humphrey Moseley, in his publishers' preface to the Beaumont and Fletcher Folio, explains matter-of-factly: "When these *Comedies* or *Tragedies* were presented on Stage, the *Actours* omitted some Scenes and Passages (with the *Author's* consent) as occasion led them" ("The Stationer to the Reader"). Many playwrights wrote plays that were too long to be performed, knowing that they would be cut in the theater. This was the common condition of playwriting, not the atypical evidence of a commitment to print.[18]

Nonetheless, the focus on long plays does show that Shakespeare was not simply a practical man of the theater, as many have held, interested only in the commercial success of his and his company's plays. Or perhaps it shows only how very practical Shakespeare's theatrical sense was, always aware of the near inevitability of abridgment, which is precisely what allowed him to exercise his unmatched abilities as a *writer,* probing and pushing the logic of his language and his characters well beyond the limits of what "our stage hath shown" (*Henry V,* Epilogue, l.13) or even what it could show. But it does not prove that he is an *author,* as the word was becoming gradually defined in the cultural and legal institutions of the day. There still is no evidence of his own desire for his plays to be printed and read.

Nonetheless, whatever resistance it demands, the triumph of Erne's book is that it is no longer possible to talk about Shakespeare and "authorship" without considering its strong claims. It has remarkably changed our sense of Shakespeare almost overnight. Even in the scholarly community, Erne's conclusions have quickly become facts, widely cited and approved. But the eagerness to accept its conclusions as they have overturned the once fixed idea of Shakespeare's indifference to print is perhaps more instructive than the argument he makes for it. The excitement the book has generated is itself evidence of how important Shakespeare is to us, and how much authorship itself matters. We want to believe in a Shakespeare who is an author, to rescue him from the necessary collaborations of the stage, even from the agency of the printing house, which, it seems to me, largely invented Shakespeare the Literary Dramatist for its own purposes rather than for those of the author it created, or for those of the playwright and writer he unquestionably was.

Notes

1. The first phrase, of course, is the title of Roland Barthes's celebrated essay, first published in English in *Image—Music—Text,* trans. Stephen Heath (London: Fortuna, 1977); the second is the title of A. D. Nuttall's recent book (New Haven: Yale University Press, 2007), published soon after his untimely death on January 24; but see also Colin McGinn, *Shakespeare's Philosophy: Discovering the Meaning Behind the Plays* (New York: HarperCollins, 2006); and Philip Davis, *Shakespeare Thinking* (London: Continuum, 2007).

2. Heywood, *The Rape of Lucrece* (London, 1608), sig. A2r; *The Lover's Melancholy* (London: 1629), sig. A2r.

3. See my *Shakespeare and the Book* (Cambridge: Cambridge University Press, 2001); Andrew Murphy, *Shakespeare in Print: A History and Chronology of Shakespeare Publishing* (Cambridge: Cambridge University Press, 2003); and Douglas Brooks, *From Playhouse to Printing House: Drama and Authorship in Early Modern England* (Cambridge: Cambridge University Press, 2000).

4. Erne, *Shakespeare as Literary Dramatist* (Cambridge: Cambridge University Press, 2003).

5. "To the Reader," in *The English Traveller* (London, 1633), sig. A3r.

6. Quoted in Evelyn May Albright, *Dramatic Publication in England, 1580–1640* (1927; repr., New York: Gordian Press, 1971), 239.

7. Quoted in E. K. Chambers, *William Shakespeare* (Oxford: Clarendon Press, 1923), 1:136.

8. William A. Jackson, *Records of the Court of the Stationers' Company* (London: Bibliographic Society, 1957), 110.

9. The term, of course, comes from Alfred W. Pollard, *Shakespeare's Folios and Quartos: A Study in the Bibliography of Shakespeare's Plays, 1594–1685* (London: Methuen, 1909), chap. 3.

10. Arthur Freeman and Paul Grinke, "Four New Shakespeare Quartos?" *Times Literary Supplement,* April 5, 2002, 17–18, found in the library catalog of Edward, 2nd Viscount of Conway, an entry for: "Loves Labours Lost by W: Sha: 1597," at least establishing the existence and the date of an earlier edition of the play. The 1598 quarto's claim that it is "Newly corrected and augmented" echoes other contemporary title page formulae that sometime accurately describe the new text (e.g., Q2 *Romeo and Juliet*) and at other times are mere publishers' puff (e.g., Q2 *1 Henry IV,* where the title page claim of "Newly corrected" is untrue).

11. For a clear and useful account of the quarto text of *Richard III*, see John Jowett's Oxford edition of the play (2000), 119–27.

12. *Henslowe's Diary,* ed. R. A. Foakes and Edith Rickert (Cambridge: Cambridge University Press, 1961), 132 (f. 68r).

13. Edward Arber, ed., *A Transcript of the Registers of the Company of Stationers of London, 1554–1640 A.D.* (1875; repr., Gloucester: Peter Smith, 1967), 3:122.

14. In this context, it is perhaps worth noting the complaint of Thomas Middleton in 1608, upset that the publication of his *Family of Love* did not take place "when the newnesse of it made it much more desired" (London, 1608, sig. A1v).

15. See Arber, 3:37, recording a supplementary leaf in Register C, dated August 4, 1600:

> As you like yt, a booke
> Henry the ffift, a booke
> Euery man in his humour, a booke
> The commedie of much A doo about
> nothing, a booke

are all entered with the notation "to be staied." Peter Blayney, in an unpublished paper, has convincingly argued that the entry's "Henry the ffift" is a mistitling of *2 Henry IV,* not least because within three weeks, Andrew Wise and William Asply "Entered for their copies vnder the handes of wardens Two bookes. the one called Muche a Doo about nothinge. Thother the seconde part of the history of kinge Henry the IIIIth with the humours of Sir John Ffallstaff: Wrytten by master Shakespere" (Arber, 3:170).

16. Blayney, "The Publication of Playbooks," *A New History of Early English Drama,* ed. John D. Cox and David Scott Kastan (New York: Columbia University Press, 1999), p. 386.

17. John Benson's 1640 edition of the *Poems: Written by Wil. Shake-speare Gent.* is instructive in this context, for, while it might be taken as a supplement to the Second Folio of 1632, it is published in a small octavo format. Adam Hooks, in a series of brilliant conference papers and in what will be a groundbreaking dissertation, has been arguing for the need to rethink the claim that print turns drama into literature, insisting on a both richer understanding of the publishing environment and of the nature of the category of literature itself. I am grateful to Hooks and András Kiséry, whose own impressive work on these topics is beginning to appear, for help formulating and clarifying the argument of this essay.

18. See Andrew Gurr, "Maximal and Minimal Texts: Shakespeare v. The Globe," *Shakespeare Survey* 52 (1999): 68–87. See also Stephen Orgel, "Acting Scripts, Performing Texts," in *Crisis in Editing: Texts of the English Renaissance,* ed. Randall McLeod (New York: AMS Press, 1994), 251–94. It would be useful to have a systematic consideration of the length of published playbooks by playwrights other than Shakespeare or Beaumont and Fletcher, and written for companies other than the King's Men.

Shakespeare as Coauthor

Jeffrey Knapp

Tracing the hands of other writers in the plays that have been traditionally ascribed to Shakespeare only has yielded a picture of
Shakespeare's career as a coauthor that is strikingly at odds with
current histories of authorship in Renaissance English drama generally. According to these histories, collective playwriting was both
the practical and the theoretical norm in English theaters until
around 1600, when the idea of single dramatic authorship first
began to surface. It makes sense, by the light of these accounts, that
evidence should suggest Shakespeare might have cowritten such
early plays as the first part of *Henry VI* and *Titus Andronicus.* It
also fits the current historical view, at least to some degree, that little evidence of substantial coauthorship has been uncovered in
Shakespearean drama written around the turn of the seventeenth
century. But the surprise from the current perspective is that the
strongest evidence of coauthorship in the Shakespearean corpus
should crop up where the supposed historical trajectory from plural to single authorship would lead us to believe it shouldn't,
toward the end of Shakespeare's career—in *Timon of Athens, Pericles, Henry VIII,* the lost *Cardenio,* and *The Two Noble Kinsmen.*
Why would Shakespeare have returned to collaborative writing
after its heyday was past, and, even more bafflingly, after he had
already achieved fame as a single author?

Some of the perplexity vanishes when the historical claim about
collaboration to authorship vanishes too. Collective playwriting, as
I've argued elsewhere, was never the practical or theoretical norm
during the English Renaissance.[1] Even though multiple authors
often collaborated on writing plays in the commercial Renaissance
theater, contemporaries typically assumed that plays were written
by single authors. But Shakespeare, thoroughly immersed in the
theater business as an actor who owned a share both in his acting

company and in the theaters where he played, came to regard the reigning authorial paradigm as an essentially literary concept that failed to capture the complexity of his aims and methods as a theatrical professional. Rather than take the time in this brief essay to demonstrate these points anew, I want instead to show how Shakespeare's return to coauthorship at the end of his career bears out a different theater history than the one that most scholars now take for granted: not the rise of the single author, but rather "an increasing readiness to acknowledge joint creations."[2]

This growing interest in multiple authorship came slowly, and it never made enough headway against the dominant single-author paradigm to move collective playwriting from the theoretical shadows entirely. In the rest of my essay, I'll survey the Renaissance book market to see how Shakespeare might have drawn on other genres of collective writing as guides to help him resolve this conceptual difficulty, and then I'll look more closely at one of his late coauthored plays, *Pericles,* to ask how Shakespeare came to understand his own coauthorial practice. The question has significant ramifications for theater history beyond the narrow issue of attribution, because whether his decision to coauthor influenced his choice of story line or his choice of story line influenced his decision to coauthor, Shakespeare's return to collective playwriting coincided with a major change in his dramaturgy: his abandonment of tragedy and his adoption of romance.

*   *   *

No one can say how many of the Renaissance publications that were advertised as single authorships were actually the products of multiple writers, but we can identify the books that were advertised as coauthorships and that therefore must have seemed, to writers or publishers in any case, to make sense as coauthorships. The most notable fact about these acknowledged cowritings is that they are relatively scarce. And the scarcest of them are works that fit the Beaumont and Fletcher model of coauthorship, which is to say, coauthorship by living contemporaries, or what I'll call contemporaneous coauthorship. Within this subgroup of acknowledged cowritings, three genres predominate: histories, devotional literature, and plays, with devotional literature providing far and away the most popular titles, and plays providing far and away the greatest number of different titles as well as the greatest number of different coauthorial partnerships. The prevalence of these genres is revealing, because the books in all three were for the most part easily divisible into units that could be parceled out to different writers: histories by reigns or years or countries; devotional literature by sermons or scriptures; plays by scenes or acts or speeches. And indeed contemporaneous coauthorships did often give credit to diffcrent writers for the different parcels of the books they jointly authored, making these coauthorships seem less like exceptions to the rule of single authorship than several single authorships bundled together. The title page of John Dod and Robert Cleaver's highly popular *Ten Sermons* (1609), for instance, specifies that Dod wrote "the six first" and Cleaver "the four last," while the title page of the first avowedly coauthored play, *The Tragedie of Gorbudoc* (1565), likewise declares that "three Acts were written by Thomas Norton, and the two last by Thomas Sackville."[3]

So authoritative was the single-author paradigm during the Renaissance, however, that even acknowledged coauthorships were regularly treated as the work of one author only. Despite the fact that both writers are named in the dedicatory letter to the most popular acknowledged coauthorship in the Renaissance, Dod and Cleaver's *Plaine and Familiar Exposition of the Ten Commandements* (1604), contemporaries nearly always referred to the book as the work of Dod alone, who came to be known as "Decalogue Dod."[4] One exception, a 1613 epigram that tells how "Dod with his Cleaver cleaves the stony rock / Of our hard hearts through their laborious pain," nevertheless ends by insisting that the two coauthors are one and the same: "Though two in Name, in Nature yet not twain." When John Aubrey reports how Beaumont and Fletcher not only "lived together" but also "lay together; had one Wench in the house between them, which they did so admire; the same clothes and cloak, &c.; between them," he too portrays a pair of coauthors as effectively one.[5] In their *Dialogicall Discourses of Spirits and Divels* (1601), the coauthors John Deacon and John Walker make the same singularizing claim about themselves: their letter to the reader recounts how the news of John Darrel's supposed exorcism of William Sommers "did so diversely affect our *minds* with a diverse and contrary *judgment* (the one very constantly *avouching,* the other no less confidently *impugning* that falsely pretended *action*)" that their friendship was nearly ruined, till "the favorable assistance of *God's holy spirit*" led them to "the very *truth* it self, . . . whereupon also, we eftsoons began to *speak both of us but one and the selfsame thing:* and (which is more) being now knit together in one *mind* and one *judgment* concerning these several matters, we determined forthwith to put down in writing, whatsoever had deliberately passed between us."[6]

One might think that Deacon and Walker's vision of coauthorship as a mutually achieved singleness would prove difficult to sustain in the more common form of acknowledged coauthorship during the Renaissance than cowriting by contemporaries: posthumous coauthorship, in which a living writer was typically said to have "corrected," "augmented," "revised," "enlarged," "continued," or "finished" the work of a dead writer or writers. The most popular posthumous coauthorship of the day, *Hero and Leander: Begun by Christopher Marloe; and Finished by George Chapman* (1598), was so unmistakably a bundle of single authorships that each poet's parcel began with a separate dedication never mentioning the other poet in the venture. But the conceptual pressure to read coauthorships as single authorships did nonetheless make it possible to treat even posthumous cowritings as the work of "one *mind* and one *judgment*." The simplest method was, again, to ignore all but one of the coauthors. When for instance *An Epitome of Cronicles . . . First, by Thomas Lanquet . . . and Now Finished and Continued . . . by Thomas Cooper* (1549) was reprinted eleven years later, its title had changed to *Coopers Chronicle . . . by Me Thomas Cooper* (1560).

Such compression could also happen without suppression. For a culture that prided itself on reviving the classics, it was conventional to assert that a dead author had been *resurrected* in a living one. Thus Ben Jonson (1616) assured Sir Henry Savile that Savile's translation of Tacitus made Jonson almost "believe, the soul of *Tacitus . . .* liv'd" again in Savile, while Thomas May (1629) countered criticisms that John Ford had drawn his play *The Lover's Melancholy* "from Shakespeare's mine" by asking "What need?—when Shakespeare still survives in you." On occasion, this transmigration of souls could even be rationalized into a straightforward bequest from the dead author to the living one. In *The Survey of London . . . Begun First by the Pains and Industry of John Stow, in the year 1598. Afterwards inlarged by the care and diligence of A[nthony].M[unday]. in the year 1618. And now compleatly finished by the study & labour of A.M. H[enry].D[yson]. and others, this present year 1633* (1633), the later author Munday explained that the earlier author John Stow had hoped to enlarge his *Survey* himself, "but prevented by infirmity, and Sickness-bringing

Death," Stow had "imparted not only his good Intentions, but best Collections also unto me."[7] Without usurping upon or otherwise disrupting the single authorship of his predecessor, a living cowriter could assert his own authorship by taking the place of the dead author as his *heir*.

*   *   *

Pericles begins with a dead author revived. In place of the living dramatist or dramatists whom the text never mentions, the prologue to *Pericles* offers us the medieval English poet John Gower, one of the sources for the play, who maintains that he has returned "from ashes" to "sing a song" he claims as "*my* rhymes." Somewhat incongruously, Gower also casts himself in the role of the living partner in a posthumous coauthorship: "I tell you what mine authors say," he declares, without informing us who these older authors might be.[8] This unstable substitution of the single author Gower for unnamed living authors and unnamed dead ones looms larger when we consider the overwhelming evidence that *Pericles* was coauthored by Shakespeare and George Wilkins.[9] By attributing their modern play to a writer who died two hundred years beforehand and who in acknowledging his debts to earlier authors speaks for the living authors in relation to himself, Shakespeare and Wilkins introduce *Pericles* as only *figuratively* a single authorship.[10]

But why would living writers use the figure of a dead writer to signify their present collaboration? The evidence we can glean of Shakespeare and Wilkins's coauthorial practice in *Pericles* suggests that they drew on the logic of posthumous coauthorship to help them suppose a unity in their contemporaneous coauthorship. As G. E. Bentley notes, the advertised practice of "separate composition" by "individual acts" in Inns of Court plays such as *Gorbudoc* became a "common" procedure in the commercial Renaissance theater as well. Like their amateur predecessors Sackville and Norton, Wilkins and Shakespeare appear to have divided the composition of *Pericles* this way, with Wilkins writing most of the first two acts and Shakespeare most of the last three.[11] This parceling out of *Pericles* suggests that the play was conceived from the start as a bundle of single authorships. But the conflation of old and new in Gower's opening resurrection gives an interesting cast to the division of labor that made Shakespeare's portion of the play the later work in the order of performance and reading, if not also of composition. When the "ancient" poet Gower claims to sing for these "latter times," he not only combines in one person the earlier and later positions of a posthumous coauthorship: he also figures the later writer as the earlier one *rcvivcd*.[12]

The first scene of *Pericles* renews this stress on a continuity between past and present while also revising the terms of that continuity. In place of Gower's ghostly revival, the play now speaks of children and inheritance: Pericles hopes to become "son to great Antiochus" by marrying his "heir." From this beginning, inheritance turns into a defining concern not only for the rest of *Pericles* but for the rest of Shakespeare's late plays generally. In the three or four years before *Pericles,* Shakespeare seems to have written nothing but tragedies: *Othello, King Lear, Macbeth, Antony and Cleopatra, Coriolanus,* and *Timon of Athens*.[13] Needless to say, these plays offered little hope that a new generation might continue or complete the work of the generation before it. In the last of the tragedies especially, this loss of generationality was tied to protagonists who overvalue their singleness. Thus Coriolanus ends his life boasting of the exceptional prowess that earned him his honorific, not inherited, name—"Alone I did it"—while Timon in his own final scene obsessively proclaims his desire to "be alone." With *Pericles,* however, Shakespeare managed to envision a future of "new joy" beyond the single life of his protagonist, which in turn created a future for himself beyond the single genre of tragedy, and the change seems tied to Shakespeare's sense of having *inherited* the tragicomedy of *Pericles* from Wilkins.[14] As most critics of the play agree, the point in the action of *Pericles* where Shakespeare makes his entrance as an author is a spectacular scene of childbirth.

A spectacularly tragic scene: the mother dies and the child is abandoned.[15] Inheritance—the transmission of resources from one generation to the next—is no simple process in *Pericles.* This is true from the first of Wilkins's scenes as well. Antiochus does not want a son-in-law, or even exactly a daughter, whom his incest makes his "mother" and "wife" as well as "child." The man who chooses to short-circuit generationality this way is not coincidentally a tyrant whose "chiefest" city, Antioch, bears his name and no one else's; he is a demonically powerful version of a single author.[16] At the end of Wilkins's contribution to the play, Pericles finds a better father-in-law in a ruler who is less "absolute" and "peremptory"— words that this second king, Simonides, applies to his daughter Thaisa's love for Pericles. Rather than force Thaisa to "frame" her "will" to his own, Simonides gives his "consent" to a marriage "agreed" upon by husband and wife that also happens to "agree" with his own desires.[17] For Wilkins, a generational future is made possible by a father who adopts a consensual rather than a conquering or imperialist approach to parenting—like the inveterate coauthor Robert Cleaver, who even in his single-authored tract on *The Patrimony of Christian Children* (1624) stresses that the book was written "with the joint consent of Mr. John Dod."[18]

When Shakespeare inherits the script of *Pericles,* however, he underscores a resistance to generationality on the part of the child as well as the father in Wilkins's portion of the play. If Antiochus does not want a son to take his place, Pericles does not want to take the place of his father: instead, he searches for a foster father from whom he can *choose* and *win* his inheritance. Shakespeare insists on the tragic consequences of Pericles' refusal to conceive of himself as determined in any substantial way by his father's authorship of him: after his own child Marina is born, Pericles leaves her with foster parents, once again denying that father and heir have any essential bond between them.[19] Further sustaining Pericles' faith that he alone has authored the "volume" of his "deeds" is the apparent death of his wife in childbirth, which echoes the fate of Antiochus's wife "who died and left a female heir." A servant of Thaisa presents Marina to Pericles as "all that is left living of your queen." By abandoning the baby, Pericles distances himself not only from the identity he shares with the child but also from the parentage he shares with the mother.[20]

Shakespeare joins Wilkins in blaming such tragic threats to generationality on an extreme, Antiochan investment in single authorship. But Shakespeare views Wilkins's consensual model of coauthorship as too weak to resolve these threats on its own, and too weak, by implication, to substantiate coauthorship in the face of the dominant single-author paradigm. One might guess that Shakespeare attributed this weakness to the awkwardness of Wilkins's having patterned consensual unity on heterosexual marriage: Shakespeare's discomfort with imagining his coauthor as his husband or wife would explain why the climax of his portion of the play should turn on Pericles' coming to terms with his heir, not his wife.[21] But Pericles' heir is female, like Antiochus's; the gender difference and, thanks to Antiochus's incest, even the sexual complications of the marriage model still pertain in Shakespeare's representation of inheritance. What's more, the renewed bond between father and child does not end up displacing marriage in the play: it leads instead to the mother's return.[22] Like other contemporaries, Wilkins and Shakespeare tried to explicate their coauthorship through fictions of consensual and generational oneness that could assimilate their collective writing to single authorship, but Shakespeare more than Wilkins insisted on heterosexual discordancies in these fictional unions and therefore on the difficulties of conflating one author or one model of authorship with another. More than Wilkins, Shakespeare also stressed the sheer variety of authorial models that *Pericles* evokes. Throughout his portion of *Pericles,* collective writing draws strength as a conceptual project from the very tensions that make the different theories of authorship in the play impossible to subsume under the "supremacy" of one hegemonic paradigm.[23] Each model as *Pericles* dramatizes them—the imperialist paradigm, which suppresses all but one author; the consensual paradigm, which makes one mind and judgment of two authors; and the generational paradigm, which treats the new author as the resurrected image of the old—possesses a narrative and cultural plausibility that denies "absolute" power to any of the others.

If Shakespeare in the first of his romances thus addressed not the emergence of single authorship but rather its possible *disintegration* as a way to conceive of playwriting, he also acknowledged that coauthorship lacked the power to "contend" successfully against single authorship as a conceptual model and therefore had to rely on the reigning paradigm for its own intelligibility. The first and last words in the play belong, after all, to Gower and Gower alone. For Shakespeare, the best face to put on this dependency was to present it as a compromise. When for instance in the final movement of Shakespeare's contribution to *Pericles* the self-isolated father embraces his daughter as "thou that beget'st him that did thee beget," the terms of their reunion suggest how the generational theory of coauthorship could be understood as striking a balance between singularity and consensus. Rather than displace one another or else become as one, Wilkins and Shakespeare could regard each other instead as both progenitor and heir: while one author originates his portion of the play and the other inherits it, the second writer might seem in the end to have developed issues from the other's script that the first writer neither recognized nor anticipated there. The last scene of *Pericles* forecasts how a similar balance between single and multiple authorship could be negotiated along consensual lines as well. Not until this final scene, when Shakespeare completes Wilkins's script, do Pericles and Thaisa ever jointly see their daughter. Their joyful response to her seems to hold the promise for Shakespeare that each cowriter of *Pericles* could in the end acknowledge the authorial role of the other while still legitimately claiming the "issue" of their collective enterprise as "mine own."[24]

Notes

1. See my "What is a Co-Author?" *Representations* 89 (2005): 1–29.
2. Brian Vickers, *Shakespeare, Co-Author* (Oxford: Oxford University Press, 2002), 10.
3. I cite the dates of first editions only. *Ten Sermons* had eleven editions between 1609 to 1634.
4. The *Ten Commandements* went through eighteen editions between 1604 and 1635. The best introduction to Dod remains William Haller's *The Rise of Puritanism* (New York: Columbia University Press, 1938), esp. 56–62. Haller mentions Cleaver only once in his entire book (120).
5. William Gamage, *Linsi-Woolsie. Or Two Centuries of Epigrammes* (Oxford, 1613), D1r-v; John Aubrey, *Aubrey's Brief Lives,* ed. Oliver Lawson Dick, 2nd ed. (1957; Jaffrey, NH: David R. Godine, 1999), 21.
6. Deacon and Walker, *Dialogicall Discourses of Spirits and Divels* (London, 1601), A5r-v.
7. Ben Jonson, *Epigrammes* (1616), no. 95, in *Ben Jonson,* ed. C. H. Herford and Percy and Evelyn Simpson (Oxford: Oxford University Press, 1925–52), 8.61; May, quoted in *The Jonson Allusion-Book: A Collection of Allusions to Ben Jonson from 1597 to 1700,* ed. Jesse Franklin Bradley and Joseph Quincy Adams (New Haven: Yale University Press, 1922), 141; John Stow, Anthony Munday et al., *The Survey of London* (London, 1633), A3r (a 1618 edition of the *Survey* contains a slightly different version of Munday's account).
8. *Pericles,* 1.0.1–2, 12 (my emphasis), and 20; I cite *The Riverside Shakespeare* (Boston: Houghton Mifflin, 1974) throughout.
9. For an excellent summary of the evidence, see Vickers, *Shakespeare.*
10. As Steven Mullaney notes in *The Place of the Stage: License, Play, and Power in Renaissance England* (Chicago: University of Chicago Press, 1988), "Gower in fact conceals as much as he reveals, especially where the genealogical entanglements of Shakespeare's sources are concerned" (148). Mullaney does not mention Wilkins. For more on the instability of Gower as a figure for authorship, see also Jeffrey Masten, *Textual Intercourse: Collaboration, Authorship, and Sexualities in Renaissance Drama* (Cambridge: Cambridge University Press, 1997), 77–78.
11. See G. E. Bentley, *The Profession of Dramatist in Shakespeare's Time, 1590–1642* (1971; Princeton: Princeton University Press, 1986), 228–34. This parceling out by acts was not the only available method of coauthorship, nor would it have prevented the authors from consulting with each other and possibly edit-

ing each other's contributions to the play. In a letter to the theatrical impresario Philip Henslowe, the actor-playwright Nathan Field asserts that he and another playwright, Robert Daborne, "have spent a great deal of time in conference" about the "plot" of a play they are cowriting (*The Henslowe Papers,* ed. R. A. Foakes, 2 vols. [London: Scolar Press, 1977], vol. 2, no. 100).

As Suzanne Gossett observes in her Arden edition of the play (London: Thomson Learning, 2004), "Almost all readers of *Pericles* note a striking change in the quality of the poetry at the beginning of the third act" (62). For the evidence that Wilkins composed the first two acts of *Pericles* and Shakespeare the last three, see esp. Vickers' and Gossett's detailed accounts of such scholars as Dugdale Sykes, who underscored the "frequent omission of the relative pronoun in the nominative case" (Sykes, quoted in Vickers, *Shakespeare,* 300) in the first two acts, which happens often in Wilkins's other writings but rarely in Shakespeare's; MacDonald Jackson, who isolated three rhyme pairs—"consist/resist," "him/sin," and "impudence/offence"—that appear in the first two acts of *Pericles* and in Wilkins's play *The Miseries of Inforct Marriage* but nowhere else in Shakespeare's attributed works; David Lake, who drew our attention to the presence in the first two acts of *Pericles* and in the *Miseries* of "rifts—a series of couplets broken by an unrhymed line, aabcc—and rafts, or couplets appearing sporadically in passages of blank verse" (as paraphrased by Gossett, ed., *Pericles,* 64); and Ernst Honigmann, who discovered that "beginning a phrase with 'which' or 'to which' or 'of which' (the so-called Latin resumptive) and . . . beginning a sentence or phrase with 'this' or 'by this' or 'to this'" (as paraphrased by Gossett, 64) happens twenty times in the first two acts of *Pericles,* yet not at all in the last three.

12. *Pericles,* 1.0.2 and 11.

13. *Pericles,* 1.1.26 and 1.0.22. Although the chronological order of Shakespeare's plays remains speculative, most scholars agree that these tragedies were written between 1604 and 1608. Even with the possible interspersal of a comedy such as *Measure for Measure,* the clustering of tragedies is striking.

14. *Coriolanus,* 5.6.116; *Timon,* 4.3.100; *Pericles,* 5.3.102.

15. Pericles immediately decides to "leave" (3.1.79) the baby at Tharsus, although he does stay with her a while before departing from Tharsus without her.

16. *Pericles,* 1.1.69, 1.0.18. Cf. Masten: "the incest . . . figures a particularly totalizing version of the (dangerous) control the author-function is said to exert" (*Textual Intercourse,* 80).

17. *Pericles,* 2.5.19, 73, 81–82, 76, 90, and 18.

18. I quote the title page of the book. In his epistle dedicatory, Cleaver explains that "I durst not be too confident of my self, nor lean too hard on mine own judgment, but entreated, and obtained the assistance of that worthy and judicious Baronet, Sir *Erasmus Dryden,* and of the reverend learned, and eminent Divine, Master *John Dod,* with others of good note" (*Patrimony,* A4r).

19. While Pericles does celebrate the recovery of a suit of armor that "my dead father did bequeath to me" (2.1.124), this is so superficial a connection that Simonides can warn observers not to undervalue the armored Pericles by mistaking "the outward habit" for "the inward man" (2.2.57).

20. *Pericles,* 2.2.3, 1.0.22 and 3.1.17–20. My thinking here derives from Stanley Cavell's *Disowning Knowledge in Seven Plays of Shakespeare* (Cambridge: Cambridge University Press, 1987). For the suppression of motherhood in the play, see esp. Janet Adelman, *Suffocating Mothers: Fantasies of Maternal Origin in Shake-*

speare's Plays, Hamlet to The Tempest (New York: Routledge, 1992), 193–99, and Coppélia Kahn, "The Providential Tempest and the Shakespearean Family," in *Representing Shakespeare,* ed. Murray Schwartz and Coppélia Kahn, 217–43 (Baltimore: Johns Hopkins University Press, 1980).

21. Interestingly, the play has little to say about homosocial friendship as a model of unity. The loyal Helicanus serves as Pericles' "substitute" (5.3.51) at Tyre, and Pericles calls him "mine own" (5.1.214), but he is also "ancient" (5.3.51), like Gower, and therefore seems less a friend than another nonbiological father figure for Pericles. To Shakespeare's mind (as I'll shortly explain) the problem with friendship is not so much the possible sexual dimension of its unity (on which see Masten, *Textual Intercourse,* esp. chap. 2), as its lack of biologically generative power.

22. Adelman claims that "the play exorcizes sexuality itself and remakes the sexual family by nonsexual means, permitting it to escape its origin in the problematic maternal body" (*Suffocating Mothers,* 196), but Caroline Bicks rightly points to Thaisa's implicit promise at the end of the play that her "sanctity" will "bend" a "licentious ear" to her "sense" upon the recovery of her husband ("Backsliding at Ephesus: Shakespeare's Diana and the Churching of Women," *Pericles: Critical Essays,* ed. David Skeele [New York: Garland, 2000], 222).

23. "Supremacy" is what Pericles attributes to his father after Simonides has reminded him of his father: "In that glory once he was; / Had princes sit like stars about his throne, / And he the sun for them to reverence; / None that beheld him but, like lesser lights, / Did vail their crowns to his supremacy" (2.3.38–42).

24. *Pericles,* 1.2.17 and 5.1.195; at Ephesus, Pericles proclaims Marina "my daughter" (5.3.13) and Thaisa calls her "mine own" (48). Steevens was the first to add a comma to Pericles' "mine own Helicanus" (5.1.214) and thus change it into the statement that Marina is "mine own, Helicanus," but the emendation is uncertain.

Early Modern Authorship in 2007

Wendy Wall

MY GOODNESS. Reading Jeffrey Knapp's "What is a Co-Author?" one would think that scholars who have argued for a collaborative notion of authorship in late sixteenth-century England simply got all of their facts wrong. Attacking the claim that single authorship was "not the norm," Knapp marshals a heap of evidence to show that many early modern people recognized writers as writers, and that works by authors were published before the modern author supposedly emerged.[1] To my mind, it's all fine and good to offer a corrective to a story in which authorship was dreamed up suddenly in 1616 or 1623. And it's certainly useful to say that facts can be assembled so as to tell a story other than the one in which authorship does not have a starring role in the culture. But it also seems clear to me that the "facts" are not unambiguous. And if the facts can be arranged to tell different and somewhat contradictory stories—which I'll caricature as "authorship was historically different in the early modern period" vs. "actually authors were much the same as we imagine"—then it's reasonable to consider what diverse stories enable us to teach and to say about literature.

I was asked to participate in this forum because my 1993 book, *The Imprint of Gender,* argued that authorship was conceptualized in Renaissance printed poetic texts in gendered and sexualized ways.[2] This project started with my skepticism over the claim that because early modern plays were collective, social, and malleable, they lacked the "authorization" that poetic texts had. After reading Arthur Marotti's work on manuscript exchange and surveying prefaces to early printed works, I realized that printed poetic texts were also collectively and collaboratively produced works with unstable boundaries and shifting attributions.[3] Because manuscript was the medium of choice for contemporary elite writers, book producers had to take some pains to shape a legitimized notion of the published *poetic* text. In showing that problems of textual fixity and attribution didn't just crop up in drama, I engaged debates about authorship.

Now I'm asked to think about whether my view of authorship has changed in light of recent work. My first thought is that there are several ongoing debates about early modern authorship. The question posed to me whenever I give a public address on Shakespeare's works is whether someone named Shakespeare actually wrote these plays or not. Most scholars, having settled that question to their satisfaction, work in a different terrain. Knapp, as I've mentioned, rejoins the debate about collaboration vs. single authorship. Other critics, taking up the obverse side of the assumption that I questioned in *Imprint,* ask whether the conditions of writing for the theater did in fact mitigate against a notion of authorship as much as has been claimed. Still other scholars zero in to consider Shakespearean authorship in particular—whether he wrote for the stage and/or page and how his actions and works fashion some idea of "the author." These arguments overlap in their rejection of oversimplified claims proclaiming the complete irrelevance of modern notions of authorship in the early modern world. One important gain of recent work is thus to incite scholars to sort out the variables so that we don't mindlessly repeat reductive versions of what has become the latest conventional wisdom (e.g., "there were no such things as authors in 1600"). But since the facts about the conditions of writing and publishing still seem sketchy and ambiguous to me, I don't feel invested in revisiting and rearranging evidence to prove that Shakespeare is an author and always was. The entire world outside of the ivory tower holds this to be true.

By all means, scholars have a responsibility to be accurate in our empirically based claims. But to my mind, there are only a few "facts" at hand to dispute. Most scholarship on the subject isn't making a splash because it unveils new facts. Instead scholars distinguish themselves by how they collate information and employ various terminologies as they arrange bits of knowledge (existing facts, new documents, new ways of reading old materials) into interpretative paradigms.

Although it clearly is a simplification, we might say that there are two early modern world pictures assumed or argued in authorship scholarship: one emphasizing the historical remoteness of categories now assumed to be obvious, another confirming that authorship and writing have more continuity with concepts today than had been imagined. Scholars, including myself, who have put more weight on the first narrative, sought a corrective to the general assumption that authors remain the same in all eras. A writer thinks up an idea; he (yes, in this period the writer is usually male) writes; his relationship to his writing is somewhat untroubled. Influenced by Foucault and armed with some facts about scripts and manuscript exchange, scholars found evidence from the early modern period that complicated this imagined scene of writing. Certainly the sixteenth century had writers and some of those writers were called authors and thought of themselves as such (did anyone dispute that?), but the legal and social arrangements supporting any one individual's assertion of authorship were quite different then than they are today. By "arrangements," I mean to point to whether or not people could own their texts legally, could sue someone who published their works, or could establish a claim to these texts in forms other than a speech act.

Given the complexity of these inquiries, including some fairly interesting disagreements about basic terminology and about what constitutes proof, citations of "facts" such as title page attributions simply won't settle the matter. Let's return to Knapp who, at one point, cites Jeffrey Masten's contention that half of all plays were collaboratively written in the period, and then observes that this "fact" indicates that half of the plays written were not.[4] This "glass half empty/ half full" conundrum confirms my somewhat banal intuition: single authorship was functional in the period, as were other modes of production. The other modes have been more interesting to me—and to some other scholars and students—because they allow us to imagine literature and writing and being as other than they are now.

Then I began to ponder the dilemma that facts are pressed into service as evidence for claims that seem incommensurate, depending on what is meant by the term "author." "Did Shakespeare have literary aspirations?" is a very different question than "did playwrights conceptualize their works as writing?" or, more broadly, "was there a place carved out in the culture for imagining a single 'authoritative' play text?" Likewise, asking if authors existed isn't the same thing as posing the question of whether modern conceptions of authorship were in play or were the norm. And establishing whether plays are legitimately "literary" objects of analysis might or might not involve looking at *representations* of author figures in works or considering how much control an author had over his written text (for this depends on what "literary" means). I'm not sure that facts aid us in collating or disentangling claims about authorial intention, "literariness," and textual fixity since the tougher questions rest in understanding these sweeping terms and their relationship to each other.

The bottom line is that this matrix of questions, weighty as they are, just hasn't been resolvable by recourse to the "facts." And so, if different plausible stories can be generated to account for poetic and dramatic production in the period, then I'm inclined to choose the story that emphasizes historical differences and thus that creates some intellectual heavy lifting and self-scrutiny; that is, it opens up important conceptual questions to consider the *discrepancy* between the sonnets' compelling articulations of poetic immortality and the lack of evidence that Shakespeare chose to put the sonnets into print. Imagining a world in which different versions of a play or a poem traveled freely beyond the confines of their authors' control is simply a launching pad, for me, for another type of interpretive question. And since the period offers ample evidence that some writers and book producers sought to shape the version of authorship that later became the norm, it's reasonable for other scholars to choose differently and to emphasize aspects and practices that link the present and past. Scholars are certainly not mandated to teach only counterintuitive narratives when they have a choice of historical stories to tell. But the "facts" give me liberty to highlight the elements of early modern literary writing that I find the most baffling: the acts and languages and lexicons that display unfamiliar and competing options for conceptualizing authorship, writing, and textual circulation. I still find it noteworthy that the works of Sidney, and of Donne, were only published posthumously, if only because this throws into relief the labor required by authors to shape a personae in print.

The thrust of some recent and provocative work has moved in the opposite direction. Lukas Erne, for instance, thoughtfully sifts historical evidence to relocate Shakespeare as a literary and not only a theatrical creator.[5] He seeks to establish that the playwright had recognizable literary pretensions, acknowledging that Shakespeare lived in a moment in which literary pretensions were made manifest in what are now considered unusual ways. In this story, it is important that Shakespeare's plays appeared in print regularly in the 1590s, roughly two years after a performance, and that some existing texts were too long to have been performed on the stage. In this story, the "bad" quartos do have some affinity with what was performed, while the longer texts are more literary (meaning conducive to reading rather than being heard). Presto: we see Shakespeare inhabiting a world in which plays get regularly printed, read, and preserved in a form other than performance. And it is the circumstantial evidence of the habits and activities of that world that allows Shakespeare to be seen as a recognizably modern author, even if we don't have facts demonstrating that he himself sought to put most of his writing into printed form.

Such an account, to my mind, is entirely plausible. And it offers an important corrective. But it remains as speculative as the view being countered; that is, some facts do support this view but they are not unambiguous and the story does prompt skeptical questions from critics with their eye on other facts. If Shakespeare had clear literary pretensions, why don't we see more evidence that he sought to put his literary versions into print and prevent performance-based versions from being published? Were these longer play versions truly sealed off from the vicissitudes of theater culture? If a person wrote a script longer than could be performed, does that necessarily mean that the longer version was thought of as "literary" by the writer? And is "literary" a matter of taste? It's hard to say.

Narrating this story requires a reinterpretation of the facts. For instance, Erne suggests that Shakespeare was offended by the printing of his poems under another name in *The Passionate Pilgrim*. Shakespeare's state of mind is derived not from something Shakespeare wrote but from Thomas Heywood's emotionally high-pitched description of some perceived publishing offense. Given the ubiquitous and conventional charges made by writers and book producers that their works had been surreptitiously published or that some audience had been scandalized by a publication, I can imagine other equally persuasive ways of reading Heywood's report. As such, it seems reasonable for scholars to disagree about how much to weigh this letter against the "fact" that that Shakespeare appears not to have had a direct hand in publishing most of his works. These are issues that scholars debate about Shakespearean authorship.

If the "critique of authorship" narrative has become standard, it is important to provide new accounts that force scholars to resift and rethink the evidence. And if one implication of the "critique of authorship" story is that Shakespeare's plays can only be treated

legitimately as performance texts, then I welcome alternative narratives. But my work will not be part of this collective revisionary
project. In fact, my sense that Shakespeare's plays are "literary"
(meaning complex writing deserving of the attention that we give
to things that can be repeatedly read), derives not from what Shakespeare thought about his writing, but from the texts themselves
(yes, I know, a risky thing to say, as if the texts have a self-evident
"nature." But I'm willing to take this risk.) My point is that some
scholars may see it useful to stay outside the game of guessing intentions or arguing authorship theories altogether but still appreciate some of the goals that corrective readings achieve.

　　Instead of helping to arbitrate what Shakespeare definitively
thought of his career (how would we prove a state of mind?), I thus
want to see how different (historically evidenced) notions of authorship illuminate our reading of texts. This is, I confess, largely a
matter of taste. I happen to be more interested in arguments that
culminate in *interpretative* rather than *empirical* analyses (just as
I'm attracted less to an individual writer's self-conception and
more to the clashing of conceptions in the culture at large). In this
regard, I find Patrick Cheney's work on Shakespearean authorship
particularly useful, since he's not as keen to establish facts about
publication dates as he is to examine how Shakespeare's texts
themselves meditate on different models of authorship: Ovidian
conceptions bleeding into Marlovian, Virgilian into Spenserian.[6] If
intentions will always remain in these circumstances hazy, why
not think instead about how competing theories of authorship arise
in textual representations of performance and writing? While such
evidence can't be used to refute empirical statements, it certainly
can reveal, as Cheney does, how discourses of the theater and of
poetry jostled uneasily but fruitfully in literature of the period. Witness the ways that *Rape of Lucrece* trades on the lexicons of blot-
ting, publication, and showing to examine ethics, politics, gender,
embodiment, and self-inscription. If all scholarly narratives about
early modern authorship, including my own, remain conjectural,
then why not foreground the *fictive* realm where ambiguity and
contradiction are so richly productive? In *Imprint of Gender* my
goal was to consider authorship only as part of a larger project of
teasing out the tropes and discourses circulating within and without texts, those figures that coalesced in the voyeurism of prefaces
and the cross-gendering of writers anxious about appearing in
print.

So I end up helping my fellow contributors make little progress on the question at hand. I think that we collectively have much to offer students in thinking broadly about what "literature" and "writing" are and how they change over time. Part of this mission involves keeping our eye on the way that "facts," marshaled so handily in our narratives about literary history, often don't sit stably in one place. And understanding the limitations on what can be proven authoritatively about authorized texts, authorship, and authority can give us license to turn more energetically to the murky terrain of complex representation. Offering tools for approaching these complexities is, after all, a not insignificant part of the teaching mission of many English Departments. I don't know for sure if Shakespeare was an author in the way that my students and the public routinely assume, but I do know that settling the question isn't as important as showing that these psychologically and socially provocative fictions have something to say, especially as they prompt us to ask more questions.

Notes

1. Knapp, "What is a Co-Author?" *Representations* 89 (2005): 1–29.
2. Wendy Wall, *The Imprint of Gender: Authorship and Publication in the English Renaissance* (Ithaca: Cornell University Press, 1993).
3. Arthur Marotti, "Shakespeare's Sonnets as Literary Property," in *Soliciting Interpretation: Literary Theory and Seventeenth-Century English Poetry,* ed. Elizabeth D. Harvey and Katharine Eisaman Maus, 143–73 (Chicago: University of Chicago Press, 1990).
4. Jeffrey Masten, *Textual Intercourse: Collaboration, Authorship, and Sexualities in Renaissance Drama* (Cambridge: Cambridge University Press, 1997).
5. Lukas Erne, *Shakespeare as Literary Dramatist* (Cambridge: Cambridge University Press, 2003).
6. Patrick Cheney, *Shakespeare, National Poet-Playwright* (Cambridge: Cambridge University Press, 2004).

"Our Bending Author": Shakespeare Takes a Bow

RICHARD WILSON

It hapned, that as they passed throow one street, Don Quixote looked up, and saw written upon a doore in great Letters, "Heere are Bookes printed," which pleased him wonderously; for till then he had never seen any Presse; and he desired to know the manner of it.

—Cervantes, *Don Quixote*

Toward the end of *Don Quixote,* the doleful knight wanders into a Barcelona printing house, "where he saw in one place drawing of sheetes, in another Correcting, in this Composing, in that mending: Finally, all the Machine that is usual in great Presses." Here he is introduced to "the Author, a good comely proper man" but "somewhat ancient," whom he wishes luck before asking about the book being printed: "they answered him that it was called *The second part of the Ingenious Knight, Don Quixote de la Mancha.*"[1] What must concern any authorship forum is how the Don wants his book burned. For as Carlos Fuentes observes, this is surely the first time a character learns how he becomes a literary product and is condemned to be a fiction. Thus, "The act of reading is both the starting point and the last stop on Don Quixote's route." For Fuentes, this episode of chill foreboding, published a year after Cervantes' death, marks the birth of the author, as it is when "reality is displaced by *another* reality made of words and paper. Where are the limits between Dunsinane and Birnam Wood?" Only Shakespeare, says Fuentes, foresees the coming of the book with the sinking feeling that makes *Don Quixote* so *sorrowful.* And when Cervantes leaves the page open where the reader knows himself read and the author written, it is easy to imagine that these two who died on the same date in 1616 were the same man, that "Will Shakespeare, the

67

comedian with a thousand faces, wrote *Don Quixote*." Thus Fuentes likens the sad knight to the Black Prince, who also knows that he is a mere character of "Words, words, words" (*Hamlet*, 2.2.192). But the alarm-bell at the coming book that for the novelist heralds "the existence of a thing called literature" had been tolled by Shakespeare in 1613 with an even closer parallel to the Barcelona story, when the page Fidele played by Imogen was asked to identify his lost master, and the time frame of *Cymbeline* was broken with a similarly uncanny reply: "Richard du Champ."[2] For as editors note, this French "champion" translates as Richard Field, the printer of Shakespeare's poems and his Stratford schoolmate, while Field is an anagram of a *faithful page*. At the time of *Cymbeline* the King's Men had just occupied the theater right beside Field's printing shop in Blackfriars, where as Adrian Johns remarks, "the topography of print could be measured in feet."[3] Thus, no wonder this most bookish of plays turns on the metaphor of printing as parenting; nor that it is the text where the future Folio is first projected to be "the world's volume" (3.4.137). But what makes Shakespeare here so like his Spanish contemporary is the melancholy with which he laments his faithful printer. For Field would, in fact, never print him again. And without "such another master," Shakespeare's page will never have *fidelity* to life:

> There is no more such masters. I may wander
> From east to occident, cry out for service,
> Try many, all good; serve truly, never
> Find such another master.
>
> (*Cymbeline*, 4.2.372–76)

"All that he hath writ / Leaves living art, but page, to serve his wit": the final words on his memorial tablet underline what the bust above commemorates, and critical fashion would now restore: the image of Shakespeare as an *author* poised quill in hand over a sheet of paper, absorbed in the rapt scene of writing his first editors, Heminge and Condell evoked when they recalled "His mind and hand went together, and what he thought, he uttered with that easiness that we have scarce received from him a blot in his papers."[4] This is the myth of the Bard in a trancelike communion with his readers enshrined in portraits like Virginia Woolf's, when her Orlando bursts upon "a rather fat, rather shabby man" sitting at the servants' table, who looks straight through him with "eyes globed and clouded," as he "turned his pen in his fingers, this way and that way . . . and then, very quickly, wrote half-a-dozen lines."[5] And it is the popular idea of the abstracted genius who devours reality that inspires films like *Shakespeare in Love* and *Molière,* where a love affair cues *Twelfth Night* or a month in the country *Le Bourgeois Gentilhomme.*[6] Yet the Stratford memorial also hints at a Cervantine *disenchantment* with the deadliness of literary authorship, when in the imagery of *Cymbeline* it insists print leaves the dramatist's "living art" with "but page, to serve his wit." So this is a tribute that adds a sharp twist to the debate about whether Shakespeare ever intended his "living art" to be *engraved,* for it confirms how at the time of his death even his greatest admirers sensed the playwright's immortality to be an eclipse of reality, experiencing the birth of the ageless author in Fuentes's terms, as the death of the mortal wit. Together with Fidele's lost faith, the gravestone throws a shadow over the theory launched by Lukas Erne with *Shakespeare as Literary Dramatist,* that the dramatist always desired publication of his words, and had his texts printed as expertly as possible, until some point around 1602 when he began to *authorize* the novel idea of a bound collected works. Erne himself considers that the primary push for publication came not from Shakespeare but "printers, publishers, and booksellers" eager to profit from "an enterprise with little or no prestige."[7] But what the tomb and *Cymbeline* instead seem to mourn is the falling away of the blackened page, the printed spectrality which demands the sacrifice that "Golden lads and lasses" onstage "all must, / As chimney-sweepers, come to dust" (4.2.262). This is a writer who never forgets that ink is made of wormwood and gall. But as book and grave both loom closer, so Shakespeare's apprehension about the stigma of print deepens, we infer, and the printing press becomes, as for Cervantes, yet another scene of death to add to the perils of representation in an age when if the author shows his face, he does "as the snail, whose tender horns being hit / Shrinks backward in his shelly cave" (*Venus,* 1033).

"Thus far, with rough and all-unable pen / Our bending author hath pursued the story": what is striking about Shakespeare's idea of authorship—it emerges from those few occasions like the one in the Epilogue of *Henry V* when he takes a bow—is how his authority is "bent" by the same bonds of subjection he gave his protagonists, who in scene after scene he imagines in an attitude not of self-determination or intentionality, but "rough and all-unable," yet wily or peasantlike subservience. And whenever he refers to "the author," we note, it is either in a traditional context of culpability—as Hamlet is said to be the "most violent author / Of his just remove" (*Hamlet,* 4.5.76)—or the dozen times he uses the word in a modern literary sense, of authorial evasion—as when Malvolio "will read politic authors" to "baffle Sir Toby" (*Twelfth,* 2.5.141). At a time when, as Johns relates, the credibility gap opened up by printing is being bridged by a book culture of goodwill and trust, Shakespeare's authors are only associated with hermeneutic crisis, like the "strange fellow" who makes Ulysses "strain" at his "drift": "That no man is the lord of anything . . . Till he communicate his parts to others" (*Troilus,* 3.3.110–12).[8] Likewise, on a stage where books "prove suspect, dangerous, even lethal," characters who "read much" are consistently depicted as treacherous or unreliable like Cassius and Brutus (*Julius,* 1.2.22).[9] So, when Troilus vows by "truth's authentic author" (3.2.168); French "authors faithfully affirm" the law (*Henry V,* 1.2.43); or Gower retails "what mine authors say" (*Pericles,* 1.1.20), credit is what is *strained,* as in these plays, we see, there is no "author in the world / Teaches such beauty as a woman's eye" (*Love's,* 4.3.291:17–18). Bent double, "our humble author" (*2 Henry IV,* Epilogue, l. 23) is as much a "crooked figure" for this writer as his suspect text (*Henry V,* Prologue, l. 15). Like the Foucault who told the Californians that though "We are accustomed to seeing the author as a genial creator . . . The truth is quite the contrary: the author is a functional principle by which, in our culture, one impedes the free circulation of fiction," it seems Shakespeare can never forget the twisted subjection of his own scene of writing, nor how "Our bending author" is obliged to bow low to the authorizing institutions, even as his servile pen is subjected to the discourse of "the story."[10] Thus, when he represents his conditions of production in *Hamlet,* he has the naughty "fellow" who speaks the Prologue to *The Mousetrap* insist not only on the collective ownership of the play, but on the cravenly contorted "stooping" required to perform it on demand: "For us and for our tragedy, / Thus stooping to your clemency / We beg your hearing patiently" (3.2.133–35).

Caught between stage and page, when he takes a bow Shakespeare comes forward, he declares, expressly "not in confidence" of *either* "author's pen or actor's voice" (*Troilus,* Prologue, ll. 23–24). Editors like to think Shakespeare himself spoke such "curtain" speeches in self-effacing cameo roles. But in *1599: A Year in the*

Life of William Shakespeare, James Shapiro contends that the Epilogue of *2 Henry IV,* which finishes by affirming "I will bid you good night, and so kneel down before you—but to pray for the Queen," is actually "the closest we get" to the author revealing himself, for there what began with "Shakespeare modestly curtsying" shifts as he "catches himself and explains to his audience that while it may look as if he's kneeling 'before them,' he's not; he's kneeling in prayer for Elizabeth." Like *Shakespeare in Love,* which has its "self-schooled, self-scanned, self-honoured, self-secure," and entrepreneurial Bard authorized in the end by Gloriana's gala appearance on the stage of the Globe, Shapiro notices no contradiction between his capitalist author, "who offers himself as a merchant" to an audience of investors, and this groveling to feudal authority.[11] But then, *1599,* Shapiro explained on accepting the 2005 Johnson Prize for Literary Biography, was all about the return of the author in place of "incomprehensible" academic theories of the self.[12] In *Secret Shakespeare,* however, I keyed Shakespeare's recurring allegiance test, in which subjects are suborned to present subjection, to the "Bloody Question" of a loyalty divided between Queen and Pope that conditioned the writer's subject position, as one born in a Catholic milieu who *resisted the resistance* to Elizabeth's "war on terror" while making a drama out of the silent refusal to be put on oath. There was an affinity, I claimed, between Shakespeare's truth games and the enigmatic gazes of Caravaggio, who in pictures like *The Calling of St. Matthew,* where no one dares to meet Christ's eye or answer his call, repeats the same hermeneutic puzzle of a self *performing secrecy,* as Leo Bersani and Ulysse Dutoit put it: "at once presenting and withdrawing itself," as if we were solicited "by a desire determined to remain hidden."[13] For the compulsion with which painter and playwright return to such scenarios of invigilation and interpellation confirms how these artists on the threshold of modernity see their own *calling* as the representation of subjectivity itself: "Unhappy that I am, I cannot heave / My heart into my mouth (*King Lear,* 1.1.90–91).

"Now, our joy . . . what can you say . . . ? Speak . . . speak again . . . mend your speech" (81–93): at the very instant when the rule of art is promulgated that to be an "authentic author" it is necessary to "look in thy heart and write!" Shakespeare makes drama out of opposition to the idea "That I . . . Must, like a whore, unpack my heart with words," demonstrating instead that although "you would pluck out the heart of my mystery" (*Hamlet,* 2.2.561–63;

3.2.336), "You cannot, if my heart were in your hand" (*Othello*, 3.3.176).[14] So, *Shakespeare in Love* got him exactly inside out when Tom Stoppard imagined his existential crisis to be a writer's block, since what his recurring execution metaphors make plain is how this most secretive of writers identified "windy suspiration of forc'd breath" (*Hamlet*, 1.2.79) with racked confession and self-expression itself with disembowelment on the scaffold.[15] By contrast, it is Shakespeare's very reluctance to *present* himself as an author, allied to the stage fright he exposes when he has "great clerks . . . Throttle their practised accents in their fears" (*Dream*, 5.1.93–97), that makes his plays apt illustrations of Foucault's theory that such "Visibility is a trap."[16] The philosopher who traced psychiatry to the confession box attributed his own desire *to write without a face* to his sensation, as a gay teenager in Vichy France, that "the obligation of speaking was both strange and boring. I often wondered why people had to speak."[17] But it is his realization that resistance relies upon that against which it struggles that offers a key to Shakespeare's "sweet and witty soul," the "honey tongue" with which the playwright is said to have accommodated himself to the great, despite notoriously associating flattery with spaniels licking candy.[18] So, it might be timely to recall Shakespeare's own picture of himself as that "bending author" who bows to the power that he bends, and to do so by considering how he presents his own *calling* not as the self-advancement of the modern literary author, but as the more contradictory desire to write without a face.

"Speak the speech, I pray you, as I pronounced it to you— trippingly on the tongue" (*Hamlet*, 3.2.1)—Hamlet's instruction to the players, misread as Shakespeare's manifesto, reminds us how he analyzed his situation in terms not of free will or self-determination, but performance to order. So, how did this writer understand the symbolic revolution by which the new cult of the sovereign author broke free of the old culture of calendar custom and state ceremonial? Dialectically; and time and again he depicted his art as a negotiation like that at Elsinore where, as Bourdieu saw, the surprise is that artistic independence has to be instituted under the tutelage of an aristocrat who presumes to direct the play like a master of revels, thus confirming that Shakespeare did not "display towards external restraints the impatience which for us appears to define the creative project." For although he would finally "owe his freedom of expression to theatre managers . . . and entrance fees paid by a public of increasingly diverse origin," financiers like

Philip Henslowe could "mould the taste of the age," which was why on Shakespeare's stage, Bourdieu argued, the first literary field was inaugurated in deference to, rather than defiance of the licensing regime, and why even as he gained autonomy, the theater writer declared ever more strongly his indifference to the public. Like the art-for-art's-sake it prefigured, the birth of the author involved a "double rupture" with power and profit. So, for Bourdieu authorship began with that sweet Shakespearean refusal to reduce theater to either a capitalist commodity or political propaganda.[19] And this is an analysis minutely confirmed by Andrew Gurr in *The Shakespearean Company,* where Shakespeare's autonomy is attributed to the "democratic, non-authoritarian management" of a crew who pretended "Motley's the only wear" by flaunting the livery of feudal servants. If the Lord Chamberlain's Men continued to be "motley-minded" (*As You Like It,* 2.7.44; 5.4.40), Gurr shows, that was because "customary suits" (*Hamlet,* 1.2.78) of a noble household fitted their "family" firm, with joint ownership of all assets, which included properties, play texts, and from 1599, the great Globe itself. But the tensions in such a royal warranty "became a supreme paradox in 1603," Gurr recounts, "when the most democratic organisation in England came under patronage of King James, the most despotic figure in the country."[20] In fact, such dependency relations were the writer's anxiety from the start, since whenever he imagined a stage it was never the commercial playhouse but always the hall of a palace.[21] Thus, Venus, "the lovesick Queen" who so resembles a geriatric Elizabeth, sets the scene for a lifetime of passive aggression toward the system he exploited, when in Shakespeare's poem she implores Adonis to cease behaving like a dumb statue: "But when her lips were ready for his pay, / He winks, and turns his lips another way" (89–90; 175). For in these texts a command performance is always such a forced occasion:

> My tongue is weary; when my legs are too, I will bid you good night, and so kneel down before you—but, indeed, to pray for the Queen.
> (*2 Henry IV,* Epilogue, ll. 28–30)

"If you look for a good speech now, you undo me; for what I have to say is of mine own making, and what indeed I should say will, I doubt, prove mine own marring": it is the deconstructive posture of Shakespeare's claim to be the maker of his meaning that it advances in self-cancelling reverse, for ever harking back to service in the great house, as cap-in-hand it proffers "First my fear, then my curtsy, last my speech" (1–6). Thus, Douglas Bruster and Robert Weimann stress how with his prologues and epilogues Shakespeare still honored the group dynamics of the great hall; while Leeds Barroll even infers from his output that he *only* wrote to order and if there was no commission "simply did not wish to write plays."[22] A first among equals, he certainly affirmed that, as Stanley Wells reminds us, he would remain a preeminent *company man,* who worked "exceptionally closely with fellow actors . . . for no other dramatist had so long a relationship with a single company," nor such solid bonds with other writers. Thus, Wells's *Shakespeare and Co.* concludes that to locate Shakespeare in his milieu "only enhances our sense of what made him unique."[23] Likewise, Bart van Es pinpoints *A Midsummer Night's Dream* as a watershed where he first realized his supreme advantage in being at once a player, sharer, and writer in a permanent "fellowship" exempt from market pressure. Shakespeare's supremacy arose, on this view, from the golden opportunity the 1594 Lord Chamberlain's warrant afforded to cover all the bases of the field.[24] These accounts are similar to Bourdieu's thesis that reconstructing the professional world of the artist "allows us to understand the labour he had to accomplish, both against these determinations and thanks to them, to produce himself as the creator, that is, as the *subject* of his own creation."[25] But the question they pose is also Bourdieu's, about what the writer gained from continuing to merge his individual interest in the impersonality of the corporate brand. What was Shakespeare's *interest in disinterestedness?* And one answer that the plays themselves suggest is that it was *safety in numbers* that gave him the freedom to write as he liked. In a system where for one of the band to roar too loudly, as his Peter Quince warns, "were enough to hang us all" (*Dream,* 1.2.72), mutual "good will" between performers and patrons was assured by subduing the playwright's intentions and identity to the métier he worked in "like the dyer's hand" (Sonnet 111), by the authorial personality behind the scenes never, in fact, stepping out of the collective line: "If we offend it is with our good will. / That you should think we come not to offend / But with good will" (*Dream,* 5.1.108–10).

"All for your delight, / *We are not here*" (114–15; my italics): if texts began to have authors, as Foucault theorized and Quince fears, to the extent that authors became subject to punishment, Shakespeare's paradoxical signature vanishing act, his reduction to the missing person who is yet a universal cipher of the world's "good will," also records the coincidence that (as Derrida countered) the "Strange Institution" of literature commenced around 1600 as "the right to say everything." Thus, if the originator of modern authorship insured his freedom of expression by remaining invisible, hiding his face in the crowd and having to be dragged to his chair, this false modesty finessed the problem that prior to the securing of the public sphere the literary field had no ground of authorization. For "How is it possible to answer for literature?" if it bows to no other institution and demands by definition the freedom of the air: "A paradox: liberation makes it an institution that is an-institutional, wild and unconditional." Derrida deduced that what literature's claim to sovereignty therefore entailed was "not irresponsibility but rather a mutation in the concept of responsibility."[26] And it is the vertigo of this process that does appear to be negotiated in *A Midsummer Night's Dream,* the work above all that identifies "good will" as a precondition of literature when, in its closing pact, Puck takes upon his fictive persona responsibility for a theater "No more yielding" to authority "than a dream." On the understanding that the "play needs no excuse" when its creator is "dead" (5.1.341–43; Epilogue, ll. 15–16), Shakespeare's "powerless theatre" thereby leaps its groundlessness to assert "the right to say everything, if only in the form of a fiction."[27] Free speech is gained by absenting authorial presence, since "*We do not come,* as minding to content you, / Our true intent is" (5.1.113–14; my italics): "Therein lies literature's secret, the . . . power to keep undecidable the secret of what it says . . . The secret of literature is the secret itself . . . 'the play's the thing'" (*Hamlet,* 2.2.581).[28] So, if it is *secrecy* about its own origins and intentions that grants literature a permit "to say everything," as Derrida thought, what is intriguing is how Shakespeare's self-concealment extends, as Richard Dutton argues, to the most startling paradox: that the reason why he never published his plays may be that he was *too much* the "company man," too loyal to collective identity to push his name, too bound by ties that went beyond a "mere contractual framework" to be the author of the book.[29] This is not the same as Eliot's dictum that art is "an escape from personality." But if we take Shakespeare to be a founder of literary authorship, it is to agree that what happens in his work is "a continual surrender of himself . . . to something more valuable . . . a continual self-sacrifice, a continual extinction of personality": "Marry, if he that writ it had . . . hanged himself . . . it would have been a fine tragedy" (*Dream,* 5.2.342–44).[30]

"Now he terrifies me," wrote Rilke of the Shakespeare of the Epilogues, "The way he draws / the wire into his head, and hangs himself / beside the other puppets, and henceforth begs mercy of the play."[31] Shakespeare's self-erasure, his drive to "hide himself from view" as if hanging beside his own creations, has indeed been decoded by Stephen Greenblatt as a burial "inside public laughter" of the "intense fear that once gripped him" of actual martyrdom. Having been traumatized by real executions of Catholics, the "genially submissive" yet "subtly challenging" writer excises his personality, on this view, "to ward off vulnerability."[32] Thus, in contrast to Caravaggio, who paints his own decapitation, the death of the author here serves "a symbolic effacement . . . for, given rope to hang himself, [he] submits instead to an aesthetic closure."[33] Such self-denial is enacted by the Williams of the plays, a series typified by the bumpkin of *As You Like It,* in which Shakespeare associates his own name, Phyllis Rackin notices, "with inarticulate, humble life obliterated by the textualized world of his betters."[34] But such also is the resistance implied when these sweet Williams cheek masters, accuse the king, or skive at Hinkley fair (*2 Henry VI,* 5.1.21). For what these winking Wills personify is in fact the truant evasion of the textualized world of authority that Shakespeare makes the story of his life: the great refusal that underlies his recalcitrance toward the printed fix of authorship itself. For as A. D. Nuttall observes in his own posthumous book, *Shakespeare the Thinker,* while his name "became a selling point," because in his own time the public "certainly caught on to the fact that Shakespeare was the man behind the plays," the writer himself appears to have feared his typographic immortality as "a freezing, a cryogenic perpetuation of something mobile" and alive.[35] Assuredly, Shakespeare was the author of his authorship, who produced himself as the "subject of his own creation." But he was also a showman embarrassed to be "a motley to the view" (Sonnet 110); and a "tongue-tied unlettered clerk" in his nightmare, mumbling "Amen" to every "form of well-refinèd pen" (Sonnet 85). And so he littered his texts with allusions to the violence of penning, printing, pressing, binding, and engraving: the morbid techniques of publishing that, as Jonathan Goldberg argues, "throw into question any identification of the *system* with a sovereign author," and mark aversion to inscription of a name in *characters.*[36] This writer who dreaded the book as a tombstone, like those brass-lettered graves that spell "the disgrace of death" for bookmen in *Love's Labor's*

Lost (1.1.1–3)—and who blackened his most bookish figure with the "inky cloak" (*Hamlet,* 1.2.78) of the letter that kills—avoided "the Graver" come to "outdo the life" until the last.[37] And even as his "project gather[ed] to a head" (*Tempest,* 5.1.1), when the future Folio was on his mind as "a book of all that sovereigns do," he sensed that "He's more secure to keep it shut than shown" (*Pericles,* 1.1.137–38). Until the very end, the author of "the world's volume" (*Cymbeline,* 3.4.137) aborted his own "birth" as an author, intent on nothing more *willfully* than that "Deeper than did ever plummet sound / I'll drown my book" (*Tempest,* 5.1.56–57).

Notes

The quote in the epigraph is from Miguel de Cervantes, *The History of Don Quixote of the Mancha,* trans. Thomas Shelton (London, 1620; repr., 4 vols., London: David Nutt, 1896), vol. 4, chap. 62, 195.

1. Ibid. and 197.

2. Carlos Fuentes, "Cervantes, or The Critique of Reading," in *Myself with Others: Selected Essays* (London: Andre Deutsch, 1988), 53–54, 58, and 63.

3. Adrian Johns, *The Nature of the Book: Print and Knowledge in the Making* (Chicago: University of Chicago Press, 1998), 68.

4. Henry Condell and John Heminge, "To the great Variety of Readers," repr., William Shakespeare, *The Norton Shakespeare,* ed. Stephen Greenblatt, Walter Cohen, Jean Howard, and Katharine Eisaman Maus (New York: Norton, 1997), 3350. All quotations of Shakespeare are from this edition.

5. Virginia Woolf, *Orlando: A Biography* (London: Penguin, 2006), 20.

6. See Robert Gottlieb, "Lit-Flicks," *New York Review of Books,* September 14 and 27, 2007, 20–22.

7. Lukas Erne, *Shakespeare as Literary Dramatist* (Cambridge: Cambridge University Press, 2003), 33.

8. Johns, *Nature of the Book,* 31–37.

9. Frederick Kiefer, *Writing on the Renaissance Stage: Written Words, Printed Pages, Metaphoric Books* (Newark: University of Delaware Press, 1998), 292.

10. Michel Foucault, "What Is an Author?" trans. Josué V. Harari, in *The Foucault Reader,* ed. Paul Rabinow (Harmondsworth: Penguin, 1984), 118–19.

11. James Shapiro, *1599: A Year in the Life of William Shakespeare* (London: Faber and Faber, 2005), 41; Matthew Arnold, "Shakespeare," in *The Oxford Authors: Matthew Arnold,* ed. Miriam Allott and Robert Super (Oxford: Oxford University Press, 1986), 8.

12. *Evening Standard,* June 15, 2005, 7.

13. Leo Bersani and Ulysse Dutoit, *Caravaggio's Secrets* (Cambridge, MA.: MIT Press, 1998), 8–9; Richard Wilson, *Secret Shakespeare: Studies in Theatre, Religion, and Resistance* (Manchester: Manchester University Press, 2004).

14. Philip Sidney, "Astrophel and Stella" (1:14), in *The Poems of Sir Philip Sidney,* ed. William Ringler Jr. (Oxford: Clarendon Press, 1962), 165.

15. For the association of "forced breath" with torture and execution, see Elizabeth Hanson, *Discovering the Subject in Renaissance England* (Cambridge: Cambridge University Press, 1998); Katharine Eisaman Maus, *Inwardness and Theater in the English Renaissance* (Chicago: Chicago University Press, 1995); and Wilson, *Secret Shakespeare*.

16. For Shakespeare's "narcissistic" terror of exposure, see Meredith Anne Skura, *Shakespeare the Actor and the Purposes of Playing* (Chicago: University of Chicago Press, 1993); for "Visibility is a trap," see Michel Foucault, *Discipline and Punish: The Birth of the Prison,* trans. Alan Sheridan (Harmondsworth: Penguin, 1977), 200.

17. Michel Foucault, "An Interview with Stephen Riggins" (Toronto, June 1982), in *Michel Foucault: The Essential Works,* vol. 1, *Ethics,* ed. Paul Rabinow (London: Allen Lane, 1997), 121–22.

18. Francis Meres, *Palladis Tamia: Wit's Treasury* (London, 1598), fols. 281v–2, repr., Samuel Schoenbaum, *William Shakespeare: A Documentary Life* (Oxford: Clarendon Press, 1975), 140. For the "tactfully suppressed grievance that Shakespeare did not love dogs as he should," because he associated sycophancy with spaniels licking candy, see William Empson, *The Structure of Complex Words* (London: Chatto and Windus, 1951), 176.

19. Pierre Bourdieu, "Intellectual Field and Creative Project," trans. Sian France, *Knowledge and Control: New Directions in the Sociology of Education* (London: Collier-Macmillan, 1971), 162–63.

20. Andrew Gurr, *The Shakespeare Company, 1594–1642* (Cambridge: Cambridge University Press, 2004), 88.

21. For discussions of this paradox, see Alvin Kernan, *Shakespeare, the King's Playwright: Theater in the Stuart Court, 1603–1613* (New Haven: Yale University Press, 1995), 178, 180, and 195; and Richard Wilson, "The Management of Mirth: Shakespeare *via* Bourdieu," in *Shakespeare in French Theory: King of Shadows* (London: Routledge, 2007), 123–39.

22. Douglas Bruster and Robert Weimann, *Prologue to Shakespeare: Performance and Liminality in Early Modern Drama* (London: Routledge, 2004), 40 and 153; Leeds Barroll, *Politics, Plague and Shakespere's Theater* (Ithaca: Cornell University Press, 1991), 17. See also Tiffany Stern, *Rehearsal from Shakespeare to Sheridan* (Oxford: Clarendon Press, 2000), 116.

23. Stanley Wells, *Shakespeare and Co.* (London: Allen Lane, 2006), 4–5, 27, and 231.

24. Bart van Es, "Company Man: Another Crucial Year for Shakespeare," *Times Literary Supplement,* February 2, 2007, 14–15.

25. Pierre Bourdieu, *The Rules of Art: Genesis and Structure of the Literary Field,* trans. Susan Emmanuel (Cambridge: Cambridge University Press, 1996), 104.

26. Jacques Derrida, "That Strange Institution Called Literature," in *Acts of Literature,* ed. Derek Attridge (London: Routledge, 1992); Jacques Derrida and Elizabeth Roudinesco, *For What Tomorrow . . . A Dialogue,* trans. Jeff Ford (Stanford, CA: Stanford University Press, 2004), 127.

27. For "Powerless theatre," see Paul Yachnin, *Stage-Wrights: Shakespeare, Jonson, Middleton and the Making of Theatrical Value* (Philadelphia: University of Pennsylvania Press, 1997), 12–13 and 21; Jacques Derrida, "The Future of the Profession or the University Without Condition (Thanks to the "Humanities"

what could *take place tomorrow*),'' in *Jacques Derrida and the Humanities: A Critical Reader,* ed. Tom Cohen (Cambridge: Cambridge University Press, 2001), 27.

28. Jacques Derrida, *Genesis, Genealogies, Genres and Genius: The Secrets of the Archive,* trans. Beverley Bie Brahac (Edinburgh: Edinburgh University Press, 2003), 18–19.

29. Richard Dutton, "The Birth of the Author," in *Texts and Cultural Change in Early Modern England,* ed. Cedric Brown and Arthur Marotti, 161 (Basingstoke: Macmillan, 1997), 161.

30. T. S. Eliot, "Tradition and the Individual Talent," in *Selected Essays* (London: Faber and Faber, 1932), 17 and 21.

31. Rainer Maria Rilke, "The Spirit Ariel (After reading Shakespeare's *Tempest*)," *Rilke: Selected Poems,* trans. J. B. Leishman (Harmondsworth: Penguin, 1964), 74.

32. Stephen Greenblatt, *Will in the World: How Shakespeare Became Shakespeare* (London: Jonathan Cape, 2004), 152 and 155.

33. Richard Wilson, "The Kindly Ones: The Death of the Author in Shakespearean Athens," in *Shakespeare in French Theory,* 160.

34. Phyllis Rackin, *Stages of History: Shakespeare's English Chronicles* (Ithaca: Cornell University Press, 1990), 244.

35. A. D. Nuttall, *Shakespeare the Thinker* (New Haven: Yale University Press, 2007), 377–78.

36. Jonathan Goldberg, *Voice Terminal Echo: Postmodernism and English Renaissance Texts* (London: Methuen, 1986), 97.

37. "To the Reader," repr., *Norton Shakespeare,* 3346: "This figure, that thou here seest put, / It was for gentle Shakespeare cut; / Wherein the Graver had a strife / With Nature, to outdo the life. . . ."

Shakespeare, the Classics, and the Forms of Authorship

Heather James

The PRESENT FORUM aims to explore the author's return to Shakespeare studies and, as I take it, the question of whether such a critical turn represents a step forward or backward. I wish to approach the issue from the perspective of the classics, with the aim of historicizing some functions of authorial returns in Shakespeare's day and in criticism since the rise of the New Historicism. Shakespeare's contemporaries thought of authors chiefly in terms of classical writers, and they regularly called on "authorities" such as Vergil, Horace, and Ovid, or Cicero, Seneca, and Tacitus, to advance their own projects. Yet they did not forge the positivistic link between the classics and the idea of the author that shows up in modern criticism. They recalled classical texts through a variety of modes, not all of which produced the heightened sense of authorial presence, even aura, associated with the most privileged mode of classical transmission, namely, imitation or sustained allusion. The various rhetorical forms in which Renaissance writers recalled the classics in fact suggest multiple and incongruent models of authority, authorship, and agency; and this diversity of forms may productively complicate what it means to say that the author has returned to Shakespeare studies.

Although humanist writers and readers sometimes thought in terms of imitation, they also called on classical authorities through the maxim, adage, sentence, and marginal gloss. Unlike imitation, which uses a poetic part to recall a textual whole, sententiae break apart poetic or prose works in search of the valuable fragment. They also differ from imitations by detaching authority from the classical author and his works. Even when a name and title (usually abbreviated) appear in a marginal note, the citation is there to help the reader retrieve the maxim, not reflect on the work as a whole. Sententiae are largely indifferent and sometimes even hostile to the issues of authorial intentions and personal agency taken up by imitation. They are taciturn when it comes to questions about the occasion for their coinage and utterance: they arise in response to nothing in particular and represent nothing other than commonplace wisdom. With similar evasion, they do not locate ideals of virtue in persons, places, and times and thus refuse to comment on the times or even to form analogies between one era and another. Critical attention understandably flows to the practice of imitation and adaptation, since each imitative act rewards study and opens up complex dialogues between one text, poet, and culture and another. Sententiae, it must be admitted, are comparatively dull if taken individually. Yet they have an important contribution to make to the present forum, since they make it clear that Renaissance writers were not necessarily waiting for the Author to Return, like some colossus with a monumental tome of his Works tucked under his arm.[1]

Although the modes of constructing authorship in the Renaissance are diverse, a remarkably uniform conception of the author took shape in literary criticism of the 1980s, when scholars of imitation in lyric and epic poetry (humanist poetics) and New Historicism (so-called cultural poetics) struck a tacit deal about authors and authority. Critics from Thomas Greene to Stephen Greenblatt agreed that studies of imitation and classical transmission had the uncontested rights to (1) authors and their aura and (2) the monumental authority of literary origins (the classics) and the canon. From the view of the New Historicism, the literary study of humanist traditions won a Pyrrhic victory by assuming the mantle of tired legitimacy and a strictly literary genealogy. The classical heritage came to suggest a set of narrowly literary relations that inexorably led, if one followed the ideological arrows, to the canon and the conservative side of the canon wars. Studies of classical imitation and allusion held on to a nominal prestige even while sinking into the "elephants' graveyard" of "source studies," which labor under the stigma of positivism to the present day.[2] Literary allusions took on the aspect of monuments to the past and losers to the more broadly cultural power of topical allusions, which seemed to release critical energies from the vertical axis of diachronic study and set them loose on a synchronic field, where they radiated outward from London to the English nation (and its neighbors and colonies), and the larger geopolitical world—skipping only the Continent, which was mostly left to traditional humanist scholarship.

In practice, studies of imitation and classical transmission continued to flourish. Those focused on epic poetry linked issues of classical transmission to antimonarchical sentiment and republicanism and, in this way, allowed literary allusions to join forces with topical ones and thus regain some of their lost glory.[3] In other quarters, studies of imitation took familiar concerns with lyric "I" and made them new by focusing them on women authors and a heroic project of recovering "other voices" in the Renaissance. In Shakespeare studies, the comparably epic project of authorial recovery is that of Patrick Cheney, who brings the diverse career models of Augustan poets to bear on the fashioning of poetic identities—and ideological dispositions—in Shakespeare's day.

Scholars of classical transmission, in short, weathered the potentially adverse tides of topical criticism, which they used to modify the directly literary character of imitation studies in Thomas M. Greene's *The Light in Troy: Imitation and Discovery in Renaissance Poetry.*[4] While critics have revised Greene's argument that the traumatic discovery of historical loss or anachronism lies at the heart of Renaissance transactions with antiquity, they have not taken issue with his conception of classical authority or noted how closely it resembles that of the New Historicists. For both sides, the classical text evokes the spectral image of stable authorial identity and intentions. Greene might not quarrel, at least too fiercely, with the slight disdain of Historicist critics for the monumental authority of the classics, since it took—in his account of Renaissance lyric—the shocking encounter with the classics to create the modern poet, who fills his pages with "the turbulent egoism, the problematic divisions and restless intensities of a voice pathetically in quest of its own integrity." The poet in question is Petrarch, and the classical monolith into which he painfully collided is Ovid, whose poem of change, the *Metamorphoses,* is made relentlessly stable by "its visual and rhetorical clarity, its calm impersonality, its security within nature, its accommodations with suffering, its refusal of psychologistic paradox, and its capacity for repose" (131).

The inverse roles that classical and Renaissance texts and their authors play in Greene's account are fascinating but, it must be admitted, more so for Renaissance poets than classical ones. The appeal and surprise of Greene's argument, of course, is that he transfers the fragility of the classical *text* in its material state—corrupt, moth-eaten, and worm-laden—to the figure and voice of the Renaissance poet, while associating the classical *work* with a lost ideal, not to be recovered by the most heroic feat of learning and textual editing. The lost ideal assumes personified form in the classical author, whereas the Renaissance poet discovers himself in the figure of corrupt and failed transmission. Although Greene and the New Historicists do not often agree, they share the view that the classical text and author enjoy a privileged but suspect monumentality.

The classics have prospered in recent days. Classical studies seem relatively free of the positivistic reading of its aims and functions that dominated the 1980s and much of the 1990s. The greater freedom of movement in the field of classical transmission is due largely to new critical energies devoted to the history of the book and, in other quarters, the rise of political readings of the classics.[5] Both types of criticism suggest the time is ripe for scholars to revisit the old idea of the classical text as a monument to the poet or Author and inspect its foundations anew. We might begin with the engravings printed in Renaissance editions of Ovid's *Metamorphoses,* which elaborately uses the trope. Thanks to the University of Virginia Electronic Text Center's Web site, "Ovid Illustrated," it has never been easier to locate and compare Renaissance engravings of Ovid and his tales.

The most important engraving of Ovid's poem-as-monument in the English Renaissance appears in George Sandys's *Ovid's Metamorphoses, Englished, Mythologiz'd, and Represented in Figures* (1632). Of the multiple interpretations suggested by the engraving, the one most consistent with New Historicism and imitation studies alike is Author-based: entrenched in the discourse of Fame, the focal point of the engraving and the book is the laureate poet. At the center of the engraving is an insignia impressed with a bust of Ovid in profile: august features, flowing locks, and toga-draped shoulders in a classic three-quarter turn. The poet's image, supported on either side by Apollo and Mercury, sits atop a classical monument or tomb. Fame personified, wielding a feathered quill in one hand and a trumpet in the other, rides the clouds above the poet, proclaiming his immortality. Ovid has transcended the grave and, as the motto at the base of the engraving tells the reader, his poem bears the deathless record of his mind:

> The sweet-tong'd Ovids Counterfeit behold,
> Which noblest Romans wore in rings of gold.
> Or would you yt which his owne pensil drew?
> The Poet, in his deathless Poems, view.

The poet indeed lives, as he himself asserts in the last word of his poem (*vivam*).

If the same monumental image is read in light of recent political criticism, however, a remarkably different set of interpretive priorities emerges. The engraving becomes less upwardly focused on the figure of Fame and more downwardly focused on the tomb, with its more than faint recollection of Ovid's death in exile at Tomis on the Black Sea. The accents of the motto change from praise for Ovid to blame for the prince who banished the "sweet-tong'd" poet, a sentence implicitly challenged by the "noblest Romans," who wore gold rings stamped with the poet's image. The invitation to view Ovid's image in his deathless poem, moreover, suggests that reading is itself an act of remembering Rome's wittiest poet, as the inscription encircling Ovid's image puts it (ROMANVS POETARUM INGENIOSISSIMVS), and his exile. The keyword in the inscription, however, appears after Ovid's name: EQVES. Ovid was a knight, as Renaissance accounts of his life often note when they discuss the exile, and, as such, he was entitled to the liberty of speech. The 1632 engraving, in this account, is profoundly concerned with the politics of Ovid's exile, silencing, and death and equally concerned with the means by which readers may regard Ovid's "continuous song" as an ongoing or "deathless" critique of the politics of that exile and others of its kind. The poem-as-monument-to-the-author, in short, is a trope in a political discourse about princes, poets, poetry, and readers.

To return to the classical text as a *specter* of authority: I have noted the ways in which this idea animates Greene's psychological portrait of the Renaissance lyric poet, burdened with the knowledge of failed and corrupt classical transmission; and I have also noted its importance to the ideological critique of literature-based studies by Marxian critics, suspicious of the apparently top-down model of classical authority. The focus on the purely spectral authority of the classical poem and author is just but, I suggest, best understood as a trope in a historical dialogue about the political conditions of writing and reading. The monumental fashioning of the author is a tactic used to counter the authority asserted by the prince at his more tyrannical. The trope of the poem-as-monument assumes its full political force, moreover, only when it is read in terms of its many material and textual productions (Sandys's various editions of his Ovid being only a few).

While the trope of the poem-as-monument depends upon the author's spectral image, that figure could not be more irrelevant to the gathering of sententiae in the printed and manuscript commonplace books of the Renaissance. One catches only glimpses of the authors behind various wise sayings, since the authority of the sententiae lies outside of the author and even beyond the individual sentence, which illustrates general topics, such as virtue, vice, life, death, learning, ignorance, goodwill, and hatred.[6] The classical author—even one as famous for his sentences as Seneca or celebrated for his wit as Ovid—is radically subordinate to the topic inserted into a literary text or a commonplace book without an obvious shift of gears. And he is fully interchangeable with other *auctores* on the same topic. In a brief consideration of sententiae, Ernst Curtius illustrates the ease with which the ancients moved from the comprehensive recall of long poems and the ability to break apart such poems into component parts and play mix and match through an account of the "philological parlor games" in the *Deiopnosophistai* ("Scholars at a Banquet"): "One recited a verse, and another had to go on with the next. One quoted a sentence, and a sentence from some other poet expressing the same idea had to be produced" (58). R. R. Bolgar notes the interest of the medieval sermon-book (compilations of anecdotes and exempla) to Renaissance humanists, once they realized the value of the "note-book and heading method" (272) to the cultivation of eloquence. One result of this interest is *De Copia,* which helped Erasmus invent the model of humanist eloquence, in which hearers may catch allusiveness without quite being able to trace any particular allusion to its origins. Authority, not authors, made the man.

In a recent chapter on the significance of Shakespeare's entry into the commonplace tradition, Roger Chartier and Peter Stallybrass discuss the paradoxical challenge to modern ideas of authorship posed by the earliest efforts to commonplace English poems and plays.[7] As they point out, the mining of texts for illustrations of topoi and exempla privileges the notion of a common perspective over the idea of the author. The work is tessellated when its sententiae are excerpted or simply marked by gnomic pointing, typographical markers indicating sententiae. Chartier and Stallybrass emphasize the use of commonplace markers (quotation marks), although there are other indexes of the noteworthy and excerptible sentence: italics, a change of font, and the marginal index that William Sherman has called the "manicule."[8] For reasons that will become apparent, I will refer to this mark—a hand with a pointing finger—as "indigitation." For Chartier and Stallybrass, the all-important authority cultivated by commonplacing has nothing to do with the author or even, in the case of plays, the character speaking the sentence. The commonplace markers do not fence off the quoted text as the property of an author but, to the contrary, demarcate a common perspective both in the sentence or maxim and in the text as shared property. Their remarks on the commonplace tradition, while informed by modern and Marxian critiques of intellectual property, are consistent with the account of sententiae provided by Quintilian: whereas Aristotle thought of them as gnome (*Rhetoric* 2.21), Quintilian called them sententiae, or "judgments," because "they resembled the decisions of public bodies" (8.5.3).[9]

My own interest focuses not on the commonplacing *of* Shakespeare's plays but the use of sententiae *within* them by characters that adopt a deliberately nonindividuating mode of speech, moral reflection, and counsel. Polonius is the most conspicuous of these characters, and it is no accident that he is a counselor to kings, one known to characters within the play—as well as readers of the play—as wise but officious. To Shakespeare's contemporaries, he may have seemed an obvious parody of Burleigh, who prided himself on his sententious speech. Shakespeare's Kent also has his moments of sententiousness when attempting to direct Lear's attention toward manifest truths and, from there, to his own errors of judgment: "Thy youngest daughter does not love thee least," he says, before hotfooting it from the personal to the general: "Nor are those empty-hearted whose low sounds / Reverb no hollowness" (1.1.151–53). That Kent depersonalizes his remarks at the very moment he is most directive suggests the consciousness that he as a character shares with his author and his audiences that the sentence, in Puttenham's Englishing, is the "directour" (gnome) or "sage sayer" (sententia).[10]

A more sustained use of sententiae appears in *Richard II,* where John of Gaunt gives himself over fully to the mode of sententiousness at the moments in the play that he struggles most violently with the conflict between his duty to the king and his conscience.

His tortured dialogue with his son after Richard has passed down the sentence of exile (to which Gaunt agreed, he says, as a counselor but not as a father) is replete with sententiae, whose counsel of patience meets with steadfast resistance on the part of Bolingbroke. This dialogue leads directly to Gaunt's emergence as a "prophet new-inspir'd" (2.1.31), which begins with a feat of eloquence that transfers majesty from the king's person to the land, customs, and people of England and ends in the face-to-face denunciation of King Richard as a tyrant. It also draws substantially for its energy on a warm-up of sententiae:

> violent fires soon burn out themselves,
> Small showers last long, but sudden storms are short.
> He tires betimes that spurs too fast betimes.
> With eager feeding food doth choke the feeder;
> Light vanity, insatiate cormorant,
> Consuming means, soon preys upon itself.
>
> (2.1.34–39)

To the student of commonplaces, these lines leap off the page in a way they do not for most modern scholars, who have concerned themselves with Gaunt's hymn to England.

One feature of Gaunt's simultaneously poetic and political rhetoric seems to me to matter to a forum on authorship and authority: when Gaunt confronts the king, he submits himself to instrumental agency. He is not the author of his words: God is. Gaunt is in fact pointing God's own finger, the *digitus dei,* at Richard II and naming him a tyrant. His personal sufferings are irrelevant, in the dramatic moment. What counts is God's word: Gaunt's sententiae point beyond the dramatic (or historical) here and now to universal and common truths. In religious, political, and quasi-typographical terms, Gaunt lends himself to God's judgment, transforming his whole person into an act of "indigitation," which Cooper's *Thesaurus* defines as an act of naming or pointing out. The meaning supplied for "Indigito, aui, are" is "To call by name: to signifie and as it were to poynt the finger at."[11] Gaunt, to sum up, is not the author of his word or sentence: he is the gnomic pointing that directs the attention of the king and the audience to God's judgment.

The final point I wish to make about the function of authors, or the Author, is simple: many of the ideas that have animated modern literary and cultural criticism have long histories in simultaneously literary and political discourses. Criticism has correctly

identified the tension between the covert mode of literary representation and the open goals of politics, but have not always given
credit to the inventors or, better, the users and continuers, of key
tropes in the literary historical cultivation of political discourse.
There are times when an Author, especially a spectral one, is helpful to the communication of a political or ideological position, and
times when a purely instrumental agency—and thus an occlusion
of authors and authorship—is more likely to serve one's turn. The
key to the author's return to Shakespeare studies, certainly where
issues of classical transmission are concerned, is to recognize the
complex and deep history of the tropes of authorship.

Notes

1. They have also received excellent critical treatments by prominent scholars, such as Richard Halpern, *The Poetics of Primitive Accumulation: English Renaissance Culture and the Genealogy of Capital* (Ithaca: Cornell University Press,
1991); Mary Thomas Crane, *Framing Authority: Sayings, Self, and Society in Sixteenth-Century England* (Princeton: Princeton University Press, 1993); and Ann
Moss, *Printed Commonplace-books and the Structuring of Renaissance Thought*
(Cambridge: Cambridge University Press, 1996). See also Paul Hammond, "The
Play of Quotation and Commonplace in King Lear," in *Towards a Definition of
Topos: Approaches to Analogical Reasoning,* ed. Lynette Hunter (Basingstoke:
Macmillan, 1991), 78–129.
2. See Stephen Greenblatt, "Shakespeare and the Exorcists," in *Shakespeare
and the Question of Theory,* ed. Patricia Parker and Geoffrey Hartman, 163–87
(New York: Methuen, 1985).
3. See David Quint, *Epic and Empire: Politics and Generic Form from Virgil to
Milton* (Princeton: Princeton University Press, 1993); and David Norbrook, *Writing
the English Republic: Poetry, Rhetoric, and Politics, 1627–1660* (Cambridge: Cambridge University Press, 1999). For a related example in the slender genres, see
Annabel Patterson, *Pastoral and Ideology: Virgil to Valéry* (Berkeley: University of
California Press, 1987).
4. Thomas M. Greene, *The Light in Troy* (New Haven: Yale University Press,
1982).
5. My own work in this area includes "The Poet's Toys: Christopher Marlowe
and the Liberties of Erotic Elegy," *Modern Language Quarterly* 67.1 (2006): 103–
27, and "Ovid and the Question of Politics in Early Modern England," *English
Literary History* 70 (2003): 343–73, as well as *Shakespeare's Troy: Drama, Politics,
and the Translation of Empire* (Cambridge: Cambridge University Press, 1997).
6. These topics are noted by Rudolphus Agricola, as quoted in R. R. Bolgar,
The Classical Heritage and its Beneficiaries (Cambridge: Cambridge University
Press, 1954), 272.
7. "Reading and Authorship: The Circulation of Shakespeare, 1590–1619," in
A Concise Companion to Shakespeare and the Text, ed. Andrew Murphy (Oxford:

Blackwell, forthcoming). I would like to thank Peter Stallybrass for allowing me to see a copy of the essay in advance of its publication.

8. See William H. Sherman, *Used Books: Marking Readers in Renaissance England* (Philadelphia: Univ of Pennsylvania Press, 2008).

9. Quoted in Curtius, *European Literature and the Latin Middle Ages* (New York: Pantheon Books, 1953), 58.

10. *The Arte of English Poesie* (London, 1589), sig. 2Dr.

11. Thomas Cooper, *Thesaurus Romanae and Britannicæ* (London, 1578).

The Author and/or the Critic

Leah S. Marcus

W E SPEAK OF THE "Return of the Author" but of course, the author
never left. Michel Foucault's essay in which he called attention to
the "author-function" as serving to "characterize a certain mode of
being of discourse" and as "the principle of thrift in the proliferation of meaning" ended with the provocative question "What difference does it make who is speaking?"[1] But Foucault's essay
dispersing the authority of the author was firmly attached to the
name of *its* author: there was never any question as to who had
written the essay asking how and why and under what conditions
it should matter to us who had written anything. Deconstruction
and other forms of post-structuralist dispersal of "Shakespeare" as
"a certain mode of being of discourse" have not so much abolished
the author-function as a defining entity in modern critical discourse as they have shifted it from Shakespeare to the critic. Even,
or perhaps especially, critics who have challenged forms of cultural
authority to which Shakespeare's name has traditionally been
attached have not been willing to relinquish their own claims to a
new form of cultural authority attached to the name of the critic as
author.

In biblical studies, a group of "Bible and Culture Collectives" has
recently served as authors: *The Postmodern Bible* was authored by
the "Bible and Culture Collective" and is still so listed on Amazon.
com and other sales venues.[2] The Collective's purpose is to introduce various forms of postmodernist literary criticism into the field
of biblical studies through seven specified "areas of engagement":
reader response criticism, structuralist and narratological criticism,
post-structuralist criticism, rhetorical criticism, psychoanalytic
criticism, feminist and womanist criticism, and ideological criticism. While recent Shakespeareans might object to some of the
emphases of this list—questioning, perhaps, the inclusion of struc-

turalism under postmodern approaches, or noting the absence of critical race studies, queer theory, and recent work in bibliography and textual scholarship—the list offers a rough approximation to recent approaches to Shakespeare that have decentered the "author" in the Foucauldian sense of the word or at least decentered many of the assumptions of an earlier author-based criticism. The nearly anonymous Bible and Culture Collective, which includes at least one scholar of the English Renaissance who is well known in that field through publications in her own name, did something interestingly audacious: with the goal of bringing new critical approaches to bear on a resistant field, they took postmodern theory at its word and effaced their own authorship in favor of an umbrella term defining their collective enterprise.

This brave anonymity has somewhat dissipated over time: *The Postmodern Bible Reader,* which follows up on *The Postmodern Bible,* is "authored" by three named editors—David Jobling, Tina Pippin, and Ronald Schleifer—and is dedicated to other members of the Bible and Culture Collective who are listed by name.[3] Still, the Collective offers an interesting contrast to Shakespeare studies, in which the work of postmodern critics over recent decades has been similarly iconoclastic in terms of its impact on a venerated field of scholarship but not similarly iconoclastic in terms of its effacement of the name of the authors. It could be countered that the Bible and Culture Collective, by effacing individual names, was actually taking on a higher form of authorship, the plural voice of God, the only voice capable of presiding in an authoritative manner over scriptural interpretation. The preface to *The Postmodern Bible Reader* refers to two waves of participants in the Collective as two "incarnations" of it (vii). Or the Collective could be understood as operating under the prestigious new "author-function" of postmodernism itself. But the example of biblical studies still serves as an instructive contrast to the field of Shakespeare studies. Why is it that postmodern critics of Shakespeare, who is second only to the Bible in terms of traditional cultural authority, have never dared to similarly relinquish our own authorship in a collective enterprise at the center of our own discipline?

To a significant degree, of course, Anglo-American academic Shakespeareans are bound by institutional demands that we publish, and prolifically, in our chosen field if we wish to continue to enjoy the privilege of being paid to read and teach Shakespeare. But the same demand for scholarly visibility exists, and is arguably even more pressing, at the most prominent schools of divinity. Perhaps biblical scholars are simply more altruistic than Shakespeareans. The closest approximation we have to the near-anonymity of the Bible and Culture Collective within Shakespeare studies is scholarly editing, a pursuit that, although rewarding on other grounds, does not grant glory in proportion to time and effort spent, and that most Shakespeareans do not undertake until they are safely tenured and often quite senior in the field.

I would suggest, however, that there may be another reason why the dispersal of earlier myths about Shakespearean "authorship" tends to be practiced under the insistent and prominent name of the critic. Although we have thrown off many of the patriarchal and genealogical assumptions within which authorship was interpreted in the past, we have not lost our need to feel that our enterprise is being guided by a trustworthy, identifiable authority figure of some kind, and that, more often than not these days, is the name of the critic. We borrow the charisma of "Shakespeare" in the process of dismantling it. If the name of Shakespeare is at least temporarily "under construction," and divested of its traditional cultural authority while new ways of looking at Shakespeare are being developed, then some of that residual authority is at least temporarily transferred to the critic who guides us safely through the fecund chaos that accompanies any major paradigm shift in our understanding of Shakespeare.

Shakespeare is indeed returning as an "author" in the field of Shakespeare studies, but not in the same sublime, unique, isolate originary genius mode by which he was once understood. Recent criticism influenced by stage historians and theorists of performance emphasizes Shakespeare's membership in a collective enterprise, the theatrical company, and the inevitably collaborative and heterogeneous nature of its productions. Recent critics who deal with questions of authorship are likely to view Shakespeare less as the presiding genius over his works and more as, in the witty formulation of Roland Barthes, a guest who can be invited into the text or into our attempts to interpret it.[4] Thus understood, the "author" is a limited historical figure who can be considered as "a variable and complex function of discourse" (Foucault, 158) and traced in interaction with other functions associated with playhouse, printing house, court and popular culture, and the like. Much of the revived interest in Shakespeare the author has crystallized around Lukas Erne's *Shakespeare as Literary Dramatist,* which acknowledges Shakespeare's deep involvement with his dramatic company but makes a case for his—and the company's—simultaneous interest in the busy commercial enterprise of London publishing by which anonymous playwrights were gradually being turned into authors of their own work, and the dramatic companies, into corporate entities concerned not only with performance but also with the publication of their play texts in more polished, often fuller, literary forms that could take a place in the world of letters beyond the stage.[5]

Erne makes a number of compelling arguments, but most of his evidence is inferential, since Shakespeare left few traces, in terms of manuscript or printed evidence, of involvement in the process of bring a play text into print. Since I am in the midst of finishing an Arden edition of John Webster's *Duchess of Malfi,* I am struck by the number of times that Erne tries to make a point about what Shakespeare is likely to have thought by invoking what Webster actually articulated about his plays and the relationship between stage and page. Erne's chapter on "The making of 'Shakespeare'" (56–77) demonstrates how title pages of late sixteenth- and early seventeenth-century editions of Shakespeare show a gradual increase in the authority of the author as opposed to the authority of dramatic performance: "they present what the dramatist William Shakespeare has originally written and is now offered to the reader. Authority, in other words, has shifted from the dramatic company to the dramatist, from the stage to the page" (77). But the proof text offered to show Shakespeare's self-conscious involvement in this process comes at the very end of the chapter and is from John Webster, not Shakespeare. In his preface to *The Devil's Law-Case* (1623) Webster struggled with the conundrum of representing dramatic action in a literary text: *"A great part of the grace of this (I confesse) lay in Action; yet can no Action euer be gracious, where the decency of the Language, and Ingenious structure of the Scene, arriue not to make vp a perfect Harmony"* (sig. A2v). This statement nicely balances a recognition of the power of action on stage and the power of a competing "grace" of inferred action, poetry, and structure as communicated in a literary text for readers. It is a strong statement that sounds reassuringly authorial to modern ears, and that says exactly what Erne needs it to say at this point in his argument. But the trouble is, it wasn't said by Shakespeare.

Similarly, in discussing the distinction between a "play," which is staged, and a "poem," which is read, Erne calls upon Webster, whose preface to *The Duchess of Malfi* (1623) insists on calling the play a "Poem" destined to last when "*the* Poets *themselues were bound vp in their winding-sheetes*" (sig. A3v). The title page specifies that the version offered readers is "The perfect and exact Coppy, with diuerse / *things Printed that the length of the Play would* / not beare in the Presentment." If we put preface and title page together, we can infer that in Webster's view, plays are likely to be shorter and poems longer and more elaborate, designed to be read by succeeding generations. But here again, the critical commentary, however valuable, comes from Webster, not Shakespeare, and is of suspiciously late date. It is perhaps not mere happenstance that both of Webster's critical pronouncements come from editions published the same year as the Shakespeare First Folio (1623), which, as many Shakespeareans have argued, played a key role in establishing Shakespeare as the celebrated author of a large body of dramatic material.

In their prefatory material to the First Folio (London, 1623), John Heminge and Henry Condell express the wish that Shakespeare had lived long enough to preside over the publication of his works: "It had bene a thing, we confesse, worthie to haue bene wished, that the Author himself had liu'd to haue set forth, and ouerseen his owne writings" but Shakespeare, by dying, "departed from that right" (sig. A3r). If he had lived, would Shakespeare have performed this task, and at what level of attention to the process of printing the plays? Here again, Webster provides an instructive point of comparison, for we have strong evidence that he corrected at least one sheet of the First Quarto of *The Duchess of Malfi* (1623) while it was in process of being printed. The two states of sigs. H1v and H2r from the inner H forme show explicit signs of authorial intervention, which I will discuss in some detail.

The first state of the quarto (usually called Q1a and reproduced here as fig. 1) is relatively straightforward.[6] On the left page (H1v) appears the beginning of 3.4, in which two "Pilgrims to the Shrine of Our Lady of Loreto" witness the Cardinal's ritualized transformation from churchman to military commander and his public disavowal of the Duchess's marriage, all of which is described in the play's most elaborate stage direction—nine lines long—at the bottom of the page. The catchword at the foot of the page is "The" and the first words below the running title at the top of the right-hand page (H2r) match the catchword, "The Hymne." In the second state of the quarto (Q1b, reproduced here as fig. 2), several things have

Shall not be at your Ceremony : fare you well,
Write to the Duke of *Malfy*, my yong Nephew,
She had by her first husband, and acquaint him,
With's mothers honesty.

Bos. I will.

Ferd. Antonio?
A slaue, that onely smell'd of yncke, and compters,
And neu'r in's life, look'd like a Gentleman,
But in the audit time, go, go presently,
Draw me out an hundreth and fifty of our horse,
And meete me at the fort-bridge.

Exeunt.

SCENA IIII.

Two Pilgrimes to the Shrine of our Lady
of Loreto.

1. *Pilg.* I haue not seene a goodlier Shrine then this,
Yet I haue visited many.

2. *Pilg.* The Cardinall of *Arragon*
Is, this day to resigne his Cardinals hat,
His sister Dutchesse likewise is arriu'd
To pay her vow of Pilgrimage, I expect
A noble Ceremony.

1. *Pilg.* No question: ——— They come.

Here the Ceremony of the Cardinalls enstalment, in the order
of a Souldier: perform'd in delivering vp his Crosse, Hat, Robes,
and Ring, at the Shrine; and investing him with Sword,
Helmet, Sheild, and Spurs: Then Antonio, the Dutchesse, and
their Children, (hauing presented themselues at the Shrine)
are (by a forme of Banishment expressed towards them by
the Cardinall, and the State of Ancona) banished: During
all which Ceremony, this Hymne is sung (to very solemne
Musique) by divers Church-men, and then Exeunt.

The

The Hymne.

Arme, and Honors, decke thy story,
To thy Fames eternall glory,
Aduerse Fortune euer flie-thee,
No disastrous fate come nigh-thee.

I alone will sing thy praises,
Whom to honour, vertu raises;
And thy fame, that's dimme-is,
Bent to Marshall discipline-is:
Lay aside all those robes lie by thee;
Crowne thy arts, with arms: they'll beautifie thee.

O worthy of worthiest name, adorn'd in this manner,
Lead brauely thy forces on, (vnder war's warlike banner:
O mayst thou proue fortunate, in all Marshall courses;
Guide thou still by skill, in arts, and forces:
Victory attend thee nigh, whilst fame sings loud thy power;
Triumphant conquest crowne thy head, and blessings, powre downe
(showres.

1. *Pilg.* Here's a strange turne of state, who would haue thought
So great a Lady, would haue match'd her selfe
Vnto so meane a person? yet the Cardinall
Beares himselfe much too cruell.

2. *Pilg.* They are banish'd.

1. *Pilg.* But I would aske what power hath this state
Of *Ancona*, to determine of a free Prince?

2. *Pilg.* They are a free state, and her brother shew'd
How that the Pope fore-hearing of her loosenesse,
Had seaz'd into th'protection of the Church
The Dukedome, which she held as dowager.

1. *Pil.* But by what iustice?

2. *Pilg.* Sure I thinke by none,
Only her brothers instigation.

1. *Pilg.* What was it, with such violence he tooke
Of from her finger?

2. *Pil.* 'Twas her wedding ring,

Which

H 2

Figure 1. First state of *The Duchess of Malfi* (1623), H1v–H2r opening. © British Library Board.
All Rights Reserved. Uncatalogued; Ashley 2207.

Armes, and Honors deck thy ſtory,
To thy Fames eternall glory,
Aduerſe Fortune euer flee-thee,
No diſtreſſe from fate come nigh-thee.

I alone will ſing thy praiſes,
Whom to honour, vertue raiſes;
And thy ſtudy, that dimme-is,
Bent to Marſhall diſcipline-is:
Lay aſide all thoſe robes lie by thee,
Crownes thy arts, with armes: they'l beautifie thee.

O worthy of worthieſt name, adorn'd in this manner,
Lead brauely thy forces on, vnder wars warlike banner:
O mayſt thou proue fortunate in all Marſhall conflict,
Guide thou high, by thy skill, in arter, and forces:
Victory attend thee nigh, whilſt fame ſings loud thy power,
Triumphant conqueſt crowne thy head, and bleſſing powre downe. (ſhowret.

1.Pilg. Here's a ſtrange turne of ſtate, who would haue thought
So great a Lady, would haue match'd her ſelfe
Vnto ſo meane a perſon? yet the Cardinall
Beares himſelfe much too cruell.

2.Pilg. They are baniſh'd.

1.Pilg. But I would aske what power hath this ſtate
Of Arragon, to determine of a free Prince?

2.Pilg. They are a free ſtate ſir, and her brother ſhew'd
How that the Pope fore-hearing of her looſeneſſe,
Hath ſeaz'd into th'protection of the Church
The Dukedome, which ſhe held as dowager.

1.Pilg. But by what iuſtice?

2.Pilg. Sure I thinke by none,
Only her brother inſtigation.

1.Pilg. What was it, with ſuch violence he tooke
Off from her finger?

2.Pilg. 'Twas her wedding-ring,

H 2   Which

The Tragedy of

I ſhall not be at your Ceremony : fare you well,
Write to the Duke of Malfy, my yong Nephew,
She had by her firſt husband, and acquaint him,
With's mothers honeſty.

Boſ. I will.

Ferd. Antonio?

A ſlaue, that onely ſmell'd of ynke, and counters,
And neer'in's like, look'd like a Gentleman,
But in the audit time, go, go preſently,
Draw me out an hundreth and fifty of our horſe,
And meete me at the fore-bridge.   Exeunt.

SCENA IIII.

Two Pilgrimes to the Shrine of our Lady
of Loreto.

1. Pilg. I haue not ſeene a goodlier Shrine then this,
Yet I haue viſited many.

2. Pilg. The Cardinall of Arragon
Is, this day to reſigne his Cardinals hat,
His ſiſter Dutcheſſe here likewiſe is arriv'd
To pay her vow of Pilgrimage, I expect
A noble Ceremony.

1. Pilg. No queſtion: ——They come.

Here the Ceremony of the Cardinalls enſtalment, in the habit
of a Souldier: perform'd in deliuering vp his Croſſe, Hat, Robes,
and Ring, at the Shrine; and inſtruing thence Antonio, his
Wife, and Children (hauing declin'd, and profeſſed themſelues at the Shrine)
are (by a forme of Baniſhment in dumbe-ſhew, expreſs'd towards them by the Cardinall, and the State of Ancona,) baniſh-
ed: During all which Ceremony, the Ditty is ſung, (to
very ſolemne Muſique) by diuerſ Churchmen; and then
                                                        Exeunt.

H   The

Figure 2. Second state of *The Duchess of Malfi* (1623), H1v–H2r opening. © British Library Board. All Rights Reserved. Shelfmark 644 f. 72.

changed. The stage direction at bottom left has obviously been partially reset, since it now spills over onto a tenth line to accommodate "*Exeunt.*" The catchword "The" remains, but it is more
crowded because of additions to the stage direction, and it has lost
its function because the title "The Hymne." has now been removed
from the top of the right-hand side and the first words on the page
after the running title are now "*Armes, and Honors, decke thy
story.*". Someone in the print shop has deliberately stripped the
"Hymne" of its title. An added note to the right of the text of the
"Hymne" suggests it is now to be understood as a "Ditty": "The
Author disclaimes this Ditty to be his." In Q1a, the "Hymne" is so
designated in the eighth line of the stage direction as well; in Q1b
that designation has been replaced by "Ditty"—a term that seems
little in keeping with the solemnity of the religious ceremony being
acted onstage, to which the sung verses, by whatever name, serve
as musical accompaniment.

What happened between the two states of the H1v–H2r opening?
Recent editors have become uncomfortable with the projections of
authorial intent than an earlier generation of editors relied on in
making emendations. But here we have material differences that
quite readily generate a narrative of authorial involvement. The
most likely narrative (though there could be others) is that Webster
came into the print shop to check on the copy, noticed in horror
that someone else's verses were being printed as his with the grand
title of "Hymne," and insisted that the printer add a note to the
right of them scornfully repudiating authorship of what he would
only term a "Ditty." The objectionable verses themselves had to be
preserved in order to avoid massive resetting of copy, but at least
Webster could register a disclaimer and deliver an implicit aesthetic judgment through the scornful word "Ditty."

This conjectural scenario is reinforced by the fact that a number
of other highly informed changes are made to the same opening. In
the first line of the stage directions, "*order*" in Q1a is changed to
the more specific "*habit*" in Q1b; and in line six, "*forme of Banishment*" is augmented helpfully to "*forme of Banishment in dumbe-
shew.*" In Q1b, that is, readers are specifically informed that the actions described in the stage direction had been performed in panto-
mime. In addition to several more minor changes, another page
from the same forme (H4r) shows a speech prefix corrected from
"Antonio" (Q1a) to "Duchess" (Q1b) and an important stage direction added: "*Enter Bosola with a Guard.*" Given the number and

type of corrections made to this forme, it seems highly likely that
Webster examined it himself, successfully insisting on changes that
made the text more accessible to readers while also downgrading
the "Hymne" to a "Ditty" and thereby pointing to the printed text's
composite origins. Here we have a likely case of the author entering
quite literally as a guest into his text as it was being printed. The
printed notice that "The Author disclaimes this Ditty to be his" reinforces the reader's apprehension of the rest of the play as genuine
Webster, since it was only the "Hymne" that "The Author" explicitly rejected.

Erne is quite clear that we would not expect Shakespeare to concern himself with printing house copy: because of the typically
slow pace of copy setting, thorough proofing of the copy would require as many visits to the printing house as there were formes to
be corrected, or an equal number of deliveries of proofs to the author for correction.[7] So when it comes to surveillance over the correction of copy, we can infer that Erne would regard Webster and
Shakespeare as having been far apart. That suggests that there may
be problems with the other cases in which Erne reasons from what
Webster said to what Shakespeare must have meant. Erne does cite
one case in which (mirabile dictu!) we seem to see Shakespeare intervening in the form taken by a printed work. The two extant copies of the third edition of *The Passionate Pilgrime* (printed by W.
Jaggard, 1612) have different title pages, one of them announcing
that the volume is *"By W. Shakespere"* and the other lacking the
authorial attribution. According to Thomas Heywood's *Apology for
Actors* (1612), Shakespeare was "much offended with M. *Iaggard*
that (altogether vnknowne to him) presumed to make so bold with
his name" (sig. G4v). Since there is a cancel title page without
Shakespeare's name, it seems reasonable to assume, as Erne does,
that Shakespeare insisted on its removal. The case is similar to
Webster's in *The Duchess of Malfi* in that we can see an author
guarding the integrity of his name by objecting to its association
with material he considered inferior to his own. But Heywood nowhere alleges that Shakespeare insisted on the cancel title page to
The Passionate Pilgrime, which had been attributed to Shakespeare
as early as the title page of the 1599 edition. And it seems odd that,
although Heywood's account of Shakespeare's disaffection was
printed in 1612, *The Passionate Pilgrime* was initially reprinted in
1613 with the name of Shakespeare still on the title page. Shakespeare may have behaved with the authorial outrage of a Webster

in this instance, or he may not have. But we are, in any case, dealing here with a volume of poems, not plays. Critics are in general agreement already that Shakespeare took more interest in the publication of his poems than of his plays, going to the trouble of providing signed dedicatory epistles for *Lucrece* (1594) and the 1594 imprint of *Venus and Adonis*. The question of his degree of investment at any level in the printing of his plays is still very much open.

While Shakespeare was incontestably in process of being constructed as an "author" by his fellow dramatists and the printers of his plays during the late sixteenth and early seventeenth centuries, the sad fact is that Shakespeare, unlike Webster, appears to have had relatively little interest in being a critic as well as an author; he has left us no body of commentary (in the manner of Webster) on his own achievement independent of the evidence provided within the plays and poems themselves. We can speculate about Shakespeare's part in the construction of his own authorship of the plays on the basis of existing evidence about promptbooks, manuscripts of plays, and early printings —and I agree with Erne and William Long that our attention to these materials has for the most part been woefully inadequate[8]—but it is too soon to imagine that we can give a reliable shape to Shakespeare's silences about key critical and textual issues We have, in gracious Barthian fashion, invited the historical figure of Shakespeare as a guest into his plays, but we have not yet invented a reliable way to gauge his presence. Some Shakespeareans have received Erne's book on *Shakespeare as Literary Dramatist* with almost a sigh of relief that we can now dispose of the annoying issues postmodern critics have raised and get back to business as usual. It need hardly be said that fostering such a rearguard movement was not Erne's intent in writing his book. If, as Foucault suggests, the author is "the principle of thrift in the proliferation of meaning," he also points out that the very achievement of authorial "thrift" contradicts our fundamental desire to invest the author with myriad, even inexhaustible powers of signification. If only because the name of Shakespeare is bound up with so much cultural capital—both academic and commercial— and is the source of so much cultural authority, it is unlikely that postmodern reinterpretations of Shakespeare will result in the author's name being reduced to the "anonymity of a murmur" (Foucault, 160). While we academic Shakespeareans are in process of deconstructing various aspects of that cultural authority among ourselves, we are willing to stand at the public barricades and defend Shakespeare against assaults (such as those by Oxfordians) on his identity and mastery. It does matter to us "who is speaking," but it is too soon for a renewal of authorial "thrift." It is too soon to close down our investigation of the ways in which Shakespeare crucially and troublingly differs from what we, or perhaps even many among his contemporaries, would consider normative authorial behavior.

Notes

1. "What is an Author?" ed. and trans. Josué V. Harari, in *Textual Strategies: Perspectives in Post-Structuralist Criticism* (Ithaca: Cornell University Press, 1979), 147, 159, and 160.

2. *The Postmodern Bible* (New Haven: Yale University Press, 1995).

3. *The Postmodern Bible Reader* (Oxford: Blackwell, 2001).

4. "From Work to Text," Harari, ed., 73–78, esp. 78.

5. Lukas Erne, *Shakespeare as Literary Dramatist* (Cambridge: Cambridge University Press, 2003).

6. My discussion here is based on the thorough analysis of the printing process by formes in David Gunby et al., eds., *The Works of John Webster* (Cambridge: Cambridge University Press, 1995), 1:576–80.

7. See Erne, 96–97; and Peter W. M. Blayney's chapter on "Proof-reading, revising, and press-correcting," in *The Texts of* King Lear *and their Origins* (Cambridge: Cambridge University Press, 1982), 1:188–218.

8. Erne, 158; and William B. Long, "Perspective on Provenance: The Context of Varying Speech-heads," in *Shakespeare's Speech-Headings: Speaking the Speech in Shakespeare's Plays,* ed. George Walton Williams (Newark: University of Delaware Press, 1997), 21–44.

Coauthors and Closed Minds

Brian Vickers

One of the defining characteristics of human knowledge is its capacity for growth. As Ben Jonson put it, in a poem of self-examination and self-criticism,

> Where do'st thou carelesse lie
>   Buried in ease and sloth?
> Knowledge, that sleepes, doth die;
>   And this Securitie,
>   It is the common Moath,
> That eats on wits, and Arts, and [oft] destroyes them both.[1]

In early modern English "securitie" meant "complacency," here the conviction that the knowledge one possesses is adequate, when it may be moth-eaten. History confirms that in the mainstream of human inquiry knowledge has never remained static. New sources come to light, old ones are reinterpreted; new paradigms are proposed, some are disputed but accepted, others are accepted but displaced or superseded, and so on. Historical scholarship uncovers neglected areas of inquiry, revalues issues formerly regarded as settled, and produces new knowledge, the product being the result of a process of inquiry and discovery that is both critical and self-critical. Francis Bacon was the first modern thinker to fully recognize growth as an innate quality of knowledge, outlining his vision in *The Twoo Bookes of Francis Bacon. Of the proficience and advancement of Learning, divine and human* (1605)—where "proficience" has the older sense of an "Improvement in skill or knowledge; progress." Bacon's dynamic concept of knowledge as something that can be continually extended included every human being's power to improve his or her ability. In his words, the *rationem totius* or "essence of the whole" is that learning disposeth the constitution of the mind not to be fixed or settled in the defects thereof, but still to be capable and susceptible of growth and reformation. For the unlearned man knows not what it is to descend into himself or to call himself to account, nor the pleasure of that "*suavissima vita, in dies sentire se fieri meliorem*" [this most happy state, to feel one's self becoming a better man day by day]. The good parts he hath he will learn to shew to the full and use them dexterously, but not much to increase them, the faults he hath he will learn how to hide and colour them, but not much to amend them; like an ill mower, that mows on still and never whets his scythe: whereas with the learned man it fares otherwise, that he doth ever intermix the correction and amendment of his mind with the use and employment thereof.[2]

By the process of self-examination and self-criticism (to "descend" into oneself), those who approach new discoveries with an open mind can improve their knowledge indefinitely; those who avoid this confrontation remain trapped in a state of ignorance or prejudice. In addition to these two categories of open and closed minds, Bacon diagnosed a third state, where systems, ideologies, or even individuals block the advancement of learning, and "are indeed but remoras and hinderances to stay and slug the ship [of knowledge] from further sailing" (ibid., 198). The "Remora remora," in our terminology, is a pelagic marine fish that uses a sucking disc on top of its head to obtain rides from other animals such as large sharks and sea turtles. In antiquity the remora was thought to attach itself to ships, slowing their progress, and the famous engraved title page to Bacon's *Instauratio Magna* shows the ship of learning returning successfully from its voyage of discovery, with some remoras observing it disgruntedly.[3]

Historical scholarship of Elizabethan drama made enormous advances over the last century, in particular in clarifying the conditions under which plays were written. When English literary history began to emerge in the eighteenth century, the normal paradigm for literary production was that of a single author, whether as poet, novelist, or dramatist. That had also been the norm for classical antiquity, despite Michel Foucault's bizarre claim that the author was a modern concept.[4] But the single-author paradigm, though appropriate for Virgil and Horace, Spenser and Milton, Fielding and Richardson, does not fit the material conditions under which drama was produced in London between 1579 and 1642. As I have observed elsewhere, the best analogy is with the *bottega* of the Renaissance painter, bronze-maker, or scupltor, where a group of craftsmen executed a contract specifying the delivery of a given artwork, of an agreed subject matter and dimension, by a specified date.[5] The analogy does not fit completely, of course (analogies are not meant to), for although Philip Henslowe fills the role of the patron who commissioned and paid for the composition, literary production was organized differently. Whereas the *bottega* was organized around a master craftsman (Filarete for the bronze doors at St. Peter's, Giovanni Bellini, Titian, or Rembrandt with their assistants), no evidence exists that Elizabethan dramatists worked for a dominant figure. From Henslowe's diary we can see that he kept many dramatists in business by his practice of offering payment in installments for the delivery of scenes or acts of the agreed play, and that he ran what have been called "drama writing syndicates."[6] In some cases the "senior" dramatist might have been the named person who received the largest payment, but in others the fee was shared equally among any number from two to four playwrights, and no master craftsman can be identified. But otherwise it is clear that collaborative writing was very common in the hotly competitive London theater world, and that perhaps a quarter to a third of all plays were coauthored.[7] Apart from John Lyly, who wrote for the special capabilities of the boy actors, almost every dramatist took part in coauthored plays: Marlowe, Heywood, Dekker, Chettle, Ford, Chapman, Webster. Even Jonson did so, although four of his coauthored plays have perished, and he fastidiously rewrote one of the survivors (*Sejanus*) in order to remove all trace of his collaborator.

Scholars and critics working on any of the dramatists mentioned above accept coauthorship as a fact of life, an inevitable feature of that amazingly productive sixty-year period in the London theater. But some readers and writers have great difficulty in seeing Shakespeare as a normal Elizabethan dramatist. We now know that George Peele wrote act 1 and three other scenes in *Titus Andronicus,* totaling 775 lines; that Thomas Middleton contributed 894 lines to *Timon of Athens;* George Wilkins supplied the first two acts of *Pericles* (1,013 lines); and that John Fletcher was responsible for 1,645 lines of *King Henry VIII* and for 1,477 lines of *The Two Noble Kinsmen.*[8] Altogether, about 6,000 of the approximately 120,000 lines in the Shakespeare canon were supplied by coauthors. We also have strong evidence that he wrote neither of the anonymously published poems recently ascribed to him, the lyric "Shall I die?" and the *Funerall Elegye* for William Peter, and I know that I am not

alone in wanting to remove "A Lover's Complaint" from *Shakespeare's Sonnets* and transfer it to John Davies of Hereford.[9]

Expressing doubts about the authenticity of some scenes in canonical Shakespeare is not a new phenomenon. It dates back to the
early nineteenth century, in the work of Charles Lamb, Henry
Weber, Charles Knight, W. A. Spalding, and James Spedding. Rejecting these doubts and asserting "the integrity of the Shakespeare
canon" is also no new phenomenon. The rationale behind these re-
jections is primarily the prestige that posterity has thrust on him.
As Ashley Thorndike wrote in 1901, scholars "have found it difficult to think of Shakspere condescending to write a play in company with another dramatist, especially when, as in *Henry VIII,* his
part is somewhat the less important."[10] But, he went on, "This ob-
jection is simply another exhibition of the common fallacy of always regarding Shakspere as a world genius and never as an
Elizabethan dramatist. Shakspere's own practices and the general
practice of Elizabethan dramatists, show that his collaboration with
Fletcher would be no cause for wonder" (35–36). The unhistorical
nature of the bardolatrous elevation of Shakespeare must be obvious to all, but such prejudices are deep-rooted. Half a century later
Marco Mincoff was making the same complaint:

> Anyone attempting to ascribe non-canonical plays or parts of plays to
> Shakespeare is faced with an even more difficult task than in other
> cases of doubtful authorship. Not so much because of the difficulty of
> recognizing his style but because of the tremendous body of prejudice
> one has to overcome. The canon of Shakespeare's works has been
> conned so religiously and invested with such an odour of divinity that
> conditioned aesthetic reflexes have been established in most critics
> which place him in a very special position—his beauties have received
> an additional glamour both through familiarity from childhood and
> through a constant chorus of praise.[11]

The ingrained resistance to accepting Shakespeare as a dramatist
sharing the normal theatrical practices of his day has not diminished in the half century since Mincoff wrote. In my contribution
to this forum, I will document this resistance in three case studies,
and examine the grounds on which it is based.

II

In 1919 the widely read scholar T. M. Parrott, who produced an
excellent edition of Chapman, recognized that act 1 of *Titus An-*

dronicus, along with two other scenes, had one prosodic feature quite unlike Shakespeare, a very low percentage of feminine endings. Other un-Shakespearean elements that Parrott identified suggested the presence of George Peele as coauthor. Over the following eighty years a succession of reputable scholars—P. W. Timberlake, John Dover Wilson, J. C. Maxwell, R. F. Hill, MacDonald Jackson, Marina Tarlinskaja, and Brian Boyd, using several different and independent analytical methods, endorsed Parrott's rejection of these scenes as un-Shakespearean, and agreed that Peele was the collaborator. In *Shakespeare, Co-Author,* I brought all this evidence together, added new tests of my own confirming Peele's coauthorship, and recorded that none of the current editions of *Titus Andronicus* took notice of these well-established scholarly findings,[12] since Peele's poor reputation had preceded him. By whatever complex process a writer acquires a reputation at a given point in time—an amalgam of inherited tradition, untested by an actual knowledge of the texts, a mixture of rumor and ignorance—Peele has been set down as a clumsy, uninventive dramatist unworthy to lace up Shakespeare's sandals, let alone jointly plot and write a play with him.

An especially revealing instance of the tendency to disqualify Peele out of hand, among even experienced scholars of English Renaissance drama, was provided by Ralph Berry, in reviewing *Shakespeare Co-Author.*[13] Berry conceded that the book had "set forth compelling arguments from many sources for the existence of various hands in 'Shakespeare'" (684), and accepted without demur the case made for Middleton, Wilkins, and Fletcher as coauthors. But although he conceded that "a non-Shakespearian hand is discernible in the early stages" of *Titus Andronicus*—in fact, the first three scenes, totaling 656 lines, and also act 4, scene 1, a further 129 lines—Berry claimed that "here, and throughout the rest of the play, a dominant mind commands the action" (685). In other words, only one dramatist could have planned the whole. Of course, this cannot be disproved, but reason suggests that the hundreds of coauthored plays that reached the stage between 1576 and 1642 must have been the result of joint planning in advance, during the writing, and perhaps even after delivery of the manuscript. Without a generally agreed plan, dramatists could hardly set to work. Having skimmed over this issue, Berry then summarized the action of the opening scene, with its dispute between the two brothers Saturninus and Bassanius over who is to become consul

of Rome, suggesting that this is the same "'hostile brother' motif
that opens *As You Like It* and is the groundplot of *The Comedy of
Errors*." Not reflecting that there must be hundreds of literary works
based on conflicts between brothers, from Cain and Abel onward,
Berry asserted that the rest of the play has an "organic logic" deriving from this opening scene, and with the help of a rhetorical question, a device much favored by Shakespeare conservators, he
reached his conclusion: "Is it seriously concluded that George and
Will got together to impose this hard, driving logic upon the raw
material?" Readers will not be surprised by his answer:

> I think not. Given that there are two metrical strata, Peele looks to have
> drafted some scenes, together perhaps with a "treatment," which
> Shakespeare took over and made into a proper play of his own. That is
> what Heminge and Condell thought. Shakespeare absorbed Peele into
> his own vision: even the repetitious and limited diction, a feature of
> Peele's style, is perfectly suited to the unvaried insistences of the main
> characters. Repetition signifies enclosure within narrow mental bound-
> aries, and that suits the "super-objective" of this drama. To elevate
> Peele to "co-author" is unearned promotion. (685)

A more attentive reading of *Titus Andronicus* would reject Berry's
claim that the play's "organic logic" springs from the opening
scene. Although it does generate much of the conflict, this does not
mean that only one dramatist planned it. Moreover, a wholly unexpected source of destruction emerges in the character of Aaron,
sketched by Peele but brought into full potential by Shakespeare in
act 2, scene 3 and following.

However, the significant point for us is Berry's condescending attitude toward Peele, who may have "drafted some scenes, together
perhaps with a 'treatment'"—presumably a plot outline or scenario
is meant—but had to wait until Shakespeare came along to make it
into "a proper play." This patronizing attitude extends to Peele's
"repetitious and limited diction," which is indeed a feature of his
style, but Professor Berry errs in stating that Shakespeare "absorbed" it as somehow suitable to the "narrow mental boundaries"
of this play. He did not; indeed, it is precisely the many differences
between Peele's style and Shakespeare's that allow us to separate
the play so clearly into two different strata. Earlier Berry had even
objected to the term "collaboration," which for him "implies some
kind of negotiation between authors, an active mutuality" (685), a
mutuality that he categorically refused to grant Peele: "Either Peele

drafted an entire play, and Shakespeare threw out nearly all of it while revising what was left, or Peele handed over a mere torso for Shakespeare to complete. In each case Shakespeare is the incontestable master. This is not a meeting of minds. . . . *Titus Andronicus* strikes me as a rewrite job, and Shakespeare's role that of playdoctor. He should get the award" (686). It is symptomatic of the unhealthy ascendancy that Shakespeare enjoys even among professional scholars of Elizabethan drama that Ralph Berry never bothered to form a firsthand knowledge of Peele's career. The fact is that Peele had a far wider experience of theater than any other dramatist working in London in 1593–94, the likely date of *Titus Andronicus,* and that several elements in the play's dramaturgy reveal his hand.[14]

Turning to the second of my three test cases, *1 Henry VI,* a similar pattern can be seen. Doubts about the play's authenticity were first expressed by Malone in 1780, and continued to be heard over the next two centuries. Many readers noticed the great variations in style throughout the play, with act 1 being regularly singled out as un-Shakespearean, together with clumsy or nonexistent joins between the various plot levels, and at least two scenes surviving alongside those they were apparently designed to displace (compare 2.4 with 2.5, 4.5 with 4.6). It was generally agreed that 2.4, the "plucking of the roses" scene, was by Shakespeare, together with several scenes in act 4 dealing with the last stand of the English hero Talbot and his son John. As a candidate for the authorship of act 1, Thomas Nashe was the strongest of those considered by H. C. Hart in 1909, and a series of largely independent studies—by Archibald Stalker in 1935, John Dover Wilson in 1952, Marco Mincoff in 1965 and 1976, Gary Taylor in 1995, and Paul Vincent in 2002—confirmed Nashe's authorship of act 1.[15] The Nashe ascription rests on several observable and quantifiable stylistic characteristics that clearly differentiate him from Shakespeare: a liking for many short sentences and brief questions, often two within a line, resulting in an oddly "staccato" utterance; and the high use of syntactical inversions, especially of subject and object, all elements that are also found in Nashe's one play, *Summer's Last Will and Testament.* Further, a considerable number of verbal parallels have been identified between act 1 of *1 Henry VI,* and Nashe's acknowledged works, sustained parallels of both words and thoughts, several deriving from literary works often used by Nashe but never by Shakespeare.

Most of this evidence was available to the four most recent editors of *1 Henry VI:* Norman Sanders for his New Penguin edition (1981), Michael Hattaway for the New Cambridge Shakespeare (1990), Edward Burns for the 3rd Arden (2000), and Michael Taylor for the Oxford World's Classics series (2003). Hattaway rightly criticized A. S. Cairncross (2nd Arden edition, 1962) for explaining away the play's many variations in style and incongruences in plot and characterization in terms of scribal error and interference by the company's book-holder. However, resolved to reject all evidence of coauthorship, Hattaway in turn attributed the many inconsistencies and "vexing problems" of the text to another convenient agent of blame, "compositorial interference" (187–95). As for the "stylistic faults" that had provoked Cairncross's orgy of emendation, Hattaway flatly denied that "quality of writing can be used . . . as a test for authorship," and he dismissed "earlier critics" (such as Mincoff) for having "generally worked impressionistically," using "various *ad hoc* stylistic methods." Done with those, Hattaway turned to Taylor's (as yet unpublished) essay, "based on vocabulary, spelling, and metrical tests, as well as on scene divisions, and orthographical and linguistic features" (42). Nobody could call Taylor's work "impressionistic," but Hattaway avoided discussing it by lumping it together with "stylistic" evidence: "I do not believe that stylistic analysis is sufficient to prove or disprove authorship, as it is likely that at an early stage in his career Shakespeare was moving freely between the various verse registers that were being deployed in the plays in which he was probably acting" (42–43). That is a glib attempt to deflect the issue, since it fails to address either the evidence of a high concentration of feminine endings in 2.4 and 4.2–4.5, characteristic of Shakespeare, or the evidence of an unusual number of syntactical inversions in act 1, characteristic of Nashe. Both elements are deeply rooted in the play's language, transcending any supposed effect caused by an actor-writer moving between various verse registers of the plays staged in the 1580s and early '90s. Hattaway closed his discussion with a defiant rhetorical question: "And even if it could be proved that the play was in whole or in part not by Shakespeare, should that affect the way in which we read or direct it?" (43). To use a rhetorical question is to assume that the answer to it is self-evident. But scholars from many disciplines would object that to ask who was responsible for the *Missa Solemnis,* the Sistine Chapel ceiling, or *King Lear,* is a legitimate and pertinent question. The link between creator(s) and creation cannot be dismissed as irrelevant.

Michael Hattaway's position on the possibility of coauthorship might be defined as "nescience." That of Edward Burns can only be described as confused. Commenting on his two predecessors as Arden editors, Burns judged that Cairncross "presents powerfully an argument for a single author, Shakespeare" (74), and dismissed the arguments for coauthorship made by H. C. Hart (1909), "based on parallels of verbal detail," as "unconvincing, and its motives unsympathetic." (What can be "unsympathetic" about trying to establish the authorship of a text?) However, despite having sided with Cairncross, Burns then decided that Hart's case for coauthorship "may intuit" a "more plausible process of writing and devising" than that offered by those who conceive of Shakespeare having projected "an epic cycle" of three interlinked plays (74–75). Indeed, Burns did more than "intuit" coauthorship, for he cited Gary Taylor's 1995 article and, despite the reservations he had expressed a page earlier, now declared himself "in broad agreement with [Taylor's] conclusion that the major identifiable contributors to the play are Shakespeare and Nashe, that Nashe is largely responsible for the first act, Shakespeare for the fourth [*sic*] and parts of the second, and that several other writers, now impossible to name, were also involved" (75). Having reached this point the reader versed in authorship studies may breathe a sigh of relief, thinking "at last we find an editor willing to concede that the many inconsistencies and incongruences in this play point to coauthorship." But within a few pages Burns veered back to nescience: "in the absence of external evidence, no *certain* division of authorship is *ever attainable. I do not believe that we can ever finally know* who wrote this or indeed many other plays of the period, nor do I believe that putting a name (or names) to it should determine our sense of *the quality and nature* of the text" (82; my italics). Shakespeare conservators often use this strategy, denying the possibility of certainty and finality—which sensible proponents of attribution studies would never make—while misdescribing the attributional scholar's enterprise. No serious scholar first ascribes an author's name to a text, as Burns later alleges ("a prior ascription would have to be made on some other basis" than empirical evidence), and then allows that to determine his or her judgment on the quality of a text, let alone its "nature" (whatever that might mean). Attribution scholars work the other way around, beginning from the perception of incongruences in the language of a text, its use of sources, characterization, and dramaturgy, and then seeking to identify the authors concerned. As far as the editors of *1 Henry VI* are concerned, we have been wasting our time.

My third test case is *Pericles,* which appeared in a quarto text (1609) but was not included in the 1623 Folio. Doubts about its authorship were expressed in the first modern edition, by Nicholas Rowe (1709), and eighteenth-century commentators lined up either to denounce its authenticity (Pope, Whalley, Steevens), or accept it as partly Shakespearean (Theobald, Farmer, Malone). In 1868 the distinguished German scholar Nicholas Delius displayed great acuity in assigning the first two acts to George Wilkins, the last three to Shakespeare. Delius's authorship division was confirmed over the next century and a half by a gallery of scholars working in Shakespearean authorship studies: F. G. Fleay, Robert Boyle, H. Dugdale Sykes, C. A. Langworthy, Ants Oras, Marina Tarlinskaja, Kenneth Muir, Ernst Honigmann, David J. Lake, M. W. A. Smith, and MacDonald Jackson. My survey of this satisfying agreement between scholars over more than a century, using several different and independent tests, appeared in 2002.[16] The following year MacDonald Jackson published a definitive study of the Wilkins-Shakespeare collaboration, an exemplary study in every way.[17] Although one modern edition (the New Cambridge Shakespeare by Anthony Hammond and Doreen Del Vecchio, 1998) dismissed any notion of coauthorship, Wilkins's contribution can be safely described as settled, for the majority of Shakespeareans.

But not all Shakespeare critics bother to keep up with scholarship. A recent issue of the *Times Literary Supplement* published a long essay by Barbara Everett, entitled "By the rough seas reft: How the 'badness' of the Pericles Quarto may be of Shakespeare's making."[18] Professor Everett is a Fellow of Somerville College, Oxford, less than a mile away from Oxford University Press, but she seems blissfully ignorant of the two books it had recently published containing abundant evidence of the coauthor's identity. Referring only to the New Penguin edition by Philip Edwards (1976), which espoused the now discredited theory that the many incoherences in the play can be put down to compositorial incompetence, Everett dismisses "textual questions" as secondary, declaring that sometimes "it is necessary to suppose that the textual is subordinate to the literary. We decide first what we are dealing with, and then discuss how the compositor printed it" (14). Writing *de haut en bas,* Everett reports the widespread feeling that the play "appears so badly written as for the most part not to be trusted to be by

Shakespeare," but dismisses the "rationalistic explanations" offered by "collaborationist scholars." Although acknowledging that *Pericles* contains "difficulties and bewilderments that may be schematized into collaboration," she categorically rejects any such explanation: "The collaborative case has grave flaws. *No known Jacobean playwright writes badly enough* to be the author of *Pericles,* and nothing suggests why the age's most successful dramatist should have chosen, or agreed to collaborate with *a writer so helplessly incapable*" (13; my emphases). The passages I have italicized are breathtaking in their combination of authoritative-sounding utterance and actual ignorance. If Everett had shown any knowledge of the sixty or so known dramatists working in Jacobean London, or even read the other work of Wilkins, she might have been qualified to make such a pronouncement. Her innocence in other matters relating to authorship attribution is shown by her reaction to a passage in Wilkins's act 1 in which the eponymous hero describes himself as "A Gentleman of Tyre, my name Pericles." Everett comments: "There is something too good for any collaborator in the entire lack of a main verb here, of a syntax, and really of a meaning." That overstatement is unaware that in 1780 George Steevens noted the large number of ellipses found in the play, and that in 1880 Robert Boyle identified this as a recurrent feature of Wilkins's style.[19]

As we can see, Everett oscillates between seeing the verse of *Pericles* as being too badly written for any known collaborator, or being too well written for anyone else but Shakespeare. She finally comes down on the side of badness, but of badness with a difference: "*Pericles* is often bad, and bad in a special way: it is archaic" (14). Conservators of the canon, resolutely rejecting the notion that the Bard needed help, have—"always already," as one used to say—another explanation for the un-Shakespearean quality of a play. Everett's commonplace observation on the "archaic" nature of the verse given to the Chorus figure Gower (whose version of the story in *Confessio Amantis* provided the main source) suddenly takes on an explanatory function. Everett suggests that "the badness of *Pericles* may be seen . . . as an ironic artefact: an antique or antic badness, invented by the author and fit for a play about love, a 'Chronicle of wasted time'" (14). This now becomes an interpretative key that explains everything "bad" about *Pericles,* namely, that the effect of badness comes from Shakespeare teaching himself to write like a botched and patchworked old script: to carefully stumble, to punctiliously ruin the flow of his paragraphs with fatally-placed internal couplets, conscientiously flattening his emergent rich late medium into a grey fustian rhythmically and verbally forty years out of date. I suspect that in the second half, where the verse gets better, it was Shakespeare, not his printers, who for pure aesthetic pleasure and consistency wrote most of it down as prose. (15)

That final sentence, with its picture of Shakespeare deliberately mangling his verse into prose "for pure aesthetic pleasure and consistency," is one of the most ludicrous suggestions ever made by an experienced Shakespeare commentator. Everett's idea that Shakespeare could deliberately write badly, so as to give the impression of an "antique badness," is reminiscent of the arguments of nineteenth-century scholars trying to preserve biblical chronology, who argued that God had deliberately created fossils so as to deceive later scientists into thinking that the earth seemed older than it was. But why should God have done this? And what sense does it make to think of Shakespeare "conscientiously flattening his emergent rich late medium into a grey fustian rhythmically and verbally forty years out of date"? Both arguments seem desperate attempts to cling to a paradigm that has been comprehensively displaced.

To revert to my starting point, it seems evident to me that those who deny the very idea of Shakespeare as a coauthor have opted out of the process by which knowledge grows. They have closed their minds, preferring to rest in a state of "securitie," in Jonson's terms, that "common Moath" that "eats on wits, and Arts." In Bacon's diagnosis, by failing to "descend into" themselves and examine their preconceptions, they accept a condition in which the mind becomes "fixed or settled in [its] defects," never amending its faults. When they enter the republic of letters as authors and book reviewers, they act as remoras to "stay and slug" the ship of learning's progress. A forum such as this provides the valuable opportunity to draw attention to these "hinderances," and to encourage others to open their minds to the fact that Shakespeare sometimes got a play written for his company with the help of a fellow dramatist. Surely no shame attaches either to his having done that, or to our recognizing it.

Notes

1. "An Ode To Himself," in *The Complete Poetry of Ben Jonson,* ed. W. B. Hunter Jr. (Garden City, NY: Doubleday Anchor, 1963), 159. The editor notes that several mss. contain the word "oft," which completes the meter.

2. *Francis Bacon: A Critical Edition of the Major Works,* ed. Brian Vickers (Oxford: Oxford University Press, 1996), 165, with annotation at 607.

3. See *The Oxford Francis Bacon XI: The Instauratio Magna Part II, Novum organum and Associated Texts,* ed. Graham Rees with Maria Wakely (Oxford: Clarendon Press, 2004), facing xxxii.

4. For a preliminary consideration of Foucault's misinterpretation, parroted by so many uncritical modern followers, see Brian Vickers, *Shakespeare, Co-Author: A Historical Study of Five Collaborative Plays* (Oxford: Oxford University Press, 2002), appendix 2, "Abolishing the Author? Theory versus History," 506–41.

5. See Brian Vickers, "Incomplete Shakespeare: Denying Co-Authorship in *1 Henry VI,*" *Shakespeare Quarterly* 58 (2007): 311–52, at 312–14.

6. See *Henslowe's Diary,* ed. R. A. Foakes, 2nd ed. (Cambridge: Cambridge University Press, 2002); Neil Carson, *A Companion to Henslowe's Diary* (Cambridge: Cambridge University Press, 1988) and "Collaborative Playwriting: The Chettle, Dekker, Heywood Syndicate," *Theatre Research International* 14 (1981): 13–23.

7. See G. E. Bentley Jr., *The Profession of Dramatist in Shakespeare's Time* (1971; Princeton: Princeton University Press, 1986), 18–21.

8. Vickers, *Shakespeare, Co-Author,* 137–500. Line counts are based on *The Riverside Shakespeare,* ed. G. B. Evans and J. J. M. Tobin, 2nd ed. (Boston: Houghton Mifflin, 1997).

9. See Brian Vickers, *"Counterfeiting" Shakespeare: Evidence, Authorship, and John Ford's* Funerall Elegye (Cambridge: Cambridge University Press, 2002), and *Shakespeare, A Lover's Complaint, and John Davies of Hereford* (Cambridge: Cambridge University Press, 2007).

10. A. H. Thorndike, *The Influence of Beaumont and Fletcher on Shakspere* (Worcester, MA, 1901; repr., New York: AMS Press, 1966), 35.

11. M. Mincoff, "The Authorship of *The Two Noble Kinsmen,*" *English Studies* 33 (1952): 97.

12. *Shakespeare, Co-Author,* 148–243. The editions I examined are the Oxford one-volume edition by E. M. Waith (1984), the New Cambridge text by Alan Hughes (1994), and the Arden 3 by Jonathan Bate (1995).

13. *Review of English Studies* n.s. 54 (2003): 648–46.

14. See *Shakespeare, Co-Author,* 138–41.

15. See Vickers, "Incomplete Shakespeare," 328–46.

16. *Shakespeare, Co-Author,* 291–332.

17. Jackson, *Defining Shakespeare:* Pericles *as Test Case* (Oxford: Oxford University Press, 2003).

18. *Times Literary Supplement,* August 11, 2006, 13–16.

19. *Shakespeare, Co-Author,* 292, 297.

"Not one clear item but an indefinite thing which is in parts of uncertain authenticity"

RICHARD DUTTON

WHY ARE THERE MULTIPLE VERSIONS of so many (nearly half) of Shakespeare's plays? For me, that is the most intriguing, frustrating, and perplexing question at the heart of any meaningful Shakespearean authorship debate, because it incorporates all the other important questions at a tangible, material, historical, textual level. If we could answer it with any assurance, we would answer so many other questions at the same time. We would understand the nature of the dramatist's relationship with his fellow actors; why he chose not to put his own plays into print; whether he wrote only for performance, or at least in part with a view to being read. There is even a good chance that we could lay to rest, once and for all, the infuriating drone of those who persist in doubting that William Shakespeare of Stratford-upon-Avon was the only begetter, more or less, of the plays accorded by modern scholarship to the dramatist of that name.

Even among literary scholars it is often not appreciated how unique is this multiplicity of Shakespearean texts, and to those outside the field it can be a source of wonder. A professor of mechanics was once pretty much gobsmacked to discover that the phrase "an enginer hoist with his own petard" is not in the First Folio text of *Hamlet,* indeed that "*Hamlet* is, or was, not one clear item but an indefinite thing which is in parts of uncertain authenticity."[1] Those of us who are less surprised at this would nevertheless do well to try to retain something of that sense of amazement at what is in fact a unique phenomenon. The very fact that there are multiple versions of the plays—and not least of some of his finest plays, among the greatest plays in the language, including *Hamlet, Othello,* and

114

Lear—is an utterly distinctive defining characteristic of Shakespeare as an "author." Analogies are sometimes drawn with the endless manuscript variants we find in the texts of such as Sidney and Donne, which were circulated for coterie consumption. But that will not answer for dramatic texts produced by a professional playwright. Among comparable contemporaries, only Jonson has left a trail of early and later versions of most of the plays reprinted in his 1616 *Works.* But in his case the certainty of Jonson's own hand in all stages of composition, and an apparent purpose—to impose himself on readers as a contemporary classic—leaves little mystery about the fact of revision, and makes it easy for us (at times, perhaps too easy) to discern Jonson's own sense of himself as an author. Or at least such a sense of himself as he wanted to make public. But we have no such pre-scripted narrative of the multiple Shakespeare texts. Nor can we draw analogies with such as Marlowe, Greene, Heywood, or Dekker, none of whom left us with such bibliographic profusion. Shakespeare is unique and sui generis in this, as in so much else.

The fact is that we do not *know* why there are multiple versions of Shakespeare's plays, or what the relationships between the various versions are. But, in the absence of that knowledge, scholars and mystics of all complexions—especially editors and bibliographers—have imagined the answers for themselves, and have in the process invented a Shakespearean "author" (or rather, a string of Shakespearean "authors") to suit themselves. So the New Bibliographers—McKerrow, Greg, and others—invented tales of textual piracy to explain the baddest of the "bad" quartos, and of adaptations for down-at-heal provincial touring to explain somewhat less bad (but still sadly sullied) versions of the plays. Such scholars were implicitly tied to a romantic or Arnoldian view of the "author" as a genius, whose words were therefore sacred, and it was their job to sift the authentic word of the master from all contaminating dross, whether it derived from the work of pirates or even the professional ministrations of Shakespeare's fellow actors. Tales of "foul papers," of scribal fair copies, and of playhouse prompt copies grew up alongside those of "bad" quartos, to help discriminate the sacred text from lesser witnesses (though few of these mythic beasts have survived to provide us with anything as unsportsmanlike as actual evidence).

In all of this, while it was customary to pay homage to Shakespeare as a consummate man of the theater, it was in practice usual to find the "authentic" texts (and so, implicitly, their "author") as far removed from playhouse contamination as possible, which often meant in "good" early quartos, where they existed. It also often involved conflating elements of various early texts, in order to reconstruct a supposed originating Shakespeare original. All of this changed markedly in the 1980s. Since the 1960s French theorists had been doing their best to kill off "the author" (an author of immanent power, most like the Shakespeare of the New Bibliographers). But Shakespeareans dodged that bullet by reconceiving him as a practicing playwright, a member of the theatrical team, part of a collective enterprise. This surfaced most memorably in the Oxford *Complete Works* under the general editorship of Stanley Wells and Gary Taylor, which confidently announced that "this edition chooses, when possible, to print the more theatrical version of each play" (xxxvii.).[2] The Shakespearean "author" had become a function of theatrical practice. And rather different myths arose. The 1603 version of *Hamlet,* for example, is politely acknowledged as a "reported text" (xxxvi) rather than vilified as a "bad" quarto. ("Reporting" may seem a more plausible and less judgmental explanation than piracy, but the evidence for it is entirely inferential.) And the hitherto little-regarded 1600 quarto of *Henry V* is accorded sufficient authority as a record of how the play was originally performed that the Dauphin does not appear at Agincourt, though the rest of the text largely follows the 1623 Folio version, where he assuredly does.

The Shakespearean "author" as collective theatrical function thus largely emerges from a different imagining of the relationships between the variant versions, where they exist. This rapidly established itself as an editorial orthodoxy, such that we find Andrew Gurr, in his own edition of Q1600 *Henry V* (the very existence of such editions of formerly despised quarto texts tells its own tale) claiming that it is a fairly respectable version of the play as it was normally performed at the Curtain or Globe in 1599: "the quarto text of *Henry V* offers the best evidence we have of what routinely happened to the scripts that the Shakespeare company bought from their resident playwright . . . the quarto [is] the prime case in point to test the view that the plays were radically altered between their first drafting and their first appearance on stage."[3] This, of course, presupposes that something like the 1623 *Henry V* existed in 1599, and that the 1600 version was crafted from it. By the same token, talk of a "reported" *Hamlet* similarly presumes that something like the 1604 version existed before that represented by Q1603 was derived from it. And so on. The new Shakespearean "author" is a great spinner of sublime but theatrically redundant verse, to be mined for the stage by his more focused fellow actors. Lukas Erne approaches this from an entirely different (i.e., not stage-centric) direction, wanting to argue that the plays were written to be read as well as performed. But his view of the relationship between the variant texts is essentially the same.[4]

I recently—and quite inadvertently—wandered back into this debate when I argued that the 1623 text of *Henry V* was more likely to have been written around 1602 than 1599.[5] And that therefore Q1600 presumably represented an originating text of the play in its own right, quite heavily indebted to the anonymous *Famous Victories of Henry V,* which was first published in 1598.[6] Only slowly did it dawn on me that this had wider implications than I had anticipated for the authorship debate, a debate in which I had once previously made a brief intervention.[7] My point in "The Birth of the Author" was to enter a small caveat about some new orthodoxies adopted, it seemed to me uncritically, in the wake of the Oxford *Complete Works,* arguing that Shakespeare is "an author of mixed authority, . . . a hybrid poet-playwright, who speaks simultaneously the different languages of which he was composed . . . [O]ne of our duties as modern readers [or practitioners] of Shakespeare is to recognize the fact of multiple voices and to discriminate between them as best we can" (90).

Like virtually everyone upto that point, I had seen the debate in terms of the two starkest extremes in the imagining of the Shakespearean "author"—the writerly/reader-focused extreme implicitly championed by the New Bibliographers, and the theater-centric extreme represented by Wells and Taylor. But my work on *Henry V* made me appreciate that the "theater-centric" side of the argument was potentially more complex than it is often represented as being, and might be reconciled more readily with the "reader-focused" side of the equation than the usual division of the kingdoms allows. If it really was the case that Q1600 was an original, independent version of the play (however inadequately transmitted to us), then the 1623 text was a later recasting of it. And both were presumably by Shakespeare. This is of real significance if *Henry V* really is "the prime case in point to test the view that the plays were radically altered between their first drafting and their first appearance on stage." In my view, the relationship between its texts is more akin to that between the 1608 and 1623 texts of *King Lear,* which since the 1980s have generally been recognized as distinct, purposely-revised versions of the play, not different witnesses to a single, lost Shakespearean original.[8] But no other multi-state play has yet been accorded quite the same status in the scholarly consensus.

To my mind, a critical question becomes: what do we *know* about the revision of play texts in the Shakespearean era—how often might it happen? why? in what circumstances? Might this be a more fruitful way into the conundrum than *supposing* that Shakespeare habitually wrote plays that were far too long to stage, presumably in order to gratify a readership of sorts, while at the same time providing his acting colleagues material to mine for the stage? In fact there is a good deal of evidence about this, enough for G. E. Bentley to announce confidently: "the refurbishing of old plays in the repertory seems to have been the universal practice in the London theatres from 1590 to 1642."[9] Like many others, he assumed this was often associated with the revival of old plays. But Roslyn Knutson, in a detailed analysis of the most telling evidence we have—Philip Henslowe's so-called *Diary*—has shown that refurbishing was far less common than we have tended to assume: "we may argue that the repertory companies in the 1590s did not see the payment for revisions to accompany a revival as a commercially necessary or profitable venture."[10] The famous revisions to *The Spanish Tragedy* and *Dr Faustus* were in fact highly anomalous. Moreover, most of the "refurbishing" we can identify in Henslowe intriguingly entailed *addition,* rather than simple revision. No one in the Henslowe records was apparently paid for *reducing* the length of plays. But then, none of his companies at that time retained "ordinary poets" with extravagant literary ambitions.

As Knutson also observes, however, "Of the sixteen plays [where Henslowe details alterations, mendings, and additions], most were altered either during their maiden run or for a presentation at Court" (12). And it is this latter category, alterations for presentation at court, that some of the heaviest work and highest costs can be identified. This must have been linked with the process which Thomas Heywood describes in *An Apology for Actors* (written ca. 1609) when he tells how the actors visited "the office of the Revels, where our Court playes have been in late daies yearely rehersed, perfected, and corrected before they come to the publike view of the Prince and the Nobility" (E1v, 1612.) So, for example, Henry Chettle was paid "for mending of the first part of Robinhood" on

18 November 1598, and received a further 10 shillings exactly a week later, in part "for mending of Robinhood for the court."[11] The following year an old and popular play, *Fortunatus* was revised, but shortly thereafter Henslowe records: "Paid unto Mr Dekker the 12 of December 1599 for the end of Fortunatus for the court at the appointment of Robert Shaw, the sum of . . . 40s"—which suggests a rather more substantial revision (128). A parallel sequence occurs a year later again, in respect of the play, *Phaeton,* in which on 14 December Dekker was paid 10s "for his pains in Phaeton . . . for the court" and eight days later a further 30s "for altering Phaeton for the court", while on 2 January 1601 William Bird was advanced 20s "for divers things about the play of Phaeton for the court."

Something of a pattern seems to be apparent here: the company revives an old play, making modest efforts to spruce it up. At which point we may surmise that they "reherse" it in front of Edmund Tilney, the Master of the Revels, hoping that it may be selected for court, who would doubtless make his views known on how it might be further "perfected" and "corrected." If they are successful in this, they call in one of their regular writers to revise it further, in line with Tilney's suggestions, perhaps modestly—perhaps more extensively. Some of these payments amount to about a third of the cost of a whole new play, so the work involved must have been considerable, and must presumably also have been considered a good investment. We in fact have *The pleasant comedie of old Fortunatus As it was plaied before the Queenes Maiestie this Christmas* (printed 1600). Some of Dekker's "pains" in this are immediately apparent: it contains a Prologue at Court and an Epilogue, both in the form of dialogues spoken by two old men. The former begins with one asking the other, "Are you then traveling to the temple of Eliza?," locating the whole play within the late mythologizing of the Virgin Queen, and defining the actors as her humble and overawed subjects. W. L. Halstead has also plausibly suggested that the Vice-Virtue subplot was a result of the late alterations, and observes that "after altering, the play was nearly 3000 lines long, and this was too long for performance in the London theatres."[12] The length of performances on the public stages is, of course, a contentious issue. But it is certainly the case that a very high proportion of the plays whose texts have survived in unusually long forms are known to have been performed at court.

There are no documents parallel to Henslowe's *Diary* for the Lord Chamberlain's Men, so there is no record of Shakespeare's employment in this mode. But it is almost inconceivable that it did not happen and not least in relation to his own plays, three of which—*Love's Labours Lost, Merry Wives,* and *King Lear*—were originally printed with the claim that they had been performed at court. Records of the titles of plays performed at court are notoriously patchy but in the period 1604–1613—Shakespeare's years with the King's Men—we can identify sixty-two plays, including repetitions: twenty-one are by Shakespeare, more than a third, against forty-one by all others combined.[13] Much though the court may have appreciated Shakespeare's plays, it goes against what we know from Henslowe and elsewhere to assume that they would expect to see them exactly as staged at the Globe or the Blackfriars. The likelihood that *some* of the revisions of Shakespeare's plays may have derived from revision for court performance seems very strong, though it has never been investigated systematically. (I am currently engaged in such an investigation.)

The "theatre-centric" approach to Shakespearean authorship, which in many ways is the modern orthodoxy—especially among editors of his plays—has been almost entirely focused on their production at the Theatre, the Globe or the Blackfriars. This has partly been because it is generally assumed that Elizabethan drama, with its minimal scenery, was highly portable, that works could be transferred with ease from the London theatres to the court, the Inns of Court, country houses and provincial civic halls. And in many respects they could. But in the case of performances at court, we know that they first went through a process of rehearsing, perfecting, and correcting, which may well have left its mark on texts that have survived. This may well, for example, have had a bearing on their length and on other issues which there is no time here to dwell upon.

The nature of the Shakespearean "author" need not, therefore, be confined to the traditional extremes of "reader-focus" and "performance-focus." If we recognize that there were multiple forms of performance, some of which may have left a special stamp on certain surviving texts, we may perhaps begin to discern a Shakespeare extremely attuned to the requirements of a range of different audiences, and prepared to recast his own material for them when the occasion demanded. If so, I may have spoken truer than I knew when I wrote that "one of our duties as modern readers of Shakespeare is to recognize the fact of multiple voices and to discriminate between them as best we can." Attention to the fact of multiple versions of so many of the plays is the essential first step in any "authorship" debate.

Notes

1. W. Johnson, "An Enginer Hoist With His Own Petard," *International Journal of Mechanical Sciences* 29 (1987): 587–600: 597.

2. Stanley Wells and Gary Taylor, general editors, *William Shakespeare: The Complete Works* (Oxford: Oxford University Press, 1986). Quotations are from the *Compact Edition,* 1988.

3. Andrew Gurr, ed., *The First Quarto of King Henry V* (Cambridge: Cambridge University Press, 2000), ix.

4. See Lukas Erne, *Shakespeare as Literary Dramatist* (Cambridge: Cambridge University Press, 2003). See especially 193–219.

5. See Richard Dutton, " 'Methinks the Truth Should Live from Age to Age': The Dating and Contexts of *Henry V*," *Huntington Library Quarterly* 68 (2005): 173–204.

6. "*The Famous Victories* and the 1600 Quarto of *Henry V*", presented at the *Shakespeare and the Queen's Men* Conference (Toronto, October 2006). To be published in a volume of conference proceedings.

7. See "The Birth of the Author." *Elizabethan Theater: Essays in Honor of S. Schoenbaum,* ed. R.B. Parker and S. Zitner (Newark: University of Delaware Press, 1996), 71–92.

8. Among the defining texts in the debate were Steven Urkowitz's *Shakespeare's Revision of King Lear* (Princeton: Princeton University Press, 1980), and *The Division of the Kingdoms : Shakespeare's Two Versions of King Lear,* edited by Gary Taylor and Michael Warren (Oxford: Oxford University Press, 1983).

9. G. E. Bentley, *The Profession of Dramatist in Shakespeare's Time, 1590–1642* (Princeton: Princeton University Press, 1971), 263.

10. Roslyn L. Knutson, "Henslowe's Diary and the Economics of Play Revision for Revival, 1592–1603," *Theatre Research International* 91 (1985): 11.

11. R. A. Foakes, ed., *Henslowe's Diary* (Cambridge: Cambridge University Press, 2002), 102. For those unused to the money, 10 shillings was half of a pound; the usual fee for a new play was between £6 and £8, plus a share in the take for an early performance. Ten shillings, then, presumably represents relatively minor work.

12. W. L. Halstead, "A Note on Dekker's *Old Fortunatus,*" *Modern Language Notes* 54 (1939), 352 Note.

13. Figures are from John Astington, *English Court Theatre* (Cambridge: Cambridge University Press, 1999).

Shakespeare Is an Author:
An Essentialist View

MICHAEL D. BRISTOL

> For me, no other choice was possible.
> —Louis, the Vampire

IF I WERE TO SAY "Shakespeare is the author of all thirty-seven plays in the collected edition known as the First Folio," what question would I be answering? Every now and then, when I tell someone at a social gathering perhaps, or on an airplane, that I am a professor of English who works on Shakespeare, the one question I can count on being asked is this: "Did Shakespeare write all those plays or was it really somebody else?" When I say, "Yes, Shakespeare really was the author," they often look disappointed or sometimes even suspicious. "Just as I thought," their looks imply, "here's another academic involved in a big cover-up." Being asked to talk about Shakespearean authorship is not the worst thing that ever happened to me on a plane, but that's another story.[1] Although I groan inwardly when someone asks me this question, I must admit that their curiosity is perfectly intelligible: they wonder if some person other than Shakespeare might have written these plays. I believe my boring, academically responsible answer to this question is right, but it has the additional virtue in this context of being fallible.[2] It is logically possible that some amazing discovery might be made that would conclusively show that someone else wrote the plays—Emilia Lanier, maybe, or Mary Sidney. This has not actually happened, but it could.[3]

There is, however, an altogether different question that my statement would be responding to, which is not asking if Shakespeare is *the* author, but rather if Shakespeare is *an* author at all. It has been suggested by a number of prominent Shakespeare scholars that these plays don't really have an "author," or more precisely that "authorship" is a misleading way to characterize their coming into existence as texts. When I'm stuck on that airplane with someone who thinks it was the Duke of Sussex who wrote those plays I feel doubly frustrated because I think their ideas are wrong, even though I can definitely make logical sense out of their concerns. When one of my colleagues wants to convince me that Shakespeare is not an author, I'm just baffled.[4] What's the argument? Do they mean that Shakespeare's *Works* are a pastiche of textual bits and pieces created by many different anonymous people and then later printed with a false attribution as the work of one person? Or do they mean that the term "author" should only apply to some precisely specified subset of all the people who write things? In that case what would be the constraints that would distinguish the special case of an "author" from the general case of all other writers and why should Shakespeare be excluded?

Actually, skepticism about the conventional view of Shakespeare as an author is not primarily motivated by an alternative theory to explain the existence of Shakespeare's *Works.* There is a deeper uneasiness about the very idea, a vague sense that any belief in an author but especially in Shakespeare amounts to a superstition. The notion of an author is a phantom, an "impoverished" concept that should be abandoned in favor of research on the "material conditions" of textual production or the history of the book.[5] Stanley Cavell calls this view iconoclasm.[6] Like Cavell I would agree that idolatry, superstition, ideological delusion, *langage de bois* are all bad, but I wonder if thinking Shakespeare is an author counts as any of these things. My own doubts are compounded by the way my skeptical colleagues like to insist on the "historicity" of the texts, appealing to all sorts of knowledge about intellectual property rights, literary patronage, theatrical performances, collaboration, bibliographical description, the history of printing, and even the chemical composition of the ink used to print the early quartos.[7] What puzzles me about all of this is why, if we're going to abandon all notions of author, intention, and work, we have any reason to care about the historical context at all. Why not just get on with jouissance, finding new and creative ways to interpret this old material without worrying about the historical circumstances in which it was created?

Frankly, I'm not very hopeful that I can make any kind of argument here that will persuade the skeptics and iconoclasts to change their minds. Much of what is being offered as an alternative to the notion that Shakespeare is the author of his works strikes me as equivocating and question-begging; and some of it seems just plain begrudging. But rather than rehearse my differences with a whole lot of people who are as honest and as sincere in their views as I hope I have been in expressing mine, I think the only thing I can do is to be as clear as possible about what I mean by saying Shakespeare is an author.

I think it makes pretty good sense to say that Shakespeare is an author, but it's not a good idea to have an inflated notion of what that means. I have explained in another context why I think the theories of "scientific bibliography" and the "ideal text" as articulated by Fredson Bowers relied on a romanticized picture of the author and on an unrealistic assessment of what critical editorial practice could achieve in restoring a reliable text of an uncorrupted original.[8] Disillusionment with the ideal of the critical edition has led to the more recent proposals to abandon the category of the author altogether.[9] But I maintain that evidence about the development of "industrial practices such as papermaking, type founding, and the production of ink . . . presuppose an intention to publish verbal artifacts, and this in turn suggests a least a limited conception of authorship."[10] I would add that any serious history of the book necessarily has to include an account of the role of authors in their production. Nor do I find the general notion of "unediting the text" by returning to the early editions particularly helpful.[11] Very few people have the kind of training that would enable them to sort out the typographical errors from those "really interesting" early modern locutions suppressed in the modern editions.[12] My own view of the situation retains the traditional view of Shakespeare as an "author" in the sense that his "singular creative agency" determines the specific ordering of language that constitutes his specific achievement. This does not imply that Shakespeare lived in a bubble or that other people weren't involved in the transmission and even the composition of his plays and poems at various stages in the history of their reproduction.[13] But a responsible account of the historical conditions in which Shakespeare worked just cannot ignore his "skilled and intentional engagement with the already existing resources of verbal expression" in the creation of his works.[14]

Printing wasn't invented for roughly 1,500 years after Virgil wrote the *Aeneid.* Shakespeare's handwriting was illegible. Milton was blind when he wrote *Paradise Lost.* Jane Austen hid her manuscript under the embroidery whenever somebody came into the room. John Stuart Mill's maid burned Carlyle's only manuscript of the first volume of *The French Revolution;* the book eventually got published in 1842. Hiroshige is the author of the *53 Stations of the Tokaido,* even though the work is not a text. I know a poet who was born with cerebral palsy. He does not have the fine motor skills to write with a pencil or even to use a computer keyboard. But he is able to compose poetry using voice recognition software that he helped to design. Before computers were available he relied on an amanuensis—like Milton—to assure that his poetry was given a material embodiment. I know another poet, a former student, actually, who lives on the street. He suffers from alcoholism and schizophrenia. Once or twice a year he turns up at my office, occasionally alarming whoever I'm talking to, to sell me the latest volume of his poetry, usually bound photocopies of handwritten verse—which is pretty good. How he pays for the photocopying is a complete mystery. Authorship isn't just paper and penmanship, though some calligraphers are certainly authors.

The use of voice recognition software and laser printing to create texts of a man's poetry means that in principle no "original manuscript" can ever exist. There is no way for anybody to know whether or not volume 1 of the published text of Thomas Carlyle's *The French Revolution* was an exact duplicate of the burned manuscript, though it seems highly unlikely. Stuff happens. My homeless friend has no publisher, though he is careful to include a © symbol on his work. In the case of Shakespeare's *Works,* we have no reliable manuscript that reveals his exact intentions. What we do have is an untidy set of early editions that includes the more or less carefully edited texts of the First Folio and a number of quartos, all of which "show errors too obvious to have escaped the eye of a proofreading author."[15] This is pretty frustrating, since any attempt to fix things up can only produce what Stanley Cavell refers to as an "editorially repossessed" text for Shakespeare's *Works.* Surely, however, no one would seriously defend the idea that you only can get recognized as an author on the condition that a clean holograph manuscript can be produced.

As I reflect on all of this I realize that for me the notion of an "author" is entirely distinct from any specific mechanism for the transcription or the transmission of a work of literature. Paper and ink and copper plates, along with voice recognition software, typesetters, rhetorical conventions, supportive spouses and friends who are willing to compensate you when one of their servants burns your manuscript all count for me as conditions for the possibility of authorship. Mechanisms like this actualize the works of authors and guarantee the possibility for their reception. But authors make their own distinctive contribution to this larger social nexus of cultural production by having something in particular to say. When I declare that someone is the author of something, what I mean by such an assertion is that a single, specific person is responsible for the creation of a specific work of literature or philosophy or graphic art. No more, no less. Well, okay. There could be two specific persons. Francis Beaumont and John Fletcher are the authors of *The Maid's Tragedy.* Charles Nordhoff and James Norman Hall are the authors of *Mutiny on the Bounty.* And I have to admit that some important works are probably not written by one or even two specific authors: *The Book of the Prophet Isaiah, The Gospel According to St. John,* maybe *The Iliad.*

My own sense of what it means to say "Shakespeare is the author of all thirty-seven plays in the collected edition known as the First Folio" amounts to a very modest claim. It suggests only that Shakespeare's relationship to Shakespeare's *Works* is a relatively straightforward instance of individual literary creativity, very much like Virgil's relationship to *Aeneid,* or Jane Austen's relationship to *Emma,* or Orhan Pamuk's relationship to *Snow.* This view is, naturally, somewhat incomplete; there is a lot more that can be said about how Shakespeare went about being an author that would look quite different from Virgil or Jane Austen, but the idea of singular creative agency does, at least, get things going. It's a way of looking at the situation that explains much of what is known about William Shakespeare and also what is known about the thirty-seven plays in the collected edition known as the First Folio. It doesn't explain everything about how the *texts* of Shakespeare's *Works* were produced, but at the moment there is no serious rival to the somewhat traditional view I've taken here.

It's fair to say that my view of "author" is essentialist, but I think it's also fair that I get to say what I mean by essentialism. The word actually means several different things in addition to its use as the currently preferred term of intellectual denunciation. The primary sense in which my usage of "author" is essentialist is taken from Karl Popper's *The Poverty of Historicism.* For Popper essentialism is related to what was once called realism, and it means that a property shared by a variety of disparate objects—let's say the white color of swans, bedsheets, and flags of surrender—can be described as a universal quality or state of whiteness. This kind of universal term refers to a "real" object in the sense that it can and should be investigated by science. So—a coin collector is interested in the concrete, sensuous properties of nickels and pennies. An economist is interested in the universal properties of money and credit. The economist is trying to get at the "essence" of exchange and to do that requires a kind of indifference to what nickels and pennies look like.[16] I'm an essentialist whenever I check my bank balance, and so are you, dear reader. If you believe that an arch can be made out of bricks, or marble, or native fieldstone and still be an arch, then you might be an essentialist. It would depend on the nature of your beliefs about your beliefs about an arch. But if you think it would be better to study how bricks are made instead of trying to understand the nature of arches, you do not thereby become a materialist, you're just changing the subject.[17] My view is, however, essentialist in another way, where essential has the sense of "definitive." This refers to those properties that are necessary for something to be whatever something it is. An ability to radiate light by means of an electrical current is essential for something to be a lightbulb; an ovoid shape is not.

For me "author" means a kind of human agent who is consciously and purposefully oriented to making something that can exist in the world, and that adds to the stock of those things that exist in the world. The idea of "adding to the stock of things that exist in the world" is the radical sense of "author," a word that comes from Latin *augere*—"to make to grow, originate, promote, increase" (*OED*). The works that authors make are generally made out of words or of other expressive media and are not, in the first instance, material objects. They most often take on material form as texts, a process that usually involves the participation of other social agents, though they might also get embodied as "performances" with or without the supervention of any textual token. On this view there are no "texts" that just somehow exist without any kind of reference to a "work" and this necessarily implies an author or authors even when we don't have a hope in hell in finding who they might have been.

My account of "author" looks like it could be a reply to Michel Foucault's influential essay "What is an Author?" except that Foucault wasn't really looking for an answer to his famous question.[18] Foucault's idea was to decenter the notion of an author, partly as a way to demystify a certain ideological notion of authorship as a constraint on interpretation. The decentering entailed two distinct maneuvers. First, he maintained that an author is not an autonomous agent, but is instead someone embedded in larger systems of social control and largely determined by those institutions. Second, on the basis of his first observation, he claimed that one cannot speak of an "author" as a person, but only of the "author-function" that exists as a feature of some—though by no means all—texts. It's hard to quarrel with the idea that authors belong to extended social networks—even the most antisocial and reclusive authors seem to know a lot of different people. Foucault's argument seems to suggest a historical treatment of the question, describing what being-an-author meant in different social and cultural settings, but there's really no sustained historical narrative in his essay. The idea that the author-function is an important feature of many texts is a useful observation, but it does not follow from this that there are no authors in the more conventional sense of the word as an actual, specific human being who did the task of writing a poem or an essay.

For me the notion of "author" always implies a person. And here my view of things flips over from a kind of essentialism to its opposite, which is not materialism, but is instead existentialism. What that means is that my existence is prior to anything else in the sense that I am stuck with what I am and have to make do with what I have as best as I can.[19] My sense of agency and identity are perhaps illusory, but I'm not off the hook and I have to take responsibility for what I've done.[20] Part of this attitude entails belief in the reality of other people, whose existence is for them what mine is for me.[21] Saying that Shakespeare is the author of Shakespeare's *Works* is really about giving credit where credit is due. And I think it's also about intellectual honesty—my own intellectual honesty. The basic theory of Shakespeare's authorship is laid out in the prefatory materials to the First Folio. Shakespeare wrote the plays, they were performed in theaters, people made unauthorized copies, Heminge and Condell did the best they could to restore as much as possible of what Shakespeare had written. I suppose you could say that Shakespeare really became an author in the "postproduction" stage, deuteronomically and after the fact, so to speak. In fact, I once did say exactly that.[22] But suggesting that Shakespeare is not an author unless and until someone comes along to produce a certain kind of edition of his works is just equivocating with the notion of an author. Authors are fictional entities created by their editors? Heminge and Condell somehow falsified the record, creating a misleading impression of Shakespearean authorship, thus giving rise to an ideologically driven sense of his cultural authority? Did I ever believe this or was the notion of decentering of authorship just more appealing for me at the time than the all-too-humanistic account of the traditional narrative?

The basic theory that Shakespeare is the author of Shakespeare's *Works* is definitely fallible and a lot of complicated detail is missing, but it can be made to work reasonably well. It accounts for a lot of what's known and it stacks up pretty well with the other relevant case studies—Ben Jonson, Michael Drayton, Edmund Spenser, or John Donne, to name only a few. To mount a serious challenge to that theory would require much more than an undefended assertion that Shakespeare's role in creating the First Folio of his works doesn't count as authorship. To claim that Shakespeare's *Works* exist only in—or as—the history of their editorial redaction is to leave unanswered the most basic question, namely, redaction of what? An alternative theory would have to provide an explicit, comprehensive account of the specific redactions involved in the production of the various texts and tell us who the authors of the various bits and pieces were. No such theory has been articulated. Under the circumstances I think we have no choice but to say unequivocally what everybody really knows is the case: "Shakespeare is the author of all thirty-seven plays in the collected edition known as the First Folio"

Notes

1. The worst thing that ever happened to me on a plane was on a flight from Shreveport, Louisiana, to Detroit. My seatmate wanted to tell me about his personal friendship with Jesus. It was a small plane; the flight lasted three hours. I thought he was indiscreet to discuss Jesus with me, a perfect stranger, but I was too polite to say so.

2. It also has the virtue of conforming to the standard usage for the word "author," which is, "person who originates or gives existence to anything," or "one who sets forth written statements; the composer or writer of a treatise or book" (*OED*).

3. Marjorie Garber, *Shakespeare's Ghost Writers: Literature as Uncanny Causality* (New York: Routledge, 1987).

4. When I encounter these assertions I want to ask, "If Shakespeare is not the author then who is?" which puts us back on that plane with a persistent stranger and the Duke of Sussex.

5. Margreta de Grazia and Peter Stallybrass, "The Materiality of the Shakespearean Text," *Shakespeare Quarterly* 44 (1993): 255–83.

6. Stanley Cavell, "Skepticism as Iconoclasm: The Saturation of the Shakespearean Text," in *Shakespeare and the Twentieth Century: The Selected Proceedings of the International Shakespeare Association World Congress, Los Angeles, 1996,* ed. Jonathan Bate, Jill L. Levenson, and Dieter Mehl (Newark : University of Delaware Press, 1998).

7. Stephen Orgel, "The Authentic Shakespeare," *Representations* 21 (1988): 1–25; Jeffery Masten, *Textual Intercourse: Collaboration, Authorship, and Sexualities in Renaissance Drama* (Cambridge: Cambridge University Press, 1997), and "Playwrighting: Authorship and Collaboration," in *A New History of Early English Drama,* ed. John D. Cox and David Scott Kastan, 357–82 (New York: Columbia University Press, 1997); David Scott Kastan, *Shakespeare and the Book* (Cambridge: Cambridge University Press, 2001); Grace Ioppolo, *Dramatists in Their Manuscripts in the Age of Shakespeare, Jonson, Middleton and Heywood: Authorship, Authority and_the Playhouse* (London: Routledge, 2006).

8. Michael Bristol, "Scientific Bibliography and the Ideal Text," in *Shakespeare's America / America's Shakespeare* (London: Routledge, 1990), 99–109. See also Anne-Mette Hjort, "The Interests of Critical Editorial Practice," *Poetics* 15 (1987): 259–77.

9. Graham Holderness, *Textual Shakespeare: Writing and the Word* (Hatfield: University of Hertfordshire Press, 2003). Holderness argues that "Shakespeare" refers to a set of texts that are basically the creation of modern editing practice. Since none of this can reliably be connected to an author's intentions, the notion of an author in this case disappears for all practical purposes. See also Randall McLeod, "The Marriage of Good and Bad Quartos," *Shakespeare Quarterly* 33 (1982): 421–31, and "Un-Editing Shak-speare," *Sub-Stance* 33–34 (1982): 26–55; and Paul Werstine, "Narratives about Printed Shakespeare Texts: 'Foul Papers' and 'Bad' Quartos," *Shakespeare Quarterly* 39 (1990): 401–18.

10. Michael Bristol, "How Good Does Evidence Have to Be?" in *Textual and Theatrical Shakespeare: Questions of Evidence,* ed. Edward Pechter (Iowa City, IN: University of Iowa Press, 1996), 41. See also Edward Pechter, "Making Love to our Employment; or, The Immateriality of Arguments about the Materiality of the Shakespearean Text," *Textual Practice* 11 (1997): 51–67.

11. Michael Bristol, "Recent Studies in Tudor and Stuart Drama," *Studies in English Literature* 38 (1998): 369.

12. I'm not convinced that most of these variants are really all that interesting, but then I'm not really as fascinated with the details of early modern social life and belief as I'm probably supposed to be.

13. Michael Bristol, "The Bias of the World," in *Big-Time Shakespeare* (New York: Routledge, 1996), 30–58. See also Lukas Erne, *Shakespeare as Literary Dramatist* (Cambridge: Cambridge University Press, 2003); Patrick Cheney, *Shakespeare, National Poet-Playwright* (Cambridge: Cambridge University Press, 2004); and, more recently, *Shakespeare's Literary Authorship* (Cambridge: Cambridge University Press, 2008).

14. Bristol, *Big-Time Shakespeare,* 53.

15. G. E. Bentley, *Shakespeare: A Biographical Handbook* (New Haven: Yale University Press, 1961), 170.

16. Karl R. Popper, *The Poverty of Historicism* (New York: HarperTorchbooks, 1964), 26–29.

17. I'm not really sure why there is so much virtue in materialism or why people are trying so hard to be more materialist than thou. And didn't we used to call this sort of approach positivism?

18. Michel Foucault, "What is an Author?" in *Textual Strategies,* ed. Josu Harari (Ithaca: Cornell University Press, 1979), 141–60. The title is a rhetorical question.

19. Hannah Arendt, *The Human Condition* (Chicago: University of Chicago Press, 1958), 175–81.

20. If I am not for myself, who will be for me.

21. If I am only for myself, what am I? I realize that it's unhistorical of me to say this, but I really don't see what the alternative would be. Historicism wants to see things the way early moderns saw them, but this is no less of a projection than my own "naive" or "humanistic" sense that I have something in common with people who lived in historically distant contexts. See Michael Bristol "And I'm the King of France," in *Presentist Shakespeares,* ed. Hugh Grady and Terence Hawkes, 46–64 (London: Routledge, 2007); James Siemon, *Word against Word: Shakespearean Utterance* (Amherst: University of Massachusetts Press, 2002); Tzachi Zamir, *Double Vision: Moral Philosophy and Shakespearean Drama* (Princeton: Princeton University Press, 2007).

22. Michael Bristol, "The First Folio as a Deuteronomic Program," in *Shakespeare's America / America's Shakespeare,* 92–99.

ARTICLES

Hamlet as Mourning-Play:
A Benjaminesque Interpretation

Hugh Grady

ONE OF THE MOST CHALLENGING and variously interpreted master-works of twentieth-century critical theory is Walter Benjamin's 1928 *Ursprung des deutschen Trauerspiele,* translated into English by John Osborne as *The Origin of German Tragic Drama.*[1] However, neither the examples Benjamin studied of the seventeenth-century baroque plays called *Trauerspiele* in German nor the term *Trauerspiel* itself has ever had much currency in the English-speaking world. If the book is familiar to readers interested in Benjamin's singular critical theory, it has been largely either because of its "Epistemo-Critical Prologue," where Benjamin first developed his antitotalizing concept of the "constellation" (which organizes ideas into selected, inter-connected groupings); or through the later prescient deconstructing demonstration of how the concept of alle-gory was a devalued binary opposite of the privileged term "sym-bol," in a relationship, Benjamin wrote, similar to that of writing to speech.[2]

For readers of Shakespeare, however, the book presents ideas and analysis little discussed in English about Shakespeare's relation to his historical moment and to the dramatic form in which he wrote his noncomic plays.[3] The first half of Benjamin's study after the prologue is devoted to a multifaceted argument that the dramatic form of the *Trauerspiel* is fundamentally different from that of an-cient Greek tragedy and needs to be distinguished from tragedy proper (*Tragödie* in Benjamin's German).[4] But since for many Ger-man critics, before and after Benjamin, *Trauerspiele* were thought of as forms of tragedy, the confusion is built into the language.[5] I will nonetheless use the German form *Trauerspiel(e)* in this essay with the understanding that Benjamin's sense of the word is meant, and not that of a broader German critical tradition.

The *Trauerspiel* as Walter Benjamin conceptualizes it is an aesthetic form that, like all others, seeks to express truths about the time in which it was constructed. But Benjamin is no New Historicist—he is much more Hegelian than that, and his periodization is large-scale. Essentially, the *Trauerspiel* is an expression of modernity, of an era of a profound subject-object split, resulting in a world of objects empty of inherent significance and of a subject who confronts the world as an alien collection of objects, seeking meaning and significance but through a structure of deferral, a movement from object to object. Since, however, one of the most common characteristics of the *Trauerspiele* Benjamin studied is their lack of a focalizing hero, there is thus an important way in which Shakespeare's *Hamlet* is not a typical example of the form. But the affinity of Shakespeare's play to the *Trauerspiel* form manifests in several other ways, as we will see,[6] even though, as I hope it is clear, Benjamin's remarks on Shakespeare's *Hamlet* as a kind of *Trauerspiel* are scattered and tangential, never developed into a full reading of the play. It is that lack in the original work that justifies the present essay.

In what follows, I will first review some salient features of Benjamin's singular and complex theory of the allegory, both as a trope and as something like a genre. But the larger part of my effort thereafter will be taken up by applying some of Benjamin's ideas to a close and detailed reading of *Hamlet* as a Benjaminesque allegory, in one sense of his multifaceted theoretical excursus—as a series of the small, "local" sets of images that Benjamin calls "fragmented allegories." These smaller units connect through a strategy of deferment and accumulate into a nonorganic unity manifesting an empty world.

Benjamin's Theory of Allegory

"Allegories are, in the realm of thoughts, what ruins are in the realm of things," Benjamin famously wrote,[7] thus emphasizing the open-ended meaning process created through the formal logic of this singular trope. Allegories disclose a world in decay, but they show how the elements of decay can be reborn as new art in a new and different era.

The most important critical concept for a Benjaminesque reading of *Hamlet* is undoubtedly this complex theory of the allegory, which Benjamin constructs (like a mosaic) over some seventy-six dense pages—and his text takes on new meaning in our own time, in the wake of more recent critical theory. In the small space available here, I will attempt to explicate Benjamin's theory of allegory primarily through examples of its application to *Hamlet,* and through an updating based on Benjamin's affinity to aspects of contemporary critical theory. I have noted Benjamin's "presentist" proclivities before.[8] Here I want to bring out other qualities of his methods relevant to the present conjuncture in Shakespeare studies as the field searches for methods that go beyond an almost exhausted New Historicism. Benjamin's insistence on reading dramas as aesthetic constructs intensely connected to their own moment of construction, but capable of constant renegotiation with changing moments of history, of the changing now or *Jetztzeit,* is one such promising approach. Benjamin's project has a historicizing dimension, but history for him is always a construct of our present moment, and he is also deeply interested in aesthetic issues of form and genre as expressions of historical moments. His analytic strategy is in some ways rooted in the 1920s, as perhaps the earliest instance of the modernist project of spatializing the temporal dimensions of the artwork, especially through a strategy of denarrativization.[9] But in his championing of fragmentation and his definition of an antitotalizing form of aesthetic unity structured through a series of deferrals, Benjamin has postmodernist dimensions as well, and these prescient postmodernist features authorize for me an incorporation into Benjamin's theory of later critical concepts. At stake is the critical usefulness of an idea defined in the late 1920s, and inevitably some of its features will require updating. What is remarkable to me, however, is how current much of the discussion remains all these decades after it was written.

The chief updating has to do with a kind of temporal structure that I see as crucial to the combination of allegories in *Hamlet,* but that Benjamin did not explicitly define. Benjamin largely avoids reference to the temporal dimension in his discussion of the plays, in common with many of the modernist-influenced critics who came after him, for whom, in their revolt against nineteenth-century realist narrativization, temporal structure was irrelevant. Instead, Benjamin developed a method of reading dramas not for narrative or other temporal elements, but for the depiction of an internal "world" expressive of the play's larger philosophical-historical moment; and for their mobilization of objects and motifs in poetic language and stagecraft, which create via "allegory" a form whose unity he characterizes as an amalgamation of signifying elements rather than an organic unity—albeit one ultimately forming an aesthetic, dissonant, nonorganic "unity" of fragments with multiple significations. I want to explore one possible configuration (or constellation) of poetic images and signifying objects creative of a "world" of this sort, an aesthetic space of fragmented allegories characteristic of modernity. However, these fragments, I will argue, participate in the play's forward movement, not at the level of narrative strictly speaking, but as part of the logic of deferral that gives structure to the play's development at formal and thematic levels—a process Benjamin referred to briefly as "substitution."[10]

The allegory as defined by Benjamin thus involves "fragmentation" in more than one sense of the word. The term refers both to the overall nonorganic unity created by this poetic trope as well as the individual units—the "fragmented allegories"—that are "amalgamated" into a dissonant unity. The most important point for Benjamin is that the *Trauerspiel*'s allegorical form never coheres into the organic unity that classical German aesthetic theory celebrated for the case of what it called "symbols"—the much-repeated example being that of a Greek sculpture of a god or goddess that unifies multiple signfications in one aesthetic object. The allegory instead *defers* meaning through a a set of "substitutions." It creates, in a phrase borrowed by Benjamin from Friedrich Creuzer, "an idea which is different from itself,"[11] as one signifier is supplemented by the next. But Benjamin also gives attention to a particular poetic strategy he found exemplified in many of the seventeenth-century *Trauerspiele* that he studied, the technique of the "fragmented allegory," by which he means either an individual visual element in the play's iconography (like Yorick's skull) or a local, relatively short set of unified poetic comparisions that does not, however, extend over the course of the entire work, but rather forms a compact unit of local meaning. We can see this kind of "allegorical fragment," to take one of many possible examples, in Fortinbras's exclamation when he discovers the carnage in *Hamlet*'s last scenes:

> O proud death,
> What feast is toward in thine eternal cell,
> That thou so many princes at a shot
> So bloodily hast struck?[12]

In terms of the work as a whole, these poetic units, he insists, "amalgamate" rather than organically cohere. In the case of *Hamlet,* as I see it, such fragmented allegories serve as elements of a larger, nonorganic structure of deferred meaning. They are fragmented allegories in two interrelated senses—in that they are themselves brief units rather than extended over the whole work, and in the sense that the larger unity of which they are parts is fragmented, not organic.

A later, deconstructive tradition encompassing Paul de Man, Jacques Lacan, and Jacques Derrida worked in detail parts of the terrain covered briefly here by Benjamin—in distinct but related terms. For Benjamin the allegorical, with its disjunctive and fragmentizing structural principle, is a formal, *aesthetic* category, characteristic of a certain kind of art. For the later deconstructors, those qualities were those of *textuality,* of the structure of language itself, so that the context for their analysis is no longer strictly aesthetic (although these critics, of course, work primarily if not exclusively with literary and literary-philosophical texts). This important difference being granted, however, I think that it is possible to create a certain intertextuality between Benjamin's theory of the allegory and later deconstructive theory. At issue here, as I mentioned, is the concept of "deferral" as a term for describing the formal logic of a certain chain of signification. The term is not prominent in Benjamin (as we saw above, he speaks rather of "substitution"), but it appears prominently in Lacan (as one of the terms describing the structure constituting desire in the Symbolic Order of the speaking "I" [13]) and Derrida (for whom it is one of the components behind his neologism *différance,* along with *differ,* referring among other things to the always incomplete sense of meaning of specific words in statements). In *Hamlet* particularly, as we will see below, the dissonant but unifying formal principle is not so much the strategy of accumulation that Benjamin emphasizes for the German *Trauerspiele* as it is a strategy of deferral or substitution.

Much of *Hamlet*'s allegorical quality thus shows up in its stage props,[14] stage effects, and imagery. Even though Benjamin does not analyze *Hamlet* in detail, it is possible to follow up on and develop much more concretely his several comments on the play in passing and interpret *Hamlet* as a special instance of the *Trauerspiel*. Specifically, I will be taking my cue from Benjamin's practice of performing close readings of those instances (and sometimes motifs) he calls fragmented allegories—most typically, as we have seen, brief passages of locally connected poetic imagery. I argue that in *Hamlet* the Ghost, the motif of unweeded garden and fallen world, the image of the beetling cliff, the satirical book, the play-within-the-play, the prayer scene, Ophelia's flowers, the graveyard and skull, the King's signet, and the "fatal stage properties" of the last scene (Laertes' poisoned sword, the pearl, and the poisoned cup) all work in the play as exactly the kind of deferring "fragmented allegories" that Benjamin discussed for the German plays—and which in Shakespeare's *Hamlet* define different facets of a fragmented world of melancholic vision.[15] These allegories for Benjamin are typically ambiguous, and in this quality *Hamlet* is quintessentially allegorical—in an ambiguity that, we will see, becomes radically pronounced in the play's ending.

The Ghost in the Emptied World

Benjamin identified Melancholy as one of the favorite motifs of baroque poetry and visual art, so that the play of the melancholy Dane is true to the baroque spirit of the *Trauerspiel* in this prominent theme. And in Shakespeare, Hamlet's melancholy is presented as the outcome of an epochal disengagement from what had been, before the death of his father, a meaningful, epic, "immanent" world.[16] He yearns for death and famously inhabits a world that has become radically devalued and empty:

> This goodly frame, the earth, seems to me a sterile promontory. This most excellent canopy the air, look you, this brave o'erhanging, this majestical roof fretted with golden fire—why, it appears no other thing to me than a foul and pestilent congregation of vapours. What a piece of work is a man! How noble in reason, how infinite in faculty, in form and moving how express and admirable, in action how like an angel, in apprehension how like a god—the beauty of the world, the paragon of animals! And yet, to me, what is this quintessence of dust? Man delights not me. (*Hamlet,* 2.2.289–98)

In statements like this one, Hamlet defines himself as a Lukácsian "demonic hero" in the throes of transcendental homelessness,[17] unable to find in this newly fallen world forms that correspond to his now unfixed but mourning subjectivity, his sense of loss. And while the loss is firmly implanted in his life-experience, and specifically in an Oedipal drama of a father's death, a mother's sexuality, a son's inarticulate longing, it is a philosophical one as well, expressive of the larger cultural-historical revolutions of Shakespeare's time. And its reverberations over the next four centuries suggest that it expresses a quality of the times that continues into our own.

Hamlet reacts to the death of his father as the death of an entire worldview. The return of his father as a ghost—with all the "questionable" resonances of the mysterious aura created in the ambiguous metaphysics of afterlife assumed in the fiction of the play's aesthetic space—in turn creates a powerful "hauntology," as Derrida calls it, an effect of presence and non-presence.[18] Among other things, the Ghost embodies Hamlet's sense of the lost world of immanent meaning, and his return asserts the continuing power of that ideal while powerfully evoking its absence. "Ghosts," Benjamin wrote, "like the profoundly significant allegories, are manifestations from the realm of mourning; they have an affinity for mourners, for those who ponder over signs and over the future."[19] And Stephen Greenblatt echoes something of this sentiment in his own terms, seeing theatrical ghosts—and especially Shakespeare's—as signifying something important about the function of the theater as art: "Ghosts, real or imagined, are good theater— indeed, . . . they are good for thinking about theater's capacity to fashion realities, to call realities into question, to tell compelling stories, to punctuate the illusions that these stories generate, and to salvage something on the other side of disillusionment."[20]

The Ghost is a potent theatrical construct with clear allegorical meanings, but Benjamin's notion of allegory is broad enough to encompass several other kinds of vehicles for allegory. What links them all is that they evoke and express different aspects of the play's projection of a fallen, emptied world and of Hamlet's predicament in the opening scenes.

The Unweeded Garden and the Beetling Cliff

The motif of the emptiness of the world under the gaze of Hamlet's depressed, melancholic vision was memorably enunciated, as we saw, in Hamlet's first conversation with Rosencranz and Guildenstern, but he was there recapitulating a theme already announced in his first soliloquy, a revelation of a state of mind that had been kept at least partially occluded in the preceding court scene—where Hamlet seemed to be lively, witty, and manic. Despite his protestation that he knows not "seems" (1.2.76), it is clear that his claim of having "that within which passeth show" (1.2.85), is equivocal, encompassing deception as well as depth of feeling. For he has not fully revealed either his wish for self-dissolution or the extent of his depression:

> O that this too too solid flesh would melt,
> Thaw, and resolve itself into a dew,
> Or that the Everlasting had not fixed
> His canon 'gainst self-slaughter! O God, O God,
> How weary, stale, flat and unprofitable
> Seem to me all the uses of this world!
> Fie on't, ah fie, fie! 'Tis an unweeded garden
> That grows to seed; things rank and gross in nature
> Possess it merely.
>
> (1.2.129–37)

The image of the garden evokes the early modern ideal of nature as a realm that must be cultivated, adapted by human labor to satisfy human needs, pruned of excess, governed, disciplined, dominated.[21] The well-tended garden is one of its most common expressions, one used by artists and poets alike, one signaled in the great interest in gardens of the period. Shakespeare had memorably used the image of the garden for a brief but telling political allegory in *Richard II,* and it recurs elsewhere in his own works.[22] Here it functions as well as a kind of implied political allegory, providing the first hint that Hamlet believes there is something rotten in Denmark. But its most obvious allegorical application at this point in the play is a psychological one, a theme to which Hamlet will return several times: the unweeded garden suggests a corruption of a female sexuality now unregulated by the social norms of marriage and patriarchy of the lost world of the past:

> Must I remember? Why, she would hang on him,
> As if increase of appetite had grown
> By what it fed on, and yet, within a month—
> Let me not think on't; frailty, thy name is woman!—
>
> (1.2.143–46)

And finally, such an allegory of female frailty is implicitly extended to encompass the entire history of humanity in the fallen world—the unweeded garden suggests the Garden of Eden after the Exile, and constitutes an indictment of the world and time out of joint, the age of emptied meaning and Machiavellian behavior in politics, sexuality, and commerce. "In allegory the observer is confronted with the *facies hippocratica* of history as a petrified, primordial landscape," Benjamin observed in a passage whose concrete application to the play can be seen here. Hamlet's baroque allegory presents history as unredeemed, full of sorrow, linked with death, revealing "the Passion of the world."[23] But there is by those very tokens the suggestion of the possibility of redemption, Benjamin would insist, of a restoration that Hamlet perceives if he cannot fathom how to bring about.

A related but quite differently inflected allegory of the susceptibility of human nature to corruption is given in the striking images of vertiginous danger in Horatio's warning to Hamlet not to follow the beckoning Ghost:

> What if it tempt you toward the flood, my lord,
> Or to the dreadful summit of the cliff
> That beetles o'er his base into the sea,
> And there assume some other horrible form,
> Which might deprive your sovereignty of reason
> And draw you into madness? think of it:
> The very place puts toys of desperation,
> Without more motive, into every brain
> That looks so many fathoms to the sea
> And hears it roar beneath.
>
> (1.4.48–53)[24]

The roaring sea is a figure for madness, the absence of reason, a chaos that can result if the boundaries within the "little world" of human mentality are dissolved through too intimate a contact with the fearful figure of the Ghost. Reason might plunge, like Hamlet himself in Horatio's mind's eye, from " the dreadful summit of the cliff," the open boundary of sanity, into the flood of the fearful unknown. The beetling cliff might also suggest another potent emblem that Hamlet will peer into later in the play, the skull, which figures both the seat of reason and the inevitability of death, that "undiscover'd country from whose bourn / No traveler returns."

The threatened dissolution of the self suggested in these allegorical fragments is a theme that plays throughout the drama, beginning with Hamlet's first remark in soliloquy "that this too too solid flesh would melt / Thaw and resolve itself into a dew (1.2.129–30), and providing much of its psychological power.[25] This threat helps prepare the audience for the ambiguities of Hamlet's "antic disposition" (1.5.173), that feigning of madness that has struck many critics since at least the eighteenth century as perhaps a courting and a succumbing to madness as much as the player's role Hamlet claims it to be later in the scene.[26]

The Satirical Book

We watch Hamlet's antic disposition on display above all with Polonius, with the hidden Claudius behind the arras and Hamlet reading a satirical book—a book that serves as a gloss to Hamlet's earlier, much recently discussed metaphor of memory as a book within his mind (1.5.104).[27] But this book serves as well as a very unobtrusive metonymy to reference other strands of the play. In the first instance, it helps establish Hamlet's status as a scholar, a university student on leave from Wittenberg. Hamlet reports the book to be a satire, the work of "a satirical slave" (2.2.196), and this reference serves as a metatheatrical allusion casting light on the satirical properties of the play *Hamlet* and prefiguring for us the more sustained metatheatrical moments of the inset play to come. Two final significations are more subtle.

As noted, the physical object of the book recalls for us Hamlet's earlier characterization of his new mind-set after the revelations of the Ghost, one in which all "baser matter" had been expunged and only the Ghost's commands lived within the "book and volume of my brain" (1.5.103). The appearance of the physical book in 2.2, in a setting in which Hamlet is being spied on by his enemies, tested for his true intentions, and engaged in bandying with Polonius in a dialogue dominated by obscure puns and double entendres is attention-getting as a possible reference to Hamlet's earlier comparison of book and brain. For the book is ambiguously and simultaneously both external and internal to Hamlet's consciousness. As the work of a "satirical slave" who has set down things that in all decency should have remained unsaid, as Hamlet points out to Polonius, the book is kept at a distance from Hamlet's own intentionality. But no audience needs an informing Ghost to understand the sly malice and irony in Hamlet's words to this tedious old fool. Looked at this way, the distance between the book and Hamlet himself is the distance between a ventriloquist and his puppet—it is illusory. Even Polonius detects the illusion, in his famous remark that there is method in this madness—although at the same time he writes it off as the happy and poignant effect of madness, blinded as he is by his theory of Hamlet's lovesickness. The hidden Claudius, we soon learn, is not so taken in, at least after he has witnessed Hamlet's insulting behavior toward Ophelia and Hamlet's not-so-veiled threats against himself in the last part of the scene. The overall effect, however, is puzzling and ambiguous, just like the book as an allegorical signifier. At the end we are simply uncertain about the state of Hamlet's mind. But Claudius's perspicuity certainly raises that fundamental interpretive problem of Hamlet's distance from the insanity he is supposedly feigning.

The critical view that Hamlet is not completely in control of his antic disposition, that the appearance of madness has in his case become the thing itself, seems to be supported by the fact that only after Hamlet's return from his aborted sea voyage does he seem truly to take in the Ghost's injunction—although pointedly through a resolution for readiness rather than any specific plan. But before that—even after he proclaims the end of his previous doubts at the conclusion of *The Mousetrap*—he always defers the moment of revenge, and in that sense the Ghost's injunction seems to be always external to him, always something to put off, or to find substitutes for.[28]

All these considerations, involving scenes both before and after Hamlet is presented to us reading a book in 2.2, suggest that the book is an ambiguous figure, and one that shifts its meaning as the theme of Hamlet's memory unfolds. Hamlet's book supplies him with matter—or pretended matter—for a curious cat-and-mouse game with Polonius:

Polonius: What do you read, my lord?
Hamlet: Words, words, words.
Polonius: What is the matter, my lord?
Hamlet: Between who?
Polonius: I mean, the matter you read, my lord.
Hamlet: Slanders, sir: for the satirical slave says here that old men have grey beards, that their faces are wrinkled, their eyes purging thick amber and plum-tree gum, and that they have a plentiful lack of wit, together with most weak hams. All which, sir, though I most powerfully and potently believe, yet I hold it not honesty to have it thus set

down; for yourself, sir, should be old as I am—if, like a crab, you
could go backward.

$$(2.2.191–202)$$

Beyond its ambiguous evocation of memory, the book serves here
as a prop for and as an emblem of Hamlet's destabilizing language,
one in which words are ends in themselves, meaning is always
multiple, and insults are delivered without, Hamlet blithely and
disingenuously suggests, being really intended. And its climactic,
indirect targeting of Polonius himself as the object of the satirical
slave's slanders against old men takes the curious form of using a
spatial metaphor—the backward walking of a crab—to describe an
impossible reversal of the arrow of time. It is one more reminder
that the time is out of joint, a preparation for Hamlet's own (antire-
alist, expressionistic) aging in the play, as he slowly metamorpho-
sizes from the young university student we meet at the beginning
to the thirty-year-old of the graveyard scene. But the language that
seems unstable here is capable of being instrumentalized, we will
learn a bit later in the play, when Hamlet uses his knowledge of
writing a "fair hand" to create an instrument of execution for Rosencrantz and Guildenstern.

Even at this point in the story, the unstable properties of Hamlet's
language are also given an instrumental dimension, as part of the
greater intrigue going on in this part of the play, when indirections
are employed to find directions out. As well as ambiguously evoking "the book and volume of my brain" as the permanent deposi-
tory of memory, this book is in addition a means of pretense and a
means of deferral. It is a sign, like Hamlet's earlier reversion to writing on erasable tables after he had used the image of an indelible
book as a metaphor for his memory, that the Ghost's injunction has
not really been assimilated, that Hamlet is doing something other
than sweeping to his revenge "with wings as swift / As meditation
or the thoughts of love" (1.5.29–30).

Hamlet's Metadramatic Turn: *The Mousetrap*

With the appearance of the players from the city—who arrive just
as Hamlet is trying to gauge the danger posed to him by Rosencrantz and Guildenstern—*Hamlet* takes an unprecedented turn.
The Spanish Tragedy had ended with its own spectacular play

within the play, a bravura court performance in which what were apparently stage deaths are revealed at the end as the real thing, the play thus emerging as Hieronimo's well-wrought instrument of revenge. In *Hamlet* Shakespeare instead situates the inset play in his drama's center and makes of it the dramatic turning point. Hamlet momentarily steps back from the role of troubled intriguer to show the audience his connoisseurship of plays, acting, and dramatic poetry. He indeed makes the play his instrument: "The play's the thing," he exalts, "Wherein I'll catch the conscience of the King" (2.2.581–82). But instead of being an instrument of violence, as in Kyd, it is in *Hamlet* an empirical probe, a means to move from uncertainty to knowledge.

Since John Dover Wilson's 1935 *What Happens in "Hamlet,"*[29] critics have been at pains to point out that Claudius's actions when he orders the play to be given over are ambiguous, susceptible to being seen as either the startling of a guilty thing (as Hamlet and Horatio assume) or as the prudence of a man who has just witnessed a blatant affront to his and his queen's dignity, an accusation of murder and lust, and a palpable threat against his person as well. For all that, however, the play soon establishes the correctness of Hamlet's and Horatio's surmise, the correctness of the Ghost on at least the central point that Claudius has murdered King Hamlet, when we are presented with the isolated figure of King Claudius confessing his guilt and trying to repent of his sin. Theodor Adorno has pointed out how human rationality can never gain direct access to the real, that it at best constructs concepts and attempts to "place" aspects of the real "under" them. However, Adorno argued, science has at least that adequacy to the real that allows technology to dominate nature. Hamlet's play, *The Mousetrap,* for all the uncertainties that its performance entailed, had that same imperfect but pragmatic adequacy.

In other ways, however, the play's metadrama is destabilizing and creative of aesthetic effects. By drawing attention to the art of playing, the play of course exposes itself as playing, as artifice, as art. As Robert Weimann put it, "*The Mousetrap* itself becomes a peculiar 'trap of *sa-voir*,' a self-conscious vehicle of the drama's awareness of the functional and thematic heterogeneity of mimesis itself."[30] Hamlet had developed this theme and inserted it back inside the fictional frame of the play, with another a fortiori argument about the greater urgency and dignity of his own situation as opposed to that of a mere actor in "a fine frenzy" of pretense. But the play continually overflows the boundaries of its own fictionality. In a few moments we hear Hamlet and the players passionately denouncing the children's drama that was undercutting the revenues of the Chamberlain's Men and the other adult actors of London, followed by a passage that steps outside of the fictional space of the narrative to name its own purposes, aesthetic and social: "For anything so overdone is from the purpose of playing, whose end, both at the first and now, was and is to hold as 'twere the mirror up to nature, to show virtue her own feature, scorn her own image, and the very age and body of the time his form and pressure" (3.2.18–22). It is, as Robert Weimann says, a "mimesis of mimesis," [31] a vertiginous assertion of the nature of art as semblance, as a "mirror" that alludes to but is Other than the society that gave it birth. And *The Mousetrap* is, of course, itself a kind of allegory, one in which the apparent signified of an "image of a murder done in Vienna" (3.2.218) becomes in turn a signifier of the murder of old King Hamlet.[32] At moments like this, Hamlet's own account of himself as a player within a de-valued world plays within our memory and establishes a metadramatic quality to all his actions. The term "antic," which Hamlet had employed to describe his deceptive actions to come, has itself roots in a world of playing—according to the *Oxford English Dictionary,* it comes from a meaning of the term as a clownlike fantastic in plays. Weimann in fact counts six different "uses of mimesis which Hamlet relates to"—as a theorist, a critic, a dramatist, a director, a chorus, and an actor.[33]

Benjamin sees the meta-aesthetic quality of motifs like this as of the essence of the baroque: "The Renaissance explores the universe; the baroque explores libraries. Its meditations are devoted to books," Benjamin wrote.[34] *Hamlet*'s play-within-the-play, like those of *A Midsummer Night's Dream* and *The Tempest,* is another such anticipation, akin to such baroque masterpieces as Pedro Calderón's 1635 *La vida es sueño* (*Life is a Dream*) or Pierre Corneille's 1636 *L'Illusion,* plays in which the illusionism of art or dream is used as a destabilizing metaphor to interrogate the certainties, and in a sense the reality, of human life. It is a motif that expresses the principle of the empty world that the various allegorical fragments of these plays had relied on for specific, local dramatic and poetic effects. It is the moment of the play, too, in which the unfixed subjectivity of the role-shifting Hamlet is inscribed within an explicitly aesthetic context.

Allegorical Deferral and the Prayer Scene

But when Hamlet's recourse to drama as a political instrument reaches its climax with apparent success, as Claudius experiences a moment of panic and ends the performance, the success does not end Hamlet's series of deferrals. In an action that has puzzled several generations of interpreters, Hamlet, right at his moment of triumph, stumbles onto a clear, unimpeded opportunity to kill Claudius at his prayers, only to decide the moment is not right.

Hamlet's explicitly expressed motivation for forgoing his momentary advantage is one of the moments of the play when its archaic, medieval material surfaces in Hamlet's own subjectivity.[35] The reason he gives for the deferral is as savage as the preceding imagery of hell and night. His decidedly un-Christian desire not just to execute his father's murderer and Denmark's usurper but to damn him as well is at once highly expressionistic and theologically puzzling. Eighteenth-century critics were shocked and dismayed by Hamlet's passion here. Samuel Johnson, for example, found Hamlet's explanation for his delay "too horrible to be read or to be uttered."[36] Beginning with the romantics, critics tended to discount these words, arguing that they were a cover for Hamlet's hesitation to kill. In the twentieth century, J. Dover Wilson thought that Hamlet's explanation for forgoing revenge was "discordant . . . with our scale of values, [yet] does not detract from our general sense of the nobility and greatness of the man." [37]

Taking a completely different tack, Arthur McGee argued that these Catholic resonances were signals to the original audience that Hamlet's mission was flawed, that the Ghost was entrapping him, successfully tempting him to effectuate his own damnation at a moment of weakness.[38] But it is impossible, I believe, to map such moments—the executed order of "not shriving time allowed" for Rosencrantz and Guildenstern repeats the same deed—into a key to the play's overall significance. Rather, we might say, they are moments of "madness," the archaic material expressive of primal emotions and extreme stress. In that way, these moments function as fragmented allegories in Benjamin's sense—in this case, they are fragments that evoke feeling and atmosphere; they are evocative of the rage and cold resolve of a revenge-hero, moments when Hamlet is not far from Hieronimo or Marlowe's Barabas. We see a world not only emptied of meaning but open to the forces of hell and damnation as well. Significantly, Hamlet situates the moment in a direful nighttime:

'Tis now the very witching time of night,
When churchyards yawn, and hell itself breathes out
Contagion to this world. Now could I drink hot blood,
And do such bitter business as the day
Would quake to look on.

                                        (3.2.358–62)

It is as if, at this moment, Hamlet has plunged over the beetling cliff
into madness, and yet the feeling it evokes is as much relief at his
apparent resolution as horror at its savagery. Again, as in the figure
of the beetling cliff, the images depict boundaries giving way, borders dissolving: graves "yawn" and hell "breathes out / Contagion." The image of drinking hot blood is a kind of inverted,
diabolical Eucharist. Hamlet seems entrapped; from one moral perspective (Christian) he is damning himself, but from another
(pagan) he is empowered: he is finally preparing himself for the
bloody necessities of carrying out his princely duty. Of course,
what follows from this vivid dramatic buildup is another deferral,
perhaps the most ambiguous one of all.

But however we evaluate the seriousness and ethics of Hamlet's
fervent wish for the damnation of Claudius, we can see the incident
as also making an important point in the play's investigation of
knowledge. Hamlet had just affirmed the possibility of reading
Claudius's subjectivity by studying his external actions as he
watched the play, and he carries on the same project here. In this
case, however, we learn that the Prince has erred in his judgment.
Claudius was unable to undertake a meaningful reformation and
instead chose to keep the effects gained by his murder rather than
relinquish them in repentance. The incident thus marks an important qualification to the possibility of reading another's interiority
by external appearances, returning us to the play's generally skeptical, Montaignean epistemology.[39] And it is one of the most remarkable of the play's several moments of deferral of revenge.

Still following the logic of deferral, Hamlet proceeds from this
postponement of revenge to a mandated conference with his
mother, in which he tries to share with her his vision of the fallen
world and her contribution to it. In the intimacy of the lady's chamber, for the first time in the play he enacts (rather than imagines)
the violent spirit of the revenge-hero—only, of course, finding the
wrong hidden target and slaying Polonius, another substitute, in
error. Without realizing it, he has slain Ophelia as well, who be-

comes the play's most unambiguous subject of madness in the famous fourth-act scenes of her disordered mourning.

Ophelia's Allegorical Bouquet

While Hamlet passively if warily accepts a hasty conveyance to England, Ophelia embodies the motif of madness in scenes that have since become iconic for their allegorical effect, in paintings and in evocative allusions like Mary Pipher's *Reviving Ophelia,* a study of suicides by adolescent females. In another image of dissolving open boundaries, Ophelia's madness is presented as a kind of dissolution of maidenly decorum, the spilling over of repressed psychic materials brought on by the two shocks she suffered in losing first her lover, second her father—a coupling that is also a textbook instantiation of the play's uncanny psychoanalytic acumen. And like virtually everything in this play, her madness is a manifestation of mourning—and an aestheticizing of it:

> Thought and affliction, passion, hell itself
> She turns to favour and to prettiness.
>
> (4.5.183–84)

This is Laertes' comment on Ophelia's allegory of the herbs and flowers, a carefully designed miniature of the play's larger motifs: rosemary for remembrance, pansies for thoughts, fennel for flattery, columbines for sexual betrayal, [40] and rue for sorrow (4.5.175–84). For herself there are a homely daisy and violets, the signifier of faithfulness, all withered at the death of Polonius.

This allegorical bouquet is the aestheticizing instrument of the kind of poetic sea change Ariel will sing about in his famous song of *The Tempest* ("Full fathom five thy father lies"). The emotions represented by herbs or flowers summarize for us much about both Hamlet the character and *Hamlet* the play: the Prince's struggle to remember, the "pale cast of thought" that sickles o'er resolution, the flattery of the court, the betrayal of Gertrude. In turning these to favor and prettiness, Ophelia enacts the aesthetic ritual of transformation that is at the heart of so much of Shakespeare's "fourth-act pathos" in the Jacobean tragedies (if I may revert to traditional genre classification for the moment) and the late romances. Desdemona with her ballad of the maid of Barbary, Antony and Cleopatra

hearing the flute-playing of Antony's retreating guiding spirit, Per-
dita's flowers in *The Winter's Tale,* the masque in *The Tempest*—all
of these involve an element of self-conscious aesthetic practices
and the use of words and images to embody feeling-tones in a patterned, "framed" manner creative of a meta-aesthetic effect. All of
them are also allegorical fragments in Benjamin's extended usage
of the term. Madness, death, eros, and aesthetic signification itself
all seem to be interrelated to each other in these famous Shakespearean moments—as they will be in so much European art of the
eras to come. And as Benjamin reminded us, the emptied world of
the *Trauerspiel,* one productive of free-floating, protean objects that
can come to stand for anything at all, is one of the richest aesthetic
forms for this combination, as *Hamlet* above all shows us.

The rich description of Ophelia's ambiguous death by drown-
ing—was it suicide or the negligence of her madness?—follows up
and extends the mood of her allegory of the flowers. It portrays the
outcome of an extended stay on the very boundary between two
different elements, water and air—"But long it could not be"
(4.7.155). She is surrounded by more allegorical flora, this time
again mingling death and the erotic:

> Of crow-flowers, nettles, daisies, and long purples
> That liberal shepherds give a grosser name,
> But our cold maids do dead men's fingers call them.
>
> (4.7.140–42)

Allegories of the Graveyard

But it is in the great graveyard scene—that piece of comic relief
that adds new social and thematic dimensions to the play and
serves to mark yet another stage of Hamlet's uncertain mental evo-
lution, encompassing such contradictory qualities as his nearness
to madness, his continuing ability to see through the surfaces of
things to their hidden natures, his fascination with death—that the
most iconic moment of all in the play takes place. In a pioneering
deconstructive reading of the play referred to above, Margaret Fergusson defined as a characteristic of Hamlet's speech his tendency
to make literal figures of speech by a "materialization" of them.[41]
Her chief example is the point when Hamlet no sooner evokes an
image of the "table of memory" (1.5.97) than he turns to his mate-

rial tables and physically writes upon them (1.5.107–10). At this point in the analysis, I believe, it makes sense to say that such a tendency is one of the play as a whole, and that it is a tendency toward visual allegories.

The graveyard scene constitutes another striking example. As a lead-in, we should recall Hamlet's direful description of his state of mind after the revelations of *The Mousetrap,*

> When churchyards yawn and hell itself breathes out
> Contagion to this world.

At the graveyard we witness such a yawning grave, but instead of demons, we meet two clowns, figures of such harmony-in-discord, such ambiguous but potent significance, that they formed the models for Beckett's existential clowns Estragon and Vladimir in *Waiting for Godot* 350 years later. The change of pace provided by these two deconstructive delvers is one of the great surprises—and great moments—of the play. They force us to rethink everything we have seen so far. Momentarily we leave behind our direct access to the deadly Machiavellian statecraft we have been immersed in and enter a plebeian world where death is commonplace, the world of politics a distant set of gossiped-about events, and social corruption is manifested directly in the rottenness of corpses:

> I' faith, if a be not rotten before a die—as we have many pocky corpses nowadays, that will scarce hold the laying in—a will last you some eight year or nine year. A tanner will last you nine year.
>
> (5.1.152–54)

In the light of their carnivalesque vision, death is revealed to us as also a moment of a life that continues in the community as it is extinguished in the individual. And the gallows humor of the two clowns adds an element of the grotesque to the play's exploration of death and corruption and provides a point of view distanced from the political intrigue we have been immersed in—one that provides Hamlet with a context for coming to terms with death as a physical, corporeal reality shared by all men and women regardless of their social estate—an inevitable triumph of nature over history and society.

The first part of the scene reaches its greatest intensity when the singing, intoxicated digger throws up a skull that Hamlet contemplates in a self-defining moment of mori memento. Unexpectedly, in a quintessentially Shakespearean moment, the skull achieves an identity—that of old King Hamlet's fool Yorick, whom Prince Hamlet describes, like a figure of Melancholy studying the transience of Mirth, to Horatio:

> a fellow of infinite jest, of most excellent fancy. He hath borne me on his back a thousand times; and now, how abhorred my imagination is! My gorge rises at it. Here hung those lips that I have kissed I know not how oft. Where be your gibes now, your gambols, your songs, your flashes of merriment, that were wont to set the table on a roar? Not one now, to mock your own grinning? Quite chap-fallen?
>
> (5.1.171–78)

The comic interlude, these lines announce, is over, and is now incorporated as merely a buildup to this epiphany. The skull is the simplest, but also the most emotionally powerful, of the play's allegorizing objects. The moment must have been iconic in the original performances as a visual invocation of a Stoic and medieval Christian practice of meditating on death; it is even more iconic now, as providing the most common of all of Hamlet's representations in the visual arts.

Beyond this identification of Hamlet with an ancient moment of wisdom, the skull also signifies and focuses other motifs of the play— notably, rottenness, death, and the extinguishing of mirth. These feelings and concepts seem to be "taken in" by Hamlet as he holds and studies the skull, in marked contrast to the externalizing logic of his earlier reaction to the Ghost's command. In a sense we can say he has finally found an object that truly corresponds to his vision of the world, with which in some sense he can identify. The universality of death that Hamlet begins to comprehend concretely will form the basis for his subsequent acceptance of the Ghost's order, hereafter seen also as an acceptance of death.

The Allegorical Signet

When Hamlet narrates his adventures on the ship to England, another signifying object proves to be a crucial part of the whole series of events and substitutions:

> I had my father's signet in my purse,
> Which was the model of that Danish seal;

Folded the writ up in form of th'other,
Subscribed it, gave't the impression, placed it safely,
The changeling never known.

(5.2.50–54)

The word "signet" derives from the French *signe* (sign) and
forms in the first instance one more link in the *Trauerspielische*
chain of allegorical fragments relating to externalization, writing,
substitution, and deferral. But the signet is also an emblem of the
royal power of Hamlet's father, and the fact that Hamlet is in possession of it (as we learn for the first time), is new and meaningful,
paralleling Prince Hal's picking up his father's crown in the famous
scene in *2 Henry IV*. In both cases, the Prince does not thereby become King—King Henry, we recall, was not really dead, and of
course Claudius remains very much enthroned in Denmark. Rather,
in each case the Prince begins to act like a king, to imagine being
King. Hamlet conspicuously takes action against a sea of troubles
for the first time in the play when he discovers the plot of death
against him and opposes it. Again like Prince Hal, Hamlet acts the
true Prince by counterfeiting, by forging new documents that defer
his own death and that designate as his substitutes his old school-
mates Rosencrantz and Guildenstern—"not shriving time allowed," as we saw earlier. Notably, he here impersonates not his
father, but Claudius, and the instrument of his stratagem is not
really the official Danish seal, but a substitute, albeit one that "was
the model of that Danish seal," his father's personal signet.

The signet is thus a very complex allegorical trope, with strong
psychoanalytic resonances relating to sons, fathers, and empower-
ment. Lacan unaccountably neglected this particular object in his
bravura reading of the play, instead seeing the Ghost as the idealized Phallus, then seeing Hamlet's stabbing of Claudius near the
end of the play as the moment when Hamlet finally addresses his
real target, the Phallus that is at once Claudius and an idealized
signifier.[42] But what of this emanation of his idealized father and
taskmaster, the sign that holds the power of life and death, that
allows Hamlet to be at once his father, his father's usurper, and
himself as dutiful son? Without attempting to place this complex
and contradictory sign precisely within Lacan's infernal machinery
of terms, we can say that the signet is both paternal and kingly, an
instrument of Hamlet's new level of activity in the world and thus
an emblem of a newfound agency and new sense of identity as a

purposeful actor; that, like the crown passed from King to Prince at the moment of succession, it confers both identity with the father and the supplanting of the father. But it manages to do all this, as I mentioned, through feigning, through substituting, through role-playing. In a play with its much-quoted advice from foolish Polonius about being true to self, Hamlet here seems to affirm a very anti-essentialist idea of the self, a very performative one.

The signet is thus a strategic relay point in the chain of deferrals and substitutions that have played through the text up to this point. At every previous moment when action is deferred—when Hamlet bandies with Polonius and the others, when he insults Ophelia, when he contrives a play as the way to settle his doubts, when he bypasses the praying Claudius, when he seeks to convert his mother to go against her new husband, when he kills Polonius, when he forges the orders of execution of Rosencrantz and Guildenstern, when he grapples with Laertes in Ophelia's grave—in all these instances, a logic of displacement, in many ways working at a formal, rather than an unconscious level, can be discerned. Hamlet's revenge-passions (and secret identifications) are clearly deflected from their true target—Claudius—and redirected to some substitute for Claudius. This logic of displacement is itself a part of the aura of the royal signet Hamlet uses—he turns it in the first instance not directly against Claudius, but against two of his instruments. But then things change. For the first time in the play, he is also striking a blow against Claudius by thwarting his execution plans and then by escaping from the ship and contriving a way back to Denmark. In his forging of the letters "in a fair hand"—the elegant style that made the forgery appear authentic—Hamlet also redirects the art of writing from what it had been in the gesture of the writing tables (an externalization of memory) to become an instrument of political intrigue and of his own agency. In this play of absences and ghosts, this turning point is narrated rather than dramatized, but it marks a crucial change in Hamlet's conduct.

Although Hamlet's substitution of letters took place before the graveyard scene, Shakespeare postponed the narration of it until after it had taken place, after Hamlet had courted "madness" one last time in his "tow'ring passion" against a Laertes who claimed to love his sister dearly and whom Hamlet clearly took as a rival for his dead beloved. His actions are puzzling, and they provoke the only sustained expression of regret that Hamlet makes throughout the entire play:

But I am very sorry, good Horatio,
That to Laertes I forgot myself;
For by the image of my cause I see
The portraiture of his: I'll court his favours.
But sure, the bravery of his grief did put me
Into a tow'ring passion.

(5.2.76–81)

But the leap into the grave with the provocative cry of "This is I, / Hamlet the Dane" is itself a brief expressive allegory. Hamlet joins Laertes and Ophelia in the grave—they are all marked for death, they are living in the boundaries between the "prison" of Denmark and the realm of death, corruption, and uncontained hell-fire. This scene is properly positioned *before* Hamlet takes up the signet seal because it shows us a Hamlet still subject to his passions, his interior self marked by open borders and hence to "madness," and still involved in a logic of deferral. But it is capable of being retrospectively "redeemed," seen to be compatible with the newly active, more focused Hamlet of the adventures of his aborted passage to England (which we only learn about after this scene) because Hamlet has now "taken in" the reality of his own death, has asserted himself in his claim to be "the Dane" as his father's successor and the enemy of his usurping uncle, and has become the restored lover of a young woman he had previously seemed to dismiss and denigrate. His actions, in short, in this light, are not madness but noble anger, based on a renewed sense of his inherited place in the Symbolic Order of his society. Like so much in the play, this scene can be read at multiple levels.

The Ambiguity of Catastrophe

While *Hamlet* surpasses the limitations of the typical *Trauerspiel* above all in its dominating, complex hero, it follows the logic of the *Trauerspiel* in its conclusion. Benjamin had praised the contingent, accidental notion of Hamlet's death as one quintessentially suited to the form's disenchanting view of the world. But he also called attention to the prevalence of mass death at the end of these plays, "the form of a communal fate, as if summoning all the participants before the highest court."[43] With four bodies "piled on the stage" at the end (joining four offstage), *Hamlet* certainly fits this aspect of Benjamin's chosen genre, and there is something close to an at-

tempt to assign guilt and innocence in these final moments, too—
Laertes' and Hamlet's mutual forgiveness, Laertes' and Horatio's
condemnations of Claudius and commendations of Hamlet, with a
discreet silence about the Queen—that is reminiscent of court proceedings in a mode quite foreign, as Benjamin underlines, to classical tragedy.

But it was also a characteristic of the radical allegorizing methodology of Benjamin's baroque *Trauerspiele* that despite the prepon-
derance of emptiness and melancholy in the representation of the
world in nearly every detail, they were also susceptible—usually
near their ending points—to a vertiginous allegorical reversal in
which redemption is glimpsed amid the gloom as a possibility, as
an alternative mode of perception of the underlying nature of the
world. Benjamin had described such a structure as one borrowed
from seventeenth-century religious emblems:

> The bleak confusion of Golgotha, which can be recognized as the
> schema underlying the allegorical figure in hundreds of the engravings
> and descriptions of the period, is not just a symbol of the desolation
> of human existence. In it transitoriness is not signified or allegorically
> represented, so much as, in its own significance, displayed as allegory.
> As the allegory of resurrection. Ultimately, in the death-signs of the ba-
> roque, the direction of allegorical reflection is reversed; on the second
> half of its wide arc it returns, to redeem.[44]

One of Benjamin's wisest commentators, Susan Buck-Morss, referred to this moment in Benjamin's allegorical interpretation as "a
dialectical move to a metalevel, at which the contradictory meanings of emblems themselves become an emblem, the sign of *their*
opposite."[45] Such a possibility swims into view within *Hamlet*
when the Prince himself unexpectedly, for the first time, begins to
speak of Providence. "Why, even in that was heaven ordinant," he
tells Horatio in explaining the lucky coincidence of his having his
father's seal—that complex symbol of coming of age and replacing
the father—with him. And Providence becomes a central theme for
Hamlet as he prepares for the fight against Laertes with the foreboding about his heart—a foreboding he puts aside with a reference to
Providence:

> Not a whit. We defy augury. There's a special providence in the fall of
> a sparrow. If it be now, 'tis not to come. If it be not to come, it will be

now. If it be not now, yet it will come. The readiness is all. Since no
man has aught of what he leaves, what is't to leave betimes?

(5.2.157–61)

This is very likely the moment Benjamin had in mind when he
praised Shakespeare for being able to strike "Christian sparks from
the baroque rigidity of the melancholic, un-stoic as it is un-Christian, pseudo-antique as it is pseudo-pietistic." [46] In this moment
Hamlet himself, we might say, becomes something of an allegorist
in a redemptory mode, finding a means to read the play's externalized, *Trauerspielische* succession of contingencies and accidents as
part of a hidden divine drama—and inviting us to do the same.

And yet at the end of the play, Horatio avoids these terms and
speaks instead of bloody contingencies, in the same mode Benjamin himself evinced in defending against earlier critics Shakespeare's treatment of Hamlet's death as something accidental and
contingent. If Hamlet offers us, near the end, as a means of reconcil-
ing himself to the unknown, a theory of divine Providence, Horatio
remains outside of paradise, still in an unweeded garden, as he
speaks:

> Of carnal, bloody, and unnatural acts,
> Of accidental judgments, casual slaughters,
> Of deaths put on by cunning and forced cause;
> And, in this upshot, purposes mistook
> Fall'n on th'inventors' heads.

(5.2.325–29)

The play thus presents us with these two alternative interpretive
frames. Hamlet dies, as Benjamin notes, contingently—"as the fateful stage-properties gather around him, as around their lord and
master."[47] He is referring to those images of poisoned honor, sexuality, and statecraft, the poisoned sword and chalice, this last en-
hanced with a "union" or pearl that, when Hamlet alludes to it in
the act of pouring the poisoned wine down Claudius's throat,
seems to symbolize both death and sex.[48] But he is also pictured by
Horatio, after all this darkness, as a soul ascending to heaven with
an angelic squadron leading him on. In short, in the event-packed
concluding moments of *Hamlet,* there is a careful balance between
a motif of continuing emptiness and another, contradictory one of
redemption and even triumph, an establishment, if not of ideal jus-

tice, then at least of an exemplary self-sacrifice that gives the lie to the play's darkest intimations about human nature through the counterexample of Hamlet's life and death.

This balance is maintained in the play's concluding words, given to the ambiguous Fortinbras, the "delicate and tender prince, / . . . with divine ambition puff'd" (4.4.9.38–39), who speaks Hamlet's second and final epitaph:

> Let four captains
> Bear Hamlet like a soldier to the stage,
> For he was likely, had he been put on,
> To have proved most royally: and for his passage,
> The soldiers' music and the rites of war
> Speak loudly for him.
> Take up the body. Such a sight as this
> Becomes the field, but here shows much amiss.
>
> (5.2.339–46)

Jan Kott, in his milestone reading of *Hamlet* as fulfilling a Shakespearean—and *Trauerspielische*—pattern of "the Grand Mechanism," of one iron age succeeded by another, has interpreted Fortinbras as a young tyrant-to-be who inaugurates a new cycle of empty history,[49] and numerous productions of the play in recent decades have followed suit, portraying Fortinbras's return as that of an invading army taking power. Although this conception is close to the spirit of Benjamin's *Trauerspiel* at one level, it misses something important at another. Of all the Machiavellian intriguers of the play, Fortinbras is the only one Hamlet admired at all, and his endorsement of his candidacy for the throne of Denmark just before his death reinforces his admiration with emphasis.

To be sure, the world of *Hamlet* remains dark at the end of the play, as empty of essential meaning at the end as it was at the beginning, and Fortinbras is at best only a well-meaning but very worldly politician, a player in the Machiavellian games of statecraft who sends thousands to their deaths over an eggshell. He is no Hamlet senior, no epic, idealized ruler of a kingdom of immanent meaning. But neither is he Claudius, the hidden serpent, murderer, adulterer, and usurper. He is, as I said above, simply the best the fallen world has to offer, and Hamlet's endorsement of him shows him as politically active, a participant in the Machiavellian arts of political-natural history till the end—in short, someone now thinking like a king even though he has come to understand the emptiness of such thinking.

What Kott's eye-opening reading of the end of the play misses is, of course, the glimpse of redemption, the fleeting moment of reversal when the series of deferrals, of bloody accidents and contingencies, come briefly into focus as the facade of some providence, of some moment when the fallen world is also an emblem of its own possible redemption. Hamlet never succeeded in setting a time out of joint aright. But he did finally face up to the imperious demands of his Ghost-father, allowing the perturbed spirit to rest and freeing the throne of Denmark of a usurper—at the cost of undertaking his own journey into the unknown country—and taking five more-or-less innocent bystanders with him as well. The last moments of the play leave us with images both of a Hamlet open to the forces of hell and damnation and a picture of him with angels bearing him to his final rest.

And then this depressed and dilatory revenge-hero is proclaimed "most likely, had he been put on, to have proven royal." Contrary to a great number of critics, however, I do not think this is to be taken as irony; it is rather part of the process of rapid, even say hasty, apotheosis and ennoblement in which Hamlet is inscribed at the play's closing moments, to balance the diabolic associations of Hamlet's words after seeing Claudius at prayer. It is not irony, but doubleness. The dark world continues, but we have all also experienced the fervent wish that it might be otherwise, that the immanent world might somehow be restored. In Hamlet's fierce depression, there burned the desire for such a transformation, and we have been given his vision, his desire—which is ultimately, of course, all art can ever give us. In Benjamin's own words, the *Trauerspiel*'s allegories "fill out and deny the void in which they are represented,"[50] proclaiming themselves to be—to gloss what Benjamin implied but left unsaid here—that new thing, an aesthetic and utopian object. Such an impossible combination of contrary perceptions is what we are left with at the end of this perfect *Trauerspiel,* which, as Benjamin implied, at once completes and abolishes the form. "A major work," Benjamin wrote, "will either establish the genre or abolish it; and the perfect work will do both."[51] He seems to have, precisely, *Hamlet* in mind. While much of the play is firmly rooted in Kyd's and Marlowe's theatrical practice and while it clearly forms part of the developing genre that Benjamin calls baroque *Trauerspiel,* the play is finally sui generis.

Nothing before or after it compares to it, even among the works of Shakespeare himself.

Notes

1. The book was written in the period 1924–25.

2. Walter Benjamin, The *Origin of German Tragic Drama,* trans. John Osborne (London: New Left Books, 1977), 159–63.

3. Susan Zimmerman, *The Early Modern Corpse and Shakespeare's Theatre* (Edinburgh: Edinburgh University Press, 2005) is a recent exception to this statement. Zimmerman takes up Benjamin's description of the German baroque *Trauerspiele* and his claim that Shakespeare's *Hamlet* shares many of the genre's features to great effect, arguing that Benjamin had grasped the larger cultural impact which both the Protestant Reformation and the incipient scientific revolution had on the concept and representation of the body in early modern England. See especially pp. 13–18.

4. Because of that fundamental distinction, the choice of the term "tragic drama" to render *Trauerspiel* in the book's title in the New Left Books 1977 translation by Osbourne is a misleading one. In the translation's text, by way of contrast, the German term is retained exclusively. The German *Trauer* variously means mourning, grief, or sorrow, so that "mourning-play" is a common translation for the German. "Plays of lamentation" is an alternative, and Fredric Jameson suggests "funeral pageant" in his, *Marxism and Form: Twentieth-Century Dialectical Theories of Literature* (Princeton: Princeton University Press, 1971), 68.

5. A similar point about the ambiguity of the relation of the terms *Tragödie* and *Trauerspiel* is made in the thought-provoking study of Benjamin's theory of the *Trauerspiel,* especially in its relations to Nietzsche, Freud, and Lacan, in Julia Reinhard Lupton and Kenneth Reinhard, *After Oedipus: Shakespeare in Psychoanalysis* (Ithaca, N. Y.: Cornell University Press, 1992), 34–59.

6. The affinity is illustrated as well by the little understood 1626 adaptation of *Hamlet* into German, *Trageodia: Der Bestrafte Brudermord oder: Prinz Hamlet aus Dännemark* (*Tragedy: Fratricide Punished; or, Prince Hamlet of Denmark*)—a work which, despite the generic designation *Trageodia* in its title (generic terminology was mobile and unstable in the baroque era, like so much else) is obviously a baroque *Trauerspiel* as Benjamin defines the term, complete with allegorizing double title. However, Benjamin scarcely refers to this work. An English translation is available in Horace Howard Furness, ed., *A New Variorum Edition of Shakespeare: Hamlet* (Philadelphia: Lippincott, 1877), 2: 121–42.

7. Benjamin, *Origin,* 178.

8. Hugh Grady, *Shakespeare's Universal Wolf: Studies in Early Modern Reification* (Oxford: Clarendon, 1996), 3–4.

9. In that way Benjamin's approach has parallels with the Modernist "spatial" hermeneutics which G. Wilson Knight applied to *Hamlet* in his *The Wheel of Fire: Interpretations of Shakespeare's Tragedies* (1930; repr. Cleveland: Meridian, 1964), 17–46. It parallels even more closely the equally Modernist and spatializing attempt to define the "world" of the play in Maynard Mack, "The World of Hamlet," *Yale Review* 41.4 (June 1952), 502–23.

10. Benjamin, *Origin,* 164–65.

11. Friedrich Creuzer, *Symbolik und Mytholgie der alten Völker, besonders der Griechen* (Leipzig: Darmstadt, 1819), 1.2, 70–71; quoted in Benjamin, *Origin,* 164.

12. William Shakespeare, *Hamlet* 5.2.308–11, *The Norton Shakespeare,* ed. Stephen Greenblatt (New York: Norton, 1997). All subsequent quotations from *Hamlet* are from this edition, which is a modified conflated text based on the Folio version, with passages from the second quarto of 1604 that were not included in the Folio text printed indented, italicized and numbered as decimals of the previous Folio lines. I will follow this numbering system in what follows, but instead of indenting and italicizing unique material from the second quarto, I will indicate in a note if a quoted passage is uniquely from the second quarto.

13. See, for example, Jaques Lacan, *Écrits: A Selection,* trans. Alan Sheridan (New York, Norton, 1977), 281 where, in a note introducing his essay "The Signification of the Phallus," he claims to have restored Freud's term "deferred action" or *Nachtrag* to "the facility from which [it] has since fallen."

14. See Jonathan Gil Harris and Natasha Korda, "Introduction: Towards a Materialist Account of Stage Properties," in Harris and Korda, eds., *Staged Properties in Early Modern English Drama* (Cambridge: Cambridge University Press, 2002), 12–13, for an earlier statement of the relevance of Benjamin's *Origin* to a study of early modern stage-props.

15. Benjamin, *Origin,* 137.

16. The term in this sense, describing a world of inherent meaning, is taken from one of Benjamin's chief sources of ideas in *Origin,* Georg Lukács, *The Theory of the Novel,* trans. Anna Bostock (Cambridge, Mass.: MIT Press, 1971), 29–39.

17. Lukács, *The Theory of the Novel,* 88–93.

18. Cf. Jacques Lacan, "Desire and the Interpretation of Desire in *Hamlet,*" *Yale French Studies* 55/56 (1977), 11–52; 50–52, who famously interprets the Ghost as an uncanny ideal Phallus "bound to nothing," which "always slips through your fingers."

19. Benjamin, *Origin,* 193.

20. Stephen Greenblatt, *Hamlet in Purgatory* (Princeton: Princeton University Press, 2001), 200.

21. Stephen Greenblatt, *Renaissance Self-Fashioning: From More to Shakespeare* (Chicago: University of Chicago Press, 1980),157–92, provides a useful discussion of this motif, especially in the passages on the razing of the Bower of Bliss in Spenser's *The Fairie Queene,* 170–73.

22. Caroline Sturgeon, *Shakespeare's Imagery: And What It Tells Us* (Cambridge: Cambridge University Press, 1935; 1966), 86–91, 164–65.

23. Benjamin, *Origin,* 166.

24. The final four lines of this passage are unique to the 1604 quarto.

25. Cf. Janet Adelman, *Suffering Mothers: Fantasies of Maternal Origin in Shakespeare's Plays* (New York: Routledge, 1992), 29. Adelman argues that these images take their origin "in the earliest stages of emergent selfhood, when the nascent self is most fully subject to the mother's fantasied power to annihilate or contaminate."

26. See Horace Howard Furness, ed., *Hamlet,* in *A New Variorum Edition of Shakespeare* (Philadelphia: Lippincott, 1877), 2:195–235, for a series of excerpts from some thirty-nine critics debating the insanity issue from 1780–1876.

27. For example, Peter Stallybrass, Roger Chartier, J. Franklin Mowery, and

Heather Wolfe, "Hamlet's Tables and the Technologies of Writing in Renaissance England," *Shakespeare Quarterly* 55, 4 (Winter 2004): 379–419; and Margaret W. Ferguson, "*Hamlet:* Letters and Spirits," in *Shakespeare and the Question of Theory* ed. Patricia Parker and Geoffrey Hartman, 292 (New York: Methuen, 1985).

28. Cf. Paul de Man, "Sign and Symbol in Hegel's *Aesthetics,*" *Critical Inquiry* 8 (1982): 761–65 and Marjorie Garber, *Shakespeare's Ghost Writers: Literature as Uncanny Causality* (New York: Methuen, 1987), 147–53. De Man borrows a distinction in Hegel between an internal, self-reflective kind of memory (*Errinerung*) and external, rote memory (*Gedächtnis*), associating the first kind with symbol, the second kind with allegory. Garber ties de Man's distinction to *Hamlet* and Hamlet's change from an initial state of internalized, "symbolic" memory in the first soliloquy to one of externalized, "allegorical" memory in need of being written down when he turns to his tables after seeing the Ghost (312–14). That second kind of external memory is highlighted in the central portions of the play between Hamlet's conversations with the Ghost and his return from his sea voyage, and it is governed by deferral.

29. John Dover Wilson, *What Happens in "Hamlet"* (Cambridge: Cambridge University Press, 1935), 154–57.

30. Robert Weimann, "Mimesis in *Hamlet,*" in *Shakespeare and the Question of Theory,* ed. Parker and Hartman, 279.

31. Ibid., 281.

32. Cf. ibid.

33. Ibid., 283.

34. Benjamin, *Origin,* 140. The identification of Shakespeare as a baroque figure was common in Germany in this era, as can be seen in the well-known work by German critic Levin Schücking, in *The Meaning of Hamlet,* trans. Graham Rawson (1937; repr. New York: Barnes and Noble, 1966), 8.

35. Phillipe Ariès, *The Hour of Our Death,* trans. Helen Weaver (New York: Knopf, 1981), 297–321, argues that the Renaissance was a period in which both Protestant and Catholic teachers tended to criticize the previous age's emphasis on the disposition of the soul at the moment of death, casting doubt on deathbed conversations and repentance, and emphasizing that a person's entire life was relevant to her salvation. In that sense Hamlet's and the Ghost's preoccupation with the state of the soul at the moment of death was medieval and anachronistic.

36. Samuel Johnson, "Notes on Shakespeare's Plays: 'Hamlet,'" *The Yale Edition of the Works of Samuel Johnson: Johnson on Shakespeare,* ed. Arthur Sherbo (New Haven: Yale University Press, 1968), 8:990.

37. Wilson, *What Happens in "Hamlet,"* 102.

38. Arthur McGee, *The Elizabethan Hamlet* (New Haven: Yale University Press, 1987).

39. I want to thank Susan Wells for suggesting this reading of this incident.

40. According to G. R. Hibbard, ed., *Hamlet,* by William Shakespeare (Oxford: Oxford University Press, 1987), 307–8n181–5.

41. Fergusson, "*Hamlet:* Letters and Spirits," 292.

42. Lacan, "Desire and the Interpretation of Desire in *Hamlet,*" 50–51.

43. Benjamin, *Origin,* 136.

44. Ibid., 232.

45. Susan Buck-Morss, *The Dialectics of Seeing: Walter Benjamin and the Arcades Project* (Cambridge, MA: MIT Press, 1991), 173.

46. Benjamin, *Origin,* 157–58.

47. Ibid., 137.

48. "Is thy union here? / Follow my mother" (5.2.279–80), Hamlet tells Claudius.

49. Jan Kott, *Shakespeare Our Contemporary,* trans. Boleslaw Taborski (New York: Doubleday, 1966), 51–65.

50. Benjamin, *Origin,* 232–33.

51. Ibid., 44.

"The verie paines of hell": *Doctor Faustus* and the Controversy over Christ's Descent

Heather Anne Hirschfeld

I N THE DEDICATION to his treatise on the creedal position that Christ descended to hell after the Crucifixion, Adam Hill warned that "there is like to be . . . great strife about the true vnderstanding of this Article in England," and that such conflict would give divines an "occasion [to] striue more bitterly one against another, then either of both do against our common aduersarye."[1] The question of the historicity as well as the meaning of Christ's descent had received attention from English reformers in the middle of the century, but Hill sensed (or wanted to prompt) a resurgence of interest in the issue in the early 1590s.[2] The controversy that resulted, preserved in a flurry of pamphlets largely drowned out by more voluble debates focused explicitly on predestination, makes strikingly visible the doctrinal flash points in the Protestant treatment of Christ's Passion, death, and resurrection. That is, in its exacting, at times seemingly scholastic, disagreements about whether or not Christ's soul literally went down to hell, the controversy reveals the reformers' investment in, as well as uncertainty about, what was necessary or essential to Christ's perfectly efficacious sacrifice. Its manifest subject was hell, but the latent content of the debate was a preoccupation with what was *enough* for Christ to do to redeem an infinite number of Christian souls.

The question of what counts as satisfactory—as "making enough," in its true etymological sense—haunts early modern Protestant theology, which had, in essence, substituted the absolute will of God for the efficacy of human penitential activity in effecting salvation. Efforts to deal with this substitution took a variety of forms in the period's religious literature but also in its drama, which displays deep concern for determining and achieving the parameters of spiritual as well as political, economic, or sexual satisfaction. And if these concerns occupy a large space in the plots of Renaissance plays, they are nowhere more explicit than in Christopher Marlowe's *Doctor Faustus* (1594), whose protagonist is tormented with questions about theological sufficiency, about what is enough for the effecting of his salvation or damnation. Faustus's torment, like the debates about Christ's descent with which it is exactly contemporary, is manifest in his obsession with hell—not only in his persistent, peculiar questions to Mephistopheles but in his overarching commitment to necromancy, the calling and raising up of dead spirits.

*   *   *

In the remainder of the essay I explore Faustus's fascination with hell in terms of a controversy related to, but distinct from, the doctrine of predestination: the sixteenth-century debate about the descent of Christ. This debate certainly has affiliations with the period's larger questions about predestination, questions that, as the 1590s Cambridge disputes make clear, were the core theological, if not ecclesiastical, concern of the late sixteenth-century Anglican Church.[3] But the controversy over Christ's descent illuminates with special intensity a set of concepts problematic for Reformation theologians. It reveals a specific conceptual instability about the definitions of sufficiency and excess, an instability, I would suggest, initiated by Protestant doctrines that eliminated the role of human activity in satisfying for sin. In its baroque efforts to identify what constitutes a sufficient sacrifice, the controversy demonstrates that the loss of human agency in the process of atonement generates questions about, and challenges to, the nature of Christ's sacrificial efficacy. Having introduced a theology that, in its opposition to Catholic belief, stressed what theologians called the "omnisufficent" nature of Christ's atonement, Protestants of different denominations found themselves in the late sixteenth century arguing not only about the limitations of human satisfaction for sin but also about what exactly constituted Christ's satisfaction.

*   *   *

A vibrant staple of medieval religious iconography and especially the cycle drama, Christ's descent into hell remained, with impor-

tant modifications, a feature of reformed theology, taking its place
in the Augsburg Confession of 1530 and as the third of the Thirty-
nine Articles of the Anglican Church of 1572. What varied, however, was the interpretation of exactly what the descent involved.
The Lutheran Formula of Concord (1580), for instance, maintains a
literal descent to a real, local hell: "It is enough to know that Christ
went to hell, destroyed hell for all believers, and has redeemed
them from the power of death, of the devil, and of the eternal damnation of the hellish jaws."[4] Calvin, on the other hand, offers a dis-
tinctly different exegesis: Christ, he explains, in order to make a
full expiation for man's sin, suffered in his soul the torment of
God's wrath, which is equivalent to the pangs of hell:

> If Christ had died only a bodily death, it would have been ineffectual.
> No—it was expedient at the same time for him to undergo the severity
> of God's vengeance, to appease his wrath and satisfy his just judgment.
> For this reason, he must also grapple hand to hand with the armies of
> hell and the dread of everlasting death. . . . The point is that the Creed
> sets forth what Christ suffered in the sight of men, and then appositely
> speaks of that invisible and incomprehensible judgment which he un-
> derwent in the sight of God in order that we might know not only that
> Christ's body was given as the price of our redemption, but that he paid
> a greater and more excellent price in suffering in his soul the terrible
> torments of a condemned and forsaken man.[5]

Calvin condemned literal readings, including the Lutheran one, as
"nothing but a story" that supported the idea of purgatory. And
against those who suggest that spiritual suffering would be impossible for Christ, Calvin endorses the glory, rather than the despair,
of Christ's pain and estrangement from God. To detractors that
claim it is "incongruous for [Christ] to fear for the salvation of his
soul," Calvin responded that, "we must with assurance, therefore,
confess Christ's sorrow, as Ambrose rightly teaches, unless we are
ashamed of the cross. Unless his soul shared in the punishment, he
would have been the Redeemer of bodies alone."[6]

The *Institutes*' explanation of the descent, designed to clarify a
Calvinist economy of Christ's sacrifice, assumes a set of basic principles about how much and what kind of activity was necessary to
make the Passion efficacious. Debora Shuger has written powerfully about the ways in which Christ's sacrifice "became a resonant
and volatile symbol for psychological and social exploration" in
the imaginative literature of the Reformation.[7] I stress here the ways

in which it both articulated and reinforced assumptions and definitions about theological sufficiency and excess. These assumptions and definitions were sources of uncertainty for English divines in the later half of the sixteenth century. The debate about the veracity and significance of Christ's descent attests to theologians' difficulty in assessing the incomprehensible, but necessarily calculable, work of the Crucifixion.

The question of Christ's descent received some attention in the middle of the century, when Christopher Carlisle spoke against the article in a public disputation in the early 1550s at Cambridge. Carlisle's positions were not published until 1582, when they appeared as a rebuttal to a treatise printed at Louvain twenty years prior by the Catholic and former Oxford scholar Richard Smith. Carlisle represents that brand of English Protestant polemic aimed directly at Catholics rather than at competing reformed sects, and in refuting Smith's belief that Christ's soul actually descended to hell to free the souls of the patriarchs and prophets, he aims at what he sees as the particularly Romish implications of the creed: It endorses the possibility of multiple levels of hell, including a *limbus patrum* and purgatory; and it also promiscuously mixes pagan and Christian concepts of the afterlife. "Perhaps we should make the pope, *Pluto,* the Cardinalle his iudges *Rodomanthus, Aecus, Minos,* and *Triptolomus,* and his *Curtesanes, Tisiphone, Megara, Alecto, Erynies,* and *Furies,* his fery man *Charon,* and his porter, *Cerbrus* [*sic*]."[8] Returning to Rufinus's argument from the fourth century and relying on humanist scholarship that translated the Hebrew *shcol* as "grave," Carlisle maintained that the "hell" of the article should be taken literally, as the place where Christ was buried. But despite the florid display of philological exactitude, the heart of Carlisle's brand of literalism was his emphasis on the absolute sufficiency of the Crucifixion for redemption, which rendered belief in any other approach to salvation unscriptural and excessive. As he writes, "If the price was paide on the crosse, was it not superfluous to be paide againe in hell?"[9]

This attack on the superfluity of the literal descent, a species of general Protestant hostility to Catholic ceremony, is echoed in John Northbrooke's 1571 treatise *Spiritus est vicarious Christi in terra,* which begins with an attack on dissimulators who "conuey all their beleefe of the Romishe faith, into their secrete bosomes" and reiterates that "Christes soule should not neede to goe downe thither" to rescue the souls of the righteous dead.[10] But Northbrooke does not dispense with the idea of the descent entirely. Rather, he adopts Calvin's hermeneutics, endorsing a metaphoric descent: "When he praied to escape death he began to goe downe: and so all his sufferynges, that he suffered afterwarde in bodie and soule, for our synnes, was his going into hell. For he felt the burden, and waight of Gods wrathe for our iniquities."[11] This suffering was essential to redemption, according to Northbrooke, and it had real effects in and on hell: "the efficacie, virtue, and power of his death and passion, did pearce through and into the verie hell it self, by his diuine power and godheade: that all the damned soules, felt their full paine, and iuste damnation for their infidelitie: and Sathan hym self, felt all the power, and strength of his tyrannie, and darknesse, was weakened, vanquished, and fallen."[12] D. P. Walker considers this kind of barely disguised delight at the suffering of damned souls an aspect of "the abominable fallacy," one of the causes for the "decline of hell" in the later seventeenth century.[13] Northbrooke, of course, does not want to refute the existence of hell; he simply wants to maintain that, contrary to certain Catholic elaborations of the creed, it was not necessary for Christ's soul to descend there literally. Christ's death and Passion, which involve an agony comparable to the experience of hell, are the "omnisufficiente Sacrifice vnto God his father." Underwriting Northbrooke's particular fixation on the descent is a broader rejection of specifically Catholic doctrines and practices that presumed that the atonement on the cross was not final and that humans participated in compensating for their sins. John Foxe makes the axis of dispute particularly clear when he explains that the "Church of *Rome*" does not understand the meaning of the Crucifixion, "as may sensibly appeare by their doctrine and institutes, by their auricular confession and satisfaction for sinnes, by their dayly sacrifices, propitiatory Masses, trentals, and Purgatory, by merites of supererogation, inuocation of Saintes, the popes pardon, & dispensations."[14] As he adds caustically, "If the reconciliation of Gods fauour purchased by Christ once for vs be perfect & perpetuall, then this dayly sacrificing for sinne, is superfluous."[15] For Foxe as for Northbrooke, superfluous belief was a willing, conscious denial of the most basic premise of Christian doctrine: that Jesus's suffering and death "should serue and suffice for euer."[16]

Some twenty years after the descent was institutionalized as one of the Thirty-nine Articles of the Anglican Church, debate about it proceeded according to the terms assumed by Carlisle, Northbrooke, and Foxe a generation or two earlier. That is, the "strife" of the 1590s revolved around the same lexicon of sufficiency, excess, necessity, and superfluity as had the earlier one. Only now the debate derived from a division within Protestantism, from reformers' difficulty in articulating for themselves and their followers what counted in the economy of Christ's sacrifice, and how. Of central concern was the status of Christ's spiritual suffering, which North-brooke, like Calvin, had taken as absolutely essential to the work of the cross. But for some theologians this notion was untenable, and they found themselves arguing in favor of a real descent in order to avoid the implications of a metaphoric one. Indeed, as Hill says, "if hell here should be taken metaphorically as some wil haue it, so may you allegorise the whole creed as doo the heretiques."[17]

Hill is worried about the hermeneutical threat of allegorizing. But his larger fear is that the metaphoric approach does not accommodate the juridical demands that would allow for the complete redemption of human sinfulness. According to a peculiar spiritual calculus that, for Hill, poses no contradiction to a view of Christ as "aboue the reach of reason," the real descent is necessary; the metaphoric descent, insufficient.[18] According to Hill, "man being seperate [*sic*] from God by the desert of sinne had fallen [into hell]," so that "it remained for the full effecting of our redemption, that man assumpted to God [i.e., Christ] should descend thither."[19] Following a similar logic Hill insists that the resurrection would be incomplete and inefficacious if Jesus did not literally go down to hell: "Christs resurrection is not a full resurrection, unlesse both partes did arise."[20] Hill offers other reasons why the literal descent was necessary: it enabled Christ's triumph over the devil and the vanquishing of death; as a miracle or mystery, it serves as a barometer to distinguish Christians from Jews, the saved and the damned. But most important to him is the compulsory, essential role of the literal descent in satisfying the demands of God's justice: "the Sonne of God by the efficacy and nature of the divinity had tarried in hell *fulfilling all things marueilouslye*."[21] For Hill, Christ's ability to complete the full redemption of man depended upon his going down to hell.

Protestant scholars who agreed with Hill in the decade to follow repeat his arguments even as they embellish particular aspects of them. The Oxford poet and linguist John Higgins, for instance, emphasizes the miraculous nature of the literal descent and, drawing on traditional images of the victoriously militant Christ, he elaborates Hill's depiction of the necessity of the descent in defeating Satan: "It was then a powerfull passage, in his sin-lesse soules free-dome and valour, for so he went to conquer the devil, and to con-found the damned in hel, from whence he returned with triumphant victory."[22] But Higgins's most significant argument in-volves a critique of the metaphoric position that Christ experienced hell in his soul as the result of estrangement from God. Such a posi-tion, according to Higgins, is a diminishment of the idea of the god-head and a threat to basic principles of the Incarnation. As he writes: "We must hold that, Iesus Christ the sonne of God, dying vpon the crosse, could neither feele nor suffer the pangs of hel, nor the ful wrath of God seazing vpon his soule; because it was neither seperated [sic] from the godhead; nor subiect vnto sin." Higgins's point here, which harkens back to Calvin's "detractors" in the 1530s, represents a fresh development in the English debate about the descent, a development underwritten by a specific understand-ing of what was required—and what was superfluous—in Christ's sacrifice. So while Higgins's commitment to the literal descent has the justifying force of patristic as well as reformed authorities, it derives more urgently from a particular interpretation, in North-brooke's terms, of "omnisufficiency." For Higgins, it is precisely sufficient that Christ suffer in his body; and it is too much—heretically so—that he suffer the pains of hell in his soul.

Such an argument had already been formulated in sermons by the learned Thomas Bilson, bishop of Winchester, in his refutation of what he calls the "novel" idea that Christ "suffer[ed] . . . the *verie paines of hell.*"[23] Those who advocate such a position, Bilson writes, though they believe it "deriued from the proportion of Gods iustice as they call it," are really operating out of "presumption of mans reason intruding into Gods secrets." Bilson insists that "we are sufficientlie redeemed by the death and bloud of Christ Iesus (without adding of hell paines to bee suffered in the soule of Christ)."[24] Certainly Christ's soul suffered, according to Bilson, only the suffering was a "pained sorrow" for human sin rather than the experience of hell, for "hell is a *totall* and *finall exclusion* of the sinfull *from* enioying the *presence* or *patience* of God," and Christ could not experience such exclusion.[25]

Bilson's treatise is explicitly concerned with defining and ex-plaining the principles of Christian satisfaction, the theological bases of Christ's "making enough" to redeem mankind: "the death and bloud of Christ Iesus we . . . set downe . . . as the sufficient price of our Redemption, and true meane of our reconciliation to God."[26] But these definitions and explanations were not shared by all divines, and their objections were articulated in different approaches to the descent. The semiseparatist minister Henry Jacob, who had attended the bishop's Paul's Cross sermons, attacked Bilson directly, insisting on a sacrificial equation that demanded soul-suffering from Christ that would preserve a direct ratio—a "proportion"—between the Messiah and mankind: "He hath borne our sinnes, as we haue receyued his righteousnes. But we attaine the righteousnes of *God* by him both in our soules and bodyes: So likewise then, He was made sinne for vs, both in his soule & body. Otherwise this similitude or comparison were vneven, and namely short on his parte, whiche ought not to be. . . . We know by Gods worde, and doe affirme, that God in his iustice regarded this proportion, that as we haue sinned both in our Bodyes & Soules, so he that was made our propitiation did purposlie and aunswerably suffer both in his Body and Soul."[27] And that suffering was the suffering of hell, if not "hell torments in the verie place & condition of the damned," nevertheless the wrath, vengeance and distance from God "which we affirme is equal to Hell itselfe."[28] Such suffering was a metaphoric descent that obviated the literal one. In this belief Jacob echoed the more mainstream Calvinist William Perkins, who is surprisingly nonchalant in his exposition of the issue in his *Exposition of the Symbole or Creed of the Apostles* (1595). Perkins unfolds four possible options for understanding the doctrine of the descent; he rejects the first two, the literal going down into hell as well as the literalist translation of *sheol* as grave, but he accepts, with some reservations, the metaphoric reading, that Christ "felt and suffered the pangs of hell and the full wrath of God seazing vpon his soule" while on the cross.[29] This reading is "good and true," Perkins says, but still not entirely "fit," so he adds a fourth reading that explains the descent as Christ's captivity in the grave, his "bondage vnder death." Perkins sums up: "These last two expositions are commonly received, and we may indifferently make choice of either: but the last . . . is most agreeable."[30] Alexander Hume, a Scottish Presbyterian schoolmaster, was much more vehement in articulating the metaphoric reading. In an attack on Hill, Hume endorses the suffering of Christ's soul in order to repudiate a literal descent, which he sees as a scandalous denial of the efficacy of the Passion. For Hume, in other words, a real or "local" descent operates "contrary to the sufficiency of Christs sacrifice," which "had paid a full ransome for our sinnes before, and left nothing behinde to be done in Hell."[31]

The controversy over Christ's descent was, in Hume's words, a debate about the "sufficiency of Christ's sacrifice," a debate about what was enough, and what was too much, for Christ to do to meet the demands of divine justice. The fascination of this issue for theologians, I would suggest, derives in part from the fact that Reformation theology so clearly rejected prospects of human satisfaction for sin. Works of satisfaction, that staple of Catholic penitential theology, were of no consequence in either Lutheran or Calvinist doctrine; indeed, as Perkins would have it, the belief in human intervention in an individual's redemption is "most damnable and wicked."[22] The debate about the descent to hell, then, transposes the human problem of satisfaction to Christ. Marlowe's *Doctor Faustus* does something similar: it begins with an explicitly discontent protagonist seeking fulfillment, and it ends by showing that protagonist's frightened glimpse of the uncertain work of the Crucifixion.

* * *

Satisfaction, in its technical sense of atoning for sin through penitential works and alms, is unavailable to Marlowe's Faustus. "Contrition, prayer, repentance—what of these?" he asks the angels in the play's second act, replacing the final two terms—confession and satisfaction—of the traditional Catholic program for penance.[33] Satisfaction in its nontechnical sense of intellectual, economic, or emotional contentment is similarly unavailable to Faustus. Indeed, the phenomenon which Harry Levin so effectively called Faustus's "overreaching," his "intellectual curiosity [that] cannot be detached from secondary motives that entrammels it, the will to power and the appetite for sensation," remains the central critical enigma and fascination of the play.[34] The opening scene, in which the protagonist dispenses with the promises of philosophy, medicine, law, and divinity before turning to magical ravishment, is the first instance of the play's alternately thrilling and horrifying depiction of what William Kerrigan considers a typically Renaissance "insistent need for *more*."[35] Numerous critics have offered compelling etiologies of this need, using various methodological frames to track its sources in Faustus's alternating displays of triumph and despair. I suggest that we see Faustus's exploits as stemming not from a "need for more"—a phrase which assumes some stable, established vantage point against which "more" takes its meaning—

but rather from a loss of enough. If, as Una Ellis-Fermor said in an early essay on Marlowe, "the central idea of the play is an idea of loss," then one of Faustus's most chilling losses has been the possibility of making or feeling enough.[36] According to this view, Faustus's pursuits across the play—his pageant pastimes in the shape of the seven deadly sins; his magnificent flights through the heavens and around the globe; his eldritch jesting with knights and commoners—look like misguided efforts to stuff himself in the absence of any internal or external barometer for gauging "enough." His final request to see Helen in order to "glut the longing of my heart's desire," is the most glorious moment of exorbitance or excess prompted by the impossibility of experiencing *satis*: "Was this the face that launched a thousand ships / And burned the topless towers of Ilium?" (5.1.93–94). These pursuits demand that Faustus traffic with hell, and my contention is that ultimately this trafficking evokes the descent debates in ways that repeat their challenges to Christ's expiatory sufficiency.

Doctor Faustus is known, of course, for its evocative portrayals of hell as *poena damni,* the enduring, ever-present pain or punishment of loss that Milton's Satan will rehearse with fresh imaginative intensity. Mephistopheles' famous description informs Faustus that hell is "Within the bowels of these elements, / Where we are tortured and remain for ever. / Hell hath no limits, nor is circumscribed / In one self place, but where we are is hell, / And where hell is, there must we ever be" (2.1.114–18). But Faustus's engagement with hell has a deliberately mobile, hydraulic, feel—he is interested in comings to and goings from the place itself. Indeed, ascents and descents are at the heart of the practice of necromancy—the summoning of dead spirits to the earthly world. The opening Chorus uses magic as a synonym: "And glutted with learning's golden gifts, / He surfeits upon cursed necromancy. / Nothing so sweet as magic is to him, / Which he prefers before his chiefest bliss" (Prol. 24–28). Faustus, too, equates the "metaphysics of magicians and necromantic books" in his first monologue, as he dispenses with all other intellectual pursuits in favor of this forbidden one. But the use of the general category of magic should not distract us from Faustus's specific interest in necromancy, which serves as a kind of compensation for the fact that, as he admits, even medicine does not allow him to "make men to live eternally, / Or, being dead, raise them to life again" (1.1.24–25). Necromancy, that "devilish exercise," gives Faustus pulsing access to infernal realms: he summons Mephistopheles only to dismiss him ("I charge thee to return and change thy shape. / Thou art too ugly to attend on me. / Go, and return an old Franciscan friar; / That holy shape becomes a devil best"); he conjures Alexander to entertain the Holy Roman Emperor; at the end of play he calls the spirit of Helen to appear for his students and then, in a moment of poetic transport, for himself. In one of the play's most caustic moments, Faustus himself is accused of being part of such otherworldly commuting, when the Archbishop of Rheims suggests that the pranks being played on the Pope are the fault of "some ghost crept out of purgatory and now is come unto your Holiness for his pardon" (3.2.80–82). The Pope agrees: "It may be so. / Go then; command our priests to sing a dirge / To lay the fury of this same troublesome ghost" (3.2.83–85). Stephen Greenblatt has addressed the persistence of—as well as hostility to—the notion of purgatory in Reformation England, and Faustus's response to the exchange seems, at least on the surface, to appeal to anti-Catholic sentiment ("Must every bit be spiced with a cross?" he asks [3.2.86]).[37] But purgatory is simply a distraction, or a prelude, to Faustus's most pressing concern: when the Pope damns "his soul forever," Faustus is prepared: "Bell, book, and candle; candle, book, and bell / Forward and backward, to curse Faustus to hell!" (3.2.93–94).

Faustus's delighted embrace of hell here can certainly be read as an effect of a Calvinist commitment to his own damnation. As John Stachniewski has suggested, Marlowe's protagonist is "a passionately detailed concentration of literal contemporary experiences of subjectivity in a theological culture so repressive that it created the rebel state of mind it reprobated."[38] Such a rebel state of mind acknowledges its own affinity with hell in order to assert a spurious power which is then taken as evidence of an already determined damnation. Or, as Faustus tells Mephistopheles, "Seeing Faustus hath incurred eternal death" (1.3.85). But scenes of hell in the play are associated not only with basic predestinarian questions of agency—of who does what—but also with questions of sufficiency, of what or how much is required from whom. Mephistopheles highlights the issue of agency when he answers Faustus's question, "Did not my conjuring speeches raise thee?"

> That was the cause, but yet *per accidens,*
> For, when we hear one rack the name of God,
> Abjure the Scriptures and his Savior Christ,

We fly in hope to get his glorious soul,
Nor will we come unless he use such means
Whereby he is in danger to be damned.

(1.3.44–49)

Mephistopheles' account teeters or vacillates, as Kristin Poole has explained in a recent essay, between uncertainty and certainty about Faustus's fate ("in hope" and "in danger" suggest that nothing has been determined, while Faustus's conjuring can be taken as the effect, rather than the cause of, reprobation).[39] But Mephistopheles goes on to show himself equally concerned with *degrees* of agency, with issues of how much or how little can be done. For he measures or quantifies Faustus's relationship to hell: "Therefore, the shortest cut for conjuring / Is stoutly to abjure all godliness / And pray devoutly to the Mephistopheles' prince of hell" (1.3.51–54).

Under Mephistopheles direction, then, hell becomes the locale for Faustus to explore problems of quantification or commensuration, of determining "enoughness." C. A. Patrides has made clear that hell has long served as an imaginative space for describing or enumerating the unspeakable infinitude of punishment for sin.[40] In his survey of early depictions of hell he cites, for instance, graphic portrayals such as John Wigmore's in 1619: "if all the agonies of the spirit of man, that euer were since life was first; if all the tyrannies of humane inuention: as hot glowing ouens; fiery furnaces; chaldrons of boyling oyle; roasting vpon spits; nipping of the flesh with pincers; parting of the nayles and finger ends with needles, and the like; if all these tortures were ioyned in one, to shew their force vpon one wretched soule, yet were they all as the biting of a flea, a very nothing, in respect of hel, where God hath shewne the power of his vengeance, in preparing that infinite, endlesse, ineffable, insufferable place of torments."[41] Marlowe's play capitalizes on this tradition to underscore the relation of such calculation to the idea of *dissatisfaction,* to the idea of not being able to make or feel enough. Marlowe's hell, in other words, is the site of eternal torment, but in such a way as to reinforce its demand rather than its supply. "No mortal can express the pains of hell" (5.1.47), the Old Man reminds Faustus, echoing the source text, *The Damnable Life and Deserved Death of Doctor John Faustus* (1592): "Hell is bloodthirsty, and is never satisfied."[42]

Mephistopheles' use of numerical terms reinforces this point. He tells Faustus, for instance, that he is "tormented by *ten thousand*

hells / In being deprived of everlasting bliss" (1.3.78–79, my italics). His descriptive efforts here may be part of the emergence in
Renaissance England of what Patricia Cahill has aptly termed the
period's "new discourses of quantification and abstraction."[43] But
they also testify to hell's special role in this play as the place that
simultaneously provokes and perplexes calculation. Faustus picks
up almost immediately on this impulse when he tries to assign a
precise, if non-numeric, value to hell. "Had I as many souls as there
be stars, / I'd give them all for Mephistopheles" (1.3.100–101).
Later Faustus will provide numerical terms: "Then there's enough
for a thousand souls," he responds to Mephistopheles promises of
magical power (2.1.87). The irony here, of course, is that Faustus
can imagine enough only in the exaggerated terms of one thousand
souls; he cannot imagine *enough for one.*

The characters' numerical excess is opposed in the following
scene by the legalistic details of the demonic contract, in which
Faustus trades his soul to Lucifer for twenty-four years of "living
in all voluptuousness" (1.3.92). The duration of the contract is not
original to Marlowe, but the juxtaposition of such specificity with
surrounding moments of computational plenitude serves as a
shocking reminder of the way the play wavers between the necessity and superfluity. According to the contract, hell is the precise
return on the exchange of a single soul for a comprehensible period
of years. But the specificity and comprehensibility of twenty-four
is belied by hell's temporal vastness, which Faustus will recognize
at the close of the play: "then thou must be damned perpetually,"
he acknowledges (5.2.52). The Bad Angel describes this vastness
with particular force:

> Now, Faustus, let thine eyes with horror stare
> Into that vast perpetual torture house.
> There are the Furies tossing damned souls
> On burning forks. Their bodies boil in lead.
> There are live quarters broiling on the coals,
> That ne'er can die. . . .
> . . . .
> But yet all these are nothing. Thou shal see
> Ten thousand tortures that more horrid be.
>
> (5.2.116–27)

Between the poles of the definite and infinite, the Bad Angel singles out a space of exorbitant numeracy: the "ten thousand tor-

tures" with which he threatens Faustus. Faustus himself repeats this kind of thinking at the close of the play, when, in the very throes of death, he continues to bargain for his soul:

> O, if my soul must suffer for my sin
> Impose some end to my incessant pain.
> Let Faustus live in hell a thousand years,
> A hundred thousand, and at last be saved.
>
> (5.3.161–65)

Faustus here comes close to transforming hell into purgatory, where souls, according to Catholic doctrine, were cleansed by suffering and from which they were eventually released. But Faustus's focus remains rooted in hell, which has for the duration of the play served both to represent and to stage his ongoing dilemma of measuring or experiencing what is enough. This is the hell of the descent debates, the hell where Christ's sufficiency is obsessively calculated and measured. This is the hell that Faustus confounds in Elysium, if we read confound not, according to a number of recent editions, as "confusing" or "failing to distinguish between," but rather according to the first OED entry for the term: "To defeat utterly, discomfit, bring to ruin, destroy, overthrow, rout, bring to nought." In Faustus's very first interview with Mephistopheles, in other words, he fashions himself as the conqueror of hell. Such triumphalism, marked by the replacement of hell with the pagan underworld, will fade by the play's close.

Competing Protestant theologies all shared a belief that no amount of human anguish could ever be enough to satisfy divine justice for sin. Faustus's tormented experience of despair, doubt, and manic exhilaration record the human toll of such a theology of insufficiency. But they also gesture to a Christological toll, a toll documented in the sixteenth-century controversy over the descent to hell. The terms of the debate demonstrate that the problem of computing expiatory penalties was pushed back onto the Savior himself, leaving Christ's own sufficiency in question. That question is the final one to haunt Faustus. Throughout the play he has made ineffectual turns to Christ, the most ghoulish of which is his repetition of "*Consummatum est*" when he signs the demonic contract. These efforts culminate in his despairing final moments, when he looks heavenward to: "See, see where Christ's blood streams in the firmament! / One drop would save my soul, half a drop. Ah, my

Christ!" (5.2.74–75, A-text). One drop or half a drop? Faustus' computational hesitancy has often been seen as yet another indication
of his religious failure. But as an attempt to calculate what is necessary not for him but for Christ, Faustus's desperate appeal actually
repeats contemporary debates about Christ's relation to hell, and
thus about what precisely was required of, and what was superfluous for, Christ's satisfaction for human sin. Unlike the rhetoric of
the theologians from either side of the debate, Faustus dies not
being sure.

Notes

1. Adam Hill, *Defence of the Article: Christ Descended into Hell* (London,
1592), A3.
2. Peter Milward, *Religious Controversies of the Elizabethan Age* (Lincoln:
University of Nebraska Press, 1977), 163–68. For a comprehensive discussion of
the controversy, see Dewey D. Wallace, Jr., "Puritan and Anglican: The Interpretation of Christ's Descent into Hell in Elizabethan Theology." *Archiv fur Reforma-
tiongeschichte* 69 (1978): 248–87.
3. See H. C. Porter, *Reformation and Reaction in Tudor Cambridge* (Cambridge: Cambridge University Press, 1958), 277–390, esp. 364–75; Peter White,
Predestination, Policy and Polemic: Conflict and Consensus in the English Church
(Cambridge: Cambridge University Press, 1992), 101–23.
4. *The Book of Concord; The Confessions of the Evangelical Lutheran Church,*
trans. and ed. Theodore G. Tappert (Philadelphia: Mühlenberg Press, 1959), 492.
5. John Calvin, *Institutes of the Christian Religion,* trans. Ford Lewis Battles
(Philadelphia: Westminster Press, 1960), 1:515–16.
6. Ibid., 517–18.
7. Debora Kuller Shuger, *The Renaissance Bible: Scholarship, Sacrifice, Subjectivity* (Berkeley: University of California Press, 1994), 5.
8. Carlisle, *A Discourse Concerning Two Diuine Positions* (London, 1582),
O7–7v.
9. Ibid., N5v–N6.
10. John Northbrooke, *Spiritus est vicarious Christi in terra* (London, 1571),
B4v, A3.
11. Ibid., Eiv.
12. Ibid., B4v.
13. D. P. Walker, *The Decline of Hell* (Chicago: University of Chicago Press,
1963), 29.
14. Hill, *Defence of the Article,* Aiiiv.
15. John Foxe, *A Sermon of Christ Crucified* (London, 1570), Fii.
16. Ibid., Eiiiv.
17. Hill, *Defence of the Article,* Giv.
18. Ibid., B2.
19. Ibid., B4v.
20. Ibid., C3v.

21. Ibid., B2, emphasis mine.

22. Ibid., C4v.

23. Thomas Bilson, *The Effect of Certaine Sermons Tovching the Full Redemption of Mankind by the Death and Bloud of Christ Jesus* (London, 1599), A2.

24. Ibid., B1.

25. Ibid., H1v.

26. Ibid., A2.

27. Henry Jacob, *A Treatise of the Sufferings and Victory of Christ, in the Work of Our Redemption* (London, 1598), A8, B4.

28. Ibid., C1.

29. William Perkins, *Exposition of the Symbole or Creed of the Apostles* (Cambridge, 1595), 301.

30. Ibid., 302. His nearly cheerful treatment of the issue as indifferent, as *adiaphora*, sounds methodologically close to Erasmus in the early sixteenth century, who, while uncertain as to the apostolic validity of the doctrine, diplomatically accepted the literal descent, telling his catechumen to treat the notion as a matter of "pious human reflections" rather than an article of faith. The substance of Erasmus's position was opposed, however, to Perkins, as Erasmus rejected the idea that Christ suffered in his soul. See Erasmus, *Explanatio Symboli Apostolorum*, trans. Louis A. Perraud, in *Collected Works of Erasmus*, ed. John W. O'Malley (Toronto: University of Toronto Press, 1998), 70:309.

31. Alexander Hume, *A Reioynder to Doctor Hil Concerning the Descense of Christ into Hell* (Edinburgh, 1594), B8v.

32. Perkins, *Exposition,* 176.

33. Christopher Marlowe, *Doctor Faustus,* ed. David Scott Kastan (New York: Norton, 2005), 2.1.17. All quotations are taken from the B-text unless otherwise specified.

34. Harry Levin, *The Overreacher, A Study of Christopher* Marlowe (Cambridge, MA: Harvard University Press, 1952), 110.

35. William Kerrigan, "*Macbeth* and the History of Ambition," in *Freud and the Passions* (University Park: Pennsylvania State University Press, 1996), 17.

36. Una Ellis-Fermor, "Faustus," in *Christopher Marlowe's Dr. Faustus: Text and Major Criticism,* ed. Irving Ribner (New York: Odyssey Press, 1966), 64.

37. Stephen Greenblatt, *Hamlet in Purgatory* (Princeton: Princeton University Press, 2001), esp. 10–102.

38. John Stachniewski, *The Persecutory Imagination: English Puritanism and the Literature of Religious Despair* (Oxford: Clarendon Press, 1991), 10.

39. Kristin Poole, "Doctor Faustus and Reformation Theology," in *Early Modern English Drama,* ed. Patrick Cheney, Andrew Hadfield, and Garrett Sullivan (New York: Oxford University Press, 2006).

40. C. A. Patrides, "Renaissance and Modern Views on Hell," *The Harvard Theological Review* 57 (1964): 217–36.

41. Ibid., 219.

42. *Christopher Marlowe: The Plays and Their Sources,* ed. Vivien Thomas and William Tydeman (New York: Routledge, 1994), 202.

43. Patricia Cahill, "Killing by Computation: Military Mathematics, the Social Body, and Marlowe's *Tamburlaine,*" in *The Arts of Calculation,* ed. David Glimp and Michelle Warren (London: Palgrave, 2004), 168.

"O for a muse of fire":
Henry V and Plotted Self-Exculpation

BRADLEY GREENBURG

> Whether this was true that so he spake, as one that gaue too
> much credit to foolish prophesies & vaine tails, or whether it was
> fained, as in such cases it commonlie happeneth, we leaue it to
> the aduised reader to iudge.

> But yet to speake a truth, by his proceedings, after he had at-
> teined to the crowne, what with such taxes, tallages, subsidies
> and exactions as he was constreined to charge the people with;
> and what by punishing such as mooued with disdeine to see him
> usurpe the crowne (contrarie to the oth taken at his entring into
> this land, upon his return from exile) did at sundrie times rebell
> against him, he wan himself more hatred, than in all his life time
> (if it had beene longer by manie years than it was) had beene pos-
> sible for him to haue weeded out & remooued.[1]

I

THE FIRST SCENE of *Henry V* presents us with a king who has set his own plots and plans, the most important feature of which is to shelter himself from responsibility. This sheltering is motivated by his desire to escape the effects of guilt, the shadow of blame or responsibility that would or might result from an action taken unsuccessfully.[2] The etiology of personal rule (the man may feel compelled to play at being king based on his personal experience) and structural rule (the man plays the king in the manner he sees as proper to a ruler) divide the possibilities of action between the king's two bodies. In Henry V's case, these two bodies are formed in the two preceding plays of the tetralogy through the constant tension between the prodigal Hal and the plotting Hal. *Henry V* yokes these two bodies together in the opening scene, but in this resolution of tension there is a crucial latent content that is key to understanding the new king, here and later: his "changed man" status is a fantasy or charade that allows Hal to displace threats to himself onto other, larger causes. Along the play's entire length Henry V counters every event that contains a potential setback or threat to his becoming "the mirrour of all Christian kings." In other words, the success of the play as a presentation of the paragon of kingship (legitimate, unifying, empire-building, and heroic, not to mention charming and eloquent) rides on Henry's ability to deflect and thereby control or manage all conflicts and challenges. The play does this by producing Henry not only as a product of the internal logic of the Henriad, but also as a function of the play's relationship to chronicle history.

My methodological schema for analyzing what I call Henry's strategy of plotted self-exculpation will make use of Harry Berger Jr.'s own exploration of the Henriad in *Making Trifles of Terrors,* where he adapts Stanley Cavell's concepts of guilt and shame. According to Cavell, "shame is the specific discomfort produced by the sense of being looked at, the avoidance of the sight of others is the reflex it produces. Guilt is different; there the reflex is to avoid discovery. As long as no one *knows* what you have done, you are safe; or your conscience will press you to confess it and accept punishment. Under shame, what must be covered up is not your deed, but yourself."[3] Cavell's work also led Berger to read Shakespeare's plays using what he calls "discourse networks," or, more specifically, ethical discourses, as a way of avoiding the so-called "epigenetic fallacy," that is, the fallacy of conducting an analysis of literary characters as if they were real people. The ethical discourses that characters deploy in their speeches or, we might say (borrowing from Wittgenstein) the language games they play are, to name the most important: those of the sinner, victim/revenger, villain, donor, saint, and hero/honor seeker.[4] When, for example, a character is describing his or her motives for behaving like a sinner, these motives are drawn from social and cultural discourses that enable such description and thus the particular role the character is assuming: the discourses comprise the world of a play. A character may take up a discourse as a way of explaining desire, in order to avoid anxiety or fear, as a means to achieve power or avoid having to wield it, and so on. Fundamentally, what this way of conceptualizing characters gets us is a method that avoids endowing characters with that nature or subjectivity they claim for themselves. It's not simply that they don't have an inside until the play hollows it out as the effect of their speech. Without the matrix of discourse formed by spoken interactions among the figures on stage, character cannot emerge at all, much less grow in complexity.

To uncover the larger discourse networks of the community of the play, we must attend to three things: the dramatic character's etiology as available in his/her speech (what motivations, emotions, habits of thought, familial/social/cultural roles, likes and dislikes, prejudices, calculations, etc. does the character pretend to assume and why?); the actions a character takes (if a king, how does he rule? if a daughter, how does she acquiesce to or resist the patriarchal discourse that envelops her?); and finally, how the structure of the drama configures such characters in relation to what we might call "outside forces," even if these are only sources (such as chronicles and other dramas). For present purposes I will apply the first two in a reading of the opening scene of *Henry V* and then triangulate this reading, rendering it more three-dimensional by adding the perspective of the play's source material.

II

In at least four pivotal scenes in *Henry V,* the play presents a king who performs a strategy of plotted self-exculpation. By this I mean that he contrives to shift responsibility to others at critical times of decision making without their being aware that this is happening. These moments—establishing claims to French territory and possibly the French throne by manipulating the Church and the insult from the Dauphin; intervening in a conspiracy of nobles who have been lured by Henry's letters of commission; threatening the Governor of Harfleur with responsibility for the rape and murder of his people if he does not capitulate; and debating the issue of loyalty the night before Agincourt (Henry: "The King is not bound to answer the particular endings of his soldiers . . .")—comprise a conspicuous habit of avoidance or, alternatively, a proactive, confrontational response to the exigencies of kingship.

As inner conditions are displaced to outer circumstances, a strategy emerges that marks the trajectory of Henry's successful rule (what in other contexts Linda Charnes calls "notorious identity").[5] The mirror of all Christian kings is not only a product of his "famous victories;"[6] he is also a product of a guilt-management strategy that incurs shame to assuage guilt. The origin of this guilt is the

Lancastrian legitimacy issue that has not disappeared with the death of Henry IV. Hal is still identified with this stain, although as Prince of Wales he has demonstrated no interest in dealing with the issue of shame. Only when he becomes king does he conspicuously attend to the causes of the "shameful" nature of the Lancastrian dynasty as evidenced by his ostentatious reburial of Richard and his building of chantries. But Henry's most important strategic shift in dealing with this legacy of guilt is to exculpate himself as king, initially by enacting a version of the saint's discourse, and then by using it to initiate the hero's discourse.[7]

At the outset, Henry V moves publicly out from under the shadow of usurpation by portraying himself as the symbol for English victimhood at the hands of the French, upon whom he will exact the revenge of empire retrieval. This discourse, however, will not of itself prove adequate to the current challenge. If the dramaturgical crux in this play is to present Henry's character as a product of the preceding plays of the Henriad with the additional imperative of raising his stature to that of Ideal English King, then it will be necessary to muster discourses other than simply those of the saint and the victim. The advantage of the saint's discourse is that it responds to a persistent question that Henry raises—"May I with right and conscience make this claim?"—and as Berger points out, this issue is "in its most significant manifestation pursued with increasing fervor through three plays by the son of Henry IV." But Berger goes on to say that the saint's discourse

> sometimes overlaps with another discourse, the hero's discourse, or discourse of honor. The saint's discourse involves a story one tells oneself . . . and one tells it to or solicits it from others primarily to persuade oneself, especially if one suspects that what one is doing may be reprehensible. But the hero's discourse involves a story one has to elicit and hear from others, a story that, like a prize, one has to win or earn by continuous displays or promises of a form of activity that in recent decades has come to be known as "laying one's body on the line." Now since this is not something that one can ask one's poor body to spend all of its time doing, there are long periods of foreplay and afterplay during which honor is maintained by words rather than deeds, or by words *as* deeds.[8]

Henry's shuttling between the discourses of saint and hero in *Henry V,* a play enacted in the shadow of *1 and 2 Henry IV* where he performs the sinner/villain's discourse as a ruse or rehearsal, establishes what will become his characteristic mode of behavior. The key features of this behavior are its plotting (its always already-plottedness), and its self-exculpation; what the play is able to produce as an effect of this behavior is a king whose fame unfolds before our eyes proleptically in anticipation of the very history the play is writing. Or, to put it another way, the main character of *Henry V* has a twofold nature: on one hand, he is the product of his *gesta,* a famous king whose exploits are foreknown; at the same time, he is a dramatic figure who constructs these exploits with the knowing anticipation of their ends and means. Yeats was right, I think, to call Henry a "ripened Fortinbras," chief figure in a play that strong-arms Henry's contemplative, weak precursors and their deeds out of the way in order to position himself as a new hero, albeit a spotted one.[9]

The tension between the saint's discourse (the story one tells oneself in order to persuade oneself of rightness/righteousness) and the hero's discourse (the story one elicits from others to support honor or honor-seeking actions) is evident in the play's representative opening scene where the hero's discourse mocks that of the saint by displaying the latter as a false, though attractive, version of Henry's character. As Berger suggests, the hero's discourse works most effectively if provoked by the saint's discourse, and the plot laid at the opening of the play demonstrates Henry's masterful deployment of this relationship. His solicitation of the proper response to his query about war functions so as to shift attention to outer circumstances, busying as it will giddy minds with value-producing foreign quarrels. This ploy is alluring because saintly (a false sense of needing to be persuaded leads those around him to leap into the breach to cooperate in the venture), but it also operates so as to open up a space for heroic discourse. The dramatic brilliance and utility of Henry's ploy is that he does not need to participate in the plots he sets in motion; the discursive game he plays works by enticing other characters to take up complementary positions to his desire. The difference in the game set in motion here as compared to the first three plays of the Henriad is clear: whereas earlier practices of kingship avoided the active enlistment of court, Church, and citizenry in favor of invoking Divine Right (Richard II) or *lex talionis* (Henry IV), Henry V begins his reign even before he inherits the crown by eliciting the kind of doubt and wonder that renders the saint's discourse as a powerful tool with which to launch the hero's discourse and the history that will record his exploits as heroic.[10] In other words, the opening gambit of the play conceptualizes a process in which Shakespeare's reading of historical source material is transformed into a dialectic of playing-out (the naturalism of a history play) and playing-with, reflecting historical narrative and reflecting on it.[11] By the opening Chorus of act 2, "the youth of England [are] on fire . . . and honour's thought / Reigns solely in the breast of every man. / They sell the pasture now to buy the horse, / Following the mirrour of all Christian kings. . . ." As Shakespeare constructs him, Henry V is a two-way mirror of all Christian kings—the saint one sees through a glass darkly, and the hero reflected back from the glass, arrayed in honor.

Henry V opens with the Archbishop of Canterbury and the Bishop of Ely in close conversation regarding a bill of disendowment that is related to a previous bill the Church barely succeeded in neutralizing. Its consequences are grim for the prelates and for the Church's material interests generally. In answer to Ely's "But what prevention?" Canterbury responds with a gnomic, "The King is full of grace and fair regard" (1.1.22–23). The bishops next engage in a kind of mild hagiography of Henry that describes him as transformed, body and spirit, into the perfect man/king. While Ely's comment that the King is "crescive in his faculty" admits, slyly, that growth is a more natural explanation than miraculousness, it is the latter that carries the greater weight. This is symptomatic of the bishops' discursive mode: miraculousness suggests that the more mundane process involved in the Prince of Wales's training and education, his coming to maturity over time in a particular context, will be suppressed in favor of the notion of dramatic incipience, a useful rhetoric in the rationalizing of policies. At this early point in the play we are led to think that the bishops have their man, a king vulnerable to manipulation by religious figures with wealth, power, and righteousness at their disposal. Like other scenes plotted to ensure the King's self-exculpation, 1.1 features older characters who are themselves deeply involved in whatever intrigue is at hand and who display concern about Henry's ability and/or willingness to exert control over the emerging situation. What is always carefully constructed in this and later scenes is this sense of a plot unfolding in the moment, a dramatic strategy that initially withholds the fact that Henry has always already outplanned and outplotted everyone. Further, he has done so in a manner that shifts responsibility while demonstrating his mastery of political tactics.

Once Henry's bona fides have been established, the question of whether the King supports the Church or Commons as regards the bill is answered by Canterbury: "He seems indifferent, / Or rather swaying more upon our part" (1.1.73–74). Canterbury admits to tilting the balance by giving the greatest sum in church history for Henry's campaign in France. Ely then asks after the King's response.

> *Ely:* How did this offer seem received, my lord?
> *Canterbury:* With good acceptance of his majesty,
>   Save that there was not time enough to hear,
>   As I perceived his grace would fain have done,
>   The severals and unhidden passages
>   Of his true titles to some certain dukedoms,
>   And generally to the crown and seat of France,
>   Deriv'd from Edward, his great-grandfather.
> *Ely:* What was th'impediment that broke this off?
> *Canterbury:* The French ambassador upon that instant
>   Craved audience—and the hour I think is come
>   To give him hearing. Is it four o'clock?
> *Ely:* It is.
> *Canterbury:* Then go we in, to know his embassy—
>   Which I could with ready guess declare
>   Before the Frenchman speak a word of it.
> *Ely:* I'll wait upon you, and I long to hear it.
>
> (1.1.83–99)

Thus it is established that the Archbishop and the King have met and agreed to a plan in which the Church will provide funds for the war in exchange for Henry's help in staving off disendowment. Canterbury and Ely now proceed to the court in anticipation of hearing what the ambassador has to say.

Although Canterbury has told Ely that his interview with the King was cut short by the need to admit the French ambassador, we find out as 1.2 opens that this has not happened.

> *King Harry:* Where is my gracious lord of Canterbury?
> *Exeter:*   Not here in presence.
> *King Harry:*   Send for him, good uncle.
> *Westmoreland:*   Shall we call in th'ambassador, my liege?
> *King Harry:* Not yet, my cousin. We would be resolved,
>   Before we hear him, of some things of weight
>   That task our thoughts, concerning us and France.
>
> (1.2.1–6)

If we stop to think about it, we realize that the ambassador has been kept waiting while the first scene unfolds—that in the play's temporal space, 1.1 is acted while Henry and the courtiers are suspended between Canterbury's dismissal due to the French ambassador's craving audience and the time designated for this audience (four o'clock). There is no indication at this point as to what the French ambassador is doing at the court, though Canterbury's "I could with a ready guess declare / Before the Frenchman speak a word of it," suggests that there are machinations in that direction as well. What is withheld in 1.1 and then revealed in 1.2 is that Henry has laid his plots with the Church and with France in order to display a strategy of conspicuous exculpation.

Act 1, scene 2 opens abruptly with a confusion about who will be called in to the King's presence. Henry's opening lines suggest a king who is burdened, his thoughts tasked with a weight that renders him paralyzed by inward reckonings, reminding us of his father's wearied, continuous postponement of crusading. The discursive game afoot at this point allows Henry to provoke those present to supply him in his saintly persona with a narrative supporting his political objectives. In view of the court, Henry will feign nonchalance, then mild hesitation at the Archbishop's authorizing of his French claims in the wake of their earlier agreement about the disendowment bill: the court will then rouse him to take actions he has already clearly planned.[12] After eliciting legitimating stories as warrants for acting, Henry's responses to the Archbishop's articulation of the Salic law and to the Dauphin's mocking gift of tennis balls unfurl the banner of the hero's discourse:

> And God forbid, my dear and faithful lord,
> That you should fashion, wrest, or bow your reading,
> Or nicely charge your understanding soul
> With opening titles miscreate, whose right
> Suits not in native colours with the truth;
> For God doth know how many now in health
> Shall drop their blood in approbation
> Of what your reverence shall incite us to.
>
> (1.2.13–20)

> And tell the pleasant Prince this mock of his
> Hath turned his balls to gunstones, and his soul
> Shall stand sore charged for the wasteful vengeance

That shall fly from them—for many a thousand widows
Shall this his mock mock out of their dear husbands,
Mock mothers from their sons, mock castles down;
Ay, some are yet ungotten and unborn
That shall have cause to curse the Dauphin's scorn.
But this lies all within the will of God,
To whom I do appeal, and in whose name . . .

(1.2.281–90)

To borrow a word from Henry, it is indeed a "conjuration" to manipulate the Archbishop and ambassador into providing a legitimating justification that allows him to shift responsibility for a
heroic course from himself to others, and to simultaneously insu-
late himself from failure.

The rhetorical force of Henry's invitation to the Archbishop to
interpret the Salic law comes from his success in sounding the
drum of humility over and over again: "God forbid, my dear and
faithful lord, / That you should fashion, wrest, or bow your
reading, / Or nicely charge your understanding soul / With opening
titles miscreate, whose right / Suits not in native colours with the
truth. . . ." It is useless to call this irony. Instead we should attend
to the latencies of the scene, specifically, Henry's already revealed
strategy of conspiring with the Church while appearing cautious
and diffident to the court. The call to arms is, he suggests, the
Church's responsibility, because he can only be "incited," "im-
pawned," his sleeping sword of war "awakened." Henry's passivity
here plays the saint's discourse to elicit the kind of support that
would endow his decision with a just inevitability; as only a pawn,
Henry shelters his kingship and himself from error, and by so doing
breaks the inherited chain of association between illegitimacy, rebellion, and deposition. Canterbury's response many lines later,
"The sin upon my head, dread sovereign" (1.2.97), is a pure expression of the discursive network that begins to construct Henry as in-
fallible. After the Archbishop's rousing speech, invoking the Black
Prince and the glory of past battles against the French, the enthusiasm for the venture catches fire and Ely, Exeter, Westmoreland, and
even "A Lord" deliver speeches urging the King on. Henry has
moved the court and clergy to agree passionately and publicly to a
course that he has himself conspicuously avoided making a case
for. His acquiescence is delayed further by his calling in of the
French ambassador.

The waiting time for the ambassador occupies a space of a dozen lines that is filled with a speech by Henry; this speech provides a transition between a hotly forged court/Church/monarchical unity of purpose and the enactment of this purpose. If the fuse has been carefully primed, it waits only to be lit. Of course, the French are about to oblige with their customary arrogance, but even as the patriotic theme—articulated in the opening speech of the Chorus in act 2 ("Now all the youth of England are on fire . . .")—unfolds, we can see how the play works to shape Henry as both the skillful political actor and the properly famous subject of history. "France," Henry says to those assembled awaiting the ambassador, "being ours we'll bend it to our awe, / Or break it all to pieces" (1.2.224). Awe is the fulfillment of Hal's prodigality, announced long ago in the corresponding scene of *1 Henry IV:* to be wondered at carries stronger force and potential than being known, and it must be supported by a particular discursive strategy. Henry continues in the same vein:

> Or there we'll sit,
> Ruling in large and ample empery
> O'er France and all her almost kingly dukedoms,
> Or lay these bones in an unworthy urn,
> Tombless, with no remembrance over them.
> Either our history shall with full mouth
> Speak freely of our acts, or else our grave,
> Like Turkish mute, shall have a tongueless mouth,
> Not worshipped with a waxen epitaph.

With this speech, which bridges a demonstration of national (or at least aristocratic and clerical) unity and the forthcoming French provocation, the play provides its already famous king with anxiety about how heroic fame is registered. This is a speech about historiography, and its figurative language constructs a proper metaphorics of risk. As Henry crosses the channel and engages the French, he will mouth over and over to his followers, and with more and more bravado, the daring implicit in the hero's discourse, the need for a leap of faith by those who join the cause. But here the anxiety is over an "unworthy urn," or to be "tombless," images that peak in the image of anonymity, if there is "no remembrance over [these bones]." The either/or that follows, success or failure, is wagered not with broken bodies, lost titles, lands, the spoil of war, but with historical memory; either Henry will earn the "full mouth" of inscribed history or a grave with a "tongueless mouth," "like Turkish mute"—silenced, castrated, his power to effect posterity cut off. The final line is pointed with the fear of lacking even the worship of a "waxen epitaph," calling attention not only to the ephemeral monument implied in "unworthy urn," since a wax tombstone or marker will not last, but especially to the transitory nature of the epitaph itself, the *words* that inscribe *deeds.* Berger's definition of the hero's discourse allows us to hear Henry's speech as the discursive game it is: the honor seeker cannot rely on deeds alone but must carefully manage words so that they prepare the appropriate memorial space in which the deeds may become inscribed.[13]

It is with the entrance of the French ambassador that Henry V begins to enact the kind of discursive strategy of emplotment, self-exculpation, *and* awe-inspiring speech making that we have anticipated since 1.2 of *1 Henry IV,* and expected from the moment Henry warned the Archbishop to "Take heed how you impawn our person, / How you awake our sleeping sword of war." Since this moment when sleeping dogs were not let lie (were, in fact, only pretending to sleep), we have awaited this famous king's cry of havoc. The unleashing occurs as Henry's other strategy, establishing his claim to "certain dukedoms," has already succeeded. The drama of the buildup for the invasion of France is heightened not by King Charles's denial of Henry's claim, which is not what the ambassador offers, but by the exchange with the Dauphin that cuts straight to the heart of the new King of England's character. The Dauphin's King Henry is Prince Hal dressed in unearned finery, more interested in dancing and drinking than in politics. The ambassador's words and, especially, the gift of a tun of tennis balls, offer the assembled English courtiers a version of their king as without balls, or without having the right idea about what balls are for (play instead of virile action). One cannot imagine a character such as Hotspur, so imbued with the hero's discourse, being sent such a mockery; only a character who has passed through other, less overtly masculine (because anxiety-ridden) discourses such as the sinner and saint, can be thus misunderstood. This part of the scene, which closes the first act, demonstrates Henry's emergence into full discursive heroism.

His strategy is to manipulate the Dauphin's challenge so as to undergird his heroic agenda while at the same time ensuring self-exculpation. Henry's response to the ambassador's hesitant query as to whether he may "freely . . . render what we have in charge" opposes his kingship to that governing the "Turkish mute," the castrated and tongueless functionary of his earlier speech: "We are no tyrant, but a Christian king, / Unto whose grace our passion is as subject / As is our wretches fettered in our prisons." This declaration invokes his previously wayward passions (prodigal, careless) with a marked difference. His ruse of Eastcheap folly is transformed into calculation, put at the disposal of any listener who finds it chilling that they may never have known this man. If when his passion was thought to be unfettered it was instead the strategic grace of emplotment, those who assumed his character to be defined by the miraculous are forced to rethink their judgment of him, which in turn endows him with a greater kingly potential. And herein lies an important element of the hero's discourse: it not only seeks honor through the support of others, but retrospectively bestows credit on those involved in making the hero. If the ambassador is chilled by this seemingly offhand, less-than-ameliorative comment, the court will smile wryly at the idea that the subjection of the King's passion to his grace also renders such passion as equivalent to an imprisoned, fettered wretch. What might this Christian king do, we wonder, if his passion were unfettered? The Dauphin's embassy refers only to a mocking catalog of Hal's profligacy ("you savour too much your youth," "there's naught in France / That can be with a nimble galliard won: / You cannot revel into dukedoms there"). Henry's answer, justly famous for its force and tone, asserts the seriousness of a king with balls who warns a mere boy that he has provoked the wrong person at the wrong game at the wrong time. As with his response to the Archbishop, Henry is again careful to make the Dauphin's blunder an opportunity to exculpate himself from any guilt in prosecuting a war with France. In returning to his theme of historical remembrance, chronicles of deaths foretold, mouths tongued with anguish and memory, he shifts responsibility to his adversary: "Ay, some are yet ungotten and unborn / That shall have cause to curse the Dauphin's scorn."

In sum, Henry's discourse as king deploys a different kind of game than the one that suited his purpose as Prince of Wales. His earlier displacement of the anxiety over Lancastrian legitimacy is now something he must actively deal with. He does so by first taking up what Berger calls the discourse of shame ("under shame, what must not be covered up is your act"), using it as a means of appropriating the hero's discourse. If at one time Hal covered up his acts by pretending to be bad, he reveals himself as a king not by "really" being good, but by ceasing the pretense of prodigality—by not covering up, but revealing, his acts. However, this description must immediately be qualified: as king, Henry reveals his acts *without* revealing his aim to avoid responsibility. That Henry is at the end of act 1 embracing shame as a mode of revelation is demonstrated by his response to Exeter's "This was a merry message." "We hope," Henry replies, "to make the sender blush at it": whereas we typically think of shame as causing a blush in the one who incurs it, Henry's staging of shame shifts guilt as responsibility to the French. Thus the catch or hitch in this discourse of shame is that it is used in the service of a fame-begetting, heroic process. In act 1, Henry has already plotted the story he elicits from others to ensure his fame; or, to state this principle more precisely, the text of the play employs a discourse is which Henry as King is animated first by the discourse of shame and then by the discourse of a hero, a shift that ensures a dramaturgical move from prodigal to warrior king.

From another vantage point, one might say that the first act of the play offers a careful and concentrated retelling of the change undergone by Hal in the *Henry IV* plays. There, the goal of Hal's change was to produce a worthy heir to the throne. In *Henry V,* this heir quickly and efficiently exceeds his father's accomplishments, and does so by plotting his way to successful ends that are foreordained. Henry's final speech in act 1 deploys fully the hero's discourse, seeking honor in response to the Dauphin's breech of decorum with the kind of masculine, martial rhetoric sure to strike the ears of those assembled.[14]

III

Thus far I have tried to demonstrate that Shakespeare created Hal/Henry V not as a "natural" hero without cunning but rather as a character who succeeds because of his strategizing and plotting. I would like to extend this reading of the Henriad with a consideration of the chronicle sources for the plays in an attempt to identify the kind of charismatic spark, the characterological quirk, that Shakespeare might have used to shape such a character. What is notable initially is that the Henry of Holinshed and Hall is far less aggressive than that of Shakespeare, a difference that can be seen from the outset of *Henry V* in Shakespeare's handling of the disendowment issue.

In introducing this issue through the Archbishop of Canterbury during 1.1, Shakespeare follows Holinshed. Canterbury remarks that the current worrisome disendowment bill is a repetition of an earlier bill—a reference to the famous disendowment bill of 1410 that detailed the benefits to secular authorities of confiscating the Church's temporal holdings.[15] In Holinshed, mention of the 1410 bill begins the account of the year 1414, and is followed by details of the Leicester Parliament called by Henry at the end of April. Holinshed writes that at this Parliament, "manie profitable lawes were concluded, and manie petitions mooued," which had been deferred until that time.[16] He then adds that "Amongst which, one was, that a bill exhibited in the parlement holden at Westminster in the eleuenth year of king Henrie the fourth (which by reason the king was then troubled with ciuill discord, came to none effect) might now with good deliberation be pondered, and brought to some good conclusion."[17] Details of the bill follow, underscoring its radical transferal of temporalities from the Church to civil authority. This disendowment bill, as did those before it, sought to transfer the considerable wealth of the Church's temporal holdings to the king's coffers, thereby enabling him to pursue policies that would strengthen the realm. The Commons pursued, at least publicly, a strategy that might be called "nationalist," taking care to avoid making any sweeping anticlerical pronouncements. The success of the disendowment would take the pressure off the Commons, since they could for the foreseeable future avoid the taxation for which the monarchy constantly claimed need. As the Church and Parliament were the two main sources of Crown revenue, and since the Lancastrian dynasty had so far spent much effort and resources putting down rebellion and was now making overtures and preparations for war or potential war with France, the jockeying for position between the parties grew even more acute.

In Holinshed, the clerical establishment, rightfully fearful of its loss of power if disendowed, was the aggressor in taking action against the bill: "This bill was much noted, and more feared among the religious sort, whom suerlie it touched verie neere, and therefore to find remedie against it, they determined to assaie all waies to put by and overthrow this bill: wherein they thought best to trie if they might mooue the kings mood with some sharpe inuention, that he should not regard the importunate petitions of the commons."[18] Enter Henry Chichele, Archbishop of Canterbury, who in Parliament "made a pithie oration, wherein he declared, how not

onlie the duchies of Normandie and Aquitaine, with the counties
of Aniou and Maine, and the countrie of Gascoigne, were by vn-
doubted title apperteining to the king, as to the lawfull and onelie
heire of the same; but also the whole realme of France, as heire to
his great grandfather king Edward the third."[19] Chichele then did
"much inuei" against the Salic law as a curb to Henry's claims on
French territories and titles. Once the archbishop had "said sufficientlie for the proofe of the kings iust and lawfull title to the
crowne of France, he exhorted him to aduance foorth his banner to
fight for his right," adding that to help in this the Church had
agreed in Convocation to grant to his highness "such a summe of
monie, as neuer by no spirituall persons was to any prince before
those daies giuen or aduanced."[20] Following these details, familiar
to any reader of *Henry V,* are lengthy descriptions of political em-
bassies and exchanges back and forth prior to anything like the
swift call to arms that characterizes Shakespeare's play. What I
want to call attention to here is the way the playwright has anticipated these political moves by creating a character who plots them
before they can be deployed against him as "sharp inventions."
Shakespeare's Henry V is not a figure borne along by the wave of
historical circumstance but rather an active participant whose an-
ticipatory moves make him not just an astute ruler, since the astute
ruler may shrewdly wait and bide his time, but rather an active
agent of his own becoming, energized by the prospect that such a
becoming is a "famous" one.

Further, the prelates in Hall's *The Union of the Two Noble and
Illustre Famelies of Lancaster and Yorke. . . .* are even more aggressive than those in Holinshed's more historiographically neutral
version of the 1414 initiatives.[21] Hall's description characterizes
the representatives of the Church in terms that leave little doubt
about how we ought to interpret their motives: "This before re-
membred bill was muche noted and feared amongst the religious
sort whom in effect it muche touched, insomuche that the fat Ab-
botes swet, the proude Priors frouned, the poore Friers curssed the
sely Nonnes wept, and al together wer nothyng pleased nor yet content. Now to finde a remedy for a mischief and a tent to stop a
wounde, the Clergy myndyng rather to bowe then breake, agreed to
offre to the kyng a greate some of money to staye this newe moued
demaund."[22] Hall notes that some in the Church were for and some
were against the offer, the latter worrying that if this strategy were
known, the Commons would accuse them of being "curruptours of

Princes and enemies of the publique wealthe." Finally, "they determined to cast all chaunces whiche mighte serue their purpose, & in
especiall to replenishe the kynges brayne with some pleasante
study that he should nether phantasy nor regard the serious peti-
cion of the importunate commons."[23] Thus the major chronicle
sources at Shakespeare's disposal clearly offer an angling church,
intent on keeping its material possessions intact, and a king content
to let fortune favor him. Little intervention on the part of the king
is needed in these circumstances. But as the final movement of the
complex work of the Henriad, the Holinshed/Hall versions of the
disendowment issue would not do; the playwright had already
constructed a character whose plotting nature was apparent early
on. If legend has often tagged such a character with the apothegm
"fortune favors the brave," Shakespeare stubbornly transformed
this to "fortune favors the planner."

But Shakespeare's sleight of hand in positioning Henry vis-à-vis
the disendowment issue in 1414 raises other questions about the
Henriad's relationship to the chronicle materials. Why would
Henry V, opening as it does at the advent of Henry's reign, pick up
Holinshed's reference to an event three years earlier? What does
1410 have to do with Henry V? According to the chronicle sources,
quite a lot, because Henry was an important player in the religious
controversies of the time, especially the Crown responses to the
Lollard threat.

As it happens, the presentation of the petition for disendowment
from the Commons in 1410 came at a time of more general instability. Because Henry IV was incapacitated due to illness, his oldest
son took over management of the Privy Council, supplanting his
father's most powerful political and religious ally, Thomas Arundel,[24] with the prince's friend and ally Thomas Beaufort, appointed
chancellor in Arundel's place earlier in the year. That the future
Henry V continued his father's precedent in burning heretics and
defending the prerogatives of the Church is clear (he was later
called "the priests' king" [*princeps presbiterorum*]),[25] but the positions of the Prince of Wales on controversial issues were nonetheless complicated and sometimes difficult to define. For example,
Henry showed considerable patience with Sir John Oldcastle, suggesting that he was loath to see a person die for his religious beliefs
and was willing on occasion to intervene personally (treason, however, was another matter).[26] But Oldcastle is not the only burned
heretic with whom Henry of Monmouth had contact, and the case

of John Badby, burned in 1410, is more suggestive in terms of Shakespeare's transformation of chronicle materials.

It should be first noted that post-Reformation writers of Lollard history (Tyndale, Bale, Hall, Foxe, Holinshed, and many more), re-configured these proto-Reformation events so as to render their principals as martyrs in the Protestant cause.[27] The difficulty that attended such rehabilitation for users of the chronicles was that it cast kings such as Henry IV and V in the role of villain. Notwith-standing the fact that guilt for the persecution, condemnation, and even sentencing of heretics fell naturally on archbishops and other targets of Protestant ire, the secular authorities not only acquiesced to such punishment but carried it out.[28] The martyrs of the first half of the fifteenth century (after Henry IV's statute *De heretico com-burendo* of 1401) are first of all Lancastrian martyrs; despite the achievements of Agincourt and other military victories, the histori-cal records of Henry V's reign, and that of his father, are of pro-nounced intolerance of religious heterodoxy. To some extent, it was possible for sixteenth-century chroniclers to finesse these awkward facts, as well as Lancastrian usurpation issues, as Hall did by begin-ning his chronicle with Henry IV's reign. Shakespeare's own strat-egy of avoidance was to ignore most of the details of religious controversy in the chronicles. Thus what Shakespeare chose to in-corporate in *Henry V,* such as the references to the disendowment issue and possible allusions to the Badby episode, are highly sug-gestive in understanding the characterological development of the king.

In Holinshed, the account of the execution in 1410 of John Badby, a Worcestershire tailor, directly follows the mention of the disendowment bill. Badby was by no means a major figure in Lol-lard intellectual circles, coming to the attention of the authorities not by any notable preaching or writing but by holding unorthodox views with little regard for secrecy. The main charge in the indict-ment against him concerned his holding stubbornly to the belief that after the Eucharistic host had been consecrated by the priest on the altar, it continued to be bread. His unwillingness to concede anything with respect to the miracle of transubstantiation put him in dangerous straits, and led him "to be brought before Thomas Peveril, the politically inconsequential bishop of the comparatively insignificant diocese of Worcester, on 2 January 1409."[29] As Peter McNiven explains in his study of Badby and the historical context that led to his execution, "The proceedings against Badby could provide an ideal occasion for illustrating the evils of Lollardy, and the orthodox fervour and determination of the authorities, before the widest of audiences."[30] Badby was in the wrong place at the wrong time.[31]

Badby's execution also came on the heels of the failure of the Commons' petition for disendowment (which Henry may have implicitly supported, or at least allowed to be set before Parliament).[32] But once the disendowment bill had failed, political equilibrium had to be restored. The Commons could not simply be punished for its cheek, since the Crown depended upon it for revenue. One way to project a coherent program of church/government orthodoxy was to collaborate in a demonstration of the severity of the retribution for violating it. In 1410, with an incapacitated king and an ambitious Prince of Wales in charge, Badby offered an ideal opportunity for such a demonstration. In 1414, a similar displacement would be effected by means of war, rechanneling reformist energies from the domestic to the foreign, busying parliamentary minds not only with foreign quarrels but also with alternate sources of revenue.

It is useful, I think, to imagine the playwright using the Badby materials as given in Holinshed to construct *Henry V,* and at root, its eponymous character. In Holinshed the account for the year 1410 begins with the disendowment bill, including Henry IV's dislike of it and his affirmation of the Church's prerogative to apprehend and punish Lollards (the Commons had asked that the king's writ be the enforcement mechanism). Holinshed goes on to describe the execution of Badby without detailing his heretical views. This is not surprising, perhaps, given the awkward task facing post-Reformation chroniclers relating pre-Reformation events in which their king and countrymen worked the wrong side of the street. But after briefly mentioning Badby, Holinshed goes into great detail about the Prince of Wales's extraordinary solicitude in attending and participating in the Lollard's execution. If, as McNiven notes, "the purpose of Badby's second appearance [after he had been condemned before Convocation] was to prove to as wide an audience as possible that he was worthy of death, and to obtain maximum publicity for the passing and carrying out of the sentence," the Church was not the only one to get in on the act. Henry's unprecedented appearance and dramatic actions at Badby's execution provide a startling ur-version of plotted self-exculpation.

Here is Holinshed's account:

> During this parlement one John Badbie a tailor . . . was brought into Smithfield, and there in a tun or pipe burnt to death, in pitifull manner. The kings eldest son the lord Henrie prince of Wales being present, offered him his pardon, first before the fire was kindled, if he would haue recanted his opinions; and after when the fire was kindled, hearing him make a roring noise verie pitifullie, the prince caused the fire to be plucked backe, and exhorting him being with pitifull paine almost dead, to remember himselfe, and renounce his opinions, promising him not onelie life, but also three pence a daie so long as he liued to be paid out of the kings coffers: but he hauing recovered his spirits againe, refused the princes offer, choosing eftsoones to tast the fire, and so to die, than to forsake his opinions. Whereupon the prince commanded, that he should be put into the tun againe, from thencefoorth not to have anie fauour or pardon at all, and so it was doone, and the fire put to him againe, and he consumed to ashes.[33]

The only detail missing from this version of events is related in the *London Chronicle*: "And Herry prynce of Walys, thanne the kynges eldest sone, consailed hym for to forsake his heresye, and holde the righte wey of holy chirche. And the prior of seynt Bertelmewes in Smythfeld broughte the holy sacrament of Godys body, with xij torches lyght before, and in this wyse cam to this cursed heretyk. . . ."[34] John Foxe's *Actes and Monuments* offers an even more elaborate version: "In this meane season, the Prior of Saynt Bartelmewes in Smythfield, brought with all solemnitye the sacrament of Gods bodye, wyth twelue torches borne before, and so shewed the Sacrament to the poore man beyng at the stake. And then they demaunded of hym how he beleued in it, he aunsweryng: that he knew well it was halowed bread, and not Gods bodye. And then was the tunne put ouer hym, and fire putte vnto hym."[35] The Prince of Wales did not just "happen" to attend the execution, nor did he come as a passive witness to the power of the monarchy to subdue unorthodox behavior. On the contrary, the staging of Badby's heresy, in which he is publicly made to reject the sacrament after a solemn and conspicuous display of orthodoxy, allows Henry to appear in dramatic fashion as an upholder of the faith while at the same time offering a merciful solution. Such coercive due process is a consistent feature of Henry's behavior as reconfigured by Shakespeare.

The extraordinary events that occurred around the burning of this otherwise insignificant heretic suggest that the Prince of Wales was not a man to sit back and let events unfold about him. When there was a political or tactical advantage to be gained, he seized it with a conspicuous intervention. And he did so in this case by pursuing a strategy that put himself in the dramatic frame of action. His participation in the burning of John Badby was a risk, but a calculated one. As McNiven points out, this was an intervention in which the prince could "impose his own individualistic solution" by effecting a recantation and offering the heretic a second chance.[36] Holinshed's language suggests Henry's Christlike overture to Badby: "to remember himselfe, and renounce his opinions, promising him not onelie life. . . ." Henry is here a potential savior, offering Badby salvation through remembrance and renunciation of sin, and the sparing of his life; the only *eternal* life he can offer is the heavenly perpetuity of three pence a day. Such a holy bribe demonstrates the prince's desire to gain Badby's cooperation in this scheme, but the latter is having none of it. At this point, instead of the triumph of turning the lost sheep back into the fold, Henry has "a scorched and unrepentant Lollard on his hands."[37] His reaction is to return Badby to the fire, but only after it is clear that Badby has deliberately chosen this fate, thereby shifting responsibility from the mechanism of power to the heretic himself. Annabel Patterson's insistence that this was "an opportunity for a dramatic public demonstration of [Henry's] own orthodoxy" ignores the possibility that orthodoxy is not the only benefit that Henry hoped to gain.[38] The impression that Shakespeare evidently took from his reading was certainly not that this was a king whose deep religious fervor superseded his political calculations.

Henry's presence at this event marks his involvement in a matter of grave and pressing interest for this period with a characteristic twist. Henry's merciful interventions—his offer of pardon and even an endowment—may well have been the kind of textual moment that becomes the raw material of a discursive game, material that a dramatist could transform for characterological purposes. It presents the prince as leaving the terrible choice to Badby himself; once he refuses to recant, the prince can wash his hands of responsibility. The example of John Badby in the chronicles thus has the makings of a strategy of displaced culpability, of deliberate emplotment, which is the hallmark of Shakespeare's king.

O for a muse of fire indeed.

Notes

I would like to thank Susan Zimmerman and the anonymous reader who worked so hard to improve this essay.

1. Both epigraph quotations from Holinshed's *The Chronicles of England, Scotland, and Ireland,* 1587 rev. ed. (London: J. Johnson, 1808), 3:58. This is the end of Henry IV's reign.

2. I am interested in countering statements like Anthony Brennan's: "We are not given any clear signal that this is a carefully constructed performance, though everything we know about Henry makes it inherently probable." *Twayne's New Critical Introductions to Shakespeare:* Henry V (New York: Twayne, 1992), 24. We *are* given clear signals and need to be doggedly attentive regarding "what we know about Henry" and how we know it.

3. Quoted in Harry Berger, Jr., *Making Trifles of Terrors: Redistributing Complicities in Shakespeare* (Stanford, CA: Stanford University Press, 1997), xii–xiii; hereafter referred to as MTT. The quotation originally appears in Stanley Cavell, *Must We Mean What We Say? Modern Philosophical Essays in Morality, Religion, Drama, Music, and Criticism* (New York: Scribner, 1969), 277–78.

4. See xiii–xix, 300–301, 222–46. It is important to note that the ethical discourses that are taken up by characters (and that, reflexively, they are taken up by) are not limited to just one. Characters often shuttle between discourses and may play them off against one another or be "unaware" (in the sense that we cannot determine their intention) that while pursuing one language game, they consistently play another. This is particularly true of the victim and revenger's discourses, which are often inextricably linked.

5. I borrow yet another conceptual phrase from Berger. In the context of a discussion of Northumberland, Falstaff, and others in *2 Henry IV,* he writes: "To shift the source of guilt and anxiety from grief to grievance, from inner condition to outer circumstance, to alienate it to some more manageable and culpable scapegoat on whom bad humors can be vented, offers the relief of action, purgation, and closure, as well as the pleasure of victimization" (142). For Charnes's term, see *Notorious Identity: Materializing the Subject in Shakespeare* (Cambridge, MA: Harvard University Press, 1993), especially 1–20.

6. I refer, of course, to the play *The Famous Victories of Henry the Fifth* that Shakespeare used as a source for his play. Reprinted in *The Oldcastle Controversy,* Peter Corbin and Douglas Sedge, eds. (New York: Manchester University Press, 1991), 145–99.

7. One of the complexities of Henry V's character is how it is built separately from that of his father (the seemingly dissolute prince who almost never has contact with him) and as a direct result of having a father whose rule is represented as at every turn impeded by these kinds of inner/outer struggles. *Henry V* presents a marked difference: a king who does not pursue this kind of discursive strategy, turning whatever inner hurts and anxieties outward without doing so reactively, as if it were always entirely personal. Henry V plans and plots instead of suffering the kind of fatigue and heaviness the crown brought to his father. I'll risk an analogy with *The Lord of the Rings.* If the crown in history plays is like the ring in Tolkien's story, Henry IV comes to possess it and then cannot help but put it on. His use of its powers drains him but he cannot do otherwise. His son, on the other hand, understands better the difference between possessing and wearing, and so reaps the benefits of potential power without bending to its soul-destroying power.

8. *MTT,* 231.

9. Anticipations of his transformation have, of course, been established earlier

in the tetralogy. See, for example, Vernon's response to Hotspur's question about the "the nimble-footed madcap Prince of Wales": "I saw young Harry with his beaver on, / His cuishes on his thighs, gallantly armed,/Rise from the ground like feathered Mercury, / and vaulted with such ease into his seat / As if an angel dropped down from the clouds / To turn and wind a fiery Pegasus, / And witch the world with noble horsemanship" (*1 Henry IV*, 4.1.95, 105–11). See also Vernon's continued praise of the Prince's rhetorical prowess at 5.2.51–68, to which Hotspur responds: "Cousin, I think thou art enamoured / On his follies" (5.2.69–70). All references to Shakespeare are from *The Norton Shakespeare*, Stephen Greenblatt et al., eds. (New York: W. W. Norton, 1997).

10. It would perhaps be better to write "as the playwright deploys them," though here and elsewhere I'll maintain the illusion that Henry controls this discourse.

11. In his Arden edition of *Henry V*, T. W. Craik contends that "Though Shakespeare read history attentively he was not fettered by it" (32). He follows this statement with a summary of liberties that Shakespeare takes with historical details; his intention is to demonstrate that the playwright made such changes when they suited dramatic force or structure. Accurate enough, but faulty in its implication as to how Shakespeare's reading of history mattered to his writing of it. Craik's Sidneyan assumption of the poet's superiority over the historian in getting at "truth" falls into a false dichotomy that Shakespeare never accedes to. The historian of Sidney's *Defence of Poesie*, "captived to the truth of a foolish world" (32), is not representative of those figures whose materials a playwright like Shakespeare used. Hall, Holinshed, Bale, Foxe, anonymous balladeers, and earlier playwrights synthesized primary, secondary, and tertiary works to construct their "histories." A close look at their work finds them often unfettered by the objective "truth" of events, nor did they seem concerned about the difficulties of uncovering the supposed "truth" of the past. Important work on this subject has been done in recent years by, among others, Michel de Certeau, *The Writing of History*, trans. Tom Conley (New York: Columbia University Press, 1988), Hayden White, *Content of the Form: Narrative Discourse and Historical Representation* (Baltimore: Johns Hopkins University Press, 1987), D. R. Woolf, *Reading History in Early Modern England* (Cambridge: Cambridge University Press, 2000) and *The Social Circulation of the Past: English Historical Culture, 1500–1730* (Oxford: Oxford University Press, 2003), J. G. A. Pocock, *Politics, Language and Time: Essays on Political Thought and History* (New York: Atheneum, 1971) and others, including Annabel Patterson and Paul Strohm, whose relevant works are listed below.

12. Contrast this with Lily B. Campbell's reading of this scene: "The sum has been offered in aid of the projected wars in France, but Shakespeare does not indicate, as does Holinshed, that the archbishop's purpose in the offer has been to turn Henry's mind to making war in France in order to get it off church revenues. Instead, Shakespeare makes the king the prime mover in the matter, representing him as seeking advice from the archbishop as his moral and spiritual mentor." It is difficult to fathom how Campbell misses Shakespeare's attentiveness to Holinshed's "indication" of the archbishop's purpose and even harder to understand how one might justify Henry's meeting with Canterbury as advice-seeking from his "mentor." See *Shakespeare's "Histories": Mirrors of Elizabethan Policy* (San Marino, CA: Huntington Library Publications, 1965), 260.

13. The first quarto offers a more concise version of this speech, altering it slightly:

> *King:* Call in the messenger sent from the Dauphin.
> And by your aid, the noble sinews of our land,
> France being ours, we'll bring it to our awe,
> Or break it all in pieces. Either our chronicles
> Shall with full mouth speak freely of our acts,
> Or else like tongueless mutes
> Not worshipped with a paper epitaph.
>
> (1.151–57)

The quarto passage does not differ essentially in its meaning, but its brevity dampens the vividness of the Folio's version as well as stripping the latter of its repetitions ("unworthy urn," "tombless," "no remembrance"). The quarto's word choice also substitutes "chronicles" for "history" and offers the collapsed "tongueless mutes" for the simile "Turkish mute" that leads to a "tongueless mouth," thus muting the Folio's hint of castration. Finally, instead of "waxen epitaph" the quarto offers "paper epitaph," which, while continuing the theme of transitoriness, offers a conceit common to the sonnets (immortality through written verse). Lost is the ancillary meaning of wax/wane implied by the Folio text. *The First Quarto of King Henry V*, ed. Andrew Gurr (Cambridge: Cambridge University Press, 2000).

14. The way shame is inverted here is akin to the dynamic that drives the story of Actaeon as explored by Berger (*MTT,* 262–87), building on Leonard Barkan's "Diana and Actaeon: The Myth as Synthesis," *English Literary Renaissance* 10 (1980): 317–59. The force is unleashed by the shamed on the shamer: Diana's turning of Actaeon into a deer and his hounds on him resembles Henry's turning tennis balls to gunstones and the French heir from aggressor to target. This is a deadly game Hal and Falstaff have played in the Henriad, as Berger notes: "In *1 Henry IV* the traces of the myth produce a more sinister network of resonances. From his first words to his final rejection, Falstaff knowingly presents himself to Harry as a target, persistently probes beneath the madcap role to lay bare the aggressive motives that Harry tries to conceal even from himself" (262–63).

15. As Margaret Aston writes: "The text explains how clerical temporalities could be used to fund 15 earls, 1500 knights, 6200 esquires and 100 almshouses, as well as maintenance for 15 universities and 15,000 priests, and additional revenues for the king. . . ." *Lollards and Reformers: Images and Literacy in Late Medieval England* (London: Hambledon Press, 1984), 21. For a text of the bill, see Anne Hudson, ed., *Selections from English Wycliffite Writings* (Cambridge: Cambridge University Press, 1978), 135–37. On disendowment in the period, see Aston's "'Caim's Castles': Poverty, Politics and Disendowment," in *The Church, Politics and Patronage in the Fifteenth Century,* ed. Barrie Dobson (Gloucester: Alan Sutton, 1984), 45–81.

16. Holinshed, 3:65.

17. Ibid.

18. Ibid.

19. Ibid.

20. Ibid.

21. Reprinted as *Hall's Chronicle,* ed. Henry Ellis (London, 1809; AMS Press, 1965); originally published 1548.

22. Ibid., 49.

23. Ibid.

24. See Christopher Allmand, *Henry V* (Berkeley: University of California Press, 1992), 39–47. See also J. F. Baldwin, *The King's Council in England During the Middle Ages* (Oxford: Oxford, 1913).

25. Walsingham's phrase. See *St. Alban's Chronicle, 1406–1420,* ed. V. H. Galbraith (Oxford: Oxford, 1937). Also used by Thomas Hoccleve in his "The Remonstrance Against Oldcastle": "Prynce of preestes our lige lord yee calle / In scorn, but it is a style of honour." *Selections from Hoccleve,* ed. M. C. Seymour (Oxford: Oxford University Press, 1991), 68 (ll. 289–90).

26. For a summary account of Henry's relationship with Sir John Oldcastle, whose heretical beliefs ran him afoul of church authority, and to whom Henry showed great patience, see the introduction to Peter Corbin and Douglas Sedge, eds., *The Oldcastle Controversy: Sir John Odcastle, Part 1 and The Famous Victories of Henry the Fifth* (Manchester, UK: Manchester University Press, 1991). See also Alice-Lyle Scoufos, *Shakespeare's Typological Satire: A Study of the Falstaff-Oldcastle Problem* (Athens: Ohio University Press, 1979), 70–80. On the differences between tolerance and treason as motivation for Henry's acting against heretics (or supposed heretics), see Aston, 26–30. For a reconsideration of the Ficket's Field "uprising" of January 1414, though one that does not change the view of Henry as calculating, see Paul Strohm, *England's Empty Throne: Usurpation and the Language of Legitimation, 1399–1422* (New Haven: Yale University Press, 1998), 63–100.

27. For a comprehensive view of these chroniclers and their works, see Antonia Gransden's seminal two-volume study: *Historical Writing in England, vol. 1, c. 550–1307* (Ithaca: Cornell University Press, 1974) and *Historical Writing in England, vol. 2, c. 1307 to the Early Sixteenth Century* (Ithaca: Cornell University Press, 1982). On the late medieval chroniclers and their methods and habits of composition, see Chris Given-Wilson, *Chronicles: The Writing of History in Medieval England* (London: Hambledon and London, 2004).

28. See Andrew Escobedo, *Nationalism and Historical Loss in Renaissance England: Foxe, Dee, Spenser, Milton* (Ithaca: Cornell University Press, 2004), chap. 1, "Traitorous Martyrs or a History to Forget?"

29. Peter McNiven, *Heresy and Politics in the Reign of Henry IV: The Burning of John Badby* (Woodbridge: Boydell Press, 1987), 199.

30. Ibid., 202.

31. We might, however, turn this around and say that, from the perspective of Archbishop Arundel, Badby was in the right place at the right time.

32. McNiven, 195.

33. Holinshed, 3:49.

34. *A Chronicle of London* (London, 1827), 92. The most comprehensive account of Badby's interrogation by Arundel and the Convocation, as well as his execution, is in John Foxe's *Actes and Monuments* (http://www.hrionline.ac.uk/johnfoxe/main/5_1570_0623.jsp). With his customary alacrity, Foxe offers a thorough narrative of Badby's unfair treatment and the extent to which the religious and secular authorities made his situation an impossible one. Foxe softens the prince's motives, however, keeping the pressure on the Catholic authorities ("it

happened that the Prince the kinges eldest sonne, was there present. Who shewing some part of the good Samaritane, began to endeuour and assay how to saue the lyfe of hym, whom the hipocriticall Leuites and Phariseis sought to put to death," 1570, 623). It is, of course, more than charitable to describe Henry's presence as happenstance, and even more polemically suspect to allow him the role of Samaritan.

35. Foxe, *Actes,* 1570, 623. Foxe also inserts a woodcut illustration of Badby's burning, with what is apparently the Prince of Wales on horseback speaking to him (1570, 624). While it is perhaps risky to place any probative value in the illustration, the representation of the prince suggests a casualness that is not flattering and that does not compare with the drama of Badby's posture and state of suffering. The illustration here perhaps works against Foxe's mitigation of royal responsibility.

36. McNiven, 221.

37. Ibid., 217.

38. *Reading Holinshed's Chronicles* (Chicago: University of Chicago Press, 1994), 132.

Eating Richard II

JEREMY LOPEZ

IN *RICHARD II* SHAKESPEARE is as unsystematic in his use of history as he is systematic in his use of poetic imagery and sustained metaphor. Students of the play have been efficient in developing critical vocabularies that express the latter fact and obscure the former. Madeline Doran noted in 1942 that Richard's character "is exhibited directly. He is a poet and he speaks poetically"; the play's images "tend to be direct or explicit, complete, correspondent, point by point to the idea symbolized, and separate from one another" (113).[1] The play's critical and theatrical traditions have borne Doran's argument out.[2] The feeling of completeness and coherence a reader or spectator gets from the poetry of *Richard II* is probably what makes it seem trivial, or at least inconsiderate, to point out the way in which virtually everything in this history play—from its elision of the majority of Richard's reign,[3] to its imagining of Woodstock,[4] to its representation of Richard's queen,[5] to its hyperbolically poetical representation of Richard himself—is a historical travesty.[6] In this play we get almost no sense of the Richard we find in Holinshed, and much less of the Richard we find in modern historical scholarship, such as Anthony Steel's or Nigel Saul's biographies of the king. Even putting factual and chronological details aside, Shakespeare gives us a Richard who is always, or can always be, solely to blame for his troubles—not a Richard who was repeatedly hemmed in by competing factions from the moment, in his early youth, of his father's untimely death; nor a Richard whose work in maintaining England's status as a European power was continually hampered by the fallout from the fiscal and military crises of the end of Edward III's reign; nor a Richard who was throughout much of his reign capable of cultivating strong internal political alliances (notably, in contrast to Shakespeare's play, with Gaunt) and of imagining and carrying out ambitious foreign policy aims (notably in his first Irish campaign).[7]

In the following pages I attempt, in three movements, to create a critical vocabulary for the study of Shakespeare's history plays and Holinshed's *Chronicles* that does justice to Shakespeare's disregard for written historical fact, and that goes beyond construing the relationship between Shakespeare and Holinshed as one of dependence, where Shakespeare's "departures" from his "sources" ultimately reinscribe the importance of those sources. In the first movement, which is as much the demonstration of a critical method for analysis of historical drama as it is an argument about *Richard II,* I argue that Shakespeare's thinking about Richard II and his use of Holinshed are imprecise:[8] understanding, or at least imagining, Shakespeare's work in this way makes it possible to see how he and Holinshed are working with the same material for purposes that are not merely entirely different, but largely unrelated. I begin by locating the traces of some of Shakespeare's imprecise, impressionistic thinking in some labored, underdeveloped poetic images that seem to me occasionally to jut out awkwardly in this densely patterned, highly symmetrical play. The palimpsestic metaphorical pattern I focus on is one that has largely gone unnoticed as such in the prolific imagery-criticism of *Richard II:* a pattern of images involving food and eating. I argue that these undeveloped, or awkwardly introduced, or clumsily artificial images are symptomatic of a form of compression analogous to that which results from the deliberate effacement of historical narrative for the sake of theatrical effect. In the images of food and eating that occur only erratically throughout the play, we see Shakespeare attempting, not always quite successfully or elegantly, to compress what he sees— and what we might see—as essential material from an antecedent text into a poetic shorthand, conferring upon it the force and energy of lyric.

In the essay's second movement, I address specifically some critical language that is conventionally brought to bear on discussions of Shakespeare's use of antecedent historical writings. My goal here is to describe how some of the entrenched habits we have developed in our reception and interpretation of medieval (and early modern) history as it has been digested by Shakespeare are simultaneously enabled by and oddly indifferent to Shakespeare's disregard for historical "facts." The essay's final movement works to trope, in the terms of the essay's first movement, and to meditate upon the implications of the way in which the historical vacuum at the center of *Richard II*'s poetic and theatrical structure has been peculiarly generative of specific but illusory historical meanings. While the processes of interpretation and reception I describe in this movement can probably be seen to be at work with respect to any early modern history play, *Richard II* is a usefully vivid representative case in that its particularly casual treatment of the monarch's reign has meant that its function in both source-study and New Historicist criticism has largely depended on various kinds of evidentiary *absence* being converted into crucially signifying *presence*. A subtitle for this essay might be found in the literary, theatrical, and interpretive processes its analysis works to describe: the transubstantiation of Holinshed.

*   *   *

In 3.2, Richard asks the land itself to revolt against Bolingbroke. "Feed not thy sovereign's foe, my gentle earth," he implores at line 11, "Nor with thy sweets comfort his ravenous sense" (12).[9] The word *ravenous* has an echo in Holinshed's excoriation of the usurping Bolingbroke:[10]

> What vnnaturalnesse, or rather what tigerlike crueltie was this . . . being so neerelie knit in consanguinitie, which ought to have moued them like lambs to haue loued each other, wooluishlie to lie in wait for the distressed creatures life, and *rauenouslie* to thirst after his bloud . . . (869, emphasis added)[11]

At something like the center of the play—in the middle of the middle act, at the moment Richard has come home to an England entirely changed from when he left it—these lines are a crucial expression of the play's sporadic but ongoing concern with consumption and eating. *Sweet* is a word with largely Lancastrian force throughout the play. Bolingbroke relishes its aggressive ambiguity, as we see perhaps most vividly in 4.1 when he reacts to the news of Mowbray's death: "Sweet Peace conduct his sweet soul to the bosom / Of good old Abraham!" (104–5).[12] Bolingbroke is the first to use *sweet* in the play, at 1.3.68, and he and his father control the metaphor through 2.1—see also 1.3.236, 1.3.306, and 2.1.13. At the end of 1.3, Bolingbroke refers to England at his banishment as the "Sweet soil . . . / My mother and nurse that bears me yet" (306–7); in the passage from 3.2 with which I began, Richard and the play's poetic patterning conspire in an attempt to deprive Bolingbroke of his consuming power, turning the earth into a barren mother or poisonous nurse.

The range of possible meanings comprised within Richard's *sweets*—its primary sense is quite general, as in *OED* 3a, "something that affords enjoyment or gratifies desire," but it also carries the proximate senses "that which is sweet to taste" (1a), "sweetness of smell" (6), "a sweet sound" (5a), and even possibly "a beloved person, darling, sweetheart" (4)—makes the subsequent *ravenous* particularly apt; what is being emphasized, or even foreshadowed, is how Bolingbroke might not have returned merely to take what is "his own," but all that the land (both as nation and as earth) can produce or offer. Shakespeare expresses an irony similar to that which we see in the passage where Holinshed uses *rauenouslie,* and a typical way of understanding the echo would be as a form of imaginative concord: Shakespeare "follows his source." Another, and I think more accurate, way of looking at it is as an opportunistic seizure, where Shakespeare forcibly enlists the almost inevitable result of Holinshed's conventional wolf-lamb antithesis in a larger and somewhat unwieldy system of images that act as a lyric gloss on Holinshed's historical narrative. The impetus toward *ravenous* can be seen to have its beginnings in the way *sweet*—a very common poetic word whose culinary connotations are far from inevitable—gets into the poetry of *Richard II:* by means of an unwieldy alimentary metaphor early in the play. In 1.3, after bidding farewell, before the imminent duel, to his cousin Aumerle, Bolingbroke turns to his father: "Lo, as at English feasts, so I regreet / The daintiest last, to make the end most sweet" (67–68). Even if one knows about the pattern of alimentary images that is going to develop out of these lines, it's hard to see what Shakespeare hopes to achieve with this odd metaphor, in which John of Gaunt is conceived as a dainty confection. Bolingbroke's obscure and self-important *regreet* is probably an opportunistic seizure of a word from Marlowe, which Shakespeare is using both for its grandiose feeling and for the way it sonically and metrically prepares for a rhyme with *sweet*.[13] The lines are stumbling hastily toward *sweet* because one path of Shakespeare's poetic imagination is twisting murkily toward Bolingbroke's surprised and surprising response to his father's suggestion that he make the best of his banishment ("who can . . . / . . . cloy the hungry edge of appetite / By bare imagination of a feast?" [1.3.294–97]), and toward Gaunt's unexpected and irritating punning passage about his name, weight, and appetite at 2.1.73–83.

Between these two rather baroque poetic moments is Gaunt's earlier speech about Richard's "fierce blaze of riot": "Light vanity, insatiate cormorant, / Consuming means, soon preys upon itself" (2.1.38–39). This passage, sharp and remarkable though it may be, is also more conventional than the other two in its expression of the relationship between power and consumption. It contains the poetic and thematic energy that we see released in an ornate frenzy in the passages on either side of it. These three passages represent two different levels of thinking about food and eating as resonant metaphors for the follies of Richard's kingship: on one level we see Shakespeare working with ideas that are conventional to his own and others' dramatization of royal power as a process of self-consumption; on another level we see him working not simply *with* material he *finds* in Holinshed, but working to impose a pattern *upon* material he has an impressionistic but vivid recollection of in Holinshed.

Most of the instances in which Richard makes an appearance in the first two-thirds or so of the *Chronicles* involve him at an elaborate ceremony or, more significantly, a meal. At the ten-year-old king's coronation, his champion Sir John Dimmocke is told to delay his challenge on behalf of Richard until

> the king was at dinner . . . The knight did as the lord marshall willed him, and so after his departure, the king hauing those lords riding afore him, was borne on knights shoulders vnto his palace, and so had to his chamber, where he rested a while, being somewhat faint with trauell, and tooke a small refection. After this, coming into the hall, he created foure new earles, before he sat downe to meal . . .
>
> (2.714)

And the feast that ensues, according to Holinshed, "passeth our vnderstanding to describe" (714). Later, in the tenth year of the reign, Gloucester is shown to believe himself and "such other lords as favored the knights burgesses in their sute against the earle of Suffolke . . . should be willed [by Richard] to a supper in London, there to be murthered. But the duke coming by some meanes to vnderstand this wicked practise, had no desire to take part of that supper, where such sharp sauce was provided . . ." (774). Richard and his uncle Gloucester's rivalry would come to a head at another dinner ten years later, after Richard returned the town of Brest to the Duke of Burgundy.

> by reason whereof no small sparke of displeasure arose betwixt the king and the duke of Glocester, which kindled vp such a flame . . . finding

matter inough to feed vpon in both their breasts, that finally it could no longer be kept down . . . In the month of Februarie, the king holding a sumptuous feast at Westminster, many of the soldiers that were newlie come from Brest preased into the hall . . . Whom as the duke of Glocester beheld, to remember how that towne was giuen vp contrarie to his mind and pleasure, it grieued him not a little . . .

(2.834)

Gloucester leaves the court after an argument with Richard and plots, over dinner, to assemble a power against the king (see 836)— the rebellion that leads to his imprisonment and death.

In among these stories of fateful dinners and consuming displeasure are some vignettes that could be seen as illustrating the dangers of excessive consumption: the death of rioters during the 1381 rebellion when Gaunt's Savoy catches fire while the rioters are drinking his wine in the cellar (738); the pride of John Littester, head of the Norfolk rebels and self-proclaimed "king of the commons," forcing noblemen and gentlemen to "serue him at the table . . . with kneeling humblie before him as he sat at meat" (745); the death, during a time of high corn prices (1389–90), of many poor people, who "through immoderate eating of nuts and apples, fell into the disease called the flix" (815); and the quarrel between the king and the bishop of Salisbury, arising, it seems, from an incident where "one of the same bishops seruants had taken a horsse-lofe frō a bakers man . . . and would not deliuer it againe" (818). It is important to emphasize that the focus on consumption in Holinshed seems incidental and narrative rather than deliberate and thematic, and that any moral pattern one constructs out of them has to be constructed.[14] His metaphors or rhetorical figures, such as "sharp sauce" above, are ad hoc rather than imposed upon the events he describes as a way of comprehending them totally. Feasting, pageantry, and conspicuous consumption are simply the stuff of monarchy—past and present—and reading around in the Chronicles does not give a sense that Holinshed is systematically more preoccupied with describing these activities in Richard's reign in particular.[15] Something like what he does by telescoping the Lists of Coventry, Gaunt's death, Richard's confiscation of Bolingbroke's lands, the second Irish campaign, and the return of Bolingbroke from several months (September 1398–July 1399) into an apparently almost simultaneous series of events, Shakespeare seems to compress all of the ideational and moralistic imagery of Holinshed's largely incidental thinking about food into moments like Gaunt's "consuming vanity" speech and his punning speech on his name. The energy that results from the compression is part of the reason the consumption-related ironies against Richard are so powerful; the force of metaphor, of poetry, is to give the audience an impression of a history it need not know. Richard becomes an emblem of the consumption-related problems that plagued his reign at every level.

Shakespeare's handling of Richard's death scene—for which he had to select from a variety of scenarios in Holinshed—gives perhaps the most vivid sense of his interest in alimentary metaphor as a crucial lens through which to view the history of the reign—though it is clear, again, that this metaphor fails to be fully incorporated into the poetic scheme of the play. There are multiple, conflicting accounts of Richard's death, given by Holinshed in volume 3, pages 13–14, and all of them involve food. In one, Richard was "euerie daie serued at table with costlie meat, like a king . . . and when the meat was set before him, he was forbidden once to touch it; . . . and so he died of forced famine" (13). In another, "he was so beaten out of hart, that wilfullie he sterued himselfe, and so died at Pomfret Castell on S. Valentines daie: a happie daie to him, for it was the beginning of his ease, and the ending of his paine: so that death was to him *daintie and sweet*" (13–14, emphasis added). And in a third, which Shakespeare more or less follows,[16] Piers of Exton and eight men go to Pomfret, where the king seems to be fed daily with royal ceremony. Exton commanded

> the esquier that was accustomed to sew and take the assaie before king Richard, to doo so no more, saieng; "Let him eat now, for he shall not long eat." Richard sat downe to dinner, and was serued without courtesie or assaie, wherevpon maruelling at the sudden change, he demanded of the esquire whie he did not his dutie; "Sir (said he) I am otherwise commanded by Sir Piers of Exton, which is newlie come from K. Henrie. . . . sir Piers entered the chamber, well armed, with eight tall men likewise armed . . ." (3.14)

Shakespeare chooses the third option, I think, not only because it is more obviously "theatrical,"[17] but also because, in place of the more predictable irony of representing the self-consumingly vain king being deprived (or depriving himself) of things to consume, it provides a picture of the still-consuming king, eating up to his last moment.

But the most vicious, if most suppressed and compressed, irony comes in the following scene, when Richard's coffin is brought on-stage. Coffins are not unusual in Shakespeare's histories (see *1 Henry VI,* 1.1 and *Richard III,* 1.2), but this one seems, like the metaphors I've been discussing, heavily artificial. One odd thing about this coffin is that it is brought on for a mere twenty-two lines, and that those lines are the last in the play; unlike in *1 Henry VI* or *Richard III,* the coffin doesn't seem to be onstage long enough to have a clear reason to be there: we've seen Richard dead already.[18] Another odd thing is that it is brought on by Exton rather than in some more obviously ceremonial way: Does it make sense for the new king, Henry IV, attempting to distance himself from the murder, to allow Exton into the presence while York, Northumberland, Fitzwater, and Henry Percy are there as well? What is the impetus behind the staging of the coffin, the cumbersome business necessary to establish its visible presence, at this point?

One part of the impetus is historical and narrative: Holinshed describes the lead-encased coffin, revealing only the king's face, that was brought from Pomfret to London "to the intent that all men might see him, and perceiue that he was departed this life" (3.14). The final moments of the play, besides being an exposition of Bolingbroke's response to his crime, are a theatrical compression of the journey of Richard's body from his northern prison to London. Again, the compression can have a potentially disruptive, clumsy feeling, but it also allows for, or is at least intended to allow for, the release of latent poetic energy—related in this case to another odd, intrusive culinary metaphor earlier in the play. In a moment in 3.2 that Samuel Johnson reasonably found somewhat infelicitous, Richard says,

> Our lands, our lives and all are Bolingbroke's
> And nothing we can call our own but death
> And that small model of the barren earth
> Which serves as paste and cover to our bones.
>
> (3.2.151–54)

In that *paste* here means "pastry crust," Richard is not only imagining his grave plot as a pie,[19] he is also, as Forker's Arden edition notes, approaching a quibble on the word *coffin* meaning "A mould of paste for a pie; the crust of a pie. A pie dish or mould" (*OED,* 4a, 4b). Like Bolingbroke's reference to Gaunt as a dainty dish, this moment strains poetic credibility. It also takes on a certain amount of thematic force from the energy that results from the compression of ideationally relevant material in Holinshed; and it proves to have a theatrical logic when it is echoed in the physical coffin in the final scene. Bringing the coffin onstage literalizes Richard's process of self-consumption, and the fantasy of nothingness, of consumption by the earth (both womb and gullet, as Gaunt imagines it at 2.1.83), which he begins to entertain as early as act 3. The point of the moment, for Henry IV and in terms of Holinshed, is deictic—all must see that the former king is dead. And in the background one can just make out the playwright's ghoulish, Titus-like laughter: Why, there he is, baked in this pie.

*　　*　　*

In the preceding pages, I have attempted to combine formalist analysis, a necessarily speculative (or imaginative) theater history, and a detailed understanding of Holinshed's narrative structure in order to arrive at a reading of *Richard II* that illuminates something of what I see as that play's rather anarchic relationship to documentary historical information.[20] My reading of Holinshed in these pages is in no way necessary to my reading of the food and eating images in Shakespeare's play. Holinshed casts a kind of indirect light on the play's language that might reveal some of the underpinnings of the play's more extravagant poetic gestures, and it is possible to see in the echoes between the two works something of the nature of verbal layering that goes into the construction of dramatic poetry. But the eating-imagery pattern I have outlined could be outlined without reference to the *Chronicles;* the larger point of my use of Holinshed has been to throw into relief the somewhat arbitrary way in which "source material" can be enlisted to authorize textual or theatrical interpretation. The formalist analysis I have developed, one goal of which has been to imagine what a literary or poetic reading of Holinshed might look like, is meant to be an antidote or counterweight to the highly conventionalized and, I suggest, misleading historical readings to which plays like *Richard II* and their antecedent, or contemporaneous, historical narratives are subjected.

In Charles R. Forker's Arden edition (2002), the section on Shakespeare's use of Holinshed is at pains to demonstrate both Shakespeare's historical accuracy (in *Richard II* "he deviated less from Holinshed than in the other histories," 124), and how relatively un-

important such accuracy is ("Although Holinshed was his principal resource, Shakespeare's inventions bulk surprisingly large in
the final result," 133). Almost every point of noncorrespondence
between the two authors is discussed in terms of the way it "signifies"; no matter how far Shakespeare's inventions stray, Holinshed
remains the point of origin from which meaning is measured, and,
at the same time, all of Shakespeare's inventions are construed as
improvements. The dangers of this equivocal method, which is
fundamental to source-study generally, are particularly evident in
Peter Saccio's *Shakespeare's English Kings*.[21] Saccio's chapter on
Richard II begins by acknowledging that modern historiography
has had much to do in correcting the Tudor view of Richard as
dramatized in Shakespeare's play and sets out its main purpose as
giving "[m]odern audiences and students . . . a summary of events
prior to the quarrel [between Mowbray and Bolingbroke]." The historical record is here treated as a kind of background noise, something we might fully expect a playwright like Shakespeare to ignore
even as we know he must have been aware of it. Over the course of
the chapter we can see Saccio responding to the massive gap between Shakespeare's history and the historical record by simply accepting the latter for the former—by accepting, that is, the play's
substitution of a poetical idea of the reign for a historical idea, so
that all of Shakespeare's departures from the source become a manifestation of something latent in and inherent to the source. Thus
on page 22, "Bushy and Green were Lancastrian officials, Bagot a
dependent of Norfolk's. All three were respectable knights, but they
received bad press from subsequent chroniclers. By the time they
reached Shakespeare they had already been turned into what the
playwright calls 'the caterpillars of the commonwealth.'" But on
page 28, the quotation marks that distinguish traditional representations from Saccio's historical inquiry have disappeared: "at
Berkeley [Bolingbroke] secured the submission of the spineless
York, and at Bristol he forced the surrender of the caterpillars and
had them executed."[22] What is understandably at stake for this kind
of criticism, the goal of which is ultimately and often primarily to
help students understand more clearly what is happening in the
play, is to render the chaotic aesthetic experience that is *Richard II*
legible in terms of and/or with respect to the more evidently coherent narrative experience of a chronicle history. The unavoidable
peril in such a method is the conflation of highly distinct forms of
writing at the expense of the specificity and complexity of both.[23]

The rhetorical problem I have been describing is all the more significant because it is not limited to literary critics who dabble in history; it is a problem faced by historians who dabble in Shakespeare, and the somewhat surprising disciplinary overlap in this regard is symptomatic of a larger scholarly or cultural impulse, perhaps essentially New Historical in character even as it certainly originates (to some extent) in the play itself, to channel historical narrative through the person of Shakespeare. Nigel Saul concludes his definitive biography, *Richard II,* by saying that while Shakespeare "distorted the historical record to suit his dramatic purpose, he nevertheless captured the essence of his subject. Perhaps the actor in Shakespeare responded to the actor in Richard. Certainly in the theatre of the medieval monarchy there was no keener actor than Richard. His tragedy was that he mistook the illusion of the stage for the reality of the world around him" (467)."[24] I want to dwell for a moment on these arrestingly casual sentences, and I hope that my criticism of them will be understood as a measure of my respect for the preceding four hundred or so pages of Saul's magisterial and brilliantly clear biography. The sentences are worth dwelling upon critically because they exemplify the kind of sloppy thinking to which Shakespeare's magnificent poetry can tempt even the most meticulous minds. Saul's "theatre of the medieval monarchy" is remarkably vague. Is he referring to all English and European monarchs throughout the entire medieval period? All medieval English kings? And regardless of whom he is referring to, how would relative theatricality in kingship be quantified? Could Richard, for example, really be said to be a keener actor than Bolingbroke?—who, after handling his return to England and rise to power with remarkable subtlety, managed to stage his coronation on St. Edward's Day and with a spectacularly effective prop, a phial of anointing-oil said to have been presented to Thomas Becket by the Virgin Mary.[25] In his next sentence, Saul seems to move from a metaphorical idea of "theater" (all kings are of necessity more or less actors) to a more literal one: Richard took "the illusion of the stage for the reality of the world around him." What "stage" can Saul be referring to? Certainly not the civic and/or liturgical medieval stage, to which not a single reference is made in the entire book. And, patron of the arts though he was, Richard did not, like the monarchs under whom Shakespeare wrote, retain court players. Suddenly, Saul's Richard seems to be the historical monarch of Saul's biography acting his own part in Shakespeare's play: 1595 is conflated with 1395 and Richard the medieval king with kingship generally. What seems to be at stake, somewhat surprisingly, in Saul's argument, is the belief that history *can be* expressed poetically—that the historical record, even once it has been meticulously reassembled and analyzed, amounts to something less than the sum of its parts. Although Shakespeare's simple central metaphor—king as actor—is commonplace, and although his play is short on any details about Richard II other than those that intersect with an audience's highly generalized and nonhistorical ideas about kingship, his magnificent poetry is invoked as a kind of necessary gloss on historical process.

Thus Saul not only ends with Shakespeare's Richard, he begins with him as well: "*Richard II* is one of the most powerful of Shakespeare's history plays. It not only contains some of Shakespeare's most impressive poetry; its lyrical pathos and aesthetic unity give it a compelling force which its author rarely subsequently surpassed" (1). The word *powerful,* I think, here glosses and ennobles the lack of correspondence between dramatic narrative and historical record. Saul responds positively, excitedly to a form of historical narrative-making that he, as a historian, is forbidden to indulge: that is, the lack of correspondence between events in Shakespeare's play and the recorded events of Richard's reign enables and is enabled by compression—of narrative, of chronology, of character and motivation; the product of this compression is a theatrical and poetic energy that audiences (readerly and theatrical) perceive as the manifestation of something "essential"—essential *because* it brazenly flouts the historical record.

I am particularly interested in the way source-minded readers of *Richard II* have conspired with Shakespeare's imagination to fill the void between the sixteenth-century stage king and the fourteenth-century monarch because of its similarity to the way New Historicist readers of the play have worked to fill the void between the events of the play and significant political events in the late sixteenth and early seventeenth centuries. Leeds Barroll's salutary illustration of the unsentimental rigor required in the examination of historical documents notwithstanding,[26] the greater part of historical criticism of *Richard II* over the past two decades has labored to identify the source of the play's energy in different forms of resonance with the Essex rebellion. Not coincidentally, I think, arguments for these resonances must be developed out of different forms of absence: the difficulty in dating the play precisely has fu-

eled a correspondingly energetic quest to identify topical allusions
that make a precise dating possible.[27] The "missing" deposition
scene in the Elizabethan quartos allows us to imagine a censorship
narrative and either a politically contentious playwright or a literary culture in which movable type is mightier than the stage.[28] The
fact that the play clearly did *not* have a galvanizing effect (and, indeed, the fact that this play may not even have been the one that
was performed) on the eve of the Essex rebellion has to a certain
degree only made the theatrical character of the rebellion and its
aftermath seem all the more important for understanding *Richard
II* as an expression, or not an expression, of Shakespeare's, or the
Elizabethan theater's, capacity for political efficacy. In Shakespeare's play, and perhaps in early modern history plays in general,
historical personages and events are important—perhaps, indeed,
intelligible—only insofar as they can be made to serve a symbolic
function, coming to seem like actors in a dramatic narrative that the
playwright simply gave a different, more coherent shape. Historical
Richard II criticism, and perhaps historiographic criticism of early
modern history plays in general, mimics and adopts the dramatist's
formal prerogative, presenting dramatic narrative as a digest of historical events, inevitably reducing one to a version of the other.

*   *   *

This essay's idiosyncratic reading of *Richard II*'s poetry, and its critique of historical criticism of the play, developed out of my experience of teaching the play to both undergraduate and graduate
students, and searching for a way of answering students' questions
about Shakespeare's "use" of history that did not make historical
inquiry seem simply like a version of literary-critical discourse. I
wanted to find a way of conveying to students that the thing we
might call "history itself"—series of temporally distant, more or
less (but not necessarily) verifiable events initiated and reacted to
by individuals with complex and contradictory motivations—can
only become legible, subject to symbolic use and interpretation,
once it ceases to exist as such. (Such an idea is certainly not new,
but is particularly difficult to express when dealing with a play,
like *Richard II,* that, by virtue of its very content, insists that the
discovery of "history itself" is not only possible, but the whole
point.) This is not to suggest, as the formalist reading with which I
began certainly might, that Shakespeare's *Richard II* does not
amount to what we might call a vision of history, or that this vision

is ideologically neutral; it is also not to suggest that "history itself" is something we can have access to, independent of readings of it, whether Shakespeare's or Nigel Saul's. What I do mean to suggest is that the pedagogically and critically convenient rhetorical formulations of source-study and New Historicism inevitably frame the search for a historical drama's ideological implications in terms of the existence—verifiable in the antecedent documents—of "history itself." Thus, to take one small example, Shakespeare's Woodstock, whitewashed and implausible when compared to the Woodstock known to Holinshed and other historians before and since, can only be an allegory for late-sixteenth-century Puritan political discourse or an index of the historical figure's "real" factionalism—and thus an allegory for the sixteenth century's revisionist medieval history. In either case, paradoxically but predictably, Shakespeare's divergence from the historical record points us in the direction of the essence of history itself, and that essence is to be found in Shakespeare.

In the model of source-study and historical criticism I have been working against throughout this essay, historical playwriting is conceived as a process of digestion, where poetic energy (mobile, figurative and productive, essential) is the product and the historical figure (temporally fixed, circumscribed by the literal, dead) is the by-product. A problem with this model is its suggestion that a playwright somehow *requires* the food of history to create poetic energy; as source studies like Saccio's or the more or less obligatory remarks at the beginning of scholarly editions of *Richard II* indicate, literary-critical conventions have not yet allowed for the creation of a vocabulary that would describe the way in which the creation of a history play is very much independent of the historical record in any and every sense—a vocabulary that does not result in every "departure" from the source being used to reinscribe the source's priority. Graham Holderness has argued that Shakespeare "had an understanding of medieval history much more complex and detailed than is generally acknowledged," and that his decision to begin *Richard II* in the last years of the monarch's reign is grounded in Shakespeare's reading of that moment in Holinshed as "the climax of [the] conflict between monarchy and feudalism which had been actively fought out throughout Richard's reign."[29] Especially when dealing with the crucial event of Richard's deposition, critics have followed Holderness's assumptions about Shakespeare's understanding of Holinshed, whether or not they agree with his claim about Shakespeare's view of the conflict between monarchy and feudalism. Thus Janet Clare's discussion of the possible censorship of Q1597 turns, in part, on Shakespeare's apparently deliberate decision to omit the king's reading of the articles of deposition which is recorded in Hall and Holinshed.[30] Barbara Hodgdon, in a book that is otherwise interested in thinking around linear relationships between source and performance, argues that "[i]n a carefully ambiguous move, *Richard II* evades the dynastic rift created by Bolingbroke's accession, mentioning neither his attempt in the Parliament to claim right by succession nor the surviving Yorkist claim in the Mortimer family . . . both of which Holinshed details."[31] Dominique Goy-Blanquet, writing in the recent *Cambridge Companion to Shakespeare's History Plays*,[32] notes that the 1587 edition of Holinshed "is often thought to have inspired the vogue of history plays" (63); and Robyn Bolam, writing about *Richard II* in the same volume, discusses the equivocal handling of Gloucester's murder and its relationship to the conflicts leading to Richard's usurpation: "[t]he sources show Gloucester as a potential threat and offer some political justification [for his murder], should Richard have done the deed—but Shakespeare does not put this in his play" (145). In this mode of analysis Shakespeare's subtlety cancels out, and is canceled out by Holinshed's relative accuracy; the complexly ambiguous theatrical and historiographical act that Phyllis Rackin has understood Shakespeare's history plays to be[33]—indeed the artistic agency of Shakespeare himself—is reduced to a dialogue between textual artifacts, whose respective meanings can be defined as a function of the calculated variation of one from the other.

While a Shakespeare who read Holinshed closely and understood him deeply is not mutually exclusive of the poetically raucous, compressing poet I have been imagining, I do think we need a way of thinking about Shakespeare's use of history in a play like *Richard II* that more accurately takes into account the kind of expediency necessary to the writing of dramatic poetry, and that locates Shakespeare more specifically in the theatrical world that was in this period producing plays like *The Famous Victories of Henry V, Look About You, The Blind Beggar of Bednal Green*—and, indeed, *2 Henry IV*. Arriving at such a way of thinking might involve restructuring the digestive metaphor with which I began this section. Consuming Holinshed's history for the sake of a career in the commercial theater, Shakespeare is a greedy, messy eater, selecting the dainty or sweet bits that appeal to him, that have not been touched by others, and ignoring the rest. The morsels he finds most delectable are not necessarily always the most nourishing for his art. We might see the product of this form of consumption as a poetic energy that fuels an artistic project that is taut in some places, flabby in others, at some times marvelously proficient and at others somewhat sweaty in its exertions; the by-product is the fatuous idea of historical process and personage that the play perpetrates upon generations of spectators and readers, teachers and students.

But this metaphor, while a useful corrective to and augmentation of the first, is not entirely satisfactory because its digestive conceit still implies a relationship of necessity between play and historical record—still implies that the character and effect of Shakespeare's poetry is a function of his distance from or proximity to prior documentary sources. My analysis in the first part of this essay was meant to offer one alternative method of making simultaneous use of Holinshed and Shakespeare in such a way as to give equal weight to some of their very different objectives. My critique in the second part of this essay was intended to close off as many easy routes of escape as possible with regard to the knotty and unavoidable rhetorical problem of talking about "history" when dealing with a play that represents historical persons and events. My goal in this third part of the essay has been to arrive at a way of describing the origin of the impulse to conflate Shakespearean history with the (or an) historical record. The impulse, I have tried to suggest, originates in a void; Shakespeare's text and Holinshed's are not connected, as by a thread, but rather in orbit around one another, and the space between them is the source of a motion that is enabled by mutual attraction and repulsion. Shakespeare's achievement in *Richard II* at least partially as the creation of something out of nothing—or nearly nothing. The plot of *Richard II* in no way depends upon the, or any, historical record, though the playwright's assessment of the importance of the historical record was certainly instrumental in the play's conception; the action of the plot proceeds, quite unlike almost any other history play of the period, as though these two years were the *only* years of the monarch's considerably longer reign; the poetry, as much as it reflects many of the thematic and imagistic preoccupations that were characteristic of Shakespeare's entire career, is unlike anything he had written before. The mechanism by which this highly unanchored structure attains meaning involves the conversion of the symbol of something into the illusion of its essence; a wafer of Holinshed becomes the spirit of Richard. In the experience of Shakespeare's *Richard II,* what is consumed by playwright and audience—a complex coalescence of historical record, popular imagination, critical tradition, actorly presence, and poetic shorthand—is converted into a figure, "Richard II," consuming vanities, consumed with sorrow, that did not exist before, though it resembles something, or some things, that did. The transubstantiation of verbal matter calls into the world a mystical, mythical being; it is a process that Richard, as we imagine Shakespeare imagined him, would have liked.

Notes

I am grateful to the following people for their comments on earlier drafts of this essay: Paula Blank, Alan Dessen, Jill Levenson, Genevieve Love, Katherine Vitale, and the anonymous reader at *Shakespeare Studies.*

1. "Imagery in *Richard II* and *Henry IV,*" *Modern Language Review* 37.2 (1942): 113–22.

2. See, for example, Richard D. Altick, "Symphonic Imagery in *Richard II,*" *PMLA* 62 (1947): 339–65; Arthur Suzman, "Imagery and Symbolism in *Richard II, Shakespeare Quarterly* 7.4 (1956): 355–70 (Suzman's claim, on 355, that perhaps "in no other of Shakespeare's plays do imagery and action so closely correspond" is typical); Karl Felsen, "*Richard II;* Three-Part Harmony," *Shakespeare Quarterly* 23.1 (1972): 107–11; Mary Grace Garry, "Unworthy Sons: Richard II, Phaethon, and the Disturbance of Temporal Order," *Modern Language Studies* 9. 1 (1978): 15–19; Allan Shickman, "The 'Perspective Glass' in Shakespeare's *Richard II,*" *Studies in English Literature* 18.2 (1978): 217–28; Scott McMillin, "Shakespeare's *Richard II:* Eyes of Sorrow, Eyes of Desire," *Shakespeare Quarterly* 35.1 (1984): 40–52; and Robert M. Schuler, "Magic Mirrors in *Richard II,*" *Comparative Drama* 38.2–3 (2004): 151–81 (see, especially, page 172, "The conceptual network of mirror-theft inversion images and ideas by which Richard so deliberately and effectively demonizes Bolingbroke in the deposition scene, and which is a touchstone of Richard's developing moral imagination, is also a key element in the play's political unconscious and in the dramatist's conception of history"). Editions of the play conventionally draw attention to its heightened poetic artificiality. Bevington's introduction to the play in his recent Longman edition (2003) is characteristic: "Balance and symmetry are unusually important in *Richard II.* . . . The play has [in the theater] become a vehicle for spectacle and striking visual effects emphasizing the symmetries of the text's attention to poetic symbolism and social ritual . . ." (745). For a useful survey of the relatively recent production history of the play, see Margaret Shewring, *Shakespeare in Performance: King Richard II* (Manchester: Manchester University Press, 1996). On page 3 Shewring says that the play's "patterned poetic language complements a deliberately balanced structure in which episodes are juxtaposed, mirrored or contrasted. . . ." A particularly vivid representation of the manifestation of this patterning in performance comes

in her description of John Barton's 1973 RSC production (120–37), which "provided a stylised visual framework which shaped the interpretation of the script" (121). See in particular the production photographs reprinted between pages 146 and 147, which include a photo of 5.5 where Richard is visited by a groom who looks almost exactly like him. In Barton's production, that Groom turned out to be Bolingbroke in disguise.

3. Shakespeare's decision to focus entirely on the last two years of Richard II's reign seems to have come in part from Hall, who starts his *Union* with the quarrel between Mowbray and Bolingbroke. Dover Wilson suggested that "in a sense Hall furnished the frame and stretched the canvas for the whole Shakespearean cycle, *Richard II* to *Richard III*," but Peter Ure has argued that although Shakespeare "may well have remembered Hall's general scheme, and perhaps some of his emphases, I cannot feel with any confidence that he actually consulted the text of Hall" (see *Richard II*, ed. Wilson [Cambridge: Cambridge University Press, 1951] liv, and *Richard II*, ed. Peter Ure [London: Methuen, 1961] xlix), and Charles R. Forker concurs with this view in the most recent Arden edition (see page 138). Lister M. Matheson ("English Chronicle Contexts for Shakespeare's Death of Richard II," in *From Page to Performance: Essays in Early English Drama*, ed. John A. Alford, 195–220 [East Lansing: Michigan State University Press, 1995]) has argued that Shakespeare seems to have taken the details of Richard's murder more from Hall than Holinshed; but on the whole it is clear that he followed Holinshed even as he ignored most of the description Holinshed gives of Richard II's reign. One reason for the play's narrow focus might be, of course, that two other recent plays, *Jack Straw* and *Thomas of Woodstock* had already covered many of the other dramatic and significant events of Richard's reign. Editorial consensus continues to be that *Woodstock* preceded *Richard II*. MacDonald P. Jackson, however, has argued on the grounds of detailed stylistic and orthographic analysis, that the play belongs to the period 1598–1608 and thus is derived from Shakespeare's. See "Shakespeare's *Richard II* and the Anonymous *Thomas of Woodstock*," in *Medieval and Renaissance Drama in England* 14 (2001): 17–65. My essay will not take a position on the relative dates of these two plays, except to say that whichever was second certainly must have been written with the first in mind.

4. Holinshed, 837, describes Gloucester as "hastie, wilfull, and giuen more to war than peece," and the description of Richard's reign given both by Holinshed and more recent historians such as Nigel Saul, Anthony Steel, and Harold F. Hutchison bear this impression out. See, especially, Saul, *Richard II* (New Haven: Yale University Press, 1997): 178–79. Paula Blank, following A. P. Rossiter's argument about the relationship between *Woodstock* and *Richard II*, says that "Shakespeare's John of Gaunt . . . seems to have had [the earlier theatrical] Woodstock in mind rather than the man Holinshed described. . . ." See "Speaking Freely about *Richard II*," *Journal of English and Germanic Philology* 96.3 (1997): 327–48. The quotation is from 329. Rossiter, in his 1946 edition of *Woodstock* (London: Chatto and Windus) describes that play's hero as "an unpriggish good-natured stoic, at once Lord Protector and a Thomas-More-like humorist" (26). If *Woodstock* was in fact written and performed before *Richard II*, it would have acted as a kind of theatrical history for Shakespeare's audience, as Blank notes. Whatever the order of the plays, the fact that both set out so deliberately to misrepresent Woodstock suggests either that there was an independent popular tradition about that figure's personality (and if there is, it is now lost to us), or that audiences did not really

have any specific sense of Woodstock as a historical personality except insofar as he was opposed to Richard II, or both.

5. Richard's queen in 1398–99 was the nine- or ten-year-old Isabelle of France.

6. More, I think, than in any of his history plays, Shakespeare is content in *Richard II* to omit minute markers of historical verisimilitude and to supply in place of such detail a vividly artificial theatrical impressionism. It is not simply that Shakespeare narrows his focus to dramatize only the last two years of Richard's reign, but also that his play seems almost entirely unaware, at any specific level, of the preceding twenty years. An interestingly characteristic example is in 1.4, after the banishment of Bolingbroke, when Green suggests Richard focus on something else:

> Now for the rebels which stand out in Ireland,
> Expedient manage must be made, my liege,
> Ere further leisure gives them further means
> For their advantage and your highness' loss.
>
> (38–41)

This is a highly vague, compressed reference to the rebellion of Art MacMurrough, king of Leinster after Richard's first Irish campaign (1395), described by Holinshed on 824–25 and 850–52. Perhaps most striking is the fact that Shakespeare does not even use MacMurrough's name. Compare Marlowe's *Edward II*, equally vague about the Irish situation confronting the titular monarch, where Lancaster refers to the dangers posed by the "wild O' Neill" (2.2.164). Compare, as well, the passage in *1 Henry IV* where the king lists the names of the prisoners Hotspur took (1.2.70–73); or the passage in *Henry V* where the king announces the names of the dead French nobles (4.8.90–98); or *1 Henry VI*, 1.6, where Salisbury enters to the walls of Orleans with the named, but never to be seen again, Sir Thomas Gargrave and Sir William Glasdale (Gargrave dies in the ambush; it's not clear what happens to Glasdale) and describes to them the history of his ransom in exchange for the Duke of Bedford's prisoner "the brave Lord Ponton de Santrailles" (1.6.6); these specific, if opaque, expositions of events and their local causes have almost no equivalent (2.1.279–88 is one exception) in *Richard II*.

7. The kind of king Shakespeare might have ended up representing had he taken into more detailed account the circumstances of Richard's coming to power and early reign would probably have been very much like a king he had already represented—Henry VI. At least part of Shakespeare's rationale for being so selective in his use of Holinshed must have been his desire to write a different kind of play—to take on a different kind of theatrical problem.

8. In this respect, Shakespeare was very much a man of his time. There is not space to take up the matter here, but the history of Richard II seems to me, from the extant plays of the period, the history with which early modern playwrights took the greatest liberties. *Woodstock,* for all its gripping and often sensational theatricality, is a historical travesty no matter what sources one looks at; *Jack Straw,* which does not even give a name to the character of the king, frequently has the feeling of a pseudoallegorical play rather than a history.

9. All references to *Richard II* come from the Arden 3 edition, ed. Charles R. Forker (2002).

10. This word occurs only seven times in Shakespeare—and, interestingly, five of these seven instances are in history plays.

11. All quotations of Holinshed are taken from the 1807 edition (London), printed in facsimile by AMS Press in 1965.

12. For a discussion of the importance of *sweet* to the verbal patterning of the play, see Altick, "Symphonic Imagery."

13. "Do greet" presumably would have worked just as well, and made more idiomatic sense: before Shakespeare's use of it here to mean simply "greet," the word means "greet again" or "greet in return." *OED* cites *1 Tamburlaine* as containing the first recorded use of *regreet:* Bajazeth says to a messenger he is sending to the king of Persia, "if before he sun have measured heaven / With triple circuit thou regreet us not, / We mean to take his morning's next arise / For messenger he will not be reclaimed, / And mean to fetch thee in despite of him" (3.1.36–40). *OED*'s other examples of this relatively rare word suggest that it was generally used in "elevated" contexts to achieve this pompous sound. Shakespeare gets a little hung up on the word in this scene, using it twice more (141, 186)—and these three instances account for 60 percent of all the word's occurrences in Shakespeare's plays. (Of the other two, one occurs in *Merchant,* 2.9.89, and is not particularly elevated or pompous; the other occurs in *John,* 3.1.241 and is similar to the instances in *Richard II.*) For an exciting account—just possibly related to the analysis in this essay—of other Marlovian seizures in *Richard II,* see Harry Berger, Jr., *Imaginary Audition* (Berkeley: University of California Press, 1989), especially 64–73.

14. This is not, of course, to say that the narrative structure of Holinshed is ideologically neutral—but rather that it does not, at the macrolevel, express its ideological biases in the compact formulations that characterize Shakespeare's, or indeed any playwright's, dramatic poetry. For the relationship between narrative form and political perspective in Holinshed, see Annabel Patterson, *Reading Holinshed's Chronicles* (Chicago: University of Chicago Press, 1994).

15. I should note, however, that this concern with consumption gets developed in other works besides Shakespeare's. See, for example, *Mirror for Magistrates* (ed. Lily B. Campbell [Cambridge: Cambridge University Press, 1938]): "Three meales a day could skarce content my mawe" ("King Richard the Second," line 35).

16. For the influence of Hall in this scene and the relationship between Hall and Holinshed, see Matheson, "English Chronicle Contexts," referred to in note 3, above. As well, the anonymous *Woodstock* is much more systematically concerned than Shakespeare's play with consumption and self-consumption in the reign of Richard II, though the form this concern takes is a preoccupation with sartorial splendor rather than food.

17. It should be noted that a scene of deprivation such as Holinshed describes in his first account could be quite theatrical—consider *Timon of Athens,* 3.6. As well, following the self-starvation narrative, however difficult, might have been the most appropriate option in terms of the play's concerns with invisibility, disappearance, and the staging of wasting or absence. On this topic, see McMillin, "Eyes of Sorrow, Eyes of Desire."

18. Stage business could, of course, establish a reason fairly easily: each other character onstage might have passed the coffin and looked upon the dead king's face while Henry was conversing with Exton. And while the coffin is not onstage nearly as long as it is in *Richard III* (the direction to exit in that play comes at line 226), it is onstage only about half as long as the coffin in *1 Henry VI.* I do, however, think the context in *Richard II* is importantly different—not only is there the prob-

lem of verisimilitude, but also the play is drawing to a close and I think it is clear that the coffin of the man whose death and dead body we have already seen is being brought onstage only to be taken off again immediately. Certainly Henry, on his way to the Holy Land before he's even off the stage, could be said to be eager to keep this ceremony as brief as possible. For these reasons, I feel the moment is somewhat, and importantly, theatrically unwieldy.

19. And/or, possibly, his own flesh. See the footnote in Ure's Arden edition for further discussion of the possible meanings of these lines, and also for Johnson's comment upon them.

20. I want to acknowledge here a general debt to James Siemon's *Word Against Word: Shakespearean Utterance* (Boston: University of Massachusetts Press, 2002), an extraordinary book whose ambitious project of "listening around" in order to describe Shakespeare as a Bakhtinian writer "orchestrating voices amid a context dense with other voices" (2) goes far beyond the very limited aims of this essay, but has invaluably stimulated my thinking about the layering of voices and texts that characterizes the dramatic representation of history.

21. Peter Saccio, *Shakespeare's English Kings* (Oxford: Oxford University Press, 2000). This book is a useful touchstone for this discussion because its goal of reaching both scholarly and popular audiences has been successful enough that the book, first published in 1977, was reissued in paperback in 2000, the dust jacket recording praise for the first edition from *Shakespeare Quarterly* and Samuel Schoenbaum alongside praise for the second from the *New York Times Book Review*. The book importantly and intentionally *represents* a way of thinking about the relationship between history and the history play, in the scholarly as well as theatrical world. Forker's edition, because it is the latest version of the play in the increasingly self-consciously definitive Arden series, seeks similar representative status, though perhaps more strictly limited within the academic community. It is hard to find much criticism dealing with the relationship between Shakespeare and Holinshed that strays very far from the orthodoxies summarized by these critics.

22. We might further add here that, untroublesome functionary though he may have been, the historical, not the Shakespearean, York was not so much "spineless" as caught in a series of impossible situations when his nephew Bolingbroke returned to claim what his other nephew Richard had unjustly taken away.

23. I use Forker and Saccio in this paragraph as synecdochic for source-study generally. The models of straightforward, usefully expository source-study of the kind editors regularly undertake are Kenneth Muir's *Shakespeare's Sources* (London: Methuen, 1957) and *The Sources of Shakespeare's Plays* (London: Methuen, 1977). Another, more recent book in this tradition is Stephen Lynch's *Shakespearean Intertextuality: Studies in Selected Sources and Plays* (Westport, CT: Greenwood, 1998). For an alternative model that provides a vocabulary for understanding different kinds of relationship between Shakespeare and Holinshed while treating the latter primarily as a separate text, see Annabel Patterson's *Reading Holinshed's Chronicles*.

24. The earlier definitive life of Richard, Anthony Steel's (Cambridge: Cambridge University Press, 1941) has very little to say about Shakespeare; it is notable, in an interesting and not precisely harmonious analogy to Saul, for locating the "essence" of Richard's personality, and the motivation for his behavior, in a clinical madness. Harold Hutchison's biography, which follows Holinshed and

the French chroniclers fairly closely on many important issues that Saul contradicts (in particular the existence of a plot on Richard's life that might have been the trigger for the arrest of Gloucester), also begins with Shakespeare's Richard but, in contrast to Saul, Hutchison is quite vehement in his view that the dramatist's "Lancastrian prejudices and distortions" ought to be "corrected by the historian." Nevertheless, the Shakespearean title of this biography, *The Hollow Crown,* suggests that Hutchison, too, has found something "essential" about the monarch to have been revealed in the play.

25. Saul notes that Richard "demonstrated a greater commitment to [Edward the Confessor's] cult than any other late medieval ruler" (311); he also notes that Richard was said to have come across the phial of oil "while searching in the Tower a year or two previously and had asked Archbishop Arundel to anoint him with it. The Archbishop had refused. There is an irony in the fact that the first king to use the oil should have been Richard's supplanter; but, given the dubious nature of his title, it is hard to think of anyone in greater need of the attributes of legitimation" (423–44).

26. See "A New History for Shakespeare's Time," *Shakespeare Quarterly* 39.4 (1988): 441–64.

27. See, for example, and most recently, Chris Fitter, "Historicising *Richard II:* Current Events, Dating, and the Sabotage of Essex," *EMLS* 11.2 2005 1:1–47. This essay makes the deliberately perverse argument that the play's connection to Essex can be seen more clearly by looking at *Richard II* in the context of the year in which it was performed (Fitter says this is 1596) rather than in the context of its (possible) performance on the eve of the 1601 Essex revolt. While the conclusion the essay arrives at—that the play is not a celebration of Essex, but an attack against him—is ostensibly the opposite of more typical New Historical readings of the play's function in the revolt, its methodology, identifying subtle critiques and points of resistance that resonate with a hypothetical critical but circumspect audience (see, especially, 15–19) is recognizably New Historicist in character.

28. See, for example, David Bergeron, "The Deposition Scene in *Richard II," Renaissance Papers* (1974); Janet Clare, "The Censorship of the Deposition Scene in *Richard II, RES* 41.161 (1990): 89–94, and Cyndia Susan Clegg, "*Richard II* and Elizabethan Press Censorship," *SQ* 48.4 (1997): 432–48.

29. *Shakespeare's History* (Dublin: Gill and Macmillan, 1985), 40 and 44.

30. "The Censorship of the Deposition Scene in *Richard II.*"

31. *The End Crowns All: Closure and Contradiction in Shakespeare's History* (Princeton: Princeton University Press, 1991): 138.

32. Dominique Goy-Blanquet, *Cambridge Companion to Shakespeare's History Plays* (Cambridge: Cambridge University Press, 2002).

33. Rackin, in *Stages of History* (Ithaca: Cornell University Press, 1990) writes that "conflicting conceptions of historical causation and historical truth and the ambiguous relationship between historical representations of past stability and a volatile theatrical present . . . provided the matrix for Shakespeare's English history play."

REVIEWS

The Third Citizen: Shakespeare's Theater and the Early Modern House of Commons
By Oliver Arnold
Baltimore: Johns Hopkins University Press, 2007

Reviewer: Chris R. Kyle

The nature of parliamentary representation in early modern England has long been a defining idea for historians interested in seeing how Parliament and Crown came into conflict in the 1640s. For Whig historians, the embryonic but growing ideas about representation in late Tudor and early Stuart England provided fertile ground leading to the Westminster system of parliamentary democracy. Parliament was the sounding board through which members of the House of Commons tested their power against an increasingly powerful Crown—a clash that "inevitably" led to complete breakdown in 1642 and civil war. Key to this process was the way in which the House of Commons saw itself as a representative assembly, "the power of the whole realm," as Sir Thomas Smith commented in *De Republica Anglorum* (1583). Given the importance of representation in early modern England as well as the centrality to political life of Parliament, in *The Third Citizen,* Oliver Arnold quite rightly wonders why "the legions of critics who followed in the footsteps of [the] pioneers" of historical materialism, never turned their attention to the House of Commons (25). It is a good question, and one whose neglect Arnold's work remedies in quite brilliant detail. He starts by examining the ideas and practices of representation prevalent in the early modern House of Commons before looking at their relationship with the notions of political representation that Shakespeare assimilated into his work, focusing on the first tetralogy, the Roman plays, and *The Rape of Lucrece.*

Arnold's readings are inherently interdisciplinary, using a detailed knowledge of parliamentary practice to proffer new and
important insights into Shakespeare's explorations of the involvement of the "common people" in the political process and how that
was mediated (and excluded) by the body politic. Arnold offers a
completely fresh perspective on *Titus Andronicus,* reading it as a
political play in which the rape of Lavinia is juxtaposed between
two overtly political elections. The centrality of muteness to the
play, most often discussed in the removal of Lavinia's tongue by
her rapists, Arnold also finds in the political actions of the common
people in the elections of Saturninus and his successor, Lucius. As
Arnold notes, "at the very moments that Saturninus and Lucius are
empowered by the 'voices and applause of every sort' . . ., the stage
is haunted by the silence of the people" (101). The people actually
remain mute, "the victims of political representation." Similarly,
for Arnold, the key to *Julius Caesar* lies in the idea of popular politics, seeing the play as in some sense, antitheatrical: "Shakespeare
figures the murder of Caesar as a betrayal of the people's will.
Shakespeare establishes an *empty* theater as the symbolic locus of
the conspiracy because a *full* theater was—in both Shakespeare's
England and . . . the Rome of *Julius Caesar*—a place of popular
judgment" (143). In these representations, the electoral process in
Coriolanus, and the idea of a single man (Jack Cade) acting on behalf of the "whole realm," Arnold clearly elucidates Shakespeare's
detailed knowledge of politics in Elizabethan and Jacobean England. Where then did Shakespeare acquire his knowledge of contemporary political practice and representation? The answer,
Arnold convincingly argues, was through his reading and knowledge of the political theory of the Commons as the representative
of all England (especially the "common people") and his own understanding and familiarity of parliamentary elections. The second
important idea that stems from Arnold's interpretation is that the
muteness or absence of those represented can also be found in the
procedures of the House of Commons in early modern England.
With the first idea I believe that he succeeds brilliantly, but it is in
the reality of parliamentary life that his foundation rests on somewhat shaky ground.

Arnold's thesis about parliamentary representation revolves
around the idea that Parliament, although claiming it represented
the whole realm, was so concerned about the secrecy of its proceed-

ings that there was a "defining contradiction between early modern representationalism's rhetoric of radical presence and its practices of secrecy and exclusion" (21). To this end Arnold marshals a powerful array of parliamentary speeches and individual events in the Commons to bolster his argument. Parliamentary writers such as John Hooker noted that any stranger who entered the Commons "ought . . . to be punished" and as Arnold notes, on many occasions strangers were punished. Arnold also rightly points to the occasions in which MPs were concerned about the dissemination of speeches and debates to a wider public outside the walls of its meeting place, St. Stephen's Chapel. As John Selden wryly commented in 1628, "shall the Counsells of Parliaments be layded on stalls and shall any thus divulge them?"[1] Secrecy was indeed the theory, and on *some* occasions, the reality that governed the proceedings of the early modern House of Commons. But was it the case, as Arnold claims, that "nearly everything the MPs did was 'hid and secret' " (18)? The answer to this is surely, no.

When in session, Parliament occupied a large part of Westminster Palace and commandeered many chambers within the walls for committee meetings. Westminster Hall, one of the main thoroughfares for MPs and peers heading to and from Parliament, remained open for business—the law courts were in session, the stallholders lining the walls continued to sell their wares, and sightseers and those with business in the area thronged the Hall and the surrounds. Westminster Palace was a very public place. A scant few steps away was the House of Commons lobby, and through the open doors, in a tiny chamber, MPs conducted their business. In the lobby, open to the public, an underclerk of the Commons received petitions, dispensed advice, and took orders for the copying of parliamentary documents. The proceedings could clearly be heard through the door, and unless at times of crisis when it was ordered closed, it remained open. That those who were not MPs flocked to hear the proceedings is clear from the opening of Parliament in 1604 when so many "commoners" crowded in to hear King James's speech that he had to repeat it the following day since many MPs could not get in. "Public access was only newsworthy, and only considered problematic, when it involved 'mass attendance' and only when the openness of the Palace was considered to have been abused." In practice, parliamentary secrecy was not routinely enforced and the rules surrounding it were enacted only on an ad hoc basis, and then rarely.[2]

Further to this is the extent to which parliamentary proceedings were dispersed to the countryside and the degree of local involvement with the House of Commons itself. The early modern period witnessed an unprecedented interest in the activities of Parliament, and this was reflected in the hundreds of letters sent back to friends, relatives, and local gentry each Parliament. Diaries of parliamentary business were taken in the House and widely copied. As Fritz Levy and Richard Cust have clearly demonstrated, parliamentary news was widespread in the localities.[3] MPs, too, especially those who represented corporate interests, were quick to communicate with their electorate when any business concerning them came before Parliament. In turn, towns and boroughs sent legal counsel, lobbyists, and local officials to Westminster to monitor or lobby for specific petitions or pending legislation. The period, too, although more in the 1620s it must be admitted than earlier, witnessed an increasing engagement between the House of Commons and the printing press. Speeches in Parliament remained largely *arcane sacra* (in print more than in scribal publication at least), but lobby documents, broadsides, parliamentary sermons, and verse satires increasingly found their way into (and out of) Parliament. This was not an institution or a House shut off from the outside world, or indeed in most cases, seeking to limit its engagement with those whom it represented. Parliament was, in fact, more like a theater with an audience/spectators, something Arnold's analysis dismisses.

Such historical evidence qualifies rather than evacuates Arnold's discussion of political representation and Shakespeare's literary outpourings. One of the key points that Arnold brings to the fore is that Shakespeare had knowledge of the English parliamentary process and indeed had the right to vote in four parliamentary elections (1597, 1601, 1604, and 1614) (22). Shakespeare's discussion of the electoral/selectorial process in *Coriolanus* displays an intimate knowledge of seventeenth-century elections, and his references to parliamentary procedure and representation owe much to the parliamentary writings of John Hooker and William Harrison. The correlation between Shakespeare's literary parliaments and contemporary parliamentary theory is too close to ignore.

Neither do I wish to imply that Arnold's reading of history is an indictment of interdisciplinary work (parliamentary historian rails at encroachment of literary critic on his domain). It is Arnold's

reading of Parliament and the tremendous intellectual and archival work that he completed that allows him to read the plays and *Lucrece* so effectively and with such a fresh approach. My copy is already dog-eared, read, and reread. The book is beautifully written and the ideas clearly articulated. Arnold has produced a simply superb analysis of political representation in Shakespeare, and *The Third Citizen* should be required reading for all Shakespeareans, early modern literary critics, and political historians. It is already on top of my graduate student reading list, and I would be surprised if anyone in the field who reads it does not immediately make it required reading. It is a work I thoroughly enjoyed and will wholeheartedly recommend to colleagues in both history and literature.

Notes

1. Robert C. Johnson, Mary Frear Keeler, Maija Jansson Cole, William B. Bidwell, eds, *Commons Debates, 1628* (New Haven: Yale University Press, 1977), 2:411–12, 416.

2. Chris R. Kyle and Jason Peacey, "'Under cover of so much coming and going': Public Access to Parliament and the Political Process in Early Modern England', in *Parliament at Work,* ed. Kyle and Peacey (Woodbridge: Boydell and Brewer, 2002), 10.

3. Fritz Levy, "How Information Spread Amongst the Gentry," *Journal of British Studies* 21.2 (Spring 1982): 11–34; Richard Cust, "News and Politics in Early Seventeenth-Century England," in *Reformation to Revolution: Politics and Religion in Early Modern England,* ed. Margo Todd, 232–51 (New York: Routledge).

Shakespeare and the Mismeasure
of Renaissance Man
By Paula Blank
Ithaca: Cornell University Press, 2006

Reviewer: Wendy Beth Hyman

And now I have only one favor more to ask (else injustice to me may perhaps imperil the business itself)—that men will consider well how far, upon that which I must needs assert (if I am to be consistent with myself), they are entitled to judge and decide upon these doctrines of mine; inasmuch as all that premature human reasoning which anticipates inquiry, and is abstracted from the facts rashly and sooner than is fit, is by me rejected . . . as a thing uncertain, confused, and ill built up; and I cannot be fairly asked to abide by the decision of a *tribunal which is itself on trial.*

—Francis Bacon

Several decades ago, historian of science Thomas S. Kuhn made the controversial claim that Western science—despite the popular fantasy of its "development-by-accumulation"—does not truly progress.[1] On the contrary, the scientific establishment resists rather than welcomes challenges to its existing paradigms. Kuhn does not so much judge this process as explain it: how could any scientist, after all, function without taking certain facts about the universe as givens? As far as science is concerned, discrepancies and anomalies simply must be regarded with great skepticism and interpreted in terms of established "paradigm-induced expectations" whenever possible (52). When not possible—when significant anomaly forces an epistemological crisis—a new paradigm will finally triumph over the old, but usually only after having encountered substantial resistance (consider the fate of Galileo). Members of the previous establishment, having resisted the change and perhaps even lacking the tools to participate in the new conversation, must assimilate or become irrelevant. What had been marginalized soon becomes the new orthodoxy, equally unequipped to recognize paradigm shifts on the next horizon.

Three and a half centuries before Kuhn, another controversial historian of science argued that long-overdue changes in natural philosophy demanded a radical paradigm shift: but this theorist, Francis Bacon, offered to provide that paradigm shift himself. Self-fashioned as a new Adam, Bacon in his prefatory epistle "The Great Instauration" (to his confrontationally titled *Novum Organon*) proposed to abolish the hegemony of Aristotle and the scholastics, and in effect discover the world anew. The sciences, he argued, were hopelessly mired in the past, resulting in a profusion of errors, a failure to understand the world as it truly is, and a stalling of intellectual progress. To address these shortcomings, Bacon offered a revolutionary new program: the unification of induction and empiricism, which he believed could change the world. For his hubris, of course, Bacon has come in for much criticism. Regardless, he was right: the scientific establishment *was* in absolutely no position to evaluate Bacon's proposals. After all, that establishment was limited to a "method of reasoning" (to borrow from another contemporary translation of *Novum Organon*) "that [was] itself on trial."

This vertiginous and urgent task of measuring the measurements—and the measurers—is the subject of Paula Blank's second book, *Shakespeare and the Mismeasure of Renaissance Man*. This well-researched, genuinely original, and nuanced study approaches the subject of measurement from a variety of perspectives, and comes to an important conclusion: on the brink of the scientific revolution (that which Bacon, for one, helped to promulgate), Shakespeare's poems and plays consistently reveal profound ambivalence about the culture's available tools of measurement, comparison, and relative justice. This in itself would be an interesting contribution to intellectual history, but Blank goes quite a bit further. It is not just that play after play demonstrates uncertainty about determinations of relative worth, but also that Shakespeare realizes how the poet, too, is imbricated in this crisis of measurement. For if merchants relied on fathoms and carpenters on ells, poets relied on verse—the "metrics" or measures of which were by no means fixed during the early modern period. By considering language from this perspective, Blank asks us to set aside mimetic or visual theories of poetry and instead consider "the extent to which Renaissance writers thought of poetry as a system of measurement, a means of evaluating oneself and one's world through verse, a rhetorical weighing of human lives and loves" (41). This hypothesis is examined in light of the Sonnets and several plays: *Othello, The Merchant of Venice,*

King Lear, Measure for Measure; the late plays as a collective entity;
and very cursorily (in an epilogue), *Hamlet.*

In order to provide a context for these philological concerns,
Shakespeare and the Mismeasure of Renaissance Man opens by
surveying "The Renaissance Art of Measurement," as the first
chapter is titled. This is a topic on which one might think little new
could be written. But rather than re-rehearse the ancient fantasy of
homo mensura, or the various Vitruvian or Platonic ideals of proportion, Blank points out the limits and inaccuracies in these systems—limits of which Shakespeare himself, she argues, was
poignantly aware (the biographical fallacy, if it is one, is a feature
of Blank's idiom throughout; e.g., "Shakespeare had reason to
imagine that 'measurement' was always and already a matter of art
rather than empirical science, a practice of making the rules that
then prescribe, rather than reveal, the dimensions of human knowledge" [17].) Whatever Shakespeare's personal beliefs, however, the
problem might well have been obvious to anyone living in early
modern England: as Blank establishes, measures varied from region
to region, from merchant to merchant, and sometimes from year to
year. The problem was so ubiquitous, it appears, that even those
laws attempting to institute some regularity only added confusion
to the system. Blank's review of the relevant statutes, and anecdotes about the kinds of misunderstandings that often arose, make
for engaging reading and show the literal dimension of "some of
the theoretical and philosophical problems of 'measuring' measures" (32).

Blank's marvelous second chapter, "Poetic Numbers and Shakespeare's 'Lines of Life,'" is at once the most traditional, the most
ambitious, and (excepting perhaps the surprisingly original chapter
on *King Lear*) the most successful in the book. The first part of chapter 2 offers a review of Renaissance poetic theory, particularly as it
concerns "enumeration," proportion, and other quasi-arithmetical
acts (Blank reminds us, for example, that Puttenham thought of the
art of meter as a "mathematicall science"). But Shakespeare, she
argues, doubted that meter, language, or measure of any kind could
forge equalities among disparate things. With reference to several
of the sonnets that seem to play deliberately with innumeracy (e.g.,
17, 103, 121, 136), Blank makes the compelling case that Shakespeare's ostensible goal of "enumerating" or "numbering" the virtues of his beloved(s) is perhaps secondary to his exploration of

whether these "rhetorical numbers" could in fact "compose a fit rule for love" (45). Consistently it appears that value in the *Sonnets* is not inherent, but rather a trick of language.

If this is true for meaning, moreover, it appears also to be true of form. That is to say, any system of measure—at the risk of tautology—can only be as strong as its instruments of measurement. Bacon knew it. The Magna Carta addressed it. And Shakespeare worried intelligently about it: not just in the content of his sonnets, but even in their very construction. This is the weighty argument of the second part of chapter 2: that we have mistaken how Shakespeare himself might have scanned his own lines—that *we* have mismeasured *him*. In short, Blank argues that the *Sonnets* must be read as rather more syllabic than iambic. The evidence seems considerable: decasyllables and hendecasyllables are customary, but the iambic pentameter paradigm can be misleading, even meaningless, when approaching such verse as, "Let me not to the marriage of true minds / Admit impediments" (116.1–2). Likewise, Blank applies her iconoclastic (I use the term admiringly) metrics to the seemingly "natural" meter of the late plays. These, she says, must be seen as freely incorporating something like quantitative verse, especially in those syllabically "short" lines (e.g., "signifying nothing"). More radically still, Blank proposes that the apparently iambic nature of Shakespeare's poetry may be as incidental, even as accidental, as the occasionally iambic nature of his prose. For Shakespeare, she writes, "Prose doesn't 'mean' one thing any more than verse does; rather, they mean in increasingly complex relations to each other" (74). It is a brave argument and beautifully defended: if the reader never believed she could find a discussion of prosody gripping, *Shakespeare and the Mismeasure of Renaissance Man* is about to prove her wrong.

The later chapters of the book draw upon Blank's hard-won theoretical paradigm: the hypothesis that in Shakespeare's plays, meaning is not absolute but established in a complex of interactions, in shifting and contingent relationships to other things. For example, in "Pounds of Flesh: Race Relations in the Venice Plays" (chapter 3), under consideration is "just *how* equal men and woman may be judged to be, pound for pound of human flesh" (80)—particularly with regards to race. "Rather than a permanent material condition, a discrete, fixed, or invariable nature," race is for Shakespeare about "a relation that arises *between* people; it is a kinship, but one that is generated among potentially shifting points of family resem-

blance" (81). This leads to some provocative reading of the racialized characters in these plays and the theme of measurement and
value. I find compelling Blank's argument with regards to Shylock.
However much it might move a contemporary audience, Shylock's
rhetorical gambit ("hath not a Jew eyes") is immaterial because
Shylock is *not* equal to Antonio in any eyes but his own. This in-
commensurability of being is then literalized in his failure to measure out a precise pound of flesh. More curious is the reading of
Iago in terms of the vectors of Spanishness and, therefore, Jewish-
ness and Moorishness. But here too the hybrid and vertiginous experience of race (one need only think of Othello's suicidal smiting
of "Turk" by "Venetian") is well taken, and no doubt, Iago partakes
of it too.

"Shakespeare's Social Arithmetics: Checking the Math of *King
Lear*" examines the problem of relative versus absolute value in
King Lear through the lens of early modern mathematical texts. In
both, the value of a figure is "contingent upon its 'place' "—its relationship to other human or numerical figures (122). What, then, is
true worth? Of course, many other critics have considered the economics of love in *King Lear,* but here, too, Blank's perspective is
fresh. The crisis of the play, it seems, is that Cordelia does *not* represent a very different value set than the King's; she too speaks in
terms of proportion, calculation, and division, such that "for Cordelia, as for Albany [and Lear], it's a matter of trying to get the math
right" (129). This sets up the haunting possibility that Lear's error
is precisely in trying to divide things equally—in mistaking arith-
metical for geometrical equalities. Distributive justice may require
fairness, but not an identity equation: especially when those thirds
are not equal (or divisible) to begin with. It is a subtle and careful
argument that ultimately shows Shakespeare taking part in a larger
cultural preference for distributing to each only according to his
desserts. Once more, of course, the system is only as strong as its
(inherently biased and interested) means of measurement.

If there is a criticism to offer about *Shakespeare and the Mismeasure of Renaissance Man,* it ironically has to do with disproportion
in the book itself. Although Blank's thick reliance on historical
sources is generally impressive, frequent use of minimally expli-
cated quotations (from the works of Aquinas, Augustine, Cicero,
Hooker, and so on) sometimes crowd out discussion of Shakespeare's plays themselves. In general, a greater integration of background material with analysis, or at least more signposting, would

have only strengthened the book further. This is especially the case in the final chapter, "The Lesbian Rule of *Measure for Measure*," of whose thirty-seven pages only nine actually discuss Shakespeare's play. As the title suggests, where earlier chapters consider metrical, racial, and economic equality, the concern here is on legal justice—equivalence and fairness under the law. For Shakespeare and his contemporaries, the "moral and mental 'spirit' of measurement" is seen to triumph over its 'letter,'" or, in other words, "equity emerges as the highest *kind* of equality—more 'equal' than others" (173). It is unfortunate to find disproportion here, since this otherwise significant book thereby loses a bit of steam at the end. But ultimately this is a complaint about structure, not content; the argument does seem of a piece with the rest of the book, if less compelling because of its brevity.

Shakespeare and the Mismeasure of Renaissance Man remains a genuinely engaging and important read to the end (no spoilers here: you'll have to read the book to learn the answer to the epilogue's question, "How smart is Hamlet?"). Blank's analysis of the fallibility of all human systems of measure successfully pushes against several critical "paradigm-induced expectations." In particular, her chapter on poetic numbers challenges how we customarily read and teach Shakespeare's *Sonnets,* and might well encourage critics seriously to rethink the question of meter in Renaissance poetry and drama. More broadly, what Blank has done is resurrect a Renaissance—as opposed to an early modern—Shakespeare: a poet whose faith is not in systems, but in mind. In art, in verse, in life (or at least, it would seem, in Shakespeare's plays) parities are forged, not found. If Blank's thesis is right, then "the mind that measures" discovers not any essential truth, but "its own latitude, its own span" (21). This is a cautionary tale, but also a deeply humane one, revealing Shakespeare's own latitude in a new light.

Notes

Epilogue is taken from Francis Bacon, "The Great Instauration," in *The Works of Francis Bacon,* ed. James Spedding, Robert Leslie Ellis, and Douglas Denon Heath, vol. 8 (Boston: Taggard and Thompson, 1863), emphasis added.

1. Thomas S. Kuhn, *The Structure of Scientific Revolutions,* 3rd ed. (Chicago: University of Chicago Press, 1996 [1962]), 2.

Voice in Motion: Staging Gender, Shaping Sound in Early Modern England
By Gina Bloom
Philadelphia: University of Pennsylvania Press, 2007

Reviewer: Carolyn Sale

Gina Bloom's *Voice in Motion: Staging Gender, Shaping Sound in Early Modern England* is on very interesting terrain. It follows in the footsteps of Bruce R. Smith's *The Acoustic World of Early Modern England* (1999), which asserts the importance of sound as a material factor in the early modern theater. Bloom's book aims to overcome the "limits" of Smith's book, and that of a related work by Wes Fokerth and Kenneth Gross, which "universalize the auditory experiences of male characters" (115), by focusing on the relationship of gender and voice on the early modern stage. Its three-pronged investigation considers the challenges facing the boy actor, who had to deal with the threat of a "cracked" or "squeaking" voice as he personated women on the early modern stage (chapter 1); Shakespeare's representations of the powers of women to exercise agency through the wielding of breath (chapter 2); and the representation of women as auditors in late Shakespeare (chapter 3). The fourth chapter analyzes the representation of Echo in George Sandys's seventeenth-century translation of Ovid's *Metamorphoses*.

On the one hand, Bloom seeks to contribute to the material history of early modern England by tracing "the materiality of spoken articulations" (2); on the other, to contribute to performance history, not only by investigating how the boy actor seeks to control his voice, but also by fashioning a theory of audience based on the relationship of audience members to the representation of female characters as "acoustic subjects" (18). The fourth chapter, although not about a dramatic text, aims to contribute to the overall investigation by extending the discussion in earlier chapters of the "vocal agency" of women. In the figure of Echo wresting from Narcissus's words the sounds and language that she needs to express her own desires, Bloom finds evidence of an "uncanny female vocal agency" (163). Given that three of the four chapters revolve, in one way or one another, around the question of female agency, and the fourth chapter is about a nondramatic text, the book's emphasis seems to fall on its gender concerns, rather than (as the introduction suggests) its contributions to performance theory. But it is in regard to the latter that this book extends a challenge that other scholars of early modern culture will want to take up.

*   *   *

The book's opening paragraph, which discusses the sounds frozen in ice in Rabelais' *Gargantua and Pantagruel* (1534), suggests one of the ways in which Bloom's book pursues Smith's into an "acoustic world": the tale, which involves sounds of a sea fight frozen in ice that are set free when the ice thaws, testifies to the enduring materiality of sound. Bloom reads the tale, however, for its hints of "the instabilities [that] render the voice susceptible to a range of forces beyond speakers' control" (2). Where Smith aimed (among other things) to consider how the Globe's wooden O functioned as an organ within which audience members were immersed in a heightened acoustic environment, and subject to the power of sound, Bloom's initial focus is on the instability of voice and the potential failure of all communication. Among the questions she asks at the outset is "If the voiced is produced by unstable bodies, transmitted through volatile air, and received by sometimes disobedient hearers, how can voice be trusted to convey an individual's thoughts to a listener?" (3). The question, while both fair and stimulating, suggests that Bloom has a predisposition toward the materials of her investigation that may affect how she pursues her project of theorizing the relation between voice and agency in early modern culture.

In chapter 1, "Squeaky Voices: Marston, Mulcaster and the Boy Actor," for example, Bloom is not so much interested in the powers of "voice" and how they are harnessed either by actors or characters in the early modern theater, but rather in where they fail or risk failing. This means that while the book has a cogent, in-depth and persuasive discussion of how *King John*'s Constance harnesses breath to do things with words, the greater part of the book focuses on "how early modern authors . . . figure the unstable voice as a function of an unmanageable body" (22). In chapter 1, this takes the form of readings of *Coriolanus* and *Antonio and Mellida* that focus on the uncertain masculinity of male characters as expressed in relation to voices that they cannot properly or fully control. The project of "[l]istening for masculinity" (25) on the early modern stage, and in particular for the ways in which "a man unable to keep his voice from squeaking manifests a breakdown in patriarchal order" (26), displaces any discussion of the *virtuosity* of the boy actor. This is odd, for while no speaker may be able fully to control where a breath travels, or whom it touches or penetrates, that is precisely what *actors* aim to do. Artists of breath as much as artists of look and gesture, early modern actors would have been continually providing their audiences (whether they were conscious of it or not) with models for harnessing and controlling their own breaths, as *Richard III's* Buckingham suggests when he claims that he can "counterfeit the deep tragedian" and "[m]urther [his] breath in middle of a word." The reader may therefore find it a strange thing to be plunged into a discussion of the "thematization and performance of vocal failure" (50) before being provided with a sense of what the voice in general, and the boy actor's voice in particular, can *do* on the early modern stage. If the book established the *power* that early modern writers imagined a person might wield by harnessing their breath and voice before delving into the boy actor's difficulties in securing this power, readers might feel that they had a larger, fuller sense of the actorly "voice" that Bloom sets out to historicize.

This might have been achieved in part with a reversal of the order of the first two chapters, which would have allowed Bloom's discussion of the constituent material of voice in chapter 2, "Words Made of Breath: Shakespeare, Bacon and Particulate Matter," to come before the discussion of the boy actor's uncertain powers in harnessing breath in "Squeaky Voices." That said, we do get a discussion of an important foundational text for Bloom's investigation in chapter 1, in her reading of Richard Mulcaster's *Positions* (1561). Mulcaster's book aims to furnish readers with exercises ranging from "lowd speaking" to "playing at the ball" whereby they might harmonize those "coparteners," body and soul. Bloom's claim is that Mulcaster focuses on the "frailty of vocal instruments," the "disciplining" of children's voices, and "the dangers of overstimulating the vocal organs" (36). Mulcaster does indeed spend some time discussing the care that those who are sick need to take if they pursue his course of "vociferation" exercises, but he discusses their dangers only in relation to the inexperienced and the ill, and contends that "*gentle* exercising of the voice" is always "whole-some." Although they involve, as Bloom notes, some "straining" of the voice (by which Mulcaster means shifts between different volumes, registers, and timbres), Mulcaster's vocal exercises are designed not to *discipline,* but to *empower.* "[P]reparatives for nimbling, and spreding the vocall powers," they aid the individual in feeling the full "powers of the soule." The larger goal is "to set the breathing at most libertie, being best discharged of impediment & let," for "[t]hough all men can tell, what a singular benefit breathing is . . . yet they can best tell, which haue it most at commaundement." Bloom's characterization of Mulcaster's text as offering "a view of human vocal organs as fragile and vulnerable to malfunction," which she casts as "a crucial observation for any history of the stage" (36), may make readers familiar with *Positions* wary of the theater history that she would derive from it. But the chapter does not, in the end, offer a discussion of the ramifications for a history of the early modern stage, concluding instead with a brief discussion of questions of gender and voice in a twentieth-century film, *Shakespeare in Love.*

With chapter 2, Bloom aims to offer a "model of vocal agency" for women by demonstrating how the "volatility of breath opens up opportunities for disenfranchised figures to intervene vocally in the play's masculinist political culture" (70). Here she pursues the introduction's claim that feminist writing has provided only an "undertheorized system of analogies between voice, body, subjectivity, and agency" (13), and aims to compensate for the "shortcomings" of Judith Butler's book *Excitable Speech* (1997), which "account[s] for the role of the body as site for the performance of speech," but "does not account for the material practice of vocal performance in the way, for example, that Derrida accounts for the material practice of writing" [14]). The book is in fact at its best when accounting for this in its readings of *King John* and *Richard III.* Both plays offer Bloom important material for demonstrating just how successfully female characters in Shakespeare can do things with breath, and the discussion of *King John* gives a little-read Shakespeare play some much-needed critical attention.

Indeed, the chapter could have benefited from a more extensive discussion of *Richard III.* Bloom focuses on the power of Margaret's curses, which put the lie to Buckingham's claim that "Curses never pass / The lips of those that breathe them in the air" (1.3.284–85) by indirectly compelling Richard to despair and yield up *his*

breath. But there is plenty to be said, too, about the play's representation of Elizabeth Woodville, for her tour-de-force manipulation of
Richard at the end of act 4 traps him into breathing a curse against
himself: "Myself myself confound / . . . if with dear heart's love, /
Immaculate devotion, holy thoughts, / I tender not thy beauteous
princely daughter" (4.4.399–405). It could be argued that the play
shows these two female characters jointly marshaling, with their
words, a material force that exerts such pressure upon Richard that
while the women may not smother him they do dispirit him.
Bloom's conclusion about Margaret—she "use[s] breath to manipulate her acoustic environment" (93)—thus seems too tame.

After its brief discussion of *Richard III,* the chapter shifts to two
other references to women and breath in the Shakespeare canon,
Othello's reference to Desdemona's "balmy breath" as he prepares
to smother her (5.2.16) and Marcus's to Lavinia's "honey breath"
when he comes upon her raped and mutilated (2.4.25). Bloom asks
readers to treat each of these instances of breath as moments of
"vocal agency" for the female characters. Desdemona's "balmy
breath," Bloom contends, "makes a case for her innocence," and
"moments like these . . . suggest that breath be read as virtually sufficient for voice" (101). And as the blood rises like a "bubbling
fountain" between Lavinia's "rosed lips / Coming and going with
[her] honey breath" (2.4.23–25), Bloom would have us believe that
Lavinia "engages in a form of dramatic dialogue with Marcus":
"The tongueless Lavinia may be denied scripted lines, but she performs certain gestures that, from an early modern perspective,
denote voice: she produces breath, which leaves her lips, commu-
nicating her message to an auditor" (102). These claims confuse
concepts central to the book's investigation. It is certainly true that
Desdemona's "balmy breath" makes her case for her, but not because it is *voice,* or a "sufficient" substitute for it, but rather because it is evidence of the *spirit* with which she is infused, and thus
evidence of her character (evidence, we must note, that Othello refuses to heed). Bloom's earlier discussion of Aristotle's *De Anima*
might enable this conclusion (for Aristotle, "soul, or form, is effectively transmitted in the breath expelled during voiced speech"
[81]) if the analysis considered whether (or to what extent) breath
is soul.

Perhaps Bloom is assuming that breath always carries audible
sound, and that this is sufficient to characterize these instances of
breath as voice despite their lack of verbal matter, but, if so, the

discussion does not make this clear. The discussion of Epicurus earlier in the chapter indicates that breath accompanies voice (97), and it is fair to claim that breath is an "*ingredient* of voice" (101, my emphasis); but while breath may indeed compose voice, as Emilia claims ("I heard / Each syllable that breath made up between them" [4.2.4–5]), it does not necessarily do so; breath is a constitutive material of voice, but not voice per se. For the linkage of breath and voice in these literary exempla to be more than figurative, Bloom would have to establish how the breath is bearing "voice"—or, to use her phrasing, "carrying the harmonious voice with it" (29).

All of this is to say that Bloom's analysis here would be all the more intriguing and substantial if, rather than making what appears to be a figurative leap to breath as voice, it stuck with breath in its nonvocal or prevocal character. Bloom would thus be able to locate more precisely the dynamics that make breath voice on the continuum between breath as a material in which no sound or voice resonates and breath that yields verbal matter. As she herself notes in her discussion of Francis Bacon's *Sylva Sylvarum,* the "slippage between breath, wind and voice is common enough that natural philosophers seeking greater precision in definition warn against it" (89). In short, to secure the "redefinition of voice" that she aims for here, and the claim that it has "profound implications for the 'silenced' female characters of the stage" (101), Bloom needs to grapple with Aristotle's contention that "voice is a sound with a meaning, and is not merely the result of any impact of the breath as in coughing." More fundamentally, in none of these literary instances can the character be said to have breath at her "commaundement." Can one really claim to exercise agency, for example, when one is *asleep?* And there is nothing in Marcus's ekphrastic speech to indicate that Lavinia is doing anything to *shape* her breath into sound as it rises and falls between her "rosed lips" unless we are to believe that Marcus likens her breath to a fountain because, doing what she can to shape sound without a tongue, she *gurgles.*

Chapter 3, "Fortress of the Ear: Shakespeare's Late Plays, Protestant Sermons, and the Audience," centers on the contention that "it is often as listeners, more than as speakers, that early modern women can most successfully disrupt and reshape their world" (12). In early modern England, Bloom contends, women could not become "acoustic subjects" unless they pursued obstructive practices or made themselves, as one Shakespeare character puts it, "senseless-obstinate" (*Richard III*, 3.1.44). Unable to achieve much agency through speech, they had to practice a form of passive aggression that she dubs "disruptive deafness" (116). They had, in short, to assert themselves through "bad hearing" (148), or behavior ranging from "inattention and distraction to misunderstanding and obstinacy" (148) by which they might mount "their resistance to aural subjugation" (117).

Bloom's theory of "disruptive deafness" is driven in part by her resistance to those critics who would reclaim Shakespeare from charges of misogyny. But is it fair to claim that Shakespeare's late plays do not "exhibit protofeminist leanings" (133) by refusing to hear the ways in which Shakespeare's female characters speak up for themselves? This refusal dominates the chapter's readings of *The Winter's Tale, Cymbeline, Pericles,* and *The Tempest.* For Bloom, for example, the voluble Paulina, who is surely one of the most forthright and fearless female speakers in all Shakespeare, may "speak persuasively at crucial moments," but as she does so in a world that privileges the aural over the oral, a world in which power resides not with speakers, but with listeners, her "vocal power" is sufficiently "diminished" (132). For Bloom, the late plays' "representations of women's persuasive speech are thus a red herring" (132). Rather than consider the incredible power that Paulina appears to exert when her "magic" seems to imbue stone with breath, the chapter focuses on claims that other female characters in the Romances engage in "aural insubordination" (142). Imogen, we hear, practices "female aural defensiveness" (140), although she is not particularly good at it. If she were, she would not succumb to Iachimo's request that he leave a trunk in her bedroom. To Cloten's subsequent aural assault Bloom claims that Imogen is a "captive audience" and "unmoved" (140). Imogen's response is in fact so vociferous, so stinging, that one of her statements—her claim that Posthumus's "Meanest garment / . . . is dearer / In [her] respect than all the hairs above [him]" (2.3.133–35)—keeps ringing in Cloten's ears. Indeed, he echoes it ("His meanest garment?" [2.3.150]), proving just how deeply her words have penetrated. It is not clear why, in her search for "vocal agency" in Shakespeare's representation of women, Bloom would not want to take account of Imogen's volubility; but in response to this reading we need to ask, what feminist theory would justify the figurative tying up of a female character's tongue in order to find in "female characters who shut their ears . . . *acoustic subjects*" (18, Bloom's italics)?

Bloom is on more promising ground with Miranda, given that *The Tempest* does furnish a lengthy exchange to which Miranda's role as auditor is important. But Miranda's contributions to this exchange suggest that she speaks true when she assures her father she listens "most heedfully" to his tale of his past in Naples (1.2.78). Miranda's questions and empathetic interjections drive forward the exchange, creating the kind of dramatic dialogue that Bloom's readings of Shakespeare find in more eccentric places. They also contradict Bloom's claim that Prospero "has conditioned his daughter to practice constructive aural defensiveness" (149). For a girl who has supposedly had "curiosity" "train[ed] out of [her]" (150), Miranda sure asks a lot of questions.

At the outset of this discussion, Bloom argues that the "agentive nature of Miranda's auditory acts" (151) have been overlooked by "critics and directors of the play," who have been for the most part "unattuned to the ways audition can be a source of agency for Miranda" (150), but Bloom's analysis could itself benefit from considering that Prospero's questions may demonstrate not that Miranda is a "bad" listener, but rather that she is a powerful one. From Prospero's words she may be wresting images, and her focus on the internal spectacle that she is generating may make it seem to Prospero that she is not listening, or listening erratically, when in fact she is riveted. In other words, even as he speaks of "being transported / And rapt" (1.2.76–77), she may be so; and contrary to Bloom's later claim in relation to the character of early modern audiences, one may be "rapt" without being "malleable" (154). But even if we were to grant that Miranda here "tunes out Prospero" (157), how are we (or early modern theatergoers) to imagine that Miranda's sense of identity is affected by her act of "bad hearing"? If she is indeed engaged in an act of "disruptive deafness," what does she gain? What does she lose? And who exactly is the "acoustic subject" that we are to imagine thrives behind the palisade of Miranda's closed ears? (The claim that Bourdieu's theory in *The Outline of a Theory of Practice* [1997], that an act is sufficient in and of itself to establish a subject, is not persuasive.)

We need to ask these questions because Bloom wants these readings to serve as the foundation for a theory of audience for the period, and it is with such a theory that the book potentially has so much to offer. We very much need theories of spectatorship for the period, and theories of the female spectator in particular, and in the absence of archival material documenting responses to the theater on the part of women audience members, we have to proceed on the method that Bloom pursues here, by considering representations of female auditors (and spectators) in Shakespeare and the work of other playwrights of the period to the female auditors (and spectators) in their audiences. These representations must bear *some* relation to the experiences and practices of early modern women theatergoers. So many pages of the chapter are devoted, however, to the language of hearing in Protestant sermons of the period, that Bloom has only limited space to give over to a discussion of the proposition (first aired in the introduction) that representations of women who shut up their ears in the Shakespearean drama demonstrate to the audience the "potential for blocked ears [to] establish their role as active participants in the creation of theatre" (18). It is not clear from the brief disquisition at the end of the chapter how the "aural resistance" of audience members produces "an ideal theatrical economy" or "cooperation" between the theater's "creators" and its "receivers" (157) or how by plugging one's ears one becomes an active participant in anything. Although it is easy enough to imagine how an attentive but critical woman listener in a play might encourage women audience members to engage critically with the play—and indeed to take the theatrical representation as not only licensing their critical audition but encouraging it, and doing so not because the "creators" wish to dupe women audience members into believing that they wish to empower them, but rather because they in good faith wish women to be as active members of their culture as their male companions— Bloom rejects any such theory of "female receptive agency" (153).

This is a shame, for to "broaden our understanding of the sort of role women were imagined to play in England's professional theater" (152), we need to do more than imagine female spectators as belligerent auditors who will mirror the "disruptive deafness" of female characters and refuse to hear certain facets of a play. The "La la la la I can't hear you" T-shirts may be popular sellers with women on eBay, but the premise behind them does not take us very far toward either a new theory of early modern audiences or a theory of "female auditory agency" in the early modern period. It certainly does not compensate for what Bloom claims as the inadequacies of Judith Butler's work, which does not, in her view, "address the agentive capacities of hearing" (143). It is in fact odd that after an era in which so much feminist work on early modern culture (and contemporary feminist theory more generally) has gone into asserting female subjectivity by reclaiming women from their association with inert matter (asserted, in the early modern period, in relation to Aristotle's *De Generatione Animalium*) that Bloom would have us think of women as material again—as the "hearing bodies" (144) in the theater blocking the dispersal of the play's voices. Maybe the "hearing bodies" of Shakespeare's female characters and female members of his audience do or did "negotiate the pressures of patriarchal institutions and misogynist discourses" (144), but Shakespearean characters from Katherina to Hamlet, who in one way or another claim that they must tell their tongues or else their hearts will break, make this a hard proposition to swallow. And as Bloom herself demonstrates so well in the first half of chapter 2, in Shakespeare political agency for women comes through their acts of *speaking.* It is also worth remembering that one of the most powerful images of political impotency comes in *Richard III,* where the citizens who listen intently to Buckingham's speech about Edward IV's imputed illegitimacy, but "[speak] not a word," are like "dumb statues or breathing stones" (3.7.24–25). They may powerfully manifest their presence as listeners, but by refusing to speak anything at all, they let a killer become a king. With the final chapter, "Echoic Sound: Sandys's Englished Ovid and Feminist Criticism," Bloom pursues the question that goes unanswered in chapter 3, "how . . . *auditory* agency . . . can, with little effort on the part of the hearing subject, be converted into the kind of *vocal* agency . . ." (160, Bloom's italics). In particular she wishes to demonstrate the "uncanny female agency" of "echoic sound" (163) in Ovid's tale of Echo and Narcissus in relation to George Sandys's 1632 translation of *Metamorphoses.* Bloom furnishes an important example of Sandys's clever poetics as translator in her account of his translation of Ovid's "ecquis adest? Adest" (Is anyone here? Here), which Sandys translates as "Is any nigh? I, Ecchoe answere made" (164). Sandys chooses a word that he may split into its constituent sounds in order to produce the echo. Bloom notes the pun (aye/I) and reads this as an important assertion of Echo's personhood. But we are not, she writes, to "leap to the conclusion that Sandys's text betrays protofeminist commitments" (173) for Sandys's translation "directly undermines Ovid's more provocative representation of the female voice" (166). By "turn[ing] Echo's reverberating, disembodied voice into self-expression," she writes, he "realign[s] [the voice] with her body and self, and [thus] places echoic sound within the range of male surveillance" (166). It is not clear from Bloom's discussion how Echo's "body" matters in Sandys's translation in a way that it does not in Ovid, or how it becomes the target of the male gaze (rather than furnishing details from Sandys's translation, Bloom offers a brief digression on feminist film theorist Kaja Silverman's *The Acoustic Mirror*). Bloom's principal contention is at any rate with Sandys's commentary on the tale, which she claims "reduces Echo to an inhuman phenomenon" (174). But in the statement to which Bloom objects, Sandys is writing not of Echo the literary character, but the echo as a material phenomenon. It is true that Sandys's prose moves deftly between character and phenomenon, and that the printer has used the same typography, "*Eccho,*" for both, but the distinction is clear enough; and Bloom makes a single statement in the commentary bear too great a burden when she asks us to view Sandys's commentary as "disciplin[ing] [Echo] for her vocal unruliness" (184) because the character poses a threat to "misogynist silencing regimes" (183). Polemics here get in the way of a more nuanced reading of the translation, one that might, for example, consider how Echo features as a figure for Sandys's own art. Echo at any rate makes an odd feminist hero. She is being punished, after all, by the embodiment of female power in the tale, Juno, for putting a man's sexuality over a woman's concerns (Echo distracts Juno with long speeches to keep her from discovering Jupiter's infidelities). The punishment, which requires Echo to spend the rest of her existence attempting to express herself through a man's words, is one that very much fits the crime. Consistently hunting down evidence of "female agency" in strange places, Bloom's book may leave readers wondering if feminist critics of early modern English literature need new quarry.

The most startling thing about this book, however, is its omission of a discussion of *Twelfth Night*. The book contains only one glancing reference to the early modern play that most readers are likely to judge most relevant to its investigation. A discussion of *Twelfth Night* would have allowed Bloom to bring together two major facets of the book, her discussion of voice and gender and her discussion of the boy actor, which might have been yoked not only around the question of the play's challenge to gender, but also around the agency of the boy actor, who uses his "small pipe" (1.4.32) not only for himself, to demonstrate his virtuosity as actor, but also for women in the audience, as he voices the speeches in which Viola challenges her culture's constructions of female physiology. It is also hard to fathom how, in a book on representations of women's voices and female echoes, Bloom could have resisted discussing Viola's claim, as Cesario, that if she loved Olivia she would "hallow [her] name to the reverberate hills" (1.5.272), an act in which the expressive he of the boy actor and the expressive she of the character are enfolded.

Twelfth Night would also have allowed Bloom to pursue a number of tantalizing propositions about breath, voice and agency scattered throughout her book. The aural and visual riddle, for example, that the two boy actors playing Viola and Sebastian present to the audience when they finally appear onstage together (they are "one voice" in "two persons" [5.1.216]) challenges the assumption that bodies and breaths, voices and souls come in the discrete vessels of unitary persons, as does Feste's philosophical lesson for Malvolio on the transmigration of souls. Bloom is not uninterested in the questions that arise from considering how individuals may exchange breath, voice, and/or soul. She asks, for example, at the outset of chapter 2, "when breath leaves the speaker's body, does it still belong to its producer?" (67). Where might we go if we pursued the proposition that the "disarticulation of voice from body" may "generate vocal power" (68) while shaking ourselves free of the assumption that bedevils Malvolio, who thinks "nobly of the soul" and "no way approve[s] [Pythagoras's] opinion" (4.2.55–56)? What happens when breath and voice move *through* persons, and when the breath, voice, and/or spirit of one person *mingles* with that of another? Such considerations would take us toward the "ideal theatrical economy" of cooperative exchange that Bloom imagines in chapter 3, though by radically different means, since they are predicated on the openness, indeed, the *permeability* of bodies, rather than their refusals and closures.

The agency here may not, however, in the end be that of the individual (or not exclusively so). If, as Bloom provocatively suggests in chapter 2, dispersal of breath is a form of agency, what form of agency do the actors participate in or create as they work their breaths? (As Bloom notes, a "mere mouthful of air can convey the [actor's] voice to multiple auditors dispersed throughout the theatre space" [104].) And what happens when an audience responds to a play, as the actor playing Prospero asks audiences of *The Tempest* to do, by yielding up their "gentle breath" (Epilogue, 11)? How might the audience bound within the wooden O *echo* a play, and what agency might it collectively exert by doing so? Can it "hallow" things to the "reverberate" walls, and what would it gain in vocal power and the "commaundement" of breath by doing so? And what role might women's voices play in all of this? (Desdemona's voice, we are told, could "sing the savageness out of a bear" [4.1.189].) Ultimately, then, while I take issue with the means by which this book finds "agency" in early modern literary representations of women, I believe it has a great deal of stimulating matter to offer on the question of the relation of breath, voice, and gender, especially to those scholars who wish to take up the challenge that Bloom raises here, by asking us to do more with the materials of breath and voice as we shape theories of the early modern stage and the dynamics of early modern audiences.

Time, Space, and Motion in the Age of Shakespeare
By Angus Fletcher
Cambridge, MA: Harvard University Press, 2007

Reviewer: Jonathan Crewe

The publication of a new book by Angus Fletcher is indeed an occasion, but not one to which it is easy to rise as a respondent. One wants to find a way of expressing due gratitude and recognition without abrogating the functions of the reviewer. Performing those functions is not made easier by the simultaneous inflation and vagueness of the blurbs accompanying *Time, Space, and Motion:* "Orphic seer," "universal scholar" (Harold Bloom); "in a class by itself," "Olympian" (John Rogers); "a lifetime of thinking about the challenges of contemporary civilization" (Knoespel); "a radically new kind of exploration" (Hollander). Admittedly, blurbs are just blurbs, the marketing necessity of which everybody understands, but the blurbs accompanying Time, Space, and Motion remain a stumbling block and a provocation. All of them elevate the book above the plane of ordinary reviewing while failing to convey a single thing about the specific character and arguments of the book. Both those characteristics make the blurbs seem like evasively hyperbolic tributes to Fletcher's legendary reputation rather than to anything contained in this book.

To set the record straight, *Time, Space, and Motion in the Age of Shakespeare* is an old-fashioned book. It shows no respect for the author to pretend otherwise or to say it in code, if that is what the blurbs are doing. It is part of Fletcher's argument that books are temporally and spatially located products of the human will, and his own book is no exception. Nor does Fletcher try to make it an exception through anything remotely like Orphic posturing. *Time, Space, and Motion* bears the stamp of its time, which is not exactly the present. Both the book's title and the nature of the undertaking savor of a grand critical humanism with little current traction or credit. In keeping with this fact, the book is devoted to studying the impact of the New Philosophy on the writing and broader mentalité of the early modern period, with chapters on Marlowe, Shakespeare, Jonson, Donne, and Milton. Of course, that impact is important, but antitheses between a decentering Renaissance restlessness and centered medieval stasis now more often comprise the materials of Renaissance survey courses than of groundbreaking books. Fletcher's preoccupation with relations between literature and science as well as his desire to reconcile their respective languages harks back, precisely, to C. P. Snow's *The Two Cultures* (1959) a work cited in *Time, Space, and Motion.* Fletcher's unifying ambition harks back as well to New Critical anxiety about the diminished claims of literature vis-à-vis science. Insofar as Fletcher reveals his own consciousness that *Time, Space, and Motion* is old, he does so by acknowledging that "several chapters of this book began life long ago" (176), but more often by lamenting the decline of criticism, poetry, and humanistic authority in "our own days of massive mediocrity" (37). The phrase, "If, then, we go back . . ." (127) captures much of the spirit of the book.

I am not saying that Fletcher has failed to keep abreast. He ranges fairly widely through the field of theory, citing Wittgenstein, Bachelard, Barthes, Foucault, de Man, Deleuze, and Rorty among others. I am saying that the critical world in which Fletcher is most at home is one in which I. A. Richards (Fletcher's named mentor), Erich Auerbach, C. S. Lewis, Kenneth Burke, William Empson, E. M. W. Tillyard, Northrop Frye, C. L. Barbour, and Frank Kermode are the names to conjure with (no shame in that). Historians, anthropologists, and cultural interpreters belonging to the same Fletcherian pantheon include Frances Yates, Lucien Febvre, Johan Huizinga, Alexandre Koyré, A. N. Whitehead, Ernst Cassirer, E. A. Burtt, Herbert Butterfield, D. P. Walker, Marjorie Nicholson, Hans Blumenberg, Arnold van Gennep, and Max Black. With one exception, to which I will come in a moment, the cutoff date for work significantly informing this book seems to be around 1985, while much of the informing work dates from before that. One inescapable consequence for many readers (although they, too, may have to be of a certain age) will be the sense of having been there if not necessarily of having done that.

So what is *that?* Although Fletcher does not speak the language of rejuvenation, much of the interest of *Time, Space, and Motion* for today's readers will be that of witnessing an unquestionably distinguished, passionate intelligence seeking to reanimate what might seem to have become superannuated topics and thought-forms. That brings me to the one exception mentioned above. Given the crucial status of Galileo, and specifically of the question of motion, in Fletcher's book, he has necessarily kept pace (more so, I suspect, than most in the early modern field) with Galileo studies and relevant histories of science. He is convinced—and who can say definitively otherwise?—that the importance and excitement of early modernity are irrevocably bound up with the advent of the New Philosophy and the attendant cross-fertilization of scientific and literary thinking.

The elements of the Galilean revolution Fletcher emphasizes (citing en passant *The Assayer, The Sidereal Messenger,* and *Dialogue Concerning the Two Chief World Systems*) include Galileo's epochal reimagining of the Book of the World as one written in mathematical symbols; his equally epochal positing of inertia as the key to understanding the local motion of bodies, including planetary ones; his positing *of* motion as the critical problem for "philosophy" in his time; his factoring in of the relative viewing position, hence the detached observer—hence the telescope and the microscope—to the production of scientific knowledge. The Galilean revolution (partly subsuming Thomas Kuhn's Copernican one) as the cognitive breakthrough of the New Philosophy excites Fletcher, as well it might. Yet in recognizing Galileo's rhetorical and even literary-critical skills, Fletcher gets to what excites him even more, namely, analogies and "crossovers" between the scientific and the literary (I use these terms for convenience rather than historical fidelity) in this period. In one perspective, crossing over means the massive breakthrough *from* scientific inquiry into literary discourse that leaves practically nothing undisturbed, and in another perspective it means the crisscrossing *between* different languages and fields of discourse in what can broadly be called the humanistic era. "Translation" accordingly becomes an even more ubiquitous phenomenon than it is usually credited with being at that time. The crossing from the scientific to the literary-rhetorical, and between them, empowered speculative intellects like that of Giordano Bruno to pursue notions of a decentered, infinite plurality of worlds to the heretical limit. In the end, nothing short of burnings at the stake could uphold the "centered" medieval world picture.

According to Fletcher, early modern translation is more than just the expression of a humanistic intellectual culture in which the respective "languages" of science and literature remain incompletely differentiated, or in which a shared preoccupation with occult forces and properties, for example, unites intellectual endeavors across the spectrum. Two-way translation attests to the unresolved ontological priority of the logico-mathematical and the metaphoric, respectively. (Perhaps that is a state of permanent irresolution, of which, as Fletcher notes, even post-structuralist thinking bears significant traces.) Translation between the languages of poetry and of mathematics among others is therefore not predetermined to be unidirectional by the certainty that one of the two languages is the original one.

All of this brings us back, finally, to Time, Space, and Motion. For Fletcher, early modern Time and Space are reconceived functions of Galilean Motion. Differently put, the New Philosophy fundamentally mobilizes the cosmos, thereby revolutionizing time, space, and individual subjectivity. (Ovid's *Metamorphoses* can thus be seen as equally informing the scientific and the poetic imagination of the time.) By setting individual subjects in motion onstage, early modern drama more fully realizes the revolutionary implications of the New Philosophy than any other cultural medium; the flourishing of drama in Elizabethan and Jacobean England is therefore no coincidence. According to Fletcher, restlessness and "hysteria" characterize the mobilized subjectivities of the early modern stage, while the dramatic soliloquy paradoxically incarnates the disturbingly cool detachment of the Galilean observer, capable of turning his scrutiny on himself. Readers of Fletcher's *Allegory: The Theory of a Symbolic Mode* (1982) will be interested to hear that he now aligns the allegorical mode with centered stasis and iconic stability rather than motion, notwithstanding an acknowledgment that for Paul de Man allegory is the rhetoric of temporality.

In Fletcher's big picture, Galilean Motion transpires either in infinitely expanded Space or, as hyperactivity, in a bounded, urban space like that of Jonsonian comedy. Time no longer transpires according, supposedly, to geocentric nature, but subject to such innovative constructions as the contract with a deadline (Faustus's twenty-four-year deal with Mephistopheles) or the interim (a Shakespearean invention through which *"action will continue* [and] *where language will not end"* [94, original emphasis]) as it does in *Timon of Athens.* Time is also sufficiently deconstructed to be personified in a play like *The Winter's Tale.* Fletcher then positions (or repositions) the major English authors previously listed within this picture.

There is something undeniably infectious, moving, and provocative about Fletcher's treatment of the authors he reveres and knows intimately; there is also no question that a powerful, idiosyncratic sensibility is on display. The energy and conviction of the book compel us, at least, to ask ourselves what we really know and think about the New Philosophy and its fallout, and even to ask ourselves whether early modern studies are now, or can be, animated by the kind of excitement Fletcher brings to them. As regards "radical innovativeness," however, matters are not quite so clear-cut. As I have already intimated, any such claim on behalf of the book needs to stipulate for exactly what innovativeness is being claimed. Fletcher himself is less than fully explicit about that, although exciting new discovery is fairly consistently implied. Other readers may be better qualified than I to judge the innovative contribution of *Time, Space, and Motion:* for my own part, I find the difficulty of distinguishing originality from grand recapitulation, fresh insight from reprocessing, almost prohibitive. Fletcher's own forms of enthusiasm and rhetorical emphasis are not necessarily the best guide to the consequential accomplishments of the book; in fact, those forms of enthusiasm and emphasis tend to erode distinctions in the book between consequential innovation and popularization. (Perhaps that is what Kenneth Knoespel means when he writes in his blurb of "an essay in the American tradition of public intellectual engagement.") In short, while I do not discount innovation in *Time, Space, and Motion,* the question strikes me as debatable. If there is such a thing as belated innovation, perhaps this is it.

Still, Fletcher legitimately insists on reconsidering Shakespeare as a "poet of nature," taking account of the traditional "woodnotes wild" sense of that term but more importantly making Shakespeare the poet of a nature-in-motion reconceived under the auspices of the New Philosophy. To the extent that alchemy is the recognized "harbinger" of "the new secular sciences," Jonson's *The Alchemist* engages directly with the "cultural manifold" or "scene of thought" (98) that is the subject of Fletcher's book. The play's luxuriant alchemical terminology as well as the strange "organic chemistry" under which stones and metals share the life of organisms add up to "a crazy code suggesting all sorts of science that has no basis in fact, but immense depths in fiction and dream" (100). Donne inevitably makes an appearance in this context as the poet who canonically articulates the disturbances arising from a New Philosophy that "calls all in doubt" ("the element of fire is quite put out; the Sun is lost, and the earth, and no mans wit can well direct him where to look for it"). In negotiating a "tortured sense of heterogeneous motions" (120), Donne also makes Wit the poetic idiom of the time in which heterogeneity can be encompassed and coherence can be recovered. For Fletcher, it is significant that Galileo is the only contemporary invoked (three times) in Milton's *Paradise Lost*. Galileo thus becomes Milton's tutelary spirit in a "new" epic that consistently "aims to dissolve ideal centers" (133) and relativizes both time and planetary motion. Newton is clearly waiting in the wings.

These very brief samplings of Fletcher's specific critical arguments may be enough to suggest their level of excitement and generous scope. Both excitement and generous scope are also implied when Fletcher connects the "intellectual" Marlowe, inventor of the new Faustian man, to J. G. Ballard, or the Milton of *Paradise Lost* to the Stanley Kubrick of *2001: A Space Odyssey*. Early and late modernity evidently both belong to an expansive "cultural manifold." In the end, however, this is not a manifold contemporary readers will necessarily feel they inhabit, either professionally or as people for whom 2001 is a date in the past rather than the apocalyptic future.

Brutal Reasoning: Animals, Rationality, and Humanity in Early Modern England
By Erica Fudge
Ithaca: Cornell University Press, 2006

Reviewer: Elizabeth Jane Bellamy

Ruminating on the totemic use of animals, Lévi-Strauss somewhat benignly conceded that it is less a case of animals being good to eat (*bon à manger*) than good to "think" (*bon à penser*).[1] But it is also the case that a genealogy of Western culture's ongoing discourse on the animal, from Aristotle to Descartes to Heidegger, reveals the unsettling extent to which the animal has persisted as not "good to think" but rather as the bearer of absolute alterity, the traumatic limit of Western thought. Heidegger's 1929–30 Freiburg lectures on "theoretical" biology, as chilling as they are sophisticated, qualify as perhaps Western philosophy's worst offender against the animal. In these lectures, Heidegger asserts that the animal has no access to being *as such;* that animals have no relationship to consciousness or selfhood; and that animals, suffering what he terms "poverty-in-the-world," can perish but they cannot accede to (a human) death.

Erica Fudge's *Brutal Reasoning,* an admirable sequel to her *Perceiving Animals: Human and Beasts in Early Modern English* (2000), can enable us to comprehend the (often depressing) extent to which early modern discourses of reason anticipate Heidegger's contention that animals have no access to being as such. Perhaps the most notorious early modern example was the "beast-machine" hypothesis of Descartes' 1637 *Discourse on the Method.* In Fudge's paraphrase,

> Descartes seems to be arguing that animals can experience the world but that their experience is not a full one. . . . This incompleteness is because animals lack thought and, crucially, the self-awareness that allows humans to fully experience their experiences. . . . Descartes's theory [his analogy between a clock and an animal], however, offered his readers something new. A clock does not "know" the time, it merely records it, and likewise, an animal did not "know" it lived, rather it merely lived. (157)

Descartes' hypothesis serves as an eerie early modern anticipation of Heidegger's modernist contention that only humans are capable of moving beyond the material world, capable of living beyond the present and possessing self-knowledge.

One haunting implication of Fudge's study is that had animals never existed, Western philosophy from antiquity to early modernity would have had to invent them. Drawing on a variety of texts, ranging from "high" philosophy to pragmatic training manuals, Fudge authoritatively demonstrates how the discourse of reason in early modern England virtually *required* the animal—that is, animal otherness—in order to define the human. This numbingly persistent early modern English turn to the animal to define the human (one might as well identify it as a topos) included such well-known names as Juan Luis Vives, George Gascoigne, Walter Raleigh, John Davies, Lodowick Bryskett, Joseph Hall, Robert Burton, Thomas Browne, and many others. But a paradox lurked within all these attempts to define human reason: the more they attempted to define the human, the more they inevitably relied upon the animal.

Among the many strengths of Fudge's study is its careful tracing of the paths through which early modern discourses of reason inherited an earlier philosophy's felt need to separate the animal and the human. She turns, for example, to Aristotle's foundational argument, in his *De anima,* that animals, dominated by the sensitive soul, lack reason, as well as to Seneca's philosophical assertion that although animals know what is good to eat, they do not know what constitutes a moral good. Fudge discusses how the early modern English discourse on reason also inherited medieval Christian philosophy's "othering" of the animal, such as Aquinas's disturbing argument that he who kills another's ox does indeed commit a sin—not, however, the sin of killing an ox, but rather the sin of inflicting loss of property on another human. Another major undercurrent of early modern English discourses of reason, according to Fudge, was the medieval bestiary tradition and its deployment of animals as mere symbols of human behavior (the sly fox, the valiant lion, etc.). These early modern discourses of reason inherited the bestiary tradition's parade of anthropomorphized animals that signified not the animal but rather the category of the human as its central focus. Fudge argues that early modern English theologians often stressed the moral responsibilities of humans toward animals. But, as was the case with Aquinas, the category of the human remained the primary object of interest. For these theologians, exhibiting kindness toward animals had less to do with the animal than with the twin virtues of serving both oneself and God.

But in early modern Europe, as Fudge patiently details, the more writers argued for the separation of the human and the animal, the more the two categories threatened to converge. In 1605, Pierre Le Loyer, to cite just one among her many examples, argued that dreaming is one of the defining aspects of human reason. But in 1607, Edward Topsell, early modern England's best known proto-zoologist, reported that dogs do, in fact, dream. Though perhaps merely dreaming of the hares they chased that day, sleeping dogs could nevertheless make use of the faculty of memory. In such a scheme, the argument for absolute animal difference (the need for the binary "reason/brute nature") began to erode the foundations of early modernity's long-standing conviction that only humans possess cognitive abilities.

As Fudge unfolds in intriguing detail, early modern England's simultaneous fascination with and dread of the potential for animal intelligence is no better evidenced than in the strange case of Morocco, the Intelligent Horse, documented anecdotally from 1590 to well into the seventeenth century. The most notorious "reasonable" animal in early modern England, a syllogizing Morocco was reportedly able, at his master Bankes's bidding, to pick out individual members of an audience, and to differentiate an honest woman from a whore. A voluble Morocco even reportedly discoursed with his owner about the hypocrisy of landlords. Though Morocco largely appealed to popular tastes hungry for public comic entertainment, the horse was disconcerting for those philosophically committed to the sovereignty of human intelligence. Ben Jonson sought to "solve" the problem of a thinking Morocco by arguing for the possibility that a human soul had entered the horse's body. Raleigh was far more pragmatic, claiming that Morocco was a product of mere training, thus restoring the comforting boundary between the animal and the human. As Fudge points out, such widely read horse-training manuals as Gervase Markham's 1607 *The English Horsemen* also had the effect of allaying anxieties about Morocco's intelligence. Though not a philosophical document, Markham's manual is thoroughly immersed in the discourse of reason as it explains how to use the whip and the rod—that is, how to inflict pain—to train a horse to count. Viewed through the lens of early modern training manuals, Morocco was not a "thinking" animal at all but rather the perfect picture of animal obedience, rightly restoring human dominion over the animal.

But certain strands of early modern discourses of reason did not rest so comfortably within the human/animal binary. As Fudge argues, to fully understand this unease, we must turn to the skepticism dominating certain schools of early modern philosophy. Revisiting antiquity, she focuses on the skepticism of the second century CE Sextus Empiricus whose *Outline of Skepticism,* published in Latin translation in 1562, exerted a major influence not only on the early modern transition from metaphysics (what we know) to epistemology (how we know what we know, and don't know), but also on the early modern need for a deeper understanding of animal being. Sextus, arguing that we cannot be sure that truth exists, called for "suspension of judgment" (118), a state of neither believing nor disbelieving. As Fudge summarizes, for Sextus reason, far from being the true marker of humanity, was merely a creation of humans for humans. In such a scheme, as she points out, pivotal for Sextus's skepticism was the category of the animal as the boundary, the limit case, of the human. Breaking ranks with prior discourses of reason, while at the same time countering critiques of a nonspeaking—hence, irrational—animal, Sextus claimed that it is not a case of animals failing to express themselves: rather, it is the human failure to comprehend them.

A knowledge of Sextus, Fudge argues, is perhaps the most useful background for understanding Plutarch's landmark thinking of animal being. Diverging widely from Aristotle, Plutarch's *Moralia* (translated into English by Philemon Holland in 1603) was an ambitious intervention into the discourse of reason, positing the notion of an ethical animal. Fudge closely reads the *Moralia,* particularly is emphasis on the animal soul and the potential for no longer excluding the animal from moral categories. As part of his attack on human reason, Plutarch argued that animals are not only reasonable but also, in fact, more virtuous than humans. Offering numerous anecdotes of animal wisdom, Plutarch asserted that animals are taught by nature: what they know, they have come to know naturally. And it is this natural reason, this status as self-taught and self-sufficient, that makes animals superior to humans. Fudge traces the influence of Plutarchanism in early modern England in such works as Thomas Wright's 1601 *The Passions of the Minde* and its claim that animals naturally know how to rear their young, unlike humans who must resort to domestic manuals on child rearing.

Montaigne's affective engagement with the animal is well documented in George Boas's 1933 *The Happy Beast in French Thought of the Seventeenth Century,* focusing on Montaigne's "Of Cruelty" and its author's distress over animal suffering as marking a key turning point in the genealogy of animal discourse since antiquity. Fudge, however, goes beyond Boas who, she argues, failed to perceive the importance of skepticism in Montaigne's animal discourse. As Fudge emphasizes, Montaigne actually turns away from the self to the *real* animal, offering the animal—or, more specifically, the mutual obligation between animal and human—as a new category for ethics. She also pushes beyond the borders of Boas's France to England to stress the influence of a skeptical Plutarchanism in early modern English discourse on the animal. She points to, for example, John Maplet's 1567 *A Greene Forest, or a naturall Historie,* which, echoing Montaigne's pondering of ethics as a shared sentience between human and animal, argued that animals do, in fact, suffer grief and pain.

Fudge's genealogy of discourse on reason makes for a powerfully charged turn to Descartes' 1637 *Discourse on the Method,* whose aforementioned "beast-machine" hypothesis offered a new—and sinister—clarification of the difference between the human and the animal. For Descartes, animals, neither reasonable, unreasonable, nor potentially reasonable, are limited by an a priori lack of reason and self-consciousness. More like an automaton—a clock, even— Descartes' animal is a mechanical entity, locked in a dialectic of mere stimulus-response. In early modern England, as Fudge discloses, Descartes' hypothesis had its detractors—most notably, William Cavendish and Robert Boyle, who argued, like Maplet many decades earlier, that animals do experience pain and are sentient. But as Fudge also notes, William Harvey's discovery of the circulation of blood via animal vivisection serves as a landmark reminder of how persistently early modernity made use of cruelty to animals to produce "human" knowledge.

Fudge's *Brutal Reasoning* joins forces with, among other studies, Bruce Boehrer's 2002 *Shakespeare Among the Animals* and Gail Kern Paster's 2004 *Humoring the Body* as key efforts to foreground early modernity's "thinking" of animal being. The relevance of these studies for early modern scholars extends well beyond a narrowly specialized interest in animals. And *Brutal Reasoning,* in particular, deserves a place on the reading list of anyone working in the broader areas of early modern philosophy and theology, early modern discourses of the body, and histories of early modern science. Some fifteen years ago, Jacques Derrida, musing on what separates the animal from the human, confessed that "the discourse of animality remains for me a very old anxiety, a still lively suspicion."[2] The same wise, welcome reluctance to foreclose on the complexities of animal-human difference—and a concomitant insistence on savoring the discourse of animality as "a very old anxiety"—is likewise reflected in Fudge's *Brutal Reasoning*.

Notes

1. Claude Lévi-Strauss, *Totemism*, trans. Rodney Needham (Boston: Beacon Press, 1963), 21.
2. Jacques Derrida, *Of Spirit: Heidegger and the Question*, trans. Geoffrey Bennington and Rachel Bowlby (Chicago: University of Chicago Press, 1989), 11.

The Dream of the Moving Statue
By Kenneth Gross
University Park: Pennsylvania State
University Press, 2006
Shylock Is Shakespeare
By Kenneth Gross
Chicago: University of Chicago Press, 2006

Reviewer: John Parker

In a new preface to *The Dream of the Moving Statue,* Kenneth Gross makes a suggestion I'd like to accept. In retrospect, he says, it seems possible to read this multifaceted study of sculpture, film, literature, philosophy, and psychoanalysis more uniformly "as a book about theater, about the work of living bodies on stage" (xii). That possibility follows from a formal trait, shared by statues and play-acting, which Gross examines with stunning acuity: to sculpture and to dramatic personae belong our bodily poise as to no other art forms. These alone of mimetic figurations take up space like we do. Where stone or some other medium serves to replicate bodies in sculpture, somebody's body is the medium for character. Character, in short, is the statue that moves. At the risk of doing a great disservice to this magnificent piece of scholarship, I am going to set aside the vast range of figures whose work Gross considers—Ovid, Charlie Chaplin, Donatello, Michelangelo, Blake, Shelley, Pushkin, Jakobson, Wittgenstein (the list could go on)—so I can concentrate on elements of *The Dream* that seem especially pertinent to Gross's overall reading of Shakespeare. According to his most recent book, Shakespearean theater in particular would seem to fulfill the hope that certain artists' fabrications might spring to real life—were only characters like Shylock not set in stone, so to speak, by the script. Shakespeare is the fantasy made flesh.

Of perhaps greatest interest to Gross in both of these books is the way that Shakespearean drama shares with sculpture not only its fullness of body but a peculiar limitation, as well, which has the power to promote a fantastic kind of self-overcoming—as though it were possible for an artwork to surpass, by means of its limits, the limit of being nothing but mimesis. Because statues are "still" in every sense of the word, because characters do nothing but talk and move, both omit what they mean to resemble: real people tend to think and feel. We have "inner lives"—or so we are told. Compared to the art of the novel or to lyric poetry, drama and sculpture permit no good likeness of internal experience. Thinking appears onstage, for example, only with enormous distortion—most notoriously in soliloquies, those incredible moments, akin to psychosis, when people converse with themselves.[1] Sculpture renders the interior even less well: at best it can suggest generic emotions or pensive moods through a fixed pose and facial expression. This is how thinking looks frozen. Imagine if your inner life boiled down to the shapeliness of a well-placed pinky; could you think at all if you had to do it while talking aloud? Yet despite this radical shortcoming, it is to sculpture and character that we habitually attribute "interiority." It's as though their deficiency in this one respect had secretly endowed them with a bizarre surfeit, making them all the more real; as though the palpable absence of any interior to these spectacular fictions best rendered after all our private experience.

In *The Dream,* Gross turns to psychoanalysis "as a way of gaining purchase on our phantasmatic intimacy with the sculpted image" (33), and from there he develops, among other elements of a complex "poetics of petrification" (30), his unique account of the interiority, insinuated by statues, that so many other cultural forms, from poetry to film to philosophy, have tried to embellish. What makes sculpture (or maybe, as it turns out, theater) so evocative in this way has specifically to do with some peculiarities of introjection. For Gross as for Freud this is the psychic correlative to an infant's swallowing, except that the mind digests nothing; it can dissolve nothing. As a consequence it's crammed with fantastic "objects"— loathed, desired, abandoned, fetishized—in the manner of a museum or *Wunderkammer.* These mental objects—"the outside brought inside" (35)—are, as it were, the grains of sand infiltrating our psyche, whose indigestible irritation produces sores that we value as pearls *when projected elsewhere.* Thus it is that our introjections can come to disquiet statues as well. Their interior is ours—though not an interior to which we might otherwise have more immediate access. Rather than seeing in statues our inner life of thought and experience, we see the unthought on which our thinking depends, the things within that we don't experience, or rather that we encounter only in and as art. Which is to say, an inner life we in no way live save during the most *superficial* experiences. Only there, for a passing hour in the museum or theater, do we witness our irrefrangible, mental possessions in all their unspeakable hardness (if by "possession" one means simply that they possess us): "That statues mirror our internal objects may also be part of what makes actual monuments such apt homes for our shifting *projections,* our castings out onto the world of those ideas we cannot bear to keep inside ourselves or recognize as our own; external statues may become the places onto which we project our most intimate opacities. We could say that actual statues allow us to restore to things inside us something of their original exteriority, even as they keep the coloring of the interior" (37).

The great value of Gross's account, as I take it, is the way that he sidesteps all the usual clichés that would see the inner life of a statue or dramatic persona as a back formation from, and supplement of, its mimetic surface. (*The statue smiles. What must she be thinking?*) For Gross the surface is all, and the fictive pretense that it might be meaningfully ruptured by some genuine sign of a deeper humanity paradoxically serves to remind us "how alien and how disruptive of what we think of as the human are our vital energies, how catastrophic, petrifying, or mechanistic a form the entry into life can assume. . . . [T]he fantasy of the animated statue may constitute [in short] an implicit critique of our optimistic pictures of human desire, and of our wish that desire and the human could peacefully occupy the same space" (135). To be human on this model means simultaneously to contain and project—to endlessly worry even as we repress—a terrible obscurity: our impotence ever to know what it is—or who or why—we are, simply because whatever we are, we are not what we think; unless, that is, we should think *precisely this* when feeling a queasy satisfaction or sublime revulsion at, for example, *The Merchant of Venice.* The Shakespearean "human," in the most uncompromising version of Gross's vision, resembles nothing so much as the golem of kabbalistic mysticism—"an anomalous entity, a categorical surd . . . less a blessing than a scandal, a threat to stable metaphysical as well as legal definitions of life and death, humanity and divinity, magic and miracle . . . The artificial golem could look like a blasphemy, a form of idolatry" (10–11). So writes Gross of a figure that appeared more prominently in his first book (on Spenser) and that serves in the latest on Shakespeare as a model for Shylock.

Meanwhile, in *The Dream,* I thought the golem made for an unexpected parallel to Hermione—although her peculiar role as a potential (and more historically specific) "blasphemy" or "form of idolatry" passes without comment. Gross nonetheless brings to light the borderline bad omens that surround her statue's "miraculous" animation. The dream of Antigonus, which duplicitously confirms beyond any reasonable doubt that Hermione has died, at the same time revives her, thus anticipating her later return even while portending the death of her prophet, who will not be redeemed. Along the same lines, Gross notes, there is "the fantasy proposed by Leontes, and taken up by Paulina, that Hermione's soul would repossess her corpse and return from the grave to terrorize him should he decide to marry again" (103); this, along with Antigonus's dream, Gross sees as a way of peripherally airing—and so exorcising—the tragedy that the play might have become, had it followed the normative pattern of Jacobean revenge, "for instance, Hermione poisoning her husband with a kiss" (108). Alternately, "Leontes could [have] readily become like Lear holding Cordelia at the end of *his* tragedy, caught between the delusive knowledge of his daughter's reanimation and the absolute certainty of her being a corpse" (104). Instead Leontes is caught by something else: "a miracle, but a secular miracle" (105)—a statue made real, if for a few terrible moments remaining deathly still. Gross does great things with this silence, as he generally does on every statue's eloquent inability ever to speak. Yet "however mysterious" Hermione's silence may ultimately be, for him "this is again a secular silence" (106).

When it comes to so emphatic a repetition of Shakespeare's secularism, I'm afraid it is required you do awake your skepticism. If nothing else, Gross's own extraordinary chapter on iconoclasm, which returns to the subject of his book on Spenser, should give rise to some questions. Gross demonstrates with unusual clarity the labor that went into freeing Judeo-Christianity from polytheistic idol worship —a labor that turns out to be unending, insofar as the iconoclastic monotheism of the Hebrew Bible, of the church fathers (and, finally, of Protestants) largely depends on the perpetual desecration of images that others hold sacred. As Gross brilliantly shows, these acts of sacrilege then tend to reconsecrate the disavowed object as an inverted picture of the attacker's own (otherwise invisible) "transcendent" godhead. Gross explores how this works in the Hebrew Bible; how the pattern survives "in Augustine's accounts of the supposedly magical statues of late-classical paganism"; consequently how "the church's own need to maintain the authority of its sacramental magic [to say nothing of its icons] . . . makes total disenchantment impossible" (50). "No iconoclasm can be pure, final, or free of fantasy," Gross concludes. "Gestures of disenchantment or revolution can be fraught with blindness, reduction, and inverted superstition and are all too likely to reanimate the very idolatry they seek to overcome" (60). In fact, for Gross, this clandestine sanctification of the objects that invite the greatest reproach as "false gods" proves so basic and inescapable it reemerges even in "what would appear to be more fully secular discourses" (50). In proof of his point he turns to two ostensibly "secular" artists of the nineteenth century—Shelley and Pushkin—to reveal how the endless seductions of sacred thinking (or if you prefer, of superstition) continually haunt their writings.

Why is the secular Shakespeare immune to such blandishment? I suspect that we're seeing here the first beginnings of what I can only describe as some kind of exceptionalism, whereby the theories and methods that Gross has worked out in painstaking detail for the rest of world literature must fail with respect to great Will, lest he stand a little too close to the herd. In *The Dream,* Shakespeare is spared any contact with Gross's (Spenserian) reading of iconoclasm (as he will later be spared any meaningful contact with Spenserian allegory), and the result is an analysis of *The Winter's Tale* that for all its sparkle and care seems to leave out what the rest of the book is then forced to supply sotto voce. For what it's worth, I do not think revenge is the tragedy that Shakespeare here courts. The "taboo" (107) that is marked by Hermione's return—in the nave of a chapel, chaste despite all, so long as her viewers allow their faith to be awakened by Paul . . . I mean, Paulina—is the historical anathema of Catholic icons, in particular Marian sculpture. Gross mentions elsewhere his skepticism of Shakespeare's alleged Catholicism but nonetheless manages to stress that "whatever his relation to Catholic thought or worship, or to specific recusant communities, the poet could imagine what it might be like to live in the shadow of a religious mythology at once needful, ruined, and under suspicion" (*Shylock Is Shakespeare,* 152). One could wish that Gross might have seen something along these same lines in the provocatively "Catholic" ending to *The Winter's Tale.* These days it seems harder to read that last scene in isolation from the history of religious suppressions preceding it, *especially* given what Gross himself has written about the tendency of iconoclastic cultures to reanimate the very idols they had wanted to shatter. In light of all that, the "difficulty" of the play's ending—for me at least—is the way its "testing of the idea of theater" (104) leads to a more worrisome aporia: is this theater really secular if "secular" means only "post-Reformation"? After *Hamlet in Purgatory*—to name only one especially fine study intervening since *The Dream* was first written—Shakespeare's secularism is perhaps the one topic on which this very wide-ranging but fifteen-year-old book might be showing its date. Everywhere else its monumental insights seem fresh and vital and hugely deserving of reanimation by this elegant paperback reprint.

*   *   *

Shylock Is Shakespeare comes across at times as a conscious exercise in the sort of fiction that *The Dream* had wanted to analyze. It opens, for example, with Gross imagining himself in conversation with Shylock. He then continues the conversation, as it were, by examining Shylock's afterlife in other works of literature, among which, it would seem from the creative approach, Gross means to include his own present efforts. These especially showcase his gifts as a writer, and it has to be said that few other Renaissance scholars now writing can turn a sentence so well. In this case he turns them in service of three contentions, the first of which stands as his title. The second is that Shylock/Shakespeare epitomizes the uncanny power of theater at its absolute best. The nature of that power follows in turn from the third and most fundamental contention of all: namely, that Shylock surpasses the world of the play "which tries to contain him" (3)—and is hence the inevitable, if recalcitrant subject of later fiction and scholarship. Shylock proves so irrepressible, we're told, by virtue of his "interior life, a thinking, more unfathomable and harrowing than that of any other character in the play" (2)—by virtue, in short, of Shakespeare's "generosity" (83), his newfound ability to give to this one character such incredible "singularity," to *lend* to Shylock "his particularity or power of idiosyncrasy" (3), which loan will of course return tenfold to the credit of Shakespeare's singular genius. So closes the circle that begins with the title.

I will admit to some serious worry, while facing this schema, that we had lost Gross to Bloom country. What saves him, in my view, is a continued (if slightly weakened) attachment to "interiority" as defined by opacity and repugnance; his definition, that is, of art's inner life as a hollow invitation to projection and stereotype, as automatism and inhumanity. Instead of getting to the core of humanity and finding there our secret, self-flattering distinction from the rest of creation, Gross still tends to find enigma, torment, conflict, a complete unknowing and wide-open possibility that we are the only gods left *and* total animals. To chalk all this up to the genius of Shakespeare differs pretty radically from the long customary claim that Shakespeare is Prospero—or Hamlet, or Lear, or any of his later, more ennobling failures. Gross would have Shakespeare acknowledge as his own a worse thing of darkness.

Of course no question has so engaged other critics—or undergraduates—as the play's relation to anti-Semitism, but Gross is the first whom I know of to openly contend that "the key to this question is that Shylock, as a piece of dramatic mimesis, takes much of his mysterious, compulsive, violent, and knowing interiority from the very language that seeks to strip him of his humanity" (83). Or to put it in other terms, "Shylock's humanity emerges exactly through rather than simply in spite of the shapes of antisemitic abuse that frame his character onstage" (10). Gross's most dazzling close readings proceed from this insight. In the course of mounting his case he unlocks the secrets of so many remarks one usually skips, and redeems from cliché the most overexposed speeches

("Hath not a Jew eyes?"), that it makes the persuasiveness of his eponymous claim seem almost beside the point, were not the readings themselves in some basic, self-reflexive manner precisely the point of his thesis: insofar as it is Shakespeare speaking through Shylock that belatedly enables a prose as rich, abstract, and lyrical as Gross's, one can see in the criticism itself what the critic would project—perhaps rightly, for once—onto his object.

For reasons of space I am going to deal in detail with just one of Gross's many astonishing meditations, but I want to praise for the record his exquisite way of handling the juxtaposition of Venice with Belmont, of Portia with Shylock, in particular the pairing of her father's caskets—one of which, remember, holds a picture of Portia entitling the bearer to receive her fair self—with Shylock's desire to have his own daughter likewise "encoffined" (43) and bent to his will. There are passages here, made with unmatched panache, that other scholars might have wagered their bodies to write. Gross devotes a real tour de force to Shylock's off-kilter self-defense at the trial, and it's this particular reading that I'll spell out at some length, as it demonstrates pretty concisely what Gross means by the "poetics of repugnancy" (ix; passim)—in particular how Shylock is supposed to earn his personhood by occupying voluntarily the slanders that fail to define him entirely. Maim him as they may, his selfhood remains proudly self-inflicted. Asked why he persists to such extremes in exercising his hatred, for example (the extremity will lead to a forced baptism), he answers that some men hate the sight of a gaping pig, some the sight of a cat; some piss themselves at the sound of bagpipes: "there is no firm reason to be rendered" for any of this, says Shylock, and none for his loathing, either: but of force a person must yield to his obsession so far "as to offend, himself being offended" (4.1.44–62).

That last phrase recurs throughout the book—sometimes without the comma, following the quarto—as the leitmotiv of Shylock's character. The speech as a whole inspires Gross, in a typical gesture, to turn momentarily away from Shakespeare, as though needing some time to catch his breath at less empyrean heights before driving on to the summit: in this case he goes first to Montaigne, then to an essay by P. F. Strawson, and what emerges at last is an entire ethics of psychology: certain behaviors are so beyond explanation, and so repugnant, Gross suggests, we must suspend our resentment on the grounds that they could not possibly have resulted from choice: poor guy, we will say, "he didn't mean it" (71; quoting

Strawson). Only some version of freedom, we learn, can provide the sufficient condition for unrelenting contempt or true approbation. Especially heinous actions that circumvent this freedom, stemming instead from some impenetrable compulsion, *compel sympathy* for the perpetrators. Here then is the source of Shylock's parodic, cynical appeal to "Christian" mercy: when he describes "his own moral passion as automatic, deterministic, and compulsive," he implicitly demands "that others suspend their resentment, for how could one resent so animal-like a hater?" (73).

If Shylock turns out to be as one-dimensional a villain as the Christians had always suspected—without any conceivable motive other than his being Jewish—this is only because he is *willfully* playing to the hilt the role in which Christian tradition has cast him. His very enthusiasm for the role, "which both strengthens his hatred and renders it uncanny" (72) according to Gross, then suggests a far deeper, more "interior" cunning. This conspiratorial inwardness again shows him further playing to type, and yet now he exceeds the type insofar as he hates Christians *because of* their hateful projections, which he epitomizes. His hatred, that is, approximates precisely the moral outrage that the Christians deny he could have, lacking it themselves. "The problem of the Jew is the problem of particularity, the problem of selecting someone from within the human species to be the site of the inhuman. Yet Shylock's speech, in its hallucinatory logic, implies that to make a Jew into an animal ends up making the whole world bestial, making it not a human community but a herd, a flock, a pack. How does a herd of goats choose a scapegoat for itself?" (74). From the simultaneous deficiency and surfeit of Shylock's character— too narrow and rapacious to contain any real humanity but by virtue of this very narrowness attaining an unvarnished reality—Gross draws his larger lessons about the theater and Shakespeare.

Unlike in *The Dream,* this time around the Reformation is central to Gross's interpretation; specifically, that the reformers annulled older ways of reading the Hebrew scriptures—by reading them in Hebrew, for one thing; for another, by learning to see "the careers of the patriarchs as more than merely empty typological symbols or shadows of a fuller, future revelation" (92). Casting aside these dead symbols, the reformers released the "plain text" in all its irreducible plenty, according to Gross, for the delectation of many. Their new hermeneutic therefore counts as a powerful precursor of his own way of reading, which would look to fictional characters as equally evasive of hermeneutic emptying. Characters such as Shylock and Jacob (to whom Shylock is likened) prove not only larger than any method used to interpret them but "larger" than the fictions from which they are endlessly escaping. The dream here is this: as an ironic *result of* the Reformation, Shylock can amount to something more than a Christian vision of *Judentum*.

I suppose one has to forgive a Spenserian and expert on allegory for wanting from Shakespeare a little something more than business as usual. Under any other conditions I would be happy to see Shakespeare's usual allergy to allegory positioned against "medieval" tradition. But Shakespeare's usual aversion only makes it all the more curious and striking that Shylock almost alone of his characters declares what he "stands for" in an openly allegorical way: "I stand for judgment" (4.1.103), he says. "I stand for law" (4.1.142). Milton normally wasn't much of an allegorist, either, except when looking back via Sin and Death to his predecessor Spenser; arguably Shakespeare paid tribute to his fallen forbears in the same way. Something about this Jewish usurer in his conflict with Christians seems to have triggered, that is, a strong nostalgia for the lost personifications of theological drama. Two traditionally medieval scenes are in this connection more central, perhaps, than Gross has allowed: I am thinking of Launcelot's small morality where he struggles between a bad and worse angel; then immediately following where he reprises the stealing of Isaac's blessing by Jacob—traditionally an allegory for how God the Father transposes his favor to the second-born Christians, just as old Gobbo's gift (a "dish of doves") will go by scene's end to the Christian Bassanio rather than Shylock.[2]

I dwell on this oversight because it seems to me of a piece with a reading of the Reformation that is surprisingly conventional for so unconventional a book and that somewhat impairs its definition of "Shakespeare." The reformers do not merely abandon typology for the literal sense, despite what they say. For Luther—to give one major example—the literal sense of the Bible in its entirety is the Word Incarnate; even the Hebrew Bible is "literally" about Jesus, and "Jesus" means Luther's self-justification. Pretty much everyone else is hell-bound and wrong, especially "Hebraists" and "scholastic theologians" who dare to believe that the Bible might have more than one meaning or differing levels of symbolic import: "I hate and detest," proclaims Luther, often and frankly, "the opinions of the rabbis on the Scriptures."[3] What he hates in particular is how they fail to admit that there is "one definite and simple understanding of Scripture"—namely, Luther's—and he condemns them for that reason to wander as "vagabonds" in the labyrinth of their own Bible, along with "the scholastic theologians, and the professors of law, who are always toiling with ambiguities" (ibid., 209).

Hopefully when we read the Hebrew Bible "literally" today we read it in a different spirit than did Luther. To me he frequently embodies the final triumph of allegorical emptying, the complete subordination of all possible polyvalence to a single deadening code, such that reading Jacob, for example, as a figure for the Protestant Church no longer even appears as an act of interpretation but pretends rather to communicate *das Ding-an-Sich:* "This striking and astounding example of the conception of the two infants who struggled with each other in their mother's womb teaches these facts about the distinction between the true and the false church," Luther allegorizes, before purporting once again to have turned against allegory: "For the sake of those who at some time or other will read the commentaries of the rabbis let us next add something of the Jewish nonsense . . ." (*Lectures on Genesis* 25.21 [in *Luther's Works,* 4:351]). Luther's rejection of the rabbis and scholastics served many purposes, but among them was not a true recuperation of literal reading (whatever that is). Gross implicitly concedes as much when he writes that "biblical characters started to be taken up by reformers as particularized *images* of a *spiritual* life that fallen human beings live *in the present*" (92; my emphasis); but he probably ought to have admitted more explicitly that biblical characters had always been taken this way. Only Protestant reformers had the audacity to call it the *literal* meaning of scripture. Medieval exegetes, by contrast, had the good sense to differentiate the literal from any more personal, presentist level (which they called the moral or tropological interpretation). To be fair to the Middle Ages, I think one has to acknowledge—against the claims of the reformers—that the literal retains its value as a category only when carefully juxtaposed with other, *relatively more* allegorical levels. Once it becomes the only level that counts, once it claims to be more than a moment in the inevitable allegoresis that I'm afraid we have to call "reading," it counts itself out.

I have spent so much time on this issue because I think it points to a deeper tension. In the end Gross has to sustain an impossible task: that of reading Shylock "in himself" as something more than merely a character, as a statue come to life, on the grounds that to do anything less would be simply to allegorize and so to deny him his full inner life, however mysterious and wounded. It would be once again to deny him his humanity, to rebaptize him in the name of literary criticism. At the same time, however, Gross is trying to argue that Shylock is Shakespeare; in other words, that Shylock is *not* irreducibly particular and idiosyncratic, uncontainable, enigmatic: he is, as in any old allegory, merely the sign of something else, supposedly more grand: in this case "Shakespeare," who (one gathers) is the truly irreducible, idiosyncratic person—being, in that case, like pretty much everyone else; hence his much touted "humanity," as well as his famous "impersonality" (172). Gross wants to find in Shylock some human element that evades any possible allegoresis. But in that case isn't Gross just imposing a fairly orthodox secular humanism? Is this book not at bottom the allegory of a "human" whose humanity amounts to the empty defiance of allegory?

While reading I was glad that the moral in the title so often faded; glad to see disappearing even the more manageable assertion that Shylock marks a turning point in Shakespeare's development, such that after *The Merchant* the playwright was enabled, through his discovery of this one character, to create all the other famous individualities—as though Shylock himself had in some sense authored those later creations. Sustaining that argument would have required a tedious comparison of those who came before Shylock with those who came after. We find instead fleeting mention of Timon, of Hamlet, of Richard III—but on sweet bully Bottom, the Bloomian candidate for Shakespeare's first human, we get nothing save for a single characterization: he is "a touchstone for understanding Shakespeare's use of Paul" (87), in particular Paul's allegories, which of course Shakespeare refutes and surpasses. Instead of any systematic argument driving home the title, that is, we mercifully get innumerable readings so lavishly "particularized" in their attention to textual detail, to the pressure of the unsaid on the said, that, for me, they ruptured the narrowness of any mere claim about a Shakespeare who "beggars description" (152). By this rather Romantic estimation, Gross's own book was bound to fail. One could wish that more books on Shakespeare failed so well. "The crucial question remains," writes Gross at one point, "what it means to keep faith with Shakespeare's fiction" (124), and I found myself closing the book in wholehearted agreement. Here it seems to mean hoping, despite a lot of evidence to the contrary, that Shakespeare escaped the theology of his day in creating his secular Bible; that our profession, keeping faith with him rather than scripture, might enjoy a brief respite from the interminable conflicts that the Good Book inspires. Would this were so.

Notes

1. A point whose outlines I draw from Margreta de Grazia, *"Hamlet" Without Hamlet* (Cambridge: Cambridge University Press, 2007), pp. 185–86.

2. See John Scott Colley, "Launcelot, Jacob and Esau: Old and New Law in *The Merchant of Venice*," in *The Yearbook of English Studies: Literature and its Audience,* I (Special Number), ed. G. K. Hunter and C. J. Rawson (Leeds, England: W. S. Maney and Son, 1980), 181–89.

3. *Lectures on Genesis* 49.3, in *Luther's Works,* American edition, 55 vols. (Philadelphia: Fortress; St. Louis: Concordia, 1955–86), 8:210.

Empire of Magic: Medieval Romance and the Politics of Cultural Fantasy
By Geraldine Heng
New York: Columbia University Press, 2003

Reviewer: Glenn Burger

Empire of Magic is one of those rare books that is both deeply rooted in the immediate historical and cultural contexts of the texts it considers *and* wide-ranging and conceptually challenging in ways that recommend it to those outside medieval or romance studies per se. Working at the forefront of a growing body of medievalist work in postcolonial, race, and gender/sexuality studies, Heng brilliantly and provocatively rethinks what she calls romance's *re-beginning* in early twelfth-century England, the reasons for traditional linkages between romance and the medieval (and the medieval and romance), as well as widening the range of texts that we might consider as romance. In the process she redefines and re-historicizes the peculiarly hybrid structures of romance as a genre in order to understand the variety and complexity of its political and ideological usefulness: "neither wholly fantastical nor wholly historical, . . . romance does not repress or evade the historical—as has sometimes been claimed—but surfaces the historical, which it transforms and safely memorializes in an advantageous form, as fantasy" (45). In "surfacing" the historical in this way, Heng argues, medieval romance engages in profound ways with the problems raised by medieval projects of imperialism, nation-building, racial and religious purification, and protocapitalist economics. And in engaging with medieval romance's hybridity, Heng challenges long-standing critical and theoretical assumptions about medieval and early modern difference and the workings of historical and cultural periodization.

In chapter 1, "History as Romance: The Genesis of a Medieval Genre," Heng argues for the origin of medieval romance, not in the vernacular courtly love narratives of Chrétien de Troyes, as has often been proposed, but in the Latin *Historia Regum Britannie,* or *History of the Kings of Britain,* composed by Geoffrey of Monmouth sometime between 1130 and 1139. Geoffrey is famous (or infamous, if we accept William of Newburgh's denunciation of the text as fiction rather than history) for his incorporation of the matter of Arthur and other romance elements within his history of Britain. And there has been much recent interest in the text's interventions within the politics of Anglo-Norman patronage, Angevin empire-building, and the relations between the native Welsh and Anglo-Norman colonial efforts in Wales during this period. For Heng, however, it is the cultural trauma of the First Crusade and its aftermath that necessitates Geoffrey's turn to the genre of romance and to the heroic "intervention of a cultural savior plucked from the distant past" (36).

In particular, Heng focuses on the fact of historical cannibalism performed by Latin Christian crusaders on Turkish Muslim cadavers at Ma'arra an-Numan in Syria in 1098 during the First Crusade (and perhaps a few months before at Antioch), citing the accounts of three independent surviving eyewitness histories of the First Crusade. Outlining the importance of eating God's body emphasized in doctrinal thinking about the Eucharist from the mid-eleventh century through the first quarter of the twelfth, as well as the fact that eating has a strong political as well as religious valence in medieval culture—given the extent to which display and conspicuous consumption of food function to mark social status and political and military power—Heng persuasively argues for the complex, even contradictory ways that cannibalism is at the heart of the medieval cultural imaginary. If the cannibal epitomizes the grotesquely subhuman, and if medieval texts of social history and popular tradition cannot conceive of the European Christian as cannibal, then "the obscenity of Christians who eat human flesh is layered over by worse terrors of self-pollution and infernal contamination issuing from the cadavers they ingest" (65). Equally important in the case of the Crusader cannibalism, the literal, horrific assimilation of the polluted other has the potential to mirror the larger assimilation of native populations taking place with the colonial activity of Latin Europeans as they establish western kingdoms in Outremer after the First Crusade. For as Heng notes, "what after all is cannibalism but a hideously somatic literalization of the language of military conquest" (31), and the discursive difficulty in dealing with the history of actual Crusader cannibalism thus mirrors the larger trauma of Latin colonialism in the East. And the Normans made up one of the larger and most important groups of knights taking part in the First Crusade; indeed, strong and intimate ties continued between the ruling class of the kingdoms of Outremer and the royal family of England into the twelfth century.

For all these reasons, Heng posits, the cultural trauma of Crusader cannibalism "required strategies of attenuation, displacement, and transformation supplied by a hybrid genre of cultural fantasy, with the emergence of the literary legend of King Arthur one generation later, in Geoffrey of Monmouth's *Historia*" (334). Heng focuses in particular on a temporary diversion Arthur undertakes while on the way to battle the forces of Rome, when he journeys to Mont Saint-Michel to rescue his kinswoman, Helena, who has been carried off by a giant. The giant is not only a rapist but a cannibal. After killing the giant, Arthur has his head cut off for display, and then recollects a giant he has also fought earlier in his career, having killed him and captured his cloak made of the beards of kings he has slain. Significantly, both giants are originally from Syria. For Heng, then, both of Arthur's encounters with giants and cannibalism tacitly memorialize the historical trauma of Crusader cannibalism while at the same time transforming that cannibalistic memory into a romance event through the heroism of King Arthur. They indicate, therefore, how romance provides Geoffrey (and later medieval writers) with a ready and safe language of cultural discussion and cultural transformation in the service of crisis and urgent contingency.

In chapter 2, "The Romance of England," Heng turns to the Middle English romance, *Richard Coer de Lyon,* whose composition and period of textual production runs from the thirteenth through the fifteenth centuries. The romance recounts a fabulous scene in which King Richard, having fallen ill from the rigors of the Crusade, longs for pork. Unable to find any in Muslim Syria, one of Richard's knights has a young, fat Saracen killed, opened up and flayed, then turned into a tasty broth. Restored, Richard devours the rest of the flesh of the Saracen and calls for the head of the same swine that he ate. When the black, grinning head of the eaten Saracen is brought before Richard, his response is extravagant laughter. Noting the performance of cannibalism here as a joke in a popular romance, akin to the beginning of *Sir Gawain and the Green Knight,* for example, one, like romance itself, with healing and aggressive properties, Heng comments that "what was a problem for resolution in Geoffrey's romances in the *Historia,* has metamorphosed into a triumphant system of symbolism in the romance of England—where the most memorably indelible equation in literature between cannibalism, romance, and empire is spectacularly arranged" (68). In a detailed, wide-ranging, and historicized account, Heng delineates the links between the discourse of cannibalism here and the appearance of the discourse of medieval nationalism and its working of England into a version of the medieval nation. Heng situates her discussion of a nationalist politics worked through in terms of a Christian king's cannibalism of a Muslim first in the epistemic shift that occurs in the long thirteenth century, following the Fourth Lateran Council of 1215, in which there develops a medieval racialized discourse of biological and spiritual difference posited on religion, color, and physiognomy. In the process she explores how the racialized politics of English nationalism here conflate distant Muslim with nearby Jew. Equally important is the romance's choice of the English language, as well as the particular forms of popular romance, as a means of asserting an imagined community that crosses and unites class, ethnic, and other differences to produce the bold experiment of nation as its end.

In chapter 3, "Warring Against Modernity," Heng's analysis of *The Alliterative Morte Arthure* (written around 1400) focuses on that text's restaging with significant difference of Geoffrey's cannibalistic episode. Characterized as a tyrant as well as cannibal, and issuing from "Genoa," rather than "Hispania"/Syria, the *Morte's* giant "is different from his predecessors because he is at once a figure of economic monstrosity—of disproportionate wealth, wrongfully acquired—and a figure of superordinate independence: conditions that define him, in the feudal system, as a monster, as much as the unconscionable appetites for human flesh and taboo forms of sexual violence" (119). Heng thus highlights the various ways that the *Morte* works as a defense of chivalric knighthood against the encroachments of economic modernity, deferentially remembering the cultural work of elite predecessors as well as disclosing "the pressure nodes of chivalric vulnerability and crisis in its own historical instant" (117).

In chapter 4, "Beauty and the East, a Modern Love Story," Heng focuses on the "Constance Group" (of which Chaucer's *Man of Law's Tale* is a part), an interlinked set of English "family romances" that develops in the fourteenth century, featuring women, and "conventional feminine performance, not transgendered mimicry" (185) at their center. In contrast to the historical prominence of female labor in certain English trades of the fourteenth century, and the associations of women with the power and portability facilitated by wealth (made memorable in a figure like the Wife of Bath), the Constance romances "show a canny understanding of just how much rhetorical force can be exercised by tapping into the deep cultural approval for traditional feminine roles, at *precisely* a time when traditional roles in social, economic, and occupational circumstances are rapidly undergoing change. Here, then, is revealed the power of a story that presents *a woman acting like a woman*" (201). Moreover, Constance, in moving from one civilization to another, is consistently depicted as moving from one family to another. In this way the model of the family becomes productively portable and instrumental in its service to discourses of the medieval nation.

In chapter 5, "Eye on the World," Hena asks what *Mandeville's Travels* as travel romance can do that other kinds of romance cannot. Foremost among such differences is the global scope of a travel romance such as Mandeville's, where the fragmented character of its narrative allows it to exceed the boundaries of nation, or a particular social class, or Latin Christendom that might bound other forms of romance, enabling "the creation of one of the most imaginative acts of cultural domination available in the Middle Ages. . . . More than in any other category of romance, travel narrative exercises its special attractions—such as the play between vast distances and close proximity, the lushly exotic and the cozily familiar—to insert its audience into an overarching system in which domination at a distance can seamlessly and seductively occur" (242). The virtual world created by such accounts transforms the world outside Europe into a collection of facts and artifacts not unlike the collections in anthropological and natural history museums today. Indeed, Heng argues, such medieval travel narratives antedate by three or four or five centuries the examples of travel writing usually cited by late-twentieth-century critical discourse on anthropology, and in some such travel romances the "role and position of the narrator is configured in ways startlingly predictive of the role and position of the 'scientific ethnographer' today" (295).

Theatre of a City: The Places of London Comedy, 1598–1642
By Jean E. Howard
Philadelphia: University of Pennsylvania Press, 2007

Reviewer: Dympna Callaghan

For reasons that we will probably never know, Shakespeare seems to have made a point of creating some geographic distance between his playgoers and the plays they watched. With very few exceptions, most famously that of *Merry Wives of Windsor* (set, obviously, in Windsor, not London), Shakespeare did not locate his plays in the geographically familiar world of early modern England. Necessarily, since London, the metropolis itself, was such a new phenomenon, the majority of the stories that playwrights chose to tell on the stages of the commercial theater in early modern England were indebted to a literary and popular tradition that was decidedly *not* about the commercial venture of which the theater was so much a part. Nor was the drama in any very direct way about day-to-day life in London. This would seem to make plays that did engage their contemporary milieu of particular historical and critical interest. Yet, as this book shows, other than those plays that fall within the rather narrowly circumscribed boundary of "city comedy," many of the plays set in the city have received little attention either from theater historians or from materialist critics concerned to unearth the gritty economic realities of early modern theater. Howard's book demonstrates that in contrast to modern critics, early modern playwrights and their audiences were— understandably—deeply interested in representations of precisely the familiar locations of the city, an interest that begins with William Haughton's *Englishmen for My Money* (1598)—the first stage comedy to boast a London setting, namely, the Royal Exchange.

This book offers a rigorously materialist account of the drama, and its success lies in the painstaking work of reading the plays in relation to complex, carefully delineated economic and social histories. *Theatre of a City* thus offers a brilliant and invaluable examination of crucial but hitherto unexamined connections between theatre and the densely packed and expanding urban milieu of metropolitan London. Howard provides a rich account of many facets of London life, and, importantly, also extends her scope beyond the usual range of "city comedies" to the much more varied and comprehensive grouping, "London comedy" (22). Once again, Howard has shifted the field of early modern studies forward, in this instance, moving us away from the canonical authors (and in many ways from authors as such) to consideration of an entirely new genre.

However, there is much more at stake in this book than even the discovery of a genre. For while only a small proportion of plays addressed contemporary London, all theatre of this period depended for its existence on the life and denizens of the city itself. As Howard points out: "The building of the early commercial theatres . . . did not . . . just magically happen. It occurred because of a particular conjunction of events that also produced other changes in the city" (15). London was characterized above all by an increasingly inescapable market economy and by the "dislocating effects of an influx of alien people, tongues, and goods, as well as the more mundane dislocations of extremely rapid demographic growth" (4). The book energetically charts these changes through a diverse range of plays from the better-known ones such as *Every Man Out of His Humor* and *The Honest Whore* to lesser known and even very ob-

scure plays. Plays of wildly different aesthetic standards became
part of the period's negotiation about the city. These include Samuel Rowley's *When You See Me, You Know Me* (1604), some of
which is set in the Counter; Shackerly Marmion's *Hollands Laeguer*
(1631), the depiction of a real-life confrontation between prosti-
tutes and constables at a Bankside brothel; and James Shirley's *The
Ball* (1632), set in the world where the English seek foreign finesse
in matters of dance and in which Luciana tells a knight, who she is
playing a trick on, that she has fallen in love with his legs.

The book is organized in terms of location and the practices of
the populations who made those locations significant: the Royal
Exchange, the prison, the bawdy house, and the ballroom. It is not,
as Howard points out, an "exhaustive catalog" of the significant
places of London comedy, but rather a series of sites whereby we
can gain some understanding of "the synergy between the city and
the theatre and the role of plays in constructing the social meanings
of place and the ideological implications of the stories that unfold
upon its terrain" (215). None of these locations are in any sense
neutral or static backdrops. Rather they serve to stage a range of
pressing social issues including demographic change, the influx of
strangers and foreigners, new money, credit, debt and financial
ruin, shifting gender roles, and the new culture of the West End. All
of the locations addressed are deeply inscribed with associations of
class and gender, so that, for example, the prison is a male world,
while the shops upstairs at the Royal Exchange are spaces dominated by women. While one gender might typically outnumber the
other in any given location, there are further connections, as Howard
argues, between masculinity and credit-worthiness and femininity
and sexual continence, or lack thereof. "[W]omen's reputations
were conventionally premised more on sexual than on financial
probity" (87) so that the counter became the site of male "social
death" while the brothel served as its female equivalent. Crucially,
all of the places in this book are sites of change, a phenomenon to
which John Stow's *Survey of London* responded with a sense of
nostalgia, a lament for the loss of an earlier time, but which Thomas
Dekker engaged as the fertile ground for irreverent satire. Plays,
Howard argues, helped London's denizens to negotiate and make
sense of the temporal ruptures forced upon them by "the world
city" in which they found themselves. Howard contends that her
"emphasis on the city in flux is meant to highlight not only the
many material changes overtaking London but also the discursive

changes and struggles necessary to make cognitive and ideological sense of life in the city" (14). What is at stake in London comedy, what is being understood, articulated, constructed, and contested, is nothing less than the imagined social reality of early modern London with its shifting occupations and identities. As Howard puts it: "In a radical sense, London comedies made London as much as they were made by it, and they made Londoners as well" (40).

Although Howard includes an incisive reading of *The Merchant of Venice,* one of the many achievements of this remarkable book is that, while it is refreshingly *not* about Shakespeare, *Theatre of a City* has radical implications for our understanding of theater in Shakespeare's London via its insistent focus on a geographically grounded temporal moment. Bringing theater history, close reading, and cultural criticism together to make sense of how drama worked not only in time but also in place, this is truly groundbreaking research that will immediately become required reading for all those interested in early modern drama and will remain a classic for many years to come.

Politics and the Passions, 1500–1850
Edited by Victoria Kahn, Neil Saccamano, and Daniela Coli
Princeton: Princeton University Press, 2006

Reviewer: Katherine Rowe

This collection of essays on the intimate relationship between Western theories of emotion and Western political thought is organized according to traditional lines of intellectual history. Each contribution is dedicated to an influential European theorist, spanning the period from Bacon's writings to Bentham's. Each reading illuminates that writer's reconfiguration of the passions to accommodate changing models of political interest, belief, and human motivation. Read sequentially, the essays unfold with remarkable

fidelity to this model. As one might expect of a collection of senior
scholars, the readings are consistently fresh, nuanced, and deeply
engaged with the writer in question. Thus, for example, John Mc-
Cormick explores Machiavelli's *Discourses* from the new perspective of an imagined readership of young *grandi,* teasing out the
author's intention to moderate their natural "desire to dominate the
people." Timothy Hampton reads Montaigne's neglected essay on
his tenure as mayor as an effort "to work out a model for a posthu-
manist political action, for a form of public service that is no longer
built upon a shared public world" (47). John Guillory traces the
emergence of modern social types—the lay intellectual and philosophical bachelor—in Bacon's meditations on the social roles of
philosopher, king, and fellow. Daniela Coli casts Hobbes as a "modernist" who articulates a counterrationalism that links passion and
reason in terms opposed to the dominant, post-Cartesian frame-
works of Western political thought. Riccardo Caporali teases out
Vico's investments in a theory of civil society in which the impulse
to "tenderness" offers an alternative to "barbarism." Howard Cay-
gill explores the implications of Kant's late reconsideration of the
passions when he began to depathologize phenomena that he had
systematically marginalized in earlier writings. Patrick Coleman
shows that Rousseau's ambivalent accounts of gratitude exemplify
profound tensions in early modern culture around the changing
terms of social obligation. Victoria Kahn tracks the inauguration of
a "new regime of politics, inscribed in the body itself" to the way
Descartes internalizes contemporary political concerns in *Passions
de l'ame* (110). None of these summaries do the essays justice, but
they should make it clear how each sets out to rethink from new
angles the philosophies of emotion these writers engage.

It is rare for a collection of essays to share a single intellectual
framework, and *Politics and the Passions* is no exception. There
are, however, some underlying premises that many of the essays
hold in common. Some of these premises are spelled out in a short
introduction by Kahn and Neil Saccamano, who map critical approaches to a political history of the passions from Norbert Elias
to Max Horkheimer, Albert Hirschman, and Michel Foucault. The
introduction digests the different contributions these theorists
make to a dominant narrative in early modern studies: that from
the end of the medieval period to the beginning of the Victorian
period, European culture saw a fundamental shift to a possessively
individualized, self-disciplining subject; that this subject evolved

to match or was part of the transformation of feudal structures to modern state formations; and that this entailed a corresponding shift in the social valuation and political meanings of everyday life—including what was to become the daily bourgeois work of disciplining the emotions, sentiments, and senses. As Kahn and Saccamano pithily frame it: "For modernity, society is that for which the inglorious life of the ancient Greek household— economics—becomes a matter of public concern" (5).

Debates about how to tell this history and critiques (often mounted by medievalists) to the specific claims early modernists regularly make about "modern" subjectivity are not the concern of this collection. (Readers should be alerted that though the title names a start date of 1500, the essays largely focus on post-1600 European political thought.) Specific challenges to the "distinctively modern subject" thesis rarely surface, even in footnotes. Thus, for example, Nancy Armstrong and Leonard Tennenhouse ground their analysis of the rise of the self-disciplining subject in Locke and Hutcheson in the claim that "modern theories of the emotions began as a refutation of the humoral model of the passions" (132). By contrast, recent work in the history of natural philosophy (John Sutton, for example) has tended to frame this shift in terms of a continuous but uneven process of revising and repurposing humoral discourse. However, simplifying—or in builder's terms, roughing out—historical structures at the early end may allow for more detail at the later end of a narrative. Armstrong and Tennenhouse connect the autonomous dramas of internal action broached by Locke and revised by Hutcheson to Victorian spectacles of extreme and nonnormative passion.

Some of the essays take a turn from local analysis of early modern passions theory to explore the payoffs for those concerned with emotion discourse in twenty-first-century politics—what the introduction observes as an ambient political surround organized by the discourses of "terror" or "compassionate" governance. The introduction singles out three essays invested in counterdiscourses that early modern passions theory can model for current issues. Judith Butler mediates on Spinoza's antinationalist and antiterritorialist concepts of political unity, offering an ethics of "nontotalizable sociality" applicable to the Israeli-Palestinian conflict (130). Neil Saccamano explores the possibilities of disidentification offered in Hume's aesthetic theory, which might serve to disrupt the totalizing affects of bourgeois economy. In a synthetic essay that concludes the collection, Frances Ferguson traces debates about liberal theories of belief, emotion, and political action derived from these early theorists, to Bentham and Mill, and finally to Stanley Fish.

Few of the essays directly engage larger methodological questions: the problem of what constitutes good practice in reading emotion theory transhistorically; the conundrum of emotion as a topic of analysis and as a social phenomenon whose decorums partly shape what's selectable for analysis. The exception is Guillory's exploration of the philosopher as a social type, which speculates about the disciplinary boundaries that preclude the kind of analysis the essay wants to pursue and which conducts a ranging conversation in its footnotes with other scholars whose concerns intersect with his own. Taken as a whole, this collection suggests that scholarship on the history of emotions has reached a maturity and depth that makes such methodological speculation both urgent and welcome.

The Jamestown Project
by Karen Ordahl Kupperman
Cambridge, MA and London: Belknap Press of
Harvard University Press, 2007

Reviewer: Jim Egan

I write this review in my office at Brown University, just across campus from the John Carter Brown Library where, some fifty-five years ago, Perry Miller delivered a talk, "Errand Into the Wilderness," that would set the terms for the study of the origins of American culture for the next few decades. Miller singled out the Massachusetts Bay Colony as the point of "coherence with which [he] could coherently begin" his story of "the movement of European culture into the vacant wilderness of America." His speech concluded with an image of those transplanted Protestants "left alone with America" with "no other place to search but within themselves." They were like so many little castaway Tom Hanks, but with Puritans instead of volleyballs for companionship.

One of the virtues of Karen Ordahl Kupperman's *The Jamestown Project* is that it indicates how much has changed in the origin stories we tell about the United States since Miller gave his talk. For one thing, far from being left alone on a vacant continent, her founding colonists seem more like social butterflies, involved with any and all groups of people, including the native inhabitants of the land, while displaying none of the interest in the kind of existential questions that defined Miller's first modern Americans. These colonists are practical people bent on making this project work however they can without dillydallying about the philosophical or spiritual implications of their behavior. Kupperman's title points to a second major change, for where Miller explicitly excludes Virginia as the starting point, Kupperman identifies Jamestown itself as the origin of America (2). What is far more important and exciting, though, is that the book spends much of its time arguing—implicitly if not always explicitly—that English commercial and political interests around the globe, but concentrated in the Mediterranean and Asia, not only must be understood in order to see America's founding "within its true context," but also that these global ventures that would have seemed irrelevant to historians just twenty years ago helped shape America's very conception and social structure.

Kupperman's focus on situating Jamestown within a broader context than would historians of a previous generation produces one of the oddities of the book: she doesn't actually get to the details of Jamestown's founding until the seventh chapter, or two-thirds of the way through her discussion. After a brief introduction that lays out her claim that Jamestown should be seen as the place where a model for successful English colonization of America would be invented, she proceeds in her first chapter, "Elizabethan England Engages the World," to explain how England saw and was seen by the world at large in the years immediately preceding Jamestown's founding. Chapter 2, "Adventurers, Opportunities, and Improvisation," focuses our attention on a number of key European and English individuals, some of whom were important in the early history of Jamestown and some of whom merely serve as examples or figures for the kind of broad experience across the known world English people brought to bear in the American colonies. While the title "Indian Experience of the Atlantic" suggests that she will give us the Native American perspective of colonization, the third chapter gives us more, for understandable reasons given the existing archive, of what Europeans said about this encounter than what the Indians themselves thought. We move from a useful discussion of English interest in a variety of things cast as "new" in the period in "English Hunger for the New," chapter 4, to a largely engaging explanation of the way the English in particular and Europeans in general imagined the globe, the American continent, and the continent's environment in chapter 5, "Grasping America's Contours." Kupperman goes on to situate Jamestown in relation to other English interests across the globe in her informative chapter 6, "A Welter of Colonial Projects," before finally giving us a picture of Jamestown in three stages that correspond to her concluding three chapters: "Jamestown's Uncertain Beginnings," "The Project Revised," and "James Cittie in Virginia."

While Kupperman writes in a generally clear prose that situates Jamestown in relation to the goings-on around the globe where I agree it belongs, I cannot recommend the book to scholars who are likely to read this journal. First, the book seems to me to be aimed at a general audience rather than a scholarly one. The book seeks to capitalize on the interest surrounding the 500th anniversary of the founding of Jamestown. I have nothing against scholars writing popular books or taking advantage of the market when they do so. Indeed, I say "bravo" to such efforts. In this case, though, the book offers very little that would be of use, not only to Shakespeare scholars but also to scholars of early modern England and/or Europe more broadly. Indeed, much of the material on world trade and America's place in that trade during the period draws on the work of such scholars. Second, when we translate scholarship for a wider audience, we sometimes rely on concepts that much recent work—often theory, but not exclusively so—has shown to be problematic at best. So, Kupperman tells her story in what has come to be termed the "Ken Burns" style of history. That is, she tells us the history as often as possible through the words of sixteenth- and seventeenth-century actors themselves and/or uses the life and adventures of particular individuals as a focal point of larger historical movements. I found myself consistently unconvinced by much of her discussion because such a method depends on taking what these actors say at face value, rather than interpreting them in relation to underlying systems of meanings of which those actors are blissfully unaware. The colonists in Kupperman's narrative speak, write, and act with an agency ungoverned by forces, discursive or otherwise, outside their control or knowledge.

The book's imagined audience of general rather than scholarly readers may account, too, for the problems I had with what appears to be one of *The Jamestown Project*'s central arguments. For in addition to her contention that American colonization be understood in a world context, she argues that the "true priority" of Jamestown "lies in its inventing the archetype of English colonization" (3). "The key to building English societies abroad," Kupperman concludes, "was discovered in Virginia and all successful colonies henceforth followed its model" (327). I have no clue just what she means here. Does she mean that seventeenth-century Virginians created a model colony whose structures were consciously followed by subsequent English colonies that survived? Given the historical record, this seems on its very face demonstrably false. She must then mean that it "invented" a model that was never used as a model but that nonetheless is important for demonstrating the foresight of its founders. Except that in order to demonstrate her point that Jamestown was such a model, even though it was never used as one, she cites the work of John Smith as the one writer who "drew the true lessons of the Jamestown experience" and, in the process, "explained to his readers . . . a fundamental understanding about human psychology" (325 and 327). The problem with such an argument is that Smith was run out of Virginia by Virginia's leaders very soon after it was founded, and though he wrote a good deal after that, every piece of scholarship I can recall agrees that few if any English readers, and certainly no one in charge of Virginia, put much stock in what he said about colonization. So, we are left to wonder about the significance of Jamestown as a model colony if the only person who recognized it as such was routinely ignored by his contemporaries.

If you are interested in a relatively general discussion of the first twenty or so years of Jamestown, *The Jamestown Project* provides a quick primer. If you need a quick summary of the way in which the American colonies were understood in relation to other English projects around the world, Kupperman's early chapters might be useful. Otherwise, I think the book offers little of value for scholars.

Lacan's Medievalism
By Erin Felicia Labbie
Minneapolis: University of Minnesota Press, 2006

Reviewer: Suzanne M. Verderber

The central thesis of Erin Labbie's *Lacan's Medievalism* is that Lacan can rightfully be considered a medievalist not only because he draws upon medieval texts in elaborating the concepts that constituted his return to Freud, but principally because his conceptualization of the unconscious situates him as a realist in the realism-nominalism debate that pervaded medieval philosophy. I would like to state at the outset that this book's proposal to expose the confluences between medieval philosophy and Lacanian psychoanalytic theory is extraordinarily ambitious because it brings together two fields that, in their scope and complexity, would require several lifetimes (or at least more than one academic career) to grasp with any confidence. This is, at least, my opinion, and I approach writing this review with a sense of my own lack of expertise in both the intricacies of the medieval debate concerning particulars and universals, and in Lacan's writings. On the other hand, Lacan himself said that "understanding" was a sham, an instance of *méconnaissance,* and that the experience of lack provokes desire and signification, and so I proceed in this spirit.

Establishing a contrast between Lacan and myriad other twentieth-century intellectuals who may be considered medievalists because of their engagement with medieval texts, including Agamben, Arendt, Bataille, and Barthes (a topic Bruce Holsinger covers in *The Premodern Condition*), Labbie argues that Lacan is a medievalist because "his methodologies follow those established by the medieval scholastic scholars who sought to determine the potential of the human subject to know and represent real universal categories" (2). Richard R. Glejzer's article "Lacan with Scholasticism: Agencies of the Letter," published in *American Imago* (1997), helps Labbie to articulate the main reason that provokes both scholars to associate Lacan's mode of thought with that of the schoolmen: "As Glejzer rightly points out, 'both scholasticism and psychoanalysis are founded on an imperative to consider a knowledge that resists signification . . .' The foundational structures of both scholasticism and psychoanalysis seek to investigate the limits of knowledge based on linguistic representation" (3). More specifically, just as the scholastic thinkers (and I believe she is referring mainly to Thomas Aquinas; she cites several times medievalist-psychoanalyst Julia Kristeva's assertion that "Lacan is a Thomist") acknowledge the limit of the ability of human reason to know God, Lacan asserts that there is a limit in the ability to know and represent the unconscious. In other words, just as Aquinas recognizes that humans cannot fully know God, Lacan asserts that the Real, the kernel of the unconscious, will forever elude the operations of the Symbolic register.

Situating Lacan on the side of the realists in the realist-nominalist debates, she takes this analogy one step further by asserting that Lacan views the unconscious as a "real universal." She defines a "real universal" as something that exists no matter what, whether or not it receives a name (nominalists, obviously, would take a different position). The unconscious, she argues, is indeed a real universal. This raises an interesting question that Labbie does not pursue in depth but is raised by this study and warrants further discussion, and which Glejzer also addresses in his article, that is, whether Lacan's linguistics is primarily that of Ferdinand de Saussure and the structuralists, as is usually stated, or is inspired by realists like Augustine, Boethius, or Aquinas. Saussure held that signifiers carve up reality and thought, that names precede things. Without the name, we do not have the thing. Lacan, of course, argued that the thing is out there anyway, in the form of the Real, and that this is, as I understand it, Labbie's basis for associating Lacan with the realists.

Following this route, she convincingly points out the paradox that the unconscious is *both* subject to history and transhistorical, the former because the psychoanalytic subject is always produced through its castration by language and law, two systems that are subject to the vagaries of history, and the latter because the unconscious is produced through the repression caused by speech: "[T]he unconscious understood as an abstract, conceptual entity, however, is precisely transhistorical in that it exists in each speaking subject throughout time, whether there is a name for it, the unconscious, or not" (9). This reminder that the unconscious is formed through the subject's acceptance of language and law, its sacrifice of jouissance to the prerogatives of civilization, sets the stage for a persuasive reply to the argument that the application of the work of Dr. Freud and his followers in the Middle Ages is ahistorical because it is only relevant to the "modern" subject. Labbie elaborates, echoing Joan Copjek's Lacanian challenge to Foucault in *Read My Desire: Lacan Against the Historicists:* [T]he unconscious as a real category is subject to these external epistemological changes, but it survives these alterations as it exceeds and evades the process of conscious registering" (19).

A final aspect of Labbie's claim that Lacan is a medievalist because he views the unconscious as a real universal is the analogy she establishes between God and the unconscious: "As Christ was proof of God's existence, desire is proof of the existence of the unconscious" (17). She argues that Lacan espoused a Thomistic approach that nevertheless accounted for his lack of faith in God, in which the unconscious, not God, is the central absent cause. Using Richard Myles's criteria for realism in *Chaucerian Realism,* she claims that Lacan is neither a *foundational* nor *intentional* realist, meaning that he neither believes "that we live in a world of beings created by a transcendent being" or that "creation is an intentional act and that human beings tend towards their creator" (28). If Lacan fails to be a foundational or intentionalist realist, he does qualify as one in four other categories of realism delineated by Myles (ethical, epistemological, semiotic/linguistic, and psychological), all of which are related to the position that language can produce knowledge, but that there is always something beyond language that eludes it and that demands a form of faith.

Nevertheless, despite this replacement of God by the unconscious as the absent cause, God is present in Lacanian theory as the face that is frequently given to the Other (symbolized as "A"), the locus that Lacan postulates is the "treasure of signifiers" and of truth for the speaking subject (the Other symbolized as a capital "A" with a slash through it would therefore signify Lacan's atheism, the fact that the symbolic order has no real foundation or basis). In addition, as Labbie points out, for Lacan, God is always dead, a reference not only to Nietzsche but to Freud's myth of the murder of the primal father, which in turn served as his explanation for the origins of monotheism and of Lacan's concept of paternity as a symbolic function. In a sense, then, if God disappears in Lacanian theory as a cause, he reappears as the imaginary embodiment of the symbolic law (as well as, to return to Lacan's reading

of Saussure, the guarantor that the signifier is connected to the signified).

What would have helped make this complex, dynamic argument
more persuasive would have been an introductory chapter explicitly detailing specifically which or whose medieval realism Lacan
assimilates. Labbie implies several times that it is the realism of
Saint Thomas, but she also mentions that of Boethius. She does not
discuss Augustine, whose semiotics was crucial to Lacan, as
Glejzer points out. So, an overview of the medieval debate over realism would have been helpful, alongside a discussion of her fundamental understanding of the Lacanian concepts at stake in the
argument (the Imaginary, Symbolic, and Real; the crossing out of
the term Woman; the object a; symbolic castration, etc). Such a
chapter would have made this otherwise stimulating book more
user-friendly, always a consideration when presenting Lacan to a
medievalist audience or vice versa (not that the two audiences are
mutually exclusive). While Labbie does assert in a footnote that her
book is not intended to be an introduction to Lacan, I would like to
echo medievalist-theorist Sarah Kay's remark in *Žižek: A Critical
Introduction* concerning the process of reading both Lacan and
Žižek: "Each reader must find his or her way of grappling with the
gaps, and will never come up with the same account twice. As with
Lacan, every reading of a Žižek text is only a possible trajectory—
which is not to say that it is not true" (16). Reading Lacan as a medievalist, Labbie does indeed carve a unique, fascinating, and
productive path through Lacan's work. But at the same time I found
myself craving Labbie's own, unique introduction to medieval realism and to Lacan.

Labbie's reading of Chaucer's *Clerk's Tale* in chapter 1 explores
Lacan's realism in relation to the concept of sovereignty, arguing
that for Lacan, sovereignty is not absolute, guaranteed by the One,
and that therefore it must find another basis. She notes Lacan's reference in Seminar VII to the role of the fool at court (a tradition in
English literature that he says began with Chaucer) as being the one
person who is able to tell the king that he is naked. Lacan's seemingly offhand reference to Chaucer provides Labbie with the pre-
text to extend Lacan's thinking on the reality of universals, and
specifically on his controversial claim that "the Woman does not
exist," through a reading of *The Clerk's Tale.* This tale, she argues,
reveals that Walter's sovereignty is *not* universal because he is subject to the command of his subjects, who demand that he take a

wife against his inclinations. Walter tries to make up for this lack in sovereignty by exerting an absolute, quasi-totalitarian sovereignty over his wife Griselda. Conversely, Griselda's absolute submission to all of Walter's outrageous demands, including that she allow her own children to be killed, a position characterized by a "singular subjective sovereignty" (54), causing her to inhabit "the totalizing position of slave" (58), raises her to the position of the universal. As the clerk makes clear in his remarks following the telling of the tale, this loyalty turns her into "*the* Woman" because no *real* woman could possibly achieve this position. Griselda becomes "a woman" again when Walter returns her children, causing her to break down in tears, and places her beside him on the throne. The juxtaposition of the tale with Lacan's crossing out of the Woman as an aspect of his engagement with universals is fascinating, but I think the links need to be more fully explained (the question of why Lacan crosses out "Woman" persists in the book, but I wish Labbie had provided a more detailed discussion of her understanding of this particularly difficult moment in Lacan's theory). It might be interesting to think of Griselda not as a sovereign in her embrace of the position of slave, but rather as a hysteric, a trait of the hysteric being not only her unending questioning of sexual difference, but also her desire to be *the* Woman and to find a master to turn her into one. Maybe Griselda thought that total submission was simply what was expected of women, a not unreasonable conclusion, and she tried hard, to say the least, to make Walter her master.

Labbie extends this discussion of sovereignty in chapter 2 in her reading of Marie de France's lay *Bisclavret,* the story of a nobleman who turns into a werewolf three days out of each week. When his suspicious wife pries the truth out of him, she repudiates him and has his clothes stolen by her paramour so that he can never again revert to human form. In wolf form, the nobleman demonstrates his courtliness to the king, who makes the noble beast a respected member of his court. When the wolf attacks the wife's paramour at court, the king assumes that he must have had a rational motive for doing so, and, discovering the wife's bad behavior, he punishes her by having her nose cut off. Her reading draws upon Giorgio Agamben's argument in *Homo Sacer* (which also takes up the lay) more than it does upon Lacan. It would have been interesting for her to reflect on this privileging of Agamben at this point in her study (what does his work offer that Lacan's lacks?), but she does not. It seems as if what psychoanalysis offers as a way of reading of this lay is its distinction between instinct and drive, which maintains a strict binary between animals and humans based upon the human alienation from instinct by language. Both Marie de France and Agamben problematize this binary by asserting that the animal is contained within the sovereign, but that the sovereign must exclude the animal, or "bare life" in order to maintain this position. But in the lay, strangely, it is the wife who tries to exclude bare life to achieve sovereignty, and the king who accepts bare life and acknowledges the fragility of sovereignty.

She juxtaposes this reading of *Bisclavret* with another tale dealing with spousal distrust and hybridity, the Old French romance *Mélusine* by Jean d'Arras, which is mentioned by Freud but not Lacan. She very insightfully juxtaposes Raymond's perception of Mélusine's tail, of the animality that she contains within her humanity, as Labbie puts it, with an analysis of Lacan's reading of the Arnaut Daniel's bawdy, obscene troubadour poem in Seminar VII, which describes the courtly lady as monstrous, smelly, and physically overwhelming. In both cases, she argues that the condition of sovereignty is the repression or sustaining of a distance from animality. In terms of the larger argument concerning real universals, she uses these texts to expand her explanation of why Lacan crosses out Woman, which is that, as in Griselda's case, no woman can fit the category; her reality always causes her to exceed it and thus to generate anxiety and disgust in the male voyeur, who really wants to see nothing "there" when he looks (as opposed to the usual narrative of castration anxiety, wherein horror or perversion is generated by the fact that nothing is there).

In the first two chapters, then, rather than mine Lacan's texts for medieval references, as one might have expected her to do in such a project (although she does this as well), Labbie uses medieval texts to extend Lacan's thinking (just as he uses medieval texts to extend his own). I think this is a wise move since it avoids "application," which maintains the boundary between theory and literature (here literature is used to explicate theory and vice versa). Her reading of Lacan's seventh seminar on ethics, that which contains his major discussion of courtly love and which has been the prime focus for medievalists interested in Lacan, is expanded in chapter 3. Here she returns to Lacan's critique of Hegelian dialectic in "The Subversion of the Subject and the Dialectic of Desire" to claim that Lacan's focus on courtly love in the seminar was provoked by the quest for a model of desire that exceeds dialectics, one that does not culminate in synthesis (by constrast, Kay explicates the Slovenian philosopher's recuperation of Hegel as a philosopher of excess in Žižek). This is so of courtly love, the scenario that allows Lacan to refine his concepts of the Real, the Thing, and the object a, all concepts that indicate excess and nonsynthesis. Indeed, as Labbie points out, Lacan finds courtly love to be a brilliant cultural achievement in its attempt to dress up and take responsibility for a failure, the failure being the fact that there is no sexual relationship.

In chapter 4, Labbie moves to another aspect of Lacan's thought that also concerns his exploration of the limits of knowledge: his relation to science. She explains how, like Freud, Lacan covets science while asserting its limits: "Lacan points out the limitations of science for the investigation of universal categories like 'virtue,' even while he continues to idealize the hard sciences" (151). His covetousness of science is reflected in his quest to find more precise means of representing his concepts than ordinary language (mathemes and knots), yet he never stops pointing out the way unconscious desire disrupts the intentionality and certainty of the cogito. Labbie demonstrates how Chaucer, in his *A Treatise on the Astrolabe,* is Lacan's *prochain* in his perception that science is imbued with desire, and this for several reasons. Citing *The Miller's Tale,* Labbie claims that the status of science as good or evil depends upon how it is used, and she notes in relation to the *Treatise* that it is addressed to Chaucer's son to "slay envy," two details that reveal that "science" is caught up in a transferential relationship involving desire, not mere mathematical objectivity. One of the complexities of this chapter that I think remains to be untangled concerns the epistemic issues raised by the comparison of Lacan's and Chaucer's views of science. Lacan is usually taken to be responding to "modern" or seventeenth-century science, and Jean-Claude Milner, whom she cites, has claimed that psychoanalytic theory is part and parcel of the episteme of modern science. What, then, does it mean to bring Chaucer's "scientific" treatise into this discussion, produced in a period when the relation between astronomy and astrology was different from what it would be after the seventeenth-century scientific revolution?

Chapter 5 concerns two gentlemen who have trouble in the bedroom: Gawain, of *Sir Gawain and the Green Knight,* and Judge Schreber, the famed psychotic whose memoirs served Freud and

Lacan as their primary case study of psychosis. Whereas Gawain
fails to have sexual relations with Bercilak's wife as he celebrates
the holidays before his date with destiny, Schreber associates the
onset of his nervous illness with the waking dream that it would
be rather pleasant to be a woman succumbing to intercourse. The
lynchpin of this comparison is that both men, she argues, are playing a game with God, Gawain in his tossing away of the girdle,
which represents the intertwining of the divine and earthly realms,
and Schreber in his transformation of himself into a woman whom
God will impregnate so that Schreber can give birth to a new
human race. More clarification of fundamental psychoanalytic concepts, and where Freud and Lacan differ on them, would have been
helpful here. Labbie does not distinguish the neurotic and psychotic structures as Lacan does, the difference hinging upon the position of the subject in relationship to the paternal function or Law
(the neurotic represses the Law, whereas the psychotic forecloses
it). She makes reference to Freud's interpretation of Schreber's
case, which Lacan refuted, which reads Schreber's psychosis as a
symptom of repressed homosexuality. Lacan, meanwhile, in this
case, asserts that the psychotic position is defined by the foreclo-
sure of the paternal function, which in turn exiles the psychotic
from the signifying chain and causes him, ultimately, to have to re-
build the cosmos from scratch (hence Schreber's grandiose, escha-
tological delusion). Is Gawain also psychotic? What would be
required to make such a claim? He, on the other hand, seems
plagued by delay, avoidance, castration anxiety, and doubt, and
perhaps could have been read also in relation to Lacan's interpretation of *Hamlet,* the story of another well-known procrastinator.

My disagreements with the details of Labbie's readings of Lacan
and medieval culture should not be taken in a negative light, but as
eager and engaged participation in the discussion that the book
raises. There is a certain richness produced by her reading of Lacanian theory alongside medieval texts, and she has managed to
help take the field of psychoanalytic medievalism well beyond the
naive "application" stage to one in which problems of historiography, epistemology, semiology, and desire, relevant not only to
medieval studies but to all engagements with the past, are pushed
to the forefront. She continues a task initiated by Bruce Holsinger,
the demonstration of the centrality of medieval modes of desire,
representation, and thought to contemporary critical theory. In this
light, objections to the use of psychoanalytic theory in medieval

studies seem absurd when, as Labbie demonstrates, we begin to glimpse the centrality of the medieval ideas to the elaboration of psychoanalytic theory.

Shakespeare's Late Style
By Russ McDonald
Cambridge: Cambridge University Press, 2006

Reviewer: Lynne Magnusson

One of the casualties of the turn to historicism and cultural studies over the last two or three decades has been the sophisticated mechanisms for the close reading of texts developed through the widespread practice in the preceding decades of the New Criticism and other formalist methods. As innumerable recent articles and books have been suggesting, the disciplinary impact of this loss is now being recognized. Returning detailed attention to the "syntax, meter, diction, repetition, figurative language, and other such verbal and poetic properties" (1) of Shakespeare's writing, Russ McDonald's new book on *Shakespeare's Late Style* participates in a revival of formalist analysis. This reemergence of formalist close analysis of texts raises many questions. Foremost among them is the question of what might be productively recovered from past practices and what needs serious rethinking to take on board the advances and the broadening of our knowledge that cultural criticism has afforded. While McDonald is quite brilliant on the former, he seems much less interested in the latter. Let me suggest how good McDonald's recovery work is.

A key strength of this book is its well-researched engagement with the critical history of its subject. A fascination with the altered texture of the dramatic verse in Shakespeare's final plays long predates mid-twentieth-century formalism. Whereas the Victorian scholars engaged in metrical tests to establish the canon and chronology (including F. J. Furnivall and James Spedding) provided some initial descriptions of the stylistic minutiae, critics like Edward Dowden initiated the efforts to interpret the manner of Shakespeare's late plays in relation to larger constructs. Dowden characterized the "phases" of Shakespeare's career, including the final phase when the dramatic poet came out of "the depths" and on to "the heights," a lofty interpretation that Lytton Strachey brushed aside in famously asserting that the combined speed and virtuosity of the late style—its effect of gesturing towards what it does not stop to fully articulate—signaled Shakespeare's boredom with drama and with life. McDonald credits A. C. Bradley with the most succinct and lucid description of the late style and the challenges it poses: "After *Hamlet* the style, in the more emotional passages, is heightened. It becomes grander, sometimes wilder, sometimes more swelling, even tumid. It is also more concentrated, rapid, varied, and, in construction, less regular, not seldom twisted or elliptical. It is, therefore, not easy and lucid and in the more ordinary dialogue it is sometimes involved and obscure, and from these and other causes deficient in charm" (30).

McDonald follows Bradley and the tradition of related commentary in accepting the assumption that there is a late style, something that can be abstracted from the multitudinous sentence forms and metrical patterns and held up, characterized (even if "sometimes" this, and "not seldom" that) as a singular "it." In this, he adheres to an understanding of style with a classical and Renaissance heritage. As George Puttenham defined this key term, "Stile is a constant & continuall phrase or tenour of speaking and writing, extending to the whole tale or processe of the poeme or historie, and not properly to any peece or member of a tale" (*The Arte of English Poesie*, 123). As Puttenham went on to make clear, and as great twentieth-century stylistic critics like Leo Spitzer, Eric Auerbach, and Morris Croll also exemplified, there are two procedures caught up in the enterprise of discerning style: the one to abstract from amidst a multiplicity of instances available for close reading a coherent and singular characterization and the other to account for the style by positing what it can be said to reflect or to have as its cause—most usually, some quality of the man, the work, the genre, or the cultural surround. Thus, rather than insisting at every point on the novelty of what he has to say, McDonald builds in an expert way on the foundations both of the tradition of stylistics and of early formulations about Shakespeare's late style. There is much to admire in this way of proceeding in a book that is the fruit of long study by an experienced scholar, especially in our era of disposable scholarship when many studies treat what went before as though it had only a five- to ten-year shelf-life.

Amidst the great variety of Shakespearean sentences, it is perhaps easier to accept that there is a "late" Shakespearean style marked off by distinctive traits of syntax, meter, and rhetorical figuration than an "early" or "middle" style. As McDonald argues, the "continual phrase" of the style makes itself felt partly by the seeming mismatch of language to speaker in the late plays. Twisted, obscure, elliptical structures may—as is often argued—fit well with Leontes' mad language in *The Winter's Tale,* but the argument for decorum to character is invalidated by the fact that the same irregularity or turbulence in the syntax occurs in Camillo's reasonable rejoinders, Florizel's lyrical protestations, or various gentlemen's quiet conversations. Where McDonald's study makes a very substantial advance on earlier criticism is in identifying the precise features of syntax, rhetorical figuration, and prosody that match up with Bradley's impressions to constitute this singular style. Dividing the syntactical traits into types of elision, divagation, and suspension (he devotes a chapter to each type), McDonald does a superb and detailed job of characterizing recurring sentence patterns. He makes his descriptions readable and interesting despite his own occasional defensive apologies for exhaustive categorization and illustration. In part, he accomplishes this by avoiding overly specialized terminology, while at the same time drawing selectively upon his own specialized expertise in the terms and distinctions of Renaissance rhetoric, traditional stylistics, and (to a lesser extent) historical linguistics. He wears his learning lightly, often offering a helpful redundancy of terms for devices (hyperbatonic, the "trespasser," disordered, "VS sentence" [115, 111]) and also shifting easily between precise technical description and suggestions about imaginative effect.

Not only does McDonald flesh out Bradley's impressionistic account of the late style as condensed, errant and convoluted, but he produces a fuller view by putting this together with the insistent aural repetition of the final romances. He posits a tension in the late style between irregularity and regularity, "threatened disorder and insistent patterning" (99): "For all its fierce abridgements, the late line is also heavy with surplus" (96). Insistent repetition of vowels, consonants, words, metrical patterns, and syntactic forms makes the style "uncommonly [McDonald's favorite adverb] musical" (181). The prevalence of sound repetition is familiar to most critics from passages in *The Tempest* like Ariel's song, "Full fathom five . . .," or Caliban's imaginative apprehension of "Sounds, and sweet airs," but, with the aid of a reasonably simple system of annotation, this book makes it clear how prevalent this verbal patterning is throughout the final romances.

It is with McDonald's insistence of the neglected topic of aural repetition that one begins to notice how his analysis could have benefited from an interest in more recent developments. He aims to rehabilitate the pleasures of alliteration and assonance and to dissociate their value to the cultured and experienced ear from the uncomfortable claims of "insecure poetry students" that they make the poetry "flow" (183). But acoustical repetition is not an easy subject to make interesting—or meaningful. Or, as Stanley Fish long since objected in "What is stylistics and why are they saying such terrible things about it?," it may be that it is too easy, or too tempting, to find ways of making it meaningful. As McDonald multiplies examples of repetition in Chapter 5, he at first confines himself to claims about the pleasures that "echoing sounds" yield to the discerning ear of the aesthetic connoisseur. But soon, repetition edges into regularity edges into order; equivalences begin to be established between the microcosmic "sonic" replications and the macrocosmic "narrative replications" of *Pericles* or *The Winter's Tale* (195), between the reassuring orderliness of sound repetition and the order worked out after chaos in romance plots, between harmonious sounds and harmonious families. "[T]he literal relations responsible for the distinctive sound of the last plays," we are told, "help physically to constitute Shakespeare's representation of the familial bond and its indisputable value in human experience. The repetition of consonants and vowels creates ligatures between words that generate a sonic atmosphere of familial security." (215) Political and cultural criticism in recent years has offered us good reasons to ask skeptical questions about what such secure pictures of family values leave out—but this is not the sort of book that asks why Hermione is silent at the end of *The Winter's Tale* or where the missing mothers are in the still-fractured families at the end of *The Tempest*. Nor does it ask, if sound repetition is so comforting, orderly, delightful and benign in the late plays, what distinguishes these poetic uses in the works of Shakespeare and Spenser (the chief comparator) from ideological or political uses in the activist rhetoric of Martin Luther King or the demagoguery of Hitler. As Mikhail Bakhtin objected, formalist stylistics tends to turn a deaf ear to the social life of language. Here, there seems to be considerable room for rethinking and asking how a renewed look at Shakespeare's style might take on board questions asked by the historicist criticism that has razed the boundaries in recent years between literary texts and social and historical contexts.

This problem is at its most evident where the book relies for its arguments about stylistic meaning-making on the methods of twentieth-century formalist or structuralist poetics. Not only did Fish's attack on stylistics show how matching small-scale linguistic structures to large-scale narrative structures could come too easily but he also argued that such claims were often circular. Is the word "divagation," for example, the most likely or neutral descriptive term to comprehend the syntactical forms of inversion, interpolation, breaking off, addition, and asyndeton that Chapter 3 treats, or does the term, from the outset, anticipate and forecast the match with the "sprawling, episodic, casually organized dramatic structures" (40) of romance? Nonetheless, the book's method, like its topic, is complex and various, and McDonald entertains many different answers to his own question, "how does a detailed acquaintance with the technical features of Shakespeare's late style help us to comprehend the plays?" (219). Often he takes his cue from "well-known critical themes" (219), as where he speculates about Shakespeare's continuing interest in language as a theme. He touches thoughtfully on the psychology of the auditor in the theatre, speculates about the changing attitudes and psychology of the author, reflects on the self-conscious artistry of the late plays, and posits a feminine aspect to the affirmation he identifies with Shakespeare's turn to romance. *Shakespeare's Late Style* goes a long way towards illuminating the fascination and complexity of Shakespeare's language in these plays, its simultaneous grace and opacity.

Cultural Capitals: Early Modern London and Paris
By Karen Newman
Princeton: Princeton University Press, 2007

Reviewer: Jean E. Howard

In *Cultural Capitals,* Karen Newman has given us a wide-ranging and invigorating investigation of how urbanization affected cultural production and urban sensibilities in early modern Paris and London. Newman selected these cities not only because of their rapid demographic growth and commercial and political importance, but also, as her title indicates, because they were crucial cultural centers. Books and ballads poured from the presses in both cities; theaters flourished; parks and bridges provided venues for new forms of urban sociability, and commercial structures such as the Royal Exchange and La Galerie du Palais put on offer an ever-more-impressive range of consumer goods. Paris and London set the standard for fashionability whether in terms of clothing, manners, carriages, or cuisine.

Newman is a gifted expositor of the texture of early modern urban life. She is as interested in the problem of city dirt and how it affected the movements and sensibilities of urban dwellers as in the analysis of Madeleine de Scudéry's romances, John Donne's poems of urban perambulation, or visual representations of the Pont Neuf. *Cultural Capitals,* then, has an unusually broad reach and embraces popular as well as elite cultural forms. At a time, moreover, when the number of comparative studies of early modern culture is dwindling, Newman's book is a striking exception. Because of her impressive linguistic skills, Newman moves with ease between English and French archives. She also has the theoretical savvy to raise interesting questions about her material. Throughout the book Newman suggestively explores the role of space, as well as time, in historical representations; queries the investigator's relationship to the archives she explores and the kinds of knowledge that can be produced from different sorts of texts; and thinks about how subjects are affected by new architectural forms, by the peculiar sensory texture of urban life, or by particular kinds

of texts, like romances or urban chorographies. Another thread
runs through the book: a concern with the ways in which the early
modern urban experience is and is not like that provided by the
more extensively studied nineteenth-century city.

A lot, then, is going on in this modestly sized book, and readers
will, I think, both appreciate the density of ideas and cultural references it provides and also sometimes wish for a more sustained
fleshing out of the theoretical issues it raises and the visual and verbal texts it evokes. Newman moves fast, not always pausing to answer fully the questions she raises. "How do texts register
sensation, sensory phenomena, and affect?" she asks (77). She answers by way of a brief discussion of Parisian mud as it figures in a
variety of French texts and of London noise as it is thematized in
Jonson's *Epicoene,* along with short discussions of Marx on the history of sensory experience, of Susan Stewart on the need for aesthetic activity to make sensory perception knowable, and of
Norbert Elias on the rise of a culture of shame in the early modern
period. Suggestive as these pages are, one leaves them feeling that
the big question Newman placed on the table has not been exhaus-
tively addressed. Some may find this a shortcoming; other readers
will simply enjoy following to their own conclusions the many
lines of inquiry the book opens up. Newman's intellectual style is
to be suggestive rather than exhaustive, but she is always deeply
intelligent.

Newman's scope of inquiry, moreover, inevitably leads to omis-
sions and oversights. When, for example, she compares Corneille's
city comedies of the 1630s and '40s to their English equivalents,
she finds them quite different. Writing of Corneille's works she
says: "Instead of tricksters, thieves, and young gallants on the make
more often for money than for love, its characters are members of a
young urban elite in search of romance, intent on urban pleasures,
on fashion, entertainment, and amatory adventure" (93). This is
more true if one compares Corneille to London city comedies written quite early in the seventeenth century, which are the English
city comedies such as *The Roaring Girl* (1611) to which Newman
refers, than to those written in the Caroline period, closer in time to
Corneille's own productions. West End comedies such as Shirley's
Hyde Park (1632) are largely free of tricksters and thieves but full
of gallants bent on fashionable pursuits and their own pleasure. In
general, Caroline London comedies more closely approximate Corneille's fictive work than do the earlier comedies of Jonson and

Middleton. A fuller engagement with Caroline theater would qualify Newman's generalizations about the differences between Corneille's city comedies and English ones.

Despite these quibbles, *Cultural Capitals* provides powerful and original analyses of a number of different kinds of cultural texts. For example, Newman's examination of the many seventeenth-century visual representations of the Pont Neuf is masterful. She argues that the bridge, which was deliberately kept free of the shops and houses found on many medieval structures, not only connected the Right Bank to the rest of the city, but also created new visual and cognitive experiences for urban dwellers of all classes. It provided a prospect, a vista, of the city in all directions; and, wide enough to accommodate coaches as well as foot traffic, it immersed those who crossed it in the hurly-burly of an urban scene in which persons of different degrees and genders mixed together in a democratizing stew. In a particularly acute section, Newman analyzes the distorted perspective that in some engravings of the bridge magnified its size and intensified for the viewer the sense of its capacity to contain multitudes and to symbolize all that was modern about the city in which they lived. By contrast, London Bridge was a narrower structure, crowded with houses and shops, and more often associated with the punishment of traitors (whose heads were famously impaled on pikes on the bridge) than with the new world of coaches and urban vistas. Newman uses Shakespeare's *2 Henry VI* to make this point, for in that play the plebeian rebel, Jack Cade, makes his tumultuous entrance to London at the head of a rebel band over London Bridge. In Shakespeare's play, the structure is associated with plebeian violence and threats to social order.

Newman presents her analysis of Cade's rebellion as a coda to her chapter on the Pont Neuf, and the juxtaposition of the chapter and its coda raises questions about the nature of the comparative enterprise on which Newman has embarked. She points out in her introduction that though her study is a comparative one, she did not intend to give equal time in each chapter to both cities and their texts because that would produce strained comparisons. This seems right, and yet the book makes readers eager for more conclusions than Newman offers about how and why the two cities and their literatures diverged as well as overlapped. While some of the *processes* of urbanization seem shared by both cities—demographic growth, concentration of market activity, centralization of services—there are also many ways in which these cities and their cultures were unique, as Newman demonstrates. So what can be said about the nature of and reasons for these similarities and differences?

Cultural Capitals is, oddly, somewhat reticent about drawing out the implications and conclusions to be drawn from its comparative approach. The book is structured as a series of juxtapositions. Sometimes those occur within a single chapter as when engravings of the Pont Neuf are juxtaposed to the London Bridge of *2 Henry VI* or Antoine Furetière's *Le roman bourgeois* is set against Ben Jonson's *Epicoene*. Sometimes a theme, like walking in the city, will be played out across several chapters using a variety of texts dealing with both London and Paris to tease out the different ways in which this activity can be inflected depending on class and circumstance. Each chapter, or section of a chapter, is interesting in and of itself, but it is not always clear what larger conclusions are being drawn from these juxtapositions. Locally, what can be learned from juxtaposing Le Pont Neuf and London Bridge? More broadly, what light is shed on these two cities and the literatures they inspired by examining the one in light of the other? What actual material connections linked the writers and artists of London to those of Paris or were there none? While Newman offers some observations on these questions, this reader would welcome a more systematic reflection on differences and similarities and their causes.

There is no doubt, however, that *Cultural Capitals* is one of the most interesting books of the year. It is invigorating to read a work of criticism that casts its net so broadly and that, in the supposedly "post-theory" world we inhabit, so obviously makes productive use of theoretical paradigms to open cultural productions to interesting and spirited investigation. The ratio of pages to smart ideas is extremely high in Newman's work, and the learning that informs every chapter is clear. Perhaps most importantly, the book vividly demonstrates the cultural impact of large-scale urbanization in the early modern period. The explosion of cultural forms that Newman examines testifies to the energy with which engravers, playwrights, poets, and satirists responded to the economic, social, and cognitive changes in which they participated and to which they gave expressive form. *Cultural Capitals* captures that energy and beckons to its further investigation.

Double Vision: Moral Philosophy and Shakespearean Drama
By Tzachi Zamir
Princeton: Princeton University Press, 2007

Reviewer: Michael D. Bristol

Once upon a time, let's say just after the middle of the eighteenth century, someone discovered that Shakespeare is a great moral philosopher. In my view this should count as a genuine discovery in the human sciences. Like all important discoveries, Shakespeare's value in moral philosophy can only be articulated in relation to developments in certain auxiliary sciences, in this case ethics, social theory, and the science of human motivation. Shakespeare's critics in the eighteenth century could draw on classical sources (Aristotle, Seneca, and the Stoics), on Christian tradition (St. Augustine), and also on new ideas about individual moral agency (the Earl of Shaftesbury, Adam Smith, Frances Hutcheson, Joseph Butler, David Hume, and others). This way of engaging with Shakespeare's plays developed into a robust tradition of interpretation that lasted for roughly 150 years, reaching a climax at the beginning of the last century in the work of A. C. Bradley and Richard Moulton.

The central category for this tradition of philosophical criticism is character, a term that basically meant something like a person's ethical or moral personality. Character criticism was eclipsed at the beginning of the last century, first by a shift of attention to the formal characteristics of Shakespeare's language and second by the development of historical inquiry. In both these interpretive traditions character criticism is frequently derided as naive, silly, and sometimes also as downright sinister in its aims. But when something is in eclipse, it hasn't really ceased to exist, it's just that something else is getting in the way of seeing it. So the work of interpreting Shakespeare in relation to moral philosophy has continued in the criticism of A. P. Rossiter, Stanley Cavell, Colin McGinn, A. D. Nuttall and Harry Berger, to name only a few examples. And of course, A. C. Bradley's *Shakespearean Tragedy* is still in print one hundred years after its first publication.

Tzachi Zamir's *Double Vision: Moral Philosophy and Shakespearean Drama* aims at sustaining this venerable tradition of criticism by showing how questions that concern philosophical inquiry help to bring out the complexity of Shakespeare's plays in fresh and interesting ways. Zamir's rediscovery of Shakespeare as a moral philosopher is itself possible because of new developments in recent moral philosophy. The work of Martha Nussbaum is central for his project, but there is also much to be learned from other contemporary philosophers, including Cavell, along with Bernard Williams, John Kekes, Alasdair McIntyre, Charles Taylor, and many others. Tzachi Zamir's larger ambition, I believe, is to bring Shakespeare-as-a-moral-philosopher out of a lengthy eclipse and back into the center of critical practice. He is admirably discrete about this, but I hope his book will contribute to a change in the focus of Shakespeare criticism.

Zamir has done an excellent job of articulating the larger project of a new Shakespeare criticism grounded in philosophical inquiry. This approach is indispensable for teaching Shakespeare and it can contribute significantly to the development of critical scholarship in the field. But then I was already convinced of the value of this general orientation before I read Zamir's book. I'm not at all sure that his book will have the impact it deserves to have in the field of Shakespeare studies, since it is likely to encounter strongly entrenched institutional resistance. For one thing, Zamir shows a marked preference for critical authorities that many people consider "humanistic" and therefore passé. Scholarship that now counts as the "cutting edge" has been concerned with the dissolution of critical categories like character and author in favor of styles of reading that dissolve Shakespeare's plays back into their local historical context. Zamir acknowledges the importance of what he calls the "cultural turn" in literary criticism, but he is very thorough in his treatment of the philosophical limitations of such orientations to literary texts. The focus of his engagement with recent criticism is the concept of social or cultural construction. "Claims regarding cultural constructs cannot simply be assumed as a priori truths blocking interpretive inquiries that may give us cause to reject them" (99). This is an important principle, one with particular relevance for the practice of historical criticism. No one can seriously contest the view that historical research can help us to see things in Shakespeare that we might otherwise miss. Understanding what Claudius meant by referring to Gertrude as the "imperial jointress of our estate" could actually shed some light on Hamlet's attitude to his mother. On the other hand, as Zamir very tactfully points out in the quotation here, scholarship is not supposed to be censorship in disguise.

Double Vision is organized in two main sections. The first part consists of three closely argued essays on Zamir's broad theoretical claims for philosophical criticism. The first two of these discussions are aimed primarily at philosophers with a view to explaining why philosophy, especially moral philosophy, needs literature. Zamir begins this discussion with a consideration of the epistemological basis of philosophical criticism. Like most readers, Zamir believes that literature has a capacity to create awareness and to amplify our knowledge. He is concerned, however, with providing a philosophical justification for these intuitions. His arguments are subtle, detailed, and very closely reasoned. The claim that literature is itself a knowledge-yielding activity is developed from Aristotle's account of practical reasoning. Although practical reasons are, strictly speaking, a "nonvalid" form of argumentation, it is nevertheless indispensable for actually living a life in the real world of contingent circumstances. Literary knowledge then is not merely a legitimate mode of "nonvalid" reasoning. Literature fosters a state of mind in which contingent claims about the good life are presented in a way that appeals to "the whole person" rather than to the specialized faculty of argumentative reasoning. "A philosophical reading of literature has an epistemological basis in two ways: in being knowledge yielding, and in being itself an inquiry into the structuralization of knowledge" (16). Literary works, according to Zamir, reveal the ways ethical maxims are embedded in lived experience.

Zamir's analysis of literature as knowledge-yielding provides the grounding for his account of the moral basis of philosophical criticism. This builds on the notion of a legitimate "nonvalid" mode of reasoning as central to the task of moral inquiry itself. Briefly, claims about the "principles" of moral philosophy cannot be "true" in the same way that the Pythagorean Theorem or Boyle's Law or Einstein's Theory of General Relativity are true. At the same time, however, the maxim that says we should not slander our neighbors has much greater salience for most of us than understanding the truth of Quantum Mechanics. I am not really able to judge whether Zamir's arguments are going to persuade my colleagues in philosophy, though for what it's worth he definitely has

Martha Nussbaum on his side. But I think Zamir's theoretical discussion should be considered very carefully by literary critics, and especially by Shakespeare scholars, many of whom have become very complacent and condescending in dismissing the possibilities for literary knowledge. Shakespeare's "texts" (there are no longer any considerations of "works") are now frequently described as merely "sites"—or opportunities—for the projection of mainly ephemeral ideological schemes. Zamir takes a much larger view of the value and importance of literature. For that reason alone I believe he needs to be taken very seriously by literary scholars.

Philosophical arguments are not the only reason for paying attention to what Zamir has accomplished, however. His discussions of individual plays demonstrate an astute grasp of the plotting of each drama and of the rhetorical features of its language. His analysis of *Richard III* addresses the question of "ethical skepticism," specifically Richard's deliberate choice of immoral conduct as a challenge to morality itself. Zamir acknowledges that Richard is modeled on the figure of the Medieval Vice—indeed Richard says so himself. But this can at best be a starting point for a more detailed "investigation into the characterization and motivation of Richard III." What Zamir is after here is what Harry Berger has called the "fatness" of a dramatic character, a complex motivational scenario "hidden in the undergrowth of language." Close reading of Richard's speeches reveals his fascination with his own ugliness and the effect it has on other people. Richard's project on this account is a vindication of the truth of his ugliness through a sustained assault on "dissembling nature" and the false face of beauty.

Most readers would agree with the suggestion that Richard's evil is a brilliantly sustained performance. Richard self-consciously reveals himself to the audience, and he is also concerned to make sure that his victims understand that he is the one responsible for their suffering and death. This is in part a form of revenge for his exclusion from the shared social life of the court and from the pleasure of love enjoyed by the beautiful people. But the larger purpose here is in actualizing the possibility for self-knowledge and self-acceptance. Richard is who he is because of the way he is seen. What Zamir finds remarkable about him is that he is willing to become the object of his own gaze, to see exactly what it is that accounts for his rejection. This ability to see himself is the basis for his "victory over dissembling nature." In choosing evil, Richard endorses the audience's condemnation of his actions, and, at the same time, challenges the ethical framework that articulates the possibility of judging him from which that judgment was initially produced. If, as Charles Taylor has suggested, a person's character is "an orientation in a space of moral questions," then *Richard III* is a profoundly disorienting work.

The discussion of ethical skepticism is developed further in Zamir's essay on nihilism in *Macbeth*. For Zamir what's striking about Macbeth is that he doesn't seem to have any fun carrying out his villainy. His ambition lacks content, there is no sense in him of why he wants to have power or what he intends to do when he gets it. Zamir calls this a lack of "motivational depth." Macbeth's nihilism is fully revealed in the "tomorrow and tomorrow" speech near the end of the play. Zamir reads this as the expression of an attitude of "postponement" or "putting off" any deeper consideration of what really matters to Macbeth. The one thing he does seem to care about is Lady Macbeth, but when she dies his reaction is that he hasn't got time right now to mourn her. But Macbeth is not only about the postponement of feelings. As a philosophical position, nihilism "rejects any process in which 'things'—states of affairs, feelings, lives, actions, dispositions—are endowed with value." The play, however, is not a philosophical position dressed up in "borrowed robes." Macbeth does not adopt nihilism as a matter of philosophical principle. His actual experience confirms over and over his sense that he lives in a world without value.

What makes all this so interesting for us is the possibility it affords to engage with such a world. For me that engagement is most powerfully articulated in the figure of Lady Macduff. Faced with her own husband's defection and with the attempts made by Ross to justify this behavior, she speaks eloquently to the complicity of powerful men in sustaining the kind of world that accepts the possibility of a Macbeth and then takes pride in "opposing evil."

> *Lady Macduff:* Wisdom! to leave his wife, to leave his babes,
> His mansion and his titles in a place
> From whence himself does fly? He loves us not;
> He wants the natural touch: for the poor wren,
> The most diminutive of birds, will fight,
> Her young ones in her nest, against the owl.
> All is the fear and nothing is the love;
> As little is the wisdom, where the flight
> So runs against all reason.

Zamir himself avoids addressing Lady Macduff's protest. Instead he takes an interest in "a build-up of sympathy to Macduff's straightforwardness and simple decency." Now the point Zamir wants to make is that Macduff is the one who in the end doesn't resist or put off his feelings; he genuinely grieves for the loss of his wife and children. And that openness to his own feelings is itself the compelling rejoinder to the existential hollowness of Macbeth.

Frankly, I prefer Harry Berger's emphasis on the complicity of Macduff, Banquo, and the other "good" thanes. And I wonder why Zamir is so ready to concede Macduff's "simple decency." But this kind of disagreement has relatively little importance in my assessment of this book. I have only admiration for the honesty of Zamir's readings and for the remarkable intelligence of his project. *Double Vision* is beautifully written, moving, witty, and convincing. The arguments presented are complex and subtle, but the reasoning is lucid. Great care has been taken here to avoid the kind of obscurity one often finds in theoretical treatments of literary questions. It will have enormous value for teachers of Shakespeare and for the artists who perform his works onstage. It should have even greater value for scholars and critics.

Index